THE STATE IN SOCIALIST SOCIETY

Edited by

Neil Harding

in association with
St Antony's College, Oxford

First published 1984 by
THE MACMILLAN PRESS LTD
London and Basingstoke
Companies and representatives
throughout the world

ISBN 0 333 34098 1 (hardcover)
ISBN 0 333 36014 1 (paperback)

Typeset in Hong Kong by
Setrite Typesetters

Printed in Hong Kong

THE STATE IN SOCIALIST SOCIETY

St Antony's/Macmillan Series

General editor: Archie Brown, Fellow of St Antony's College, Oxford

Archie Brown and Michael Kaser (editors) SOVIET POLICY FOR THE 1980s
S. B. Burman CHIEFDOM POLITICS AND ALIEN LAW
Renfrew Christie ELECTRICITY, INDUSTRY AND CLASS IN SOUTH AFRICA
Wilhelm Deist THE *WEHRMACHT* AND GERMAN REARMAMENT
Julius A. Elias PLATO'S DEFENCE OF POETRY
Ricardo Ffrench-Davis and Ernesto Tironi (editors) LATIN AMERICA AND THE NEW INTERNATIONAL ECONOMIC ORDER
Bohdan Harasymiw POLITICAL ELITE RECRUITMENT IN THE SOVIET UNION
Neil Harding (editor) THE STATE IN SOCIALIST SOCIETY
Richard Holt SPORT AND SOCIETY IN MODERN FRANCE
Albert Hourani EUROPE AND THE MIDDLE EAST
          THE EMERGENCE OF THE MODERN MIDDLE EAST
A. Kemp-Welch (translator) THE BIRTH OF SOLIDARITY
Paul Kennedy and Anthony Nicholls (editors) NATIONALIST AND RACIALIST MOVEMENTS IN BRITAIN AND GERMANY BEFORE 1914
Richard Kindersley (editor) IN SEARCH OF EUROCOMMUNISM
Gisela C. Lebzelter POLITICAL ANTI-SEMITISM IN ENGLAND, 1918–1939
C. A. MacDonald THE UNITED STATES, BRITAIN AND APPEASEMENT, 1936–1939
Patrick O'Brien (editor) RAILWAYS AND THE ECONOMIC DEVELOPMENT OF WESTERN EUROPE, 1830–1914
Roger Owen (editor) STUDIES IN THE ECONOMIC AND SOCIAL HISTORY OF PALESTINE IN THE NINETEENTH AND TWENTIETH CENTURIES
Irena Powell WRITERS AND SOCIETY IN MODERN JAPAN
T. H. Rigby and Ferenc Fehér (editors) POLITICAL LEGITIMATION IN COMMUNIST STATES
Marilyn Rueschemeyer PROFESSIONAL WORK AND MARRIAGE
A. J. R. Russell-Wood THE BLACK MAN IN SLAVERY AND FREEDOM IN COLONIAL BRAZIL
Aron Shai BRITAIN AND CHINA, 1941–47
Lewis H. Siegelbaum THE POLITICS OF INDUSTRIAL MOBILIZATION IN RUSSIA, 1914–17
David Stafford BRITAIN AND EUROPEAN RESISTANCE, 1940–1945
Nancy Stepan THE IDEA OF RACE IN SCIENCE
Guido di Tella ARGENTINA UNDER PERON, 1973–76
Rosemary Thorp and Laurence Whitehead (editors) INFLATION AND STABILISATION IN LATIN AMERICA
Rudolf L. Tőkés (editor) OPPOSITION IN EASTERN EUROPE

Contents

Preface

Students of Communist regimes or those that style themselves socialist quickly become aware that the state formations which constitute a large part of their concern are different in kind from those of the non-socialist world. They are different in the scope of their powers and their degree of intervention into society and the economy. They are differently perceived by their citizens, and their rulers have different modes of justifying or legitimating their regimes. The relationship between the state and the individual, political parties, trade unions and other partial organisations is, clearly, quite different from that prevailing under Western liberal democracy. What this volume seeks to do is to bring some of these threads together, to give an account of the generic character of these state formations, and to notice at least some of their species differentiation. Its aim is to provide an extensive and varied picture both of Western and of indigenous theorising about the nature of the state, and as representative a coverage of the problems of its institutional development as is practicable within the confines of one volume.

With two exceptions the chapters of this book were presented as papers in a conference of the Communist Politics Group of the Political Studies Association of Great Britain which met in September 1981 at the University of Wales Conference Centre, Gregynog, Powys. The papers were subsequently redrafted in the light of discussion at the Conference and updated to July 1982. I know that I would be echoing the sentiments of the authors in thanking the discussants of their papers – Mary McAuley, David McLellan, Tony Kemp-Welch, Alex Pravda, Tony Saich and Alexandras Shtromas – for introducing the lively and informed discussions which each generated.

We were fortunate indeed that Mary McAuley subsequently volunteered a chapter on the nationalities' question in the Soviet Union which complemented so well Peter Rutland's chapter on this important problem, and that Sharon Zukin, at short notice, kindly agreed to fill the gap on the development of the Yugoslav State which the original Conference programme had intended to cover.

NEIL HARDING

Acknowledgements

My thanks to the Social Science Research Council for a Personal Research Award, 1981–2, and to the British Academy for research funding to pursue work on the development of Soviet theories of the state, to St Antony's College, Oxford, for its hospitality during that year, to Archie Brown as general editor of the series for his assiduous and expert help in preparing this volume, and to the Centre for Soviet and East European Studies, University College, Swansea, for financial assistance which made possible the initial conference at which these papers were presented.

N.H.

List of the Contributors

ARCHIE BROWN is Fellow of St Antony's College, Oxford, and Lecturer in Soviet Institutions at the University of Oxford.

DAVID S. G. GOODMAN is Lecturer in the Department of Politics at the University of Newcastle upon Tyne.

NEIL HARDING is Senior Lecturer in the Department of Political Theory and Government and in the Centre for Russian and East European Studies, University College, Swansea.

RONALD J. HILL is Associate Professor of Political Science and Fellow of Trinity College, Dublin.

JOHN HOFFMAN is Lecturer in the Department of Politics at the University of Leicester.

PAUL G. LEWIS is Senior Lecturer in Government at the Open University.

MARY McAULEY is Senior Lecturer in the Department of Government at the University of Essex.

PETER RUTLAND is Lecturer in the Department of Politics at the University of York.

SHARON ZUKIN is Associate Professor in the Department of Sociology at Brooklyn College of the City University of New York.

List of Abbreviations and Glossary

ASSR Autonomous Soviet Socialist Republic. Political and administrative unit within the USSR below the level of Union Republic.

CCP Chinese Communist Party.

CPSU Communist Party of the Soviet Union.

FEC Federal Executive Council (of Yugoslavia).

IPSA International Political Science Association.

KC Central Committee (of the Polish United Workers' Party).

KGB Committee for State Security.

Komsomol Young Communist League.

KW Committee of *Województwo* or Province of Poland.

KZ Factory Committee.

NEP New Economic Policy. Introduced in 1921 to moderate the austerity of the earlier period of War Communism.

NIK Supreme Control Chamber (of Poland).

Nomenklatura List of posts that can be filled only with the confirmation of a specified committee of a Communist Party.

NPC National People's Congress (legislature of China).

PCF French Communist Party.

PLA People's Liberation Army.

PRC People's Republic of China.

PUWP (or PZPR) Polish United Workers' Party.

RSFSR Russian Soviet Federated Socialist Republic. The largest of the fifteen Union Republics of the Union of Soviet Socialist Republics.

1 Socialism, Society, and the Organic Labour State

Neil Harding

The problem of characterising Communist regimes runs through all the chapters of this volume. It is a problem which is as unavoidable as it is hazardous. We evidently do have a psychological and pedagogic need to classify political systems into types according to the character-istics they share and those that set them apart from others. This concern is as old as the study of politics itself and we do no more than tread somewhat warily in the footsteps of Aristotle. Warily because in our case the landscape that greets us is strewn with half-finished buildings and ruins – totalitarianism, institutional pluralism, cor-poratism – each no sooner erected than lapsing into dereliction. The problems involved in attempting to apply these models to Communist regimes are explored in the next chapter of this volume and the details need not detain us here. We would only note that, in the case of the theory of totalitarianism many commentators feel that, while in-structive as a comparative analysis of the shared characteristics of Communist regimes, at a particular point in their development, and fascist political structures and practices, it proved too abstracted and rigid. It lacked the capacity to accommodate the quite abrupt changes in Communist regimes that took place almost simultaneously with its dissemination in the 1950s. As to institutional pluralism and corporat-ism, they both suffer from the defect of attempting to view Soviet politics and the relationships between the individual, society and the state, through the prism of Western theories. They consequently tend to ignore the unique and particular character of Communist regimes and the intentions of their important political actors.

Any adequate characterisation of these regimes ought to comply with a number of exacting specifications. It ought, obviously, to

1

locate those particular and specific elements that mark off these regimes from others. It ought to be able to encompass their whole historical development rather than one limited phase. It ought, finally, to make articulate the intentions of the actors involved and explore how far their institutions and political practice conform to their goals. We are, in short, concerned not with a generalised comparative paradigm, but with a unique mode of discourse and political practice.

This introductory chapter sets out to make explicit a tradition of theorising the relationships between society and the state indigenous to these regimes. It is a tradition that has its roots in Marx and nineteenth-century aspirations to formulate a 'science of society', so it is there that we must begin. We will follow its theoretical development through the writings of Bukharin, Lenin and Trotsky and its practical enforcement under Stalin. By that time the internal logic of the organic labour state and its attendant political practices had been firmly established, and these, while by no means frozen or static, severely constrained the options available to Stalin's successors. The presuppositions of this political tradition about the role of the state, the rights of the individual and the perogatives of social groups, developed within the logic of Russian Marxism and were, subsequently, imposed with varying degrees of success upon post-war Eastern Europe. They were, for a time at least, voluntarily imitated even by those Communist regimes, like China and Yugoslavia, that were not subject to Soviet military occupation.

We ought, in particular, to note how increasingly remote this political tradition became from the assumptions of Western political theory. There never was, either in Russia, or in China, or in much of Eastern Europe, any strong liberal tradition. The powerful mythology of social contract theory, in whose terms government is established to protect individual and group rights and to guarantee the life, liberty and estates of its citizens and is, therefore, limited by those ends, never impressed itself at all deeply on the popular consciousness. There never has been in Russia, and certainly not under the Soviet regime, any widespread conception of the individual or of social groups disposing of rights that can be exercised *against* the executive, openly to oppose its plans, limit its pretensions, or establish spheres into which it ought not to intrude. In both constitutional theory and in actual practice, as we shall see, individuals and groups are only conferred such rights as tend to promote and enhance *the state's* objectives. Their exercise of those rights is expressly limited by that very large condition. The distribution of awards, honours and social prestige is, likewise, directly linked to functional contribution to the goals set by the state. Even the definition of citizenship is determined by the same criteria. Elections are occasions not for calling governments to account for their administration and to argue the desirability of their continued tenure of power; they are, on the contrary, mobilisations of the citizenry affording the opportunity to express unanimous support of state plans. We are, clearly, dealing with a political tradition that inverts many of the basic assumptions of Western political thought, and to render it intelligible we must explore the development of its own internal rationale.

RIVAL MODELS OF THE STATE IN MARX

We must begin by considering the ambiguity of Marx's prescriptions for the state in socialist society, an ambiguity that, due to the canonisation of Marx and the veneration of the orthodoxy he established, has had a continuing influence on the communist movement.

There are, in Marx, two differing sets of objectives, two vying conceptions of socialism to which there correspond two divergent models of the state. The problem is not that Marx was entirely silent about the relationship between state and society under socialism, but that on the infrequent occasions that he was drawn to discuss the problem, he suggested mutually exclusive alternatives.

Marx's Model One has as its objective the liberation of man from the relations of domination and subordination that derived from the division of labour within the productive process and within society.

As producer, man was confronted and dominated by the very machines he had himself created which instead of being an object for him made of him the object. The patterns of domination within the productive process were reflected in law and guaranteed by the coercive might of the state. In his economic relations the worker was subordinated to the will of the capitalist and even to the inanimate machinery that deployed him. In his civic relations he was subordinated to the interests of the ruling class expressed in law and enforced by the state. Private property and the state were central elements of man's alienation from his true species being. This *true* being of man could be realised only by doing away with both to allow the uncoerced flowering of free, conscious, co-operative association and labour. We have here a sort of philosophical determinism in which the demand is made that society be remade to fit a particular view of man's essential or species being.

We should also be aware that Marx's early specification of the nature of man, and therefore of the socialism that would suit him, was largely derived from a tradition within socialist thought that stretched back to Fourier and was, in Marx's lifetime, carried on by Proudhon. This strand of socialism was in conscious rebellion against the de-humanising effects of large-scale machine industry on the one hand, and the rapidly growing industrial conurbations on the other. Machine industry, with its intricate division of labour, converted craftsmen omnicompetent within their trade, and therefore able to work independently on their own account, into detail labourers trained to perform a tiny fraction of the old craft and therefore comprehensively dependent upon factory production. It destroyed the independence of artisan and peasant alike, making servile wage labourers of them. The growth of towns of unnatural dimensions bred extravagance and luxurious decadence on the one hand and penury on the other.

This anti-industrial, anti-urban, populist socialism was in part a demand for the restitution of the happy mean. It sought to make available to all, that moderate amount of property that would guarantee the independence of each. It recognised the necessity of setting limits to sumptuary norms and was consciously prepared to bargain away the prospect of prosperity in favour of freedom. In Proudhon's celebrated epigram, 'enough is *better* than a feast.'

The structures of administration favoured by this species of socialism were entirely consonant with their objectives. Being advocates of rounded individuality moulded in variety of employment they stood opposed to the division of labour within emergent modern industry. So too, most forcibly, did the young Marx, attributing to division of labour a primary causal role in inducing alienation. They believed independent self-acting labour to be *the* moralising agency in man's existence and held that, to be attractive, labour had to be varied. On both counts the young Marx agreed. Uncoerced creative labour he took to be definitive of man's species being, and variety of employment of its essence. We ought to note, furthermore, that on the one occasion when he outlined the sorts of pursuits that would occupy unalienated man he saw him as hunter, fisherman, shepherd and critic,[1] and not as collier, fitter, assembly-worker and salesman. Marx's whole project to put an end to alienation is distinctly tinged with the Agrarian anti-industrial socialism from which he derived so much of his early inspiration. Finally, it is clear that the young Marx was broadly in agreement with Proudhon that socialism had more to do with absence of coercion and external authority than it did with the pursuit of plenty.

The question now arises of what forms of social organisation would realise Marx's objectives in this humanist model that aspires to free the individual of dependence upon capital and the state? Clearly, within the productive process not only private ownership of the forces of production would have to go, but so too would the patterns of domination and subordination inherent within the divisions of labour. As to the conduct of public affairs, Marx, perhaps for fear of falling into the error of the utopians in constructing a blueprint of the future, was extremely guarded. His remarks on the matter were sporadic and sparse. We are obliged therefore to make some connections Marx himself did not make.

Of the forms of administration Marx proposed only one would serve in the task of eliminating alienation, and that was the form of the Paris Commune of 1871. The Commune, according to Marx's account of it, proceeded *immediately* to the elimination of the standing army, the police and the judiciary. Their functions were to be appropriated by the people in arms. It followed that in so far as coercive power was now fused with the population at large the state no longer existed. For the state, in Marx's account of it, comprised *separate* bodies of armed men standing outside of and above society. Louis Bonaparte's Imperial regime, with its swollen executive, its host of irresponsible officials and its vastly expanded standing army, was, in Marx's account, the apogee and terminus of the bourgeois state, 'its most prostitute, its most complete, and its ultimate political form. It is the state power of modern class rule, at least on the European continent.'[2] It was against this monstrous power which was clogging all the vital pores of French society that the Commune raised its revolt and in so doing proclaimed the state redundant. 'The true antithesis to the *Empire itself* – that is to the state power... was *the Commune*.'[3]

> This was, therefore, a Revolution not against this or that, legitimate, constitutional, republican or Imperialist form of State power. It was a Revolution against the *State* itself, of this super-naturalist abortion of society, a resumption by the people for the people of its own social life.[4]

In the final draft of *The Civil War in France*, Marx repeatedly talks of 'the destruction of the State power',[5] 'the antagonism of the Commune against the State',[6] and 'the, now superseded, State power'.[7]

The ideal of the Commune, 'the unchangeable goal of the workmen's revolution',[8] was a vision of:

> All France organised into selfworking and selfgoverning communes, the standing army replaced by the popular militias, the army of state-parasites removed, the clerical hierarchy displaced by the schoolmaster, the state judge transformed into Communal organs... the state functions reduced to a few functions for general national purposes.[9]

All officials were to be elected, all subject to recall, and paid at workmen's wages. In this way the administration of society was to be kept permanently accountable and revocable, unable to establish interests or objectives separate from those of society or to cloak itself in secrecy and mystery. In short, 'Public functions ceased to be the private property of the tools of the Central Government.'[10] The scale of administration was to be enormously reduced, the centralised nation state was no longer to be the unit of civic and political life: it was to be dissolved into a multitude of self-governing communes in which the individual could feel a real sense of participation and control – a real identification of his will with that of the community. 'The unity of the nation', Marx affirmed, was 'to become a reality by the destruction of the State power.'[11]

The Commune, it is clear, qualified as a socialist form of administration *only* in so far as it set out a model for transforming the relationships of domination and subordination among men. It is certain that its very modest *economic* measures, the most audacious of which eliminated night-work for bakers, were of little or no importance in leading Marx to recommend it as 'the political form at last discovered under which to work out the economic emancipation of labour';[12] the model administrative structure for realising socialism. The Commune signified the appropriation by society of all its lost powers on the basis of small-scale administrative units in which the individual not only participated in deliberating public policy but also in executing it. For the Commune was to be at once a legislative executive, judicial, policing and defensive body and its members were to be engaged in all its functions.

It is rather odd, given Marx's general concerns, that the one sphere of public life that seemed to lie outside the purview of the Commune was the economic. The transformation of the ownership relations within society was nowhere alluded to, and, true to the decentralised ethos of the Commune, the regulation of national production was vaguely entrusted to 'united co-operative societies'.[13] It was, of course, the case that the inspiration behind the Commune derived more from Proudhon than from Marx. Its decentralised structure, its preoccupation with eliminating patterns of domination and subordination, its concern to break up the centralised nation-state into self-governing units of local administration – all of this fitted the agrarian, populist and anti-urban bias of at least one wing of European socialist thought. Marx's adoption of these themes and the triumph of society over the state that they represented, was enthusiastic but short-lived. They smacked too much of the schemes of his populist and anarchist rivals. More important, their emphases were thoroughly at odds with the objectives of the mature Marx, which had to do not with dismantling industrial society and the state but with expanding and refining them.

What we might term Marx's Model Two, was concerned not with alienation but with eliminating exploitation. *Its* protest against capitalism was not so much with its failure to secure freedom as with its failure to provide for the security and welfare of the vast majority. The principal deficiencies of commodity production were held to be that its objective being profit maximisation it must lead to increasingly ruthless extraction of surplus value and, therewith, to the tendency to immiserisation of the working class. Second, production for an unregulated market would necessarily generate crises of overproduction, unemployment, destruction of productive forces and failure to satisfy felt needs. The severe and evident problems of unregulated and anarchic capitalist production could, Marx felt, only be overcome by the state owning and controlling the productive forces of society. It would eliminate the anarchy of production through rational planning and ensure general well-being through the equitable distribution of the social product. Such a radical transformation of ownership relations would, however, generate bitter resistance from the possessing classes. It followed that, both for the initial *repressive* task of putting down the opposition of the owners and for the subsequent *constructive* task of planning national production and distribution, the socialists would have to dispose of a tightly centralised structure of coercive power and a very considerable body of administrative expertise.

The state form explicitly linked to these objectives was the dictatorship of the proletariat. In Marx's references to it (eleven in all)[14] it is characterised as a highly centralised, expressly coercive and transitional form of the state. It is to be employed by the proletariat to put down bourgeois opposition and to centralise forces of production, communications and credit in the hands of the proletarian state.

Within this model the whole of Marx's emphasis is upon the transformation of *ownership* relations. It is this objective that determines the centralising and coercive structure he has in mind. He refuses, even when drawn by suspicious contemporaries, to be tempted into any discussion of its administrative structures and how they were to be kept accountable to the class on behalf of whom they were to act.

The objectives of the transitional period which the dictatorship of the proletariat was to superintend were (i) to eliminate exploitation by transferring ownership of the productive forces to the state, and (ii) to maximise production through state planning and through relating wages directly to productivity. Within the transitional state the category of wage labour (the alienating condition of Model One) was not to be done away with, it was to be universalised. There were to be no idlers, no non-productive able-bodied adults. Men (and women) were to be related to one another as labourers, and the principle of distributive justice that was to order their relationships was precisely the relative duration and intensity of their labour – *that* was to apportion rewards. Reward was to be made according to function and contribution to the maximisation of production. It was, therefore, explicitly a principle of inequality: 'labour, to serve as a measure, must be defined by its duration or intensity, otherwise it ceases to be a standard of measurement. This *equal* right is an unequal right for unequal labour.'[15] What we have here is 'society as the ensemble and union of men engaged in useful work',[16] whose co-ordinating mechanism and guarantor is the state. It is a second edition of Saint Simon's organic labour state in which managerial, technocratic and positivist notions of the objectives, and therefore the administrative structures of socialism, had their origin. It left its deep impress upon Marx's idea of the transitional phase, and it resurfaced, as we shall see, with renewed vitality in Russia in the 1920s.

It was from Saint Simon that Marx imbibed the particular vision of socialism that was to inform his ill-elaborated notion of the dictatorship of the proletariat. Society, in Saint Simon's view, was a single co-ordinated organism whose parts were, therefore, by nature, kept subordinate to the whole.[17] For Marx too, 'Civil society embraces the whole material intercourse of individuals within a definite stage of the development of productive forces.'[18] The objective of this single social body was the maximisation of socially useful production and the fullest satisfaction of the needs of all those who played their part in the industrial system. 'The production of useful things is the only reasonable and positive aim that political societies can set themselves.'[19] This formulation quite clearly sets Saint Simon's thought radically apart from the classical political economists. It rejected their proposition (and that of the Agrarian socialists) that economic life was the province of the individual or autonomous group and lay, therefore, outside the sphere of politics. Saint Simon, and subsequent theorists and builders of the organic labour state, inverted this axiom. For them, society has no other identity or purpose apart from useful production which, therefore, constitutes the whole of politics. Social relations are relations entered into for the purpose of production since society is a productive system. According to Marx, *'The relations of production in their totality constitute what are called the social relations, society*, and specifically, a society at *a definite stage of historical development.'*[20] The social, productive, and political spheres of life have no separable autonomy as the classical economists and liberal theorists had taught. They are, in the Saint Simonian tradition, conflated. Suffused with the same essential productive goal they are run together and made identical. 'Politics', Saint Simon insisted, 'is *the science of production*, that is, the science whose object is the order most favourable to every kind of production.'[21] The time was not far distant, he prophesied, when 'political economy ... will itself comprise the whole of politics'.[22] Marx was to make this the guiding light of his whole system: 'the anatomy of civil society is to be sought in political economy'.

   A number of important implications flowed from this setting of social purpose. In the first place it was clear that in this model the objective of society was not pre-eminently the realisation of man's freedom in political and legal equality, as social contract theorists had argued. Saint Simon's tart response to their contention was that 'Savages combine to hunt, to wage war, but surely not to gain liberty; for in this respect they would do better to remain isolated.' It followed that 'By no means does one associate in order to remain free.'[23] The object of association being production, the bases of social relations were necessarily located within the productive process. In Saint Simon's account, 'in his social relations every man should consider himself to be engaged in a company of workers'.[24] There was in Marx a similar essentialism that made him blind to the virtues of social variegation and eccentricity, and led him 'to see almost all social organisation as dependent on the mode of production . . . This in turn entails a tendency to view society as if it were a factory run by the state.'[25] Society, in the marxist tradition, is not merely ultimately reducible to a mode of production but is no more than it. The history of social relations is, therefore, enclosed in the manner in which men produce. 'The whole of human history', Trotsky tells us, 'is the history of the organisation and education of collective man for labour, with the object of attaining a higher level of productivity.'[26]

To conceive of society as essentially a mechanism of production had, both for Saint Simon and for Marx, certain highly important structural and administrative implications. For its efficient operation the social system of production demanded differentiation of function and division of labour. It demanded too (overtly in Saint Simon and implicitly in Marx) a central co-ordinating and directing agency commanding the scientific knowledge and administrative skills appropriate to its large responsibilities. This administrative structure, operating initially on the national level but progressively co-ordinating the industrial system of the entire globe, would, however, be different in principle from existing governments. Hitherto political government had reflected the social organisation of military societies. Groups of individuals had asserted their will over other individuals through the preponderance of coercive power they disposed of. In industrial society such a foundation for government was irrelevant and harmful. 'Governments will no longer command men.'[27] Their functions were, rather, to ensure that useful work was properly organised, and to put down the vicious ambitions of parasites and idlers to consume yet not to produce. What was required in the positive age and in industrial society was knowledge, not coercive power. The men of science in Saint Simon's Credo 'will establish laws of social hygiene for the social body, and in their hands politics will become the complement of the science of man'.[28] Their findings, based upon observation of indisputable facts, would be applied to all political, social and economic questions, all of which were resolvable through 'scientific demonstrations, absolutely independent of all human will'.[29] The nature of their authority, as co-ordinators of the productive organism and planners of the single social workshop, derived from their proven understanding of the workings of industry and society. In so far as politics became a science it was to lose its arbitrary and wilful essence. It was to be the benign non-coercive administration of things. Where

Saint Simon is more honest than some of his disciples is in his frank acceptance that the ability to participate in elaborating a science of man is far from a universal attribute. It is, on the contrary, given only to a relatively small number within society. When politics ascends to the status of a science it will, like all sciences, demand considerable training and intellectual capacity of its practitioners. Like all sciences it must demand for its qualified exponents an exclusive sphere of competence, with the inferred right of silencing untrained competitors and quacks whose remedies threaten more to aggravate than to relieve social malaise:

> But when politics has risen to the ranks of the sciences of observation, which must be before too long, the conditions of capacity will become clear and fixed, and the cultivation of politics will be entrusted exclusively to a special class of scientists who will impose silence on all twaddle.[30]

Under the Soviet dictatorship of the proletariat, as we shall see, an exactly similar animus against industrial democracy, deriving from the same preoccupation with maximising production, was to prevail. There were, of course, considerable differences between Marx's accounts of the nature and functions of the future administration of society. In particular, Marx followed Saint Simon's own disciples in arguing that the planned control of social production could only be accomplished by transferring ownership of the means of production from private individuals to the state. Indeed Marx's model of the dictatorship of the proletariat was distinguished precisely by its tendency to identify socialism as state ownership. According to the ten-point programme of *The Manifesto of the Communist Party*, credit was to be centralised in the hands of the state 'by means of a national bank with state capital and an exclusive monopoly'.[31] The means of communication and transport were to be similarly centralised in its hands, and there was to be a rapid 'Extension of factories and instruments of production owned by the State'. Finally, the state would decree 'Equal liability of all to labour. Establishment of labour armies.'[32] In all of this there was a certain fit between Marx's objectives and the policies recommended. If the objectives are elimination of exploitation and inequality, of anarchy of production and wastefulness, and the bountiful production of goods to satisfy expanded needs, *then* it seemed clear that a single central authority would have to organise social production and to decide upon and allocate its surplus. It would therefore need to own the forces of production. We have here a schema different in kind from the vague and permissive plan of the Commune, which left 'the united co-operative societies to regulate national production upon a common plan'.[33]

Marx, in his mature writings (with the exception of his accounts of the Commune), spoke very little about the forms of administration that would return to society all its lost powers so as to restructure the relations of domination and subordination among men; he was now absorbed with the relationship of men to *things* – to their forces of production. Within the work process itself, Marx and Engels were quite clear that, since modern large-scale factory methods were to remain as the basic productive mechanism of socialist society, then the patterns of domination and subordination inherent in this system of production would have to be retained. The material benefits of the industrial system, they concluded, could not be enjoyed without suffering the loss of autonomy the system necessarily entailed. Transforming private ownership of the means of production into social or state ownership would in no way diminish the need for authority and subordination within industry; these 'are things which, independently of all social organisation are imposed upon us'.[34] The working day would be 'fixed by the authority of the steam, which cares nothing for individual autonomy', and 'must be observed by all, without any exception'.[35] Division of labour would have to be authoritatively allocated; the several processes within the factory, conducted in its different shops, would have to be systematically co-ordinated by a single will, and the larger the factory the more despotic the control would have to be. Marx, too, in *Capital*, and in the *Grundrisse*, conceded that, within the industrial work process, even under socialism, the worker could not hope to realise the dream of free uncoerced productive activity that had inspired his early writings. Labour under socialism would remain a realm of necessity. Marx and Engels came to realise that the early dream was incompatible with the maintenance of the modern industrial system. They had chosen Saint Simon's path, which consciously acknowledged that the object of society was productive activity not freedom, and that the price to be paid for increased material comfort under *any* social system was a loss of autonomy and liberty:

If man, by dint of his knowledge and inventive genius, has subdued the forces of nature, the latter avenge themselves upon him by subjecting him, in so far as he employs them, to a veritable despotism independent of all social organisation. Wanting to abolish authority in large-scale industry is tantamount to wanting to abolish industry itself, to destroy the power loom in order to return to the spinning wheel.[36]

How could it be otherwise than that the form of central government would replicate the patterns of despotic authority within the mode of production?

Whereas Marx's account of socialism in his writings on the Commune concentrated exclusively on the structures of administration through which man could reassert his control over the deliberation and execution of public policy, his accounts of the dictatorship of the proletariat were notable for their studied indifference to the forms of government or the mechanisms that would ensure its accountability. The Commune model expressed the principles and forms of administration that would serve to realise one of Marx's accounts of the goal of socialism – *the transformation of the patterns of authority* within society. The dictatorship of the proletariat outlined *the transformation of property relations* that would be necessary to realise the quite distinct and separable goals of ending exploitation, organising the national economy and ushering in the realm of plenty. Historically it was these objectives that gave the ideology of Marxism its mobilising power. Though the actual term 'dictatorship of the proletariat' fell into general disuse during the Second International, it was undoubtedly its tough-minded content, its promise to end exploitation and charge retribution upon the capitalists, that provided the basis of the appeal of Marxism to the industrial workers. This Marxism was addressed not to humanity as a whole, nor to the fiction of 'society' (and in this it distinguished itself from all species of Utopianism), but to the oppressed and poor and exploited. It was a programme of *their* redemption. Its emphases and objectives were class-exclusive and were attainable only through the economic and political expropriation of the bourgeoisie.

That Marx himself recognised that he had produced incommensurable accounts of the ends of socialism, which therefore entailed radically different recommendations for the form of the state, is fairly evident. It is, above all, very telling that Marx himself carefully and consistently avoided identifying the Commune as a form of the dictatorship of the proletariat. So long as Marx was alive, Engels too was similarly careful.[37]

What we have in Marx, as in the socialist tradition generally, are two differing sets of objectives to which there correspond differing and incompatible models for the administration of public affairs. Direct democracy presupposes severe limitations upon the size of the administrative unit. General participation in deliberating and executing public policy must, realistically, presuppose the volume of business to be relatively restricted and its complexity manageable by the average level of intelligence and education. It is fairly clear that a structure embodying these characteristics, admirable as it might be in the cause of emancipation, could not serve in the business of planning and directing a complex industrial economy and ensuring an equitable distribution of its product. It could not serve the tasks of producing abundance and equality. It was fitted (as Marx conceded) to the populist slogan of cheap government.[38] Technocratic Marxism was, by contrast, necessarily wedded to the twin principles of centralisation within the state and subordination within the workplace. It had grandiose aspirations not merely for the size of individual productive units but for the planning and direction of the entire national and international economy. This would require, on an exalted plane, authoritative directions on the social division of labour and allocation of resources. Only a centralised authority could dictate, as it would have to, the measure of labour and of consumption.

It was partly because the Commune model was tarred with the anarchist brush and smacked too much of asceticism and anti-industrialism that it all but vanished from Marx's writings after 1871 and from the vocabulary of marxists during the career of the Second International. It took a popular revolt to oblige a reluctant Marx to acknowledge the Commune and it was not resuscitated until the next great popular upsurge in the Russian revolution of 1917. It was, as we shall see, fairly quickly discarded by the Bolsheviks as soon as they recognised that it was incompatible with their aspirations for a planned economy. They, too, subsequently tried to efface its memory by presenting the dictatorship of the proletariat and the organic labour state as the foundation myth of modern communism and by re-writing their own history. And yet wherever Communist states have asserted their independence from Soviet control they have, in differing ways, gone back to the Commune alternative. In Yugoslavia and in China this has been the case, and in the uneasy post-war politics of Eastern Europe its modified formulations continue to reverberate.

THE BOLSHEVIK RESOLUTION OF THE DUALISM IN MARX

It is often presumed that the Bolsheviks took power with a ready-made conception of the dictatorship of the proletariat. Comment-ators, deeply aware of the fusion of party and state that was to take place, presume that it was quite natural for the Bolsheviks to begin by simply transferring the organisational model of the party to the state. And so tight centralisation, hierarchical subordination of lower administrative bodies to higher ones, rigid division of labour and authoritative allocation of function came to be imposed upon state and society by simple transferral from the model of the party.

This was, however, certainly *not* the way in which the Bolsheviks justified the revolutionary seizure of power, nor does it reflect their intentions during the first nine months in power. During this period the dictatorship of the proletariat was seldom alluded to, and the theme of democratic centralism, as applied to state institutions, did not surface until the early 1920s. It is little noticed how implacably anti-statist was the motivation and justification of the Bolshevik Revolution. Nor is it sufficiently recognised how the extravagant libertarianism, and the anarchic centrifugal forces it encouraged, were themselves causal factors necessitating the subsequent imposition of tight centralisation.

By late 1916 Lenin was convinced that capitalism had finally ex-hausted its potential. The war was a manifestation of the worldwide contradictions of international finance capitalism.[39] Remorseless pursuit of economic territory brought militarism in its train, in-creasingly oppressive state structures within the imperialist countries, and slaughter on a grandiose scale to the peoples of the world. As the imperialist war progressed it brought ruination, famine and economic collapse to much of central and eastern Europe. Lenin clearly believed that he was witnessing the death-throes of capitalism as a mode of production. He was confident beyond any doubt that capitalism had reached its historical terminus.

Monopoly Capitalism had tried every expedient available to it to retain its political power and reproduce its mode of production, but all to no avail. Capital had been exported on a huge scale to reap the super-profits of colonial investment. Armament expediture had been enormously increased, tariff barriers established, state capitalist intervention in the economy and the subordination of the Labour movement had been accomplished but still the global economy of finance capitalism continued its downward spiral and the countries of

Europe suffered military and economic devastation. There were now no other recourses available to capitalism; it was dying on its feet. Indeed, in Lenin's view it was already putrefying, as the stench of death in Europe bore witness.

As a mode of production, capitalism in its parasitic finance capitalist stage was finished. It followed, therefore, in the accounts of Bukharin and of Lenin, that the political superstructure – the state – that it had reared had now become equally redundant. This was the more so because, in the era of finance capitalism, according to their analyses, the state and the mode of production had become inseparably linked. It was, after all, the state that sustained the armies, navies, armaments, industries and administrative bureaucracies, so vital for colonial expansion and the protection of exported capital. It was the imperialist state that created tariff barriers so that monopoly prices could be protected, the state that imposed the direct and especially the regressive indirect taxes to furnish the national debt which, in its turn, afforded lucrative outlets for finance capital. It was the state, in short, that guaranteed the reproduction of the mode of production of finance capitalism. It had therefore imperatively to be controlled and directed by the magnates of finance capitalism, and so, in Lenin's view, it was. The state itself now became a terrain of plunder for the monopolists, a vehicle for organising national production and, increasingly, a cudgel to put down opposition and criticism, especially that voiced by the socialist parties.

The singular feature of the imperialist state formation, its whole historical originality, was that *it* now dictated the form of development of the productive forces rather than they it. It was Bukharin who first hit upon the heresy of the superstructure determining the base.[40] This was, he felt, particularly evident during its wartime death agonies. The imperialist state had emerged as the last mighty fortress of the capitalist economic formation, utilising the coercive power it disposed of to intimidate the population, using fiscal powers and wholesale direct intervention to control and organise the entire national economy.[41] Whole sectors of industry had been mobilised under its direction, its sumptuary norms set by the state through control of wages and rationing. Trade unions had been deprived of the right to strike, workers prohibited from moving jobs and tied as indentured men to the service of state capitalism: 'They are transformed into bondsmen, attached, not to the land, but to the plant. They become white slaves of the predatory imperialist state, which has absorbed into its body all productive life.'[42] All the local, trade, professional and political organisations of society were sub-ordinated to its will and incorporated in its structure. The essence of imperialist ideology was its insistence upon the monolithic uniformity of the embattled nation. It fostered a spurious organic corporatism in its assertion that all this was necessary for national survival in the life-and-death struggle with other state-capitalist trusts. This was its justification for trampling upon the civic and political rights won in the epoch of competitive capitalism, and its pretext for the assault on militant socialists and trade-union leaders. The state had, in the epoch of imperialist war, entirely subordinated society for its own purposes. It now disposed of the whole national economy and the entire work-force, which it parasitically exploited to ensure the highest return for finance capital and the growth of coercive power to sustain its stranglehold upon society: 'the state power ... sucks in all areas of production; it not only embraces the general conditions of the ex-ploitative process; the state becomes more and more a direct exploiter, which organises and directs production as a collective capitalist.'[43] Thus there arose, Bukharin contended, the finished form of the im-perialist state, monolithic in structure and totalitarian in pretension, contemptuous of democratic rights and suspicious of group autonomy, militarist and expansionist. It was 'The New Leviathan, beside which the fantasy of Thomas Hobbes seems but a child's plaything',[44] for Hobbes's state was mighty yet limited in its pretensions, but this state formation aimed at 'absorbing within the domain of state regulation everyone and everything'.[45]

The conclusion that Bukharin and Lenin arrived at by late 1916 was sophisticated in its theoretical background, it was passionately argued and was certainly radical. Monopoly capital was shown to be parasitic upon the whole world and tended to hinder innovation and develop-ment of the productive forces. It had outlived its historical mission. The imperialist state was shown to be dictatorial and oppressive. It had devastated the autonomy of society and reduced the worker to a slave. It had lured the socialist parties and trade unions into its embrace so that 'they were actually nationalised by this *imperialist* state, that they transformed themselves into labour departments of the military machine'.[46] Capitalist monopoly tended to retard tech-nological innovation and therefore undermined the great pro-gressive role of competitive capitalism to constantly revolutionise the forces of production. It could only live by parasitically absorbing into itself all the vital forces of society and of the national economy. The time had finally come when overripe capitalism, and its perfected state formation, had become not merely redundant but cancerous. The time had come to vanquish the state and restore society to its lost vitality.[47]

These radical conclusions, which informed Lenin's whole strategy throughout 1917, necessarily led him to consider the forms of administration that would replace the imperialist state. It did not take him long to recognise the startling similarities between the model of the imperialist state that he and Bukharin had theorised, and the 'parasitic excrescence' that Marx had described in his account of Louis Bonaparte's regime. And what had replaced this imperial regime? It was, of course, the Commune. Lenin now rescued from the oblivion into which it had fallen Marx's account of the Commune, and made of it the practical programme of the Bolsheviks from April 1917 to April 1918. His insistence that the party change its name and adopt the title Communist was, precisely, meant to indicate that they had now become proponents of a 'state of which the Paris Commune was the prototype'.[48] All, literally *all*, the population, Lenin insisted, were to be drawn into the administration of the common affairs of society. Through their soviets, which were the contemporary form of the Commune, through their factory councils, regimental committees, co-operative societies and, especially, by participation in a universal militia, the people were to resume their self-administration. The whole objective now was to build

> Democracy from below, democracy without an officialdom, without a police, without a standing army; voluntary social duty guaranteed by a *militia* formed from a universally armed people.[49]

All the features that Marx had extolled in the Commune, Lenin reproduced in the soviets. 'Only the Commune can save us, so let us all perish, let us die, but let us have the Commune.'[50] All officials were to be made revocable and accountable, all to be paid at workmen's wages. All the powers arrogated to the state were to be reabsorbed by the populace organised in their soviets, which not only deliberated upon public policy but executed it as well. Legislative, executive, judicial and policing functions, all were fused in the armed people. In this fusion of powers the soviets were incomparably more advanced and more democratic than the 'talking shops' of bourgeois parliamentary structures.[51] This, for Lenin, represented above all a recovery by society of its lost control of its own affairs. It was to end the paralysing habit of giving and accepting imperative commands from the Centre, it was to abolish castes of officials on the one hand

and servile subjects on the other. Its objective was to shatter 'the old, absurd, savage, despicable and disgusting prejudice' that only the rich and educated could govern,[52] and to induct the whole population into their own self-administration. As late as April 1918, Lenin still insisted

> All citizens must take part in the work of the courts and in the government of the country. It is important for us to draw literally all working people into the government of the state. It is a task of tremendous difficulty. But socialism cannot be implemented by a minority, by the Party. It can be implemented only by tens of millions when they have learned to do it themselves.[53]

We should be clear that what Lenin had in mind was a transformation of authority patterns benefiting society at the cost of the state, rather than a radical restructuring of the ownership relations in the economic base. The economy was, on the national plane, to be brought under the control of the people via the national bank. The 'single State Bank, the biggest of the big', having control and supervision of all credits, acting as a ready-made instrument of book-keeping and accountancy on a national basis, would therefore 'constitute as much as nine-tenths of the Socialist apparatus', it was 'the "state apparatus" that we *need* to bring about socialism'.[54] Capitalism, in its finance capitalist stage, had at last elaborated in the banks, in the trusts and cartels that had centralised resources and nationalised the productive and distributive systems, those mechanisms of control that made Saint Simon's ideal of the administration of things a practicable proposition. These 'new means of control', Lenin pointed out, 'have been created *not* by us, but by capitalism in its military-imperialist stage.'[55] Nor was there any need to reserve control over them to the well-educated and scientifically trained as in the Saint-Simonian model: 'Capitalism simplifies the functions of "state" administration; it makes it possible to cast "bossing" aside.'[56] The simplified structures of management of the banks and the trusts were, Lenin believed, accessible to all, and consequently it was possible to 'set in motion a state apparatus consisting of ten if not twenty million people, an apparatus such as no capitalist state has ever known'.[57] Socialism was simply a matter of turning around the structures created by state capitalism and perfected during the war, making them accessible to popular control and obliging them to serve public needs not private greed. Socialism was 'merely state-capitalist monopoly which is made to serve the interests of the whole people'. State-monopoly capitalism had created 'a complete *material* preparation for socialism, the threshold of socialism'.[58]

But Lenin was insistent that this did not mean that private owner-ship of capital resources would be violated. On the contrary, nationalisation would guarantee the 'shares, bills, receipts, etc. Not a single one of these certificates would be invalidated if all the banks were amalgamated into a single state bank.' Such a move 'would not deprive any owner of a single kopek'.[59] Similarly, compulsory trustification of industry simply 'expedites capitalist development'[60] under the control of the state. All industries and consumer associa-tions were to be grouped into vertical trusts in order to ensure the efficient regulation of economic life.[61] But again, Lenin was insistent, 'it must be repeated that this unionisation will not in itself alter property relations one iota and will not deprive any owner of a single kopek'.[62]

On the local plane, within each enterprise, the existing manage-ment, provided that it did not engage in sabotage of the new regime, was to be preserved but was to be subjected to workers' control. Factory committees were to have access to all books and balance-sheets, they were to discuss all policy projections and set minimum production figures. Above all they were to ensure that the owners did not sabotage the productive system nor engage in excessive pro-fiteering. The factory committees were not, however, to expropriate the existing owners nor even displace the existing management. The decree on workers' control (14 November 1917) made clear the limitations under which control was to operate. It was to check and keep accountable, but not to own nor to administer. 'The control commission ... has no right itself to seize and administer an enterprise.'[63]

Lenin's conception of Soviet democracy clearly went a good deal further than Marx's sketch of the Commune. In particular, Lenin be-lieved that on the basis of the mechanisms of supervision of the national economy developed by finance capitalism, it was at last possible for society as a whole to resume radical democratic control of its economic life and yet to preserve and enhance its nationwide, systematic and planned character. In this optimistic, highly theorised prospectus it seemed that, at last, the freedom and self-activity of the Commune form could be reconciled with a planned and regulated ad-ministration of things. It appeared that the great conundrum of the marxist theory of the state, its persistent duality, had been overcome.

Yet, still, what stands out in Lenin's whole account of the project for Socialism in Russia, is his agreement with Marx's emphasis in the Commune model, that Socialism is to be defined as a free and conscious relationship of man to man. Its characteristic feature is its elimination of the patterns of domination and subordination, an end to the bossing that had hitherto prevailed. Neither Marx in the Commune model, nor Lenin in 1917 and early 1918, was concerned with utilising the state to effect a wholesale restructuring of prevailing property relations. Socialist ownership, it was inferred, would extend itself through its technical superiority and natural attractiveness. Socialism, in the first flush of the Soviet Republic, was conceived of as a free relationship among men rather than as a transformation of property relations. Participatory administrative patterns and an end to the prerogatives of office-holders were its hallmarks. Universal participation was to be secured through the simplified patterns of administration inherited from finance capitalism. Spontaneity, local initiative, and an end to 'stereotyped forms and uniformity imposed from above'[64] were to be guaranteed through the proliferation of agencies of self-administration. Yet the planned development of the economy and an equitable distribution of its product could simultaneously be achieved through popular control of the vertically structured banks and industrial trusts. In the naive enthusiasm of their early months in power the Bolsheviks believed they had at last resolved Marx's apparently incompatible accounts of the goals of socialism and the relationship between state and society into a coherent whole.

ISOLATION AND DICTATORSHIP

The optimism of the early months of the Revolution could not long survive the series of crises it had to face by the spring of 1918. Famine was, by this time, biting hard into the urban centres. The peasants, having seized the land and abrogated the debts and mortgages that hitherto had obliged them to produce for the market, retreated into subsistence farming. The consequences for the towns were dire. By late spring they were in the grip of famine. Industry was in a state of chaos, and transport, especially the railways, had been strained by the war to the point of breakdown. Despite Lenin's advice, the factory committees, with accelerating radicalism, had unleashed a campaign of wholesale expropriation and expulsion of the old management, making the restitution of centralised co-ordination imperative. The plethora of self-governing communes, councils and committees and the loosely structured hierarchy of soviets, found themselves faced, in the summer of 1918, by food, fuel and transport crises, by internal civil war and the predatory intervention of hostile states. The Bolsheviks, if they were to retain any credibility, had to satisfy those primal and minimal demands of government to defend its territory and to feed its population. In the plight of Russia at that time, both required herculean effort and the growth of centralised coercion.

To deal with this aggregation of crises the Bolsheviks had to centralise the meagre resources at their command. They rapidly established a standing army under Trotsky, staffed largely by the old officer corps. They founded an Extraordinary Commission to Combat Counter-Revolution (the infamous Cheka) under Dzerzhinsky. These two bodies formed not only the coercive structure of the regime but also the actual governing and executive administration over a large part of Soviet territory for the next two years at least:[65] 'the two pillars of traditional government, the army and the police, were reformed, responsible to the central power and completely independent of the Soviets and the control of the rank and file'.[66] Meanwhile the civilian government, The Council of People's Commissars, though responsible to the Executive Committee of the Soviets according to the letter of the constitution, almost from the start usurped the latter's powers and built up a bureaucratic apparatus of a broadly conventional type. The Soviet institutions, particularly the unwieldy Executive Committee, proved incapable of dealing with the pressing problems of famine and war with the speed and resolution required. They were swiftly infiltrated at all levels by the Bolsheviks and acquiesced remarkably quietly in what was represented as a temporary transfer of power for the duration of the civil war. They had, already, in late 1918, become the largely dignified or decorative elements of the constitution and ever more remained so.[67]

It was not until mid-1920, when the regime had seen off the worst military challenges, that the Bolshevik leadership had time to ponder and theorise the governmental structure that had been extemporised in the previous two-and-a-half years. There was considerable pressure from within the Party and from sections of the urban workers for all-round relaxation now that the military crisis was over. The Workers' Opposition and Democratic Centralists protested against the undue centralism and bureaucratic necrosis of party and state, they demanded more autonomy for local party and state bodies and the application everywhere of the democratic principle instead of the system of appointments from above. By this time, however, Lenin, Trotsky and Bukharin were aware of the receding prospects for the revolution in Europe. Each month of post-war stabilisation made it increasingly unlikely. The international revolution upon which they had pinned all their hopes, without which, they all agreed, they would be ruined, had not materialised. The revolution in Russia was thrown in upon its own ruined resources. The war had, as we have seen, left Russian industry and transport in chaos, which the revolution and the expropriations of the workers'-control movement exacerbated. Then came the civil war, adding its quota of destruction and depletion of men, machinery and rolling stock. By the end of the civil war the economic situation was more desparate than ever. The towns were again starving, trade between town and country had virtually collapsed, the population of the principal urban centres had shrunk by two-thirds, pathetically few factories were in operation, and those that were produced only intermittently, for want of fuel or parts or raw material. 'No country' Lenin concluded 'has been so devastated as ours.'[68] The urban working force, the erstwhile proletarian base of the regime, had been reduced to one-third of its 1913 numbers. It had been exhausted by years of famine, cold and typhus, diminished by exodus to the villages, diluted by peasant and youth recruitment and its best forces mobilised and sacrificed on the fronts of the civil war. As Lenin conceded, it had reaped no benefits from its class rule. On the contrary, it 'had suffered distress, want, starvation and a worsening of its economic positions such as no other class in history had suffered. It's not surprising that it is uncommonly weary, exhausted and strained.'[69] The proletarian vanguard, Lenin reminded his more utopian comrades, lay 'bleeding and in state of prostration'.[70]

> consider this carefully – our proletariat has been largely declassed; the terrible crises and closing down of the factories have compelled people to flee from starvation. The workers have simply abandoned their factories; they have had to settle down in the country and ceased to be workers. That is the economic source of the proletariat's declassing and the inevitable rise of petty-bourgeois, anarchist trends.[71]

These petty-bourgeois elements had penetrated 'deep into the ranks of the proletariat and the proletariat is declassed, i.e. dislodged from its class groove. The factories and mills are idle – the proletariat is weak, scattered enfeebled.'[72]

We have here a very strange circumstance indeed. At the very time that Lenin, Bukharin and Trotsky arrived at their conclusion about the declassing of the proletariat they began a self-conscious reorientation of the regime's justification. Their thorough elaboration of the dictatorship of the proletariat coincided with their discovery of the declassing of the proletariat.[73] Lenin at least had the honesty to acknowledge, albeit in appalling understatement, 'that the fact that the proletariat is declassed is a handicap'.[74] Above all, of course, it meant that its dictatorship would have to be exercised exclusively by its party.[75]

The situation, as the Bolshevik leadership quite openly acknowledged in the latter half of 1920, was briefly this. The regime was isolated in a world of predatory and mighty nation states. The prospects for world revolution receded by the month. Internally, industry and trade were at their lowest ebb, had indeed almost ceased. Even after a modest recovery in 1921 to 1922, Preobrazhensky estimated that 'Industrial production stands at no more than about one fifth of the pre-war level.'[76] The regime, which had long since alienated the peasantry, found itself faced with a numerically tiny and declassed urban workforce. The truth of the matter was, Lenin three times reminded the Eleventh Party Congress, that the Communists were isolated with Russia. They had, therefore, to build their policies on the frank recognition that 'we are but a drop in the ocean of the people'.[77] The prognosis for the regime looked desperate. Unless it could elaborate structures and policies that would deal with internal and international isolation and restore the ruined economy, the beacon of socialism flickering fitfully in Russia would be extinguished. *It was these extraordinary and quite unanticipated difficulties that the new model of the dictatorship of the proletariat was constructed to remedy.*

Bereft of the international support which they hitherto had believed alone could save them, with a declassed proletariat and a minimal internal social base, with a ruined industrial infrastructure, the Bolsheviks had no other available recourse to maintain their sway other than the power of the state. State power would have to resurrect industry, recreate and re-educate the proletariat, and suborn society to its purposes. But what model of state power was available to them that would show them how this might be done? The only state form that had achieved anything comparable was the imperialist state. The barons of finance capital had also comprised a tiny minority of the population, and had had to ruthlessly impress their will upon society in order to sustain their own mode of production. They, too, had had to reform, re-educate and discipline the working class. They had had to establish the armed might of the embattled state-capitalist trust simply in order to survive in the hostile world environment. And the way in which they had succeeded was sketched out in the Bolsheviks' own theorised account of the imperialist state. The finance capitalists had audaciously utilised the state, expanded its coercive power, boldly intervened to manage and direct the whole economy, had dominated society and incorporated the working class to serve their interests. They had put down faction and opposition and insisted upon the conformity and accountability of all to the single co-ordinated politico-economic productive system they had created. 'State capitalism', Bukharin declared, 'saved the *capitalist* state by an active and conscious intervention in production relations. Socialist methods will be a continuation of this active process of organisation.'[78] What was arrived at now was not the smashing of the great Leviathan but 'the dialectical transformation of the bourgeois dictatorship into the proletarian'.[79]

It is clear that the same method is formally necessary for the working class as for the bourgeoisie at the time of state capitalism. This organisational method exists in the co-ordination of all proletarian organisations with one all-encompassing organisation, i.e. with the state organisation of the working class, with the *Soviet state of the proletariat*. The 'nationalisation' of the trade unions and the effectual nationalisation of all mass organisations of the proletariat result from the internal logic of the process of transformation itself. The minutest cells of the labour apparatus must transform themselves into agents of the general process of organisation, which is systematically directed and led by the collective reason of the working class, which finds its material embodiment in the highest and most all-encompassing organisation, in its state apparatus. Thus the system of state capitalism dialectically transforms itself into its own inversion, into the state form of workers' socialism.[80]

The form and structure of the dictatorship of the proletariat was explicitly derived from the Bolsheviks' own theorised model of the imperialist state, and is unintelligible unless this relation is acknowledged. In both models 'the economically active subject' was the state and the state alone.[81] Both grasped the essential proposition that, to survive in the modern world, states had to dominate and bring coherent organisation to the entire economic infrastructure. The superstructure of organised coercion was to determine the economic base of society rather than vice versa. And the greater the concentration of power in the hands of the state, the swifter and more radical would be the transformation of the economic and social base. 'For this reason, revolutionary state power is the mightiest lever of the economic revolution.'[82] The road to socialism, according to Trotsky at this time, 'lies through a period of the highest possible intensification of the principle of the State . . . the most ruthless form of State, which embraces the life of the citizen authoritatively in every direction'.[83]

In the Commune model, as we have seen, the objective was to transform all those patterns of domination and subordination that had characterised relationships between men both within the productive process and in public and political life. The transformation of ownership relations was a secondary and derivative concern, that is it was to be pursued where appropriate in order to accomplish the primary objective. Socialism in this first account was defined in terms of relationships of egalitarian participation in the deliberation and execution of public policy and control over the productive process. Under the new specification of socialism, contained in the dictatorship of the proletariat, the earlier model was stood on its head. Socialism was now exclusively defined as a relationship of men to things; as an ownership relationship rather than a social relationship. It now consisted wholly in state ownership of the means of production and not at all in patterns of popular control and accountability.

By November 1918 Lenin introduced a distinction between the form of *government* and the form of the *state*.[84] There were in history, he maintained, the most varying administrative structures under the general rubric of the bourgeois state, but their *essence* was always the same. Their varying forms were but conventional and convenient administrative adaptations, whereas their class interest, that which really characterised the essential nature of the state, remained the same. In just the same way a dictatorship 'may also be exercised by a handful of persons, or by an oligarchy, or by a class, etc.'.[85] We are led by this essentialist reasoning to Lenin's stark conclusion, which reverses the position he had adopted a year previously: '*The form of government* has absolutely nothing to do with it.'[86] As we have seen, the Commune qualified as a socialist model of administration solely because it commended 'forms of government' through which permanent popular control could be exercised over all aspects of the deliberation and execution of public policy. Now, Lenin, pursuing the crude reductionism of class analysis, maintains that the forms of government through which a class exercises its power are a matter of irrelevance.

The same sophistical reasoning was to be applied to the administration of industry and the management of individual plants. Socialism, according to Trotsky's narrow definition, consisted in state ownership of the forces of production and not at all in collegial forms of decision-making, workers' control or industrial democracy:

> The dictatorship of the proletariat is expressed in the abolition of private property in the means of production, in the supremacy of the whole Soviet mechanism of the collective will of the workers, and not at all in the form in which individual enterprises are administered.[87]

The terminus in this progression was the redefinition of Socialism as that system of social ownership that best conduced to maximum economic efficiency and productivity. 'The creation of Socialist society means the organisation of the workers on new foundations, their adaptation to those foundations, and their labour re-education, with the one unchanging end of the increase in the productivity of labour'.[88] Society was now conceived of as one great factory, 'a single automatically working mechanism'.[89] It was, indeed, asserted that discipline, one-man management, the necessity of centralised planning and direction – in short, hierarchy and subordination – were intrinsic to the transitional phase. The objective of socialism now became the maximisation of production through the rational allocation of resources, including labour power, and the planned co-ordination of the whole economy. '*All* citizens are transformed into hired employees of the state. *All* citizens become employees and workers of a *single* country-wide state "syndicate".'[90] 'The whole of society', Lenin continued, 'will have become a single office and a single factory.'[91] The whole population, in Trotsky's view, was to be treated 'as the reservoir of the necessary labour power',[92] and 'Socialist industry is a trust of trusts'.[93]

The distinctions between citizen and worker, republic and mode of production, were already being eliminated. Henceforth, political rights were made an adjunct of socially useful work, and status, wages, honours and awards were distributed according to productivity. The principle of distributive justice that was to apply was the same as in the Marxian original version of the dictatorship of the proletariat – men were to be measured by their work. All of this was perfectly captured in what was trumpeted as the new principle of socialism: 'from each according to his ability to each according to his work'. These distinctive principles of the organic labour state were first formulated by Lenin, Trotsky and Bukharin in the period from spring 1918 to mid-1920. They have had a preponderant influence upon the social and political attitudes and institutions of Soviet-type regimes from that time until the present day. They constitute the unchallengeable core of Soviet-style socialism.

It was entirely clear to the Bolshevik leaders that this new specification of the nature of socialism was fundamentally incompatible with their original Commune model. Indeed they recognised that the sorts of attitudes and institutions it had given rise to were directly antagonistic to their new objectives. The objectives of their first model (as with Marx's) had been to smash the old authoritarian patterns of administration in the workshops, in society and in the state. The organic labour state which they called the dictatorship of the proletariat (which was itself modelled in the mirror image of the imperialist state), unequivocally demanded authoritative, or even despotic, one-man management in industry and the unquestionable jurisdiction of the centralised state to manage and remake society. The first shot in this campaign came in April 1918 when Lenin insisted:

We must learn to combine the 'public meeting' democracy of the working people – turbulent, surging, overflowing its banks like a spring flood – with *iron* discipline while at work, with unquestioning obedience to the will of a single person, the Soviet leader, while at work.[94]

Industrial democracy was distinguished, in Lenin's eyes, from political democracy. 'Industry', he contended 'is indispensable. Democracy is a category proper only to the political sphere.'[95] Even more categorically, in a phrase that might encapsulate the spirit of the organic labour state, Lenin insisted 'Industry is indispensable, democracy is not.'[96] The programme of industrial democracy (which had recruited the mercurial Bukharin to its ranks) henceforth became a dangerous syndicalist deviation which Lenin and Trotsky fought vehemently against – especially when it raised its head in the Party. The last defenders of the goals of industrial democracy, the Workers'

Opposition, finally succumbed in the spring of 1921 to a barrage of fierce and personal invective from Lenin,[97] administrative measures that effectively exiled its leaders, and a formal declaration by the tenth Party Congress that membership of the faction was incompatible with membership of the Party.

In the Commune model the diffuse collegial self-administration of the proletariat was to refashion and eventually to absorb the state. Under the dictatorship of the proletariat the state was expressly charged with refashioning, re-educating and eventually absorbing the proletariat. Just as the magnates of finance capital had had to utilise state power against sections of their own bourgeois class, so too the state power of the proletariat would have to be turned inwards against sections of the proletariat. For the proletariat, the Bolsheviks increasingly asserted, was not all of a piece. It had inherited divisions and prejudices from the old regime. It had been disorientated, diminished and declassed in the awful traumas of the revolution. In a backward country it lacked the cultural and organisational means to defend itself against petty-bourgeois infiltration from the great peasant mass around it.

As a consequence, according to Trotsky, there enters into the composition of the proletariat 'various elements, heterogeneous moods, different levels of development. Yet the dictatorship pre-supposes unity of will, unity of direction, unity of action.'[98] The dictatorship of the proletariat therefore 'became possible only by means of the dictatorship of the party', because only 'the Communists express the fundamental interests of the working class'.[99] By concentrating the will of the class and transcending the particular interests of trades and regions, the proletarian state, more than the weakened proletariat itself, became the true vehicle of proletarian interest. The state now became the dominant and essential organisational focus and authoritative institution of the class to which all other more partial and localised organisations, such as trade unions and workers councils, had to be subordinated. According to Bukharin, 'The state organisation is the most far-reaching organisation of the class in which it concentrates its entire strength ... in which the ruling class is organised specifically as a *class* and not as a small part or small group of a class.'[100] Confronted with a proletariat that had lost its class attributes, that was restive and undisciplined, the Bolsheviks had no option but to turn this concentrated force 'inward by constituting a factor of the self-organisation and the compulsory self-discipline of the working people'.[101] A principal task of the dictatorship of the proletariat became, paradoxically, the creation of a proletariat in the place and in the proportion needed by the state, imbued with attitudes favourable to the maximisation of productivity and free from autonomous defensive organisations that might have frustrated these goals.

In 1920, Lenin, Trotsky and Bukharin all favoured the militarisation of labour, the absorption of the trade unions by the state and the planned mobilisation of the entire labour force on the production front. Since, by their reasoning, socialism was defined as a system of ownership relations promoting the maximisation of production, and not at all in terms of its forms of administration, there could be no incompatibility between militarisation of the economy or dictatorial one-man direction, and socialism. On the contrary, socialism, in certain situations, might well be promoted and enhanced by these means. It was not matters of principle that made Lenin, in late 1920, criticise Trotsky's plan to militarise labour and absorb the unions into the state, but rather the prudent realisation that the regime was for the time being too weak to bear the determined opposition of the trade unions.

But if the unions were not to be actually absorbed by what Trotsky accurately dubbed 'The Labour State', there was general agreement with him that the unions must accept their role as ancillary agencies of the state and executants of its plans. Their functions were:

> to organise the working class for the ends of production, to educate, discipline, distribute, group, retain certain categories and certain workers at their posts for fixed periods ... in order to lead the workers into the framework of a single economic plan.[102]

Lenin was in complete agreement. The continued pretensions of the unions to interfere in the management of factories 'must be regarded as positively harmful and impermissible'.[103] The unions' tasks were to mobilise the mass behind state plans to 'enlist the working class', to engage in production propaganda, to organise disciplinary courts in the workplace, to enthuse the workers, monitor their performance and to admonish the recalcitrant or lazy.[104] They were to become an 'apparatus of revolutionary repression against undisciplined, anarchical parasitic elements in the working class'.[105] The unions, Lenin asserted, 'cannot refuse to share in coercion' to achieve the labour re-education needed, and to eliminate 'the prejudices and backwardness of the masses'.[106] They had no separate or autonomous existence from the party and the state. They were simply the 'transmission belts' connecting the various 'machines' of the national economy to their motor or prime mover, which was the state.[107] The unions were, to continue the mechanical allusion, to be no more than cogs and wheels in 'the automatically working mechanism of national production'.[108]

We have already seen that labour within the organic labour state was to be rewarded according to its intensity and duration. It followed therefore that the main function of the trade unions, which had hitherto been to negotiate collective agreements specifying hourly or weekly time-rates for differing groups of workers, had become superfluous and damaging. The labour principle was, as we have seen, one of inequality which tied individual reward to individual effort. Time-rates would therefore have to be supplanted by piece-rates. According to a decree of 21 February 1921, 'wage contracts for all Soviet, nationalised, public and private enterprises must, wherever possible, be based on piecework rates and a bonus system'.[109] Norms were to be introduced for all productive labour, with heavy penalties and bonuses for under- and over-fulfilment.[110] The idea of the crude performance-wage typical of the early severe stages of capitalist accumulation, was now trumpeted, even in the Constitution, as the principle of socialism. Preobrazhensky, at least, was more honest:

> NEP hastened the transition to a new wage system, and at present that system is for the most part based on the same principles as wages under capitalism: the more an individual turns out, the more he gets paid.[111]

In terms of its distributive principle, Preobrazhensky conceded, Soviet Russia 'has not gone very far from capitalism'.[112] The difference was that, potentially at least, the performance-wage could be more rigorously and universally applied. The ideal, according to Trotsky, was 'a sliding scale adaptable to all individual changes in the productivity of labour'.[113] In June 1921 Lenin even complained that, 'The system of distributing food on the egalitarian principle has led to equalisation, which sometimes proves to be an obstacle to increasing output.' Even food rations, he insisted, ought to be utilised 'as a political instrument ... to reduce the number of those not absolutely needed and to encourage those who actually are'.[114]

Gradually, regressively, the liberal provisions of the Soviet Labour Code, which had prompted Preobrazhensky's fears that socialist accumulation would be impeded (by comparison with the rate of primitive capitalist accumulation) by a humanitarian concern for the welfare and living conditions of the workers, were rescinded. Broader and broader categories of workers were mobilised and subjected to military discipline. The early stringent limitations on overtime, employment of minors and women, were attenuated. According to the new Labour Code of December 1918 all employees were to carry labour-books, which were to be comprehensive dossiers of individual productivity, benefits received, sick-leave granted, fines levied and disciplinary measures imposed.[115] Without a valid work-book the individual could not travel, could not find employment, could not obtain rations or accommodation. In this one measure the state hit upon its most potent means for the economic, and therefore political, control of its population. In April 1919 workers were prohibited from changing their work or place of employment 'without the written consent of the present employer'.[116] For those miscreants who persistently violated labour discipline or disrupted production, Compulsory Labour Camps were introduced, already, in May 1919. The labour state was laying the groundwork for the creation of an indentured workforce that had been so prominent a characteristic of the imperialist-state formation. As in the model of the imperialist state, the labour movement and individual workers were to be subordinated to the state, mobilised to fulfil its plans, rewarded according to the sumptuary norms set by the state, and disciplined and punished for any disruption of its productive system.

In part, the Bolsheviks' increasing intolerance towards alternative specifications of socialism and the role of the state stemmed from their recognition that the original formulations were corrosive of the centralised authoritarian direction that they felt to be necessary for the revival of Russian industry. This hardened, with the formulation of the dictatorship of the proletariat, into a more generalised antagonism to the whole of what is conventionally called politics, and this a-political stance was to have a lasting and disastrous impact upon the style of Soviet-type administrations. Faithful to the Saint Simonian original from which it derived, the dictatorship of the proletariat proclaimed the end of politics, in the sense of parties and factions competing for support on the basis of rival platforms and manifestoes with differing specifications of national goals. Politics in this sense, the Bolsheviks believed, was a feature of the regime's adolescence. It had passed away, to be replaced by a more mature application of scientific reason to the problems of industrialising society and maximising production. 'Henceforth', Lenin asserted in December 1920, to, of all audiences, the All-Russian Congress of Soviets which was supposedly the sovereign political body of the state, 'less politics will be the best politics.'[117]

It is often maintained, by those concerned to point up the 'democratic' essence of Leninism in comparison with the dictatorial regime imposed by Stalin upon party and state, that during Lenin's tenure of office the Party at least remained the forum for vital and animated debate. So indeed it was, to an extent at least. But this was despite, rather than because of, Lenin's pleadings. He complained bitterly about the 'luxury' of an open party debate on the trade-union question – it ought to have been quietly settled in a Party Commission;[118] 'it was a great mistake to put up these disagreements for broad Party discussion and the Party Congress'.[119] Disagreements, separate platforms and genuine debate, far from being indices of health and vitality, indicated to Lenin that 'The Party is sick. The Party is down with the fever.'[120] Disputation was a sign of morbidity not health.[121] His own displeasure and anxiety at this pre-Congress debate shone through everything he wrote. 'Personally, I am sick and tired of it.'[122]

Throughout late 1920 and down to his last writings in 1923, Lenin waged a consistent and bitter campaign against the Old Bolsheviks' fixation with theoretical disputation that surfaced in an indefatigible ability to produce theses, platforms, resolutions, and amendments to amendments, all couched in excellent dialectic, when what was needed was the ability to organise, to learn from concrete experience, to discipline oneself to the unglorious slog of punctual and persistent application to practical tasks. There was enough and too much of 'the intellectualist conceit of the Communist literati',[123] 'Incessant Meeting Sitters',[124] so effectively satirised by Mayakovsky, 'prepared at a moment's notice to write "theses", issue "slogans" and produce meaningless abstractions'.[125] In Lenin's eyes, 'production work is more interesting than the rectifying of a minute theoretical disagreement'.[126] The Party, he as much as declared, was full of theoretical masturbators. It had precious few administrators and experts and didn't know how to use those it had. 'We don't know how to collect evidence of practical experience and sum it up. We indulge in empty "general arguments and abstract slogans".'[127] The dictatorship of the proletariat, in this sense, entailed the imperative of remaking the Party, re-educating and retraining its personnel to make them effective and efficient managers of the national economy – a persistent and continuing concern of Soviet-type regimes. It was better by far, Lenin concluded, to have the services of one avowedly bourgeois expert who really knew his job, than to enjoy the sympathy of a dozen useless marxists schooled in exegetics.[128] The specialist, consequently, should be respected, should be learnt from, not commanded, and should be materially rewarded commensurate with his large contribution to production. 'Before the expert', Trotsky prophetically concluded, 'there opens up a boundless field of activity.'[129]

The functions of all the media of communication, of the trade unions and of education generally, were to act as centres for production propaganda. Lenin's exhortations to the Press were blunt and clear:

> Let us have less political fireworks, fewer general arguments and abstract slogans from inexperienced Communists who fail to understand their tasks; let us have more production propaganda.[130]

The faithful carrying-out of his instructions – for the press to avoid clashes of personality and conflict of policy – is painfully apparent to anyone obliged to read the newspapers of communist regimes. Their content is hardly political in the conventional sense, since their objective, from Lenin's time onward, has been to mobilise and enthuse the mass for the fulfilment of production norms. Their preoccupations have been with the exemplary individuals, collectives and enterprises that have pioneered more efficient means of economising on costs and maximising production. They have, with a vengeance, made up for Lenin's censure that 'Our press does not publicise those really exemplary local organisations which have practical experience.'[131] Even electricity-generating stations were to be used as centres of enlightenment for inducting the mass into the plans for revitalising industry and into the technology that would be its basis. (The parallels with Saint Simon's temples of science and enlightenment dedicated to Newton are strikingly similar in naivety.)

The administration of things was, in the eyes of the Bolsheviks, not at all a matter for disputation. On the basis of what is, the figures show what has to be done:[132] 'in the dry columns of figures and in the equally dry explanation of them, we can hear the glorious music of socialism in birth.'[133] Socialism, Trotsky concluded, 'is a balance-sheet'.[134]　But where disputation and politics ceased, the expert stepped in. Specialists and experts alone commanded the skills and experience to set the whole intricate structure of the planned economy into synchronised motion. They had, therefore, to be treasured as the apple of the eye of the organic labour state and given payment and authority commensurate with their status. The original animus against the bourgeois *spetsy*, the revolutionary prejudice that *all* could deliberate, plan and manage the affairs of society and of the economy, would have to be ruthlessly purged. On pain of being made redundant to the whole new mode of production the Communists would have to learn from the experts, but for the moment they certainly could not manage without them. For the time being, the proletariat, the whole workforce, and even the Party to a large extent, would have to subordinate themselves to the authority of the old experts and managers:

> it is precisely these people whom we, the proletarian party, must appoint to 'manage' the labour process and the organisation of production, for there are *no* other people who have practical experience in this matter.[135]

Until the workers themselves had acquired the requisite technical and managerial skills there could be no other solution compatible with the rapid development of the productive forces. To perpetuate the collegial system of management and decision-making was, in the view of Trotsky and Bukharin, simply to multiply ignorance.[136] What was imperatively required was a new model that would restore the link between the technical intelligentsia and the working class that had been broken by the prejudices on both sides that had arisen during the revolution. The solution, as Bukharin (and Lenin) perceived it in 1920, was that within the factories and plants the workers were to submit to the authority of the technical intelligentsia, but the intelligentsia in its turn was to be answerable 'in the last analysis to the collective will of the working class, which will find its expression in the state-economic organisation of the proletariat'.[137] Within this structure, therefore, 'working-class control' was to be exercised *only* at the state level and was emphatically denied at the local or plant level. What the social and economic organisation required was:

> the greatest exactitude, the unconditional and undisputed discipline, speed in decision-making, unity of will, and therefore minimal consultation and discussion, a minimal number of councils, maximal unanimity.[138]

Once again the guarantee of socialism was to consist *solely* in party control over the state. All in authority were to be appointed by, and answerable solely to, the state. The responsibility of managers and officials to local, plant, regional or industrial constituencies was expressly disavowed. The *nomenklatura* system practised in all Soviet-type regimes, in which all important managers and officials are appointed by and answerable to the central state, is and must be intrinsic to the planned economy and the organic labour state. It is the managers and officials who decide the promotional prospects, perks and status of their underlings, but it is the state that does likewise for *them*. By reserving to itself the power to decide where people shall work and what the nature of their work shall be, by keeping under its control the avenues of promotion and advancement of the entire workforce, the organic labour state has created for itself powers of social control over its entire population that are far more important to its stability than naked coercion. It can, and does, deploy a whole barrage of economic, educational and promotional sanctions against any dissident, and only in the comparatively rare instances when these fail does it need to have recourse to the penal system. Its stability is based upon the truth that very few men are prepared to martyr themselves for their principles. Even fewer rebel when they know that the educational and economic prospects of their children and relatives will be grievously affected by their dissidence. The moral and social constraints of doing well by one's family and loved ones (at the least not harming their interests) are systematically counterposed to personal principle. Even to make a stand poses an acute moral dilemma which only the very toughest can sustain.

We should at this stage recognise that, until 1928 at least, the vision of the organic labour state remained no more than a theorised projection. It was, as Lenin conceded, a dictatorship without a proletariat and a mode of production without large-scale industry.[139] The very weakness of the Bolshevik regime prevented the implementation of the vision and forced the 'temporary retreat' to the milder and more permissive policies of the New Economic Policy. For external consumption, however, the Bolsheviks insisted all the more stridently upon the dictatorship of the proletariat as the only form of state appropriate to the transitional phase. The very first of the Conditions for Admission to the Communist International, drafted by Lenin and presented to the Second Congress in July 1920, obliged all Communists to defend and propagandise it.[140] The dictatorship of the proletariat was adopted as the foundation myth of modern communism by generations of militant marxists. There were few, even in

1920, who would have been aware of the alternative and original justi-ficatory rationale of the Bolshevik regime. Communism announced itself to the world not in the libertarian garb of the Commune but in the steely armour of the dictatorship of the proletariat. Particularly for foreign consumption it cultivated a tough, uncompromising and ruthless image which proved quite successful in the depressed and turbulent 1920s and 1930s. It was also, of course, indispensable for the rise of Stalin.

For all the tough-minded utterances of the Bolsheviks, especially as directed to the Communist International, for all their insistence upon the need for tight centralisation and the planned mobilisation of national resources by the state, little progress was in fact achieved in the course of the 1920s. The one seemingly emphatic sign of advance was in the growth of the personnel employed by the state, from 600 000 at the end of 1917 to four million by 1928.[141] But this 'progress', as Lenin had tried to alert his colleagues in 1923, was largely the result of the creation of sinecures, of duplication of effort and the remorseless production of red tape. A very large apparatus had been created, but the growth of personnel seemed to stand in inverse proportion to the extensiveness of their useful functions. The threat of bureaucratism, of a swollen executive parasitically leeching the vitality from industry struggling to re-establish itself, seemed genuine enough. Lenin's response, in the last of his writings, was to advise a swingeing reduction of this great apparatus that, in his view, was not merely useless but harmful and parasitic. His abiding pre-occupation while in power was to increase gross production, produc-tivity and exchange, and therewith to increase the economic surplus available to the state, If, proportionate to these indices, the machinery and expenses of state administration had excessively expanded (and he had no doubt that they had), then they had to be drastically reduced. And if, by like token, the Party had been swollen by careerists and cluttered with deadwood veterans – trained in dialectic and conspiratorial method but quite hopeless at organising production – then it needed to be severely purged. Neither Party nor state was an end in itself. Neither was sacrosanct. Both existed to subserve the objectives of the productive system, to co-ordinate and promote its development, and to achieve the highest possible surplus in the hands of the state. On pain of frustrating these goals both party and state machines would, he believed, have to reform themselves. They had to become more economical in their use of resources and more efficient in deploying them.

Even during his own lifetime, however, Lenin could do little to curb the remorseless growth of vast bureaucratised Commissariats which, in the era of the New Economic Policy and government withdrawal from close supervision over the economy, had little to do. Industry only gradually recovered, the dispersed proletariat slowly returned to the towns, and only in 1928 did the urban industrial workers regain their 17–18 per cent share of the population. Agriculture remained overwhelmingly within private hands, and the landholding peasants and the self-employed actually increased from 67 per cent of the population in 1917 to 75 per cent in 1928. It followed, therefore, that this overwhelming majority was largely outside the sphere of state economic compulsion and was, in consequence, largely outside its effective political control as well.[142] It could be argued that the state, in 1928, was less intrusive for most citizens and less able to control and direct the heights of the economy than the highly interventionist tsarist regime had been. There was, without any doubt, a discrepancy between the extensiveness of the machinery of state and its effectiveness in planning the economy and modernising the productive process. There was a large gap between the pretensions of the dictatorship of the proletariat to mobilise all labour and all resources under the centralised planned direction of the state, and what actually existed in the Soviet Union. It was Stalin's dubious privilege to bring practice back into line with theory.

STALIN AND THE REALISATION OF THE ORGANIC LABOUR STATE

The decade from 1918 to 1928 was, as we have seen, characterised by audacity and even extremism in formulating the theory of the organic labour state, which was followed by a pragmatic acceptance that weakness and isolation made it impossible to realise. The decade from 1928 to 1938 was, on the contrary, characterised by theoretical inertia (in the sense that Stalin simply appropriated the formulations of 1920)[143] coupled with ruthless audacity and extremism in realising all of the conditions for the practical operation of the organic labour state.

In the decade up to 1938 the great immensity of Soviet society was more radically transformed than any society in history had been in so short a time. Almost nobody in Russia was, in 1938, where he had been in 1928. The old Bolsheviks, the revered leaders of the October

Revolution and the intellectual heart of the Party, had been physically eliminated. The trade-union, Soviet and Party structures had been ruthlessly purged and their leading bodies almost wholly replaced. Between 1934 and 1939, according to Stalin, half-a-million Party members were promoted to replace the old elite.[144] Entire social groups had been eliminated, millions had died or had been deported from their home regions in the forced collectivisation of agriculture, millions more perished in the forced labour of the *gulag* and in the appalling conditions that prevailed in the huge construction projects, millions more had been uprooted to supply labour to the new industrial towns. It was a cataclysm such as no other modern society had endured.

The class structure of Soviet society had been abruptly transformed. If in 1928 approximately three-quarters of the population had been self-employed, by 1938 this category had shrunk to insignificance. The goal of the integral labour state, of transforming *all* into the salaried employees of a single economic mechanism, had been ruthlessly achieved.

Most important, the two five-year plans had, at an unspeakable cost in torment, built up a powerful heavy industrial infrastructure. Total production had quadrupled within a decade.[145] A vast new industrial workforce had been created in the place, number and proportion that state plans required. Here, for the first time in history, was an industrial workforce made to the specification of the masters of the state machine. It was a workforce that owed its existence, its expectations, its knowledge of the world, indeed its literacy, to that same state that controlled all its avenues of movement, promotion, or even physical survival. The state now firmly controlled the educational, employment and career prospects of the entire population. These were, and still remain, the mightiest levers of this unique state form. The cement of the system was, and continues to be, the state's almost boundless power of patronage.

The state now decided who should work at what, and, of crucial importance in a land-mass as vast as the Soviet Union encompassing the full range of climatic extremes and with as large a disparity in cultural provision, it dictated *where* one should work. It set norms for all productive work, rewarding most highly those whose contribution to the fulfilment of the Plan was considered most exemplary. Payment was strictly according to performance and differentials were enormously extended. Sharply defined gradations were established within the working class and between it and the managerial and technical elite. Within the state administration and the army, pay differentials, perks and the insignia of office now became more exaggerated than they had been even under the tsar. The egalitarian inspiration of the Revolution, which resented and challenged the legitimacy of these divisive policies, had now to be confronted and denigrated. '*Uravlinovka* (levelling down) has as its origins the peasant outlook, the psychology of equal division of goods' and this, Stalin insisted, 'has nothing in common with Marxian socialism'.[146] According to Molotov, 'Bolshevik policy demands a resolute struggle against egalitarians as accomplices of the class enemy, as elements hostile to socialism.'[147] The watchword of 'equality' was dispensed with and in its place 'socialist emulation' or 'socialist competition' tied reward firmly to the skill, intensity and duration of labour. In this way the 1938 *History of the Communist Party of the Soviet Union* (short course) could reflect with evident satisfaction that, 'In the USSR is realised the Socialist principle: "From each according to his ability, to each according to his work." '[148] The most typical aspect of this state-promoted labour competition was the Stakhanov movement which started in 1935 and which sought to popularise the extraordinary (and contrived) productivity of dedicated shock-workers. The more these industrial commandos allegedly produced, the more the norms for everyone else were raised, and the more depressed the living standards of the majority became.

Preobrazhensky had, in 1924, believed that the political victory of the working class entailed a considerable economic impediment, in that the rate of accumulation could not be as large, for the reason that 'the working class...cannot treat its own labour power, its health and working conditions in the same way as the capitalist did'.[149] It did not, however, take long for Soviet economists, with Strumilin in their van, to grasp the fact that *precisely because* the state disposed of an effective monopoly as an employer of labour it could (given adequate coercive resources) impose its sumptuary norms, its hours and conditions of work and its labour discipline upon the entire population. Once it had done so, then it could obviously control the rate of accumulation and the size of the social surplus more effectively than any other productive system known to history.[150] According to some East European critics this is *the* principal distinguishing characteristic of the mode of production now known as 'developed socialism'. It is the central political bureaucracy that 'has at its exclusive command the basic means of production'.[151] that sets the norms of consumption for the population and determines the duration and intensity of labour. It determines the size of the social surplus (or the funds available for investment) and decides upon its allocation. It was precisely these characteristics that fitted what we refer to as the organic labour state to preside over the rapid industrialisation of a backward country. Marxism in this guise became pre-eminently an ideology of modernisation appealing to the intelligentsia of the underdeveloped world as a short cut to industrialisation and national grandeur.

But rapid industrialisation clearly required the maximum accumulation of capital reserves in the hands of the state. This, in turn, presupposed that wages and the norms of consumption should be depressed to the minimum compatible with the reproduction of labour power. High prices and low wages and a policy of 'utmost economy in the interests of accumulation'[152] were essential. Preobrazhensky now acknowledged that primitive socialist accumulation would have to 'take place through the temporary sacrifice of the masses, inequality and oppression'.[153] If followed that the powerful defensive organisations of labour, the trade unions, would have to be broken and reformed to promote rather than frustrate the goal of 'socialist accumulation'. The organic labour state was, by its nature, obliged to deprive the workers of their means of self-defence. Already in 1920 Bukharin, Lenin and Trotsky were broadly agreed that the unions would have to be militarised and absorbed into the state structure and should concern themselves exclusively with mobilising and enthusing the mass for the achievement of state plans. They were to be the executants of labour discipline, the transmission-belts through which the central apparatus set in motion the several parts of the single mechanism of production. By 1929 the trade unions had been so emasculated that they had lost all right to participate in the settlement of wages. It was declared that, in the epoch of the Plan 'the collective agreement as a form of regulating wages has outlived its usefulness'.[154]

The most basic defence mechanisms of the workers had been effectively destroyed; the trade unions were converted into what Carr refers to as 'production unions'.[155] Strikes were (and still are) punished with the most extreme retribution, for in the organic labour state the greatest threat must always be the organised withdrawal of labour. (For this reason, Solidarity in Poland could not long co-exist with the Communist government; threatening its control of labour it threatened the basis of its political power.) It was under Stalin during the period of the first two five-year plans that Soviet workers were reduced to an atomised mass and their trade unions became agencies of the state. The results were predictable enough. The decade from 1929 to 1939 saw a reduction in the real wages of all groups of workers (apart from the tiny numbers of Stakhanovites) by approximately 50 per cent.[156] A vast, impoverished and indentured labour force tied to its place of work and prohibited from striking had been created within a decade. It was kept in its place partly by creating a small aristocracy of labour, dependent for its privileges upon the regime, and partly by the enforcement of draconian legislation which visited the most severe penalties for breach of discipline, absenteeism, and sabotage or theft of public property. Above every worker hung the threat of the knock on the door at night and consignment to corrective labour.

Nowhere except in the Soviet Union was there such a large industrial workforce so devoid of the characteristics that, according to Marx, defined the proletariat. It had no autonomous national organisations and no means of independent articulation.[157] It could not, therefore, attain to any generalised conception of the exploitable structure in which it was locked. Here, with a vengeance, 'was a working class the like of which the history of mankind had never known before'.[158] These characteristics of a declassed workforce deprived of organisation and articulation, subjugated by violence and reduced to subsistence wages, were precisely the characteristics discerned by Lenin and Bukharin in their accounts of the plight of the workers under the ideal-typical Imperialist state formation. All the devices of capitalist accumulation under monopoly capitalism were deployed and refined in the organic labour state. It was Stalin who implemented them in the Soviet Union and who represented the triumph of the state over society in general, and the workers' organisations in particular, as the accomplishment of *socialism*.

The forced integration of all resources and labour power into a single productive mechanism was not of course restricted to the industrial workers and the peasantry. The intelligentsia, and especially the creative artists, were allotted their clearly delimited function in the organic plan. Art, like every other facet of social life, was to subserve the interests of production. Under Stalin it became the function of the artist to inspire the mass with a vision of heroic endeavour and the insurmountable will of workers to overcome all obstacles. The subjects the artist was to depict never gave in to self-pity or anxious self-doubt, they were never pessimistic, never concerned with the flaws and deficiencies of the present, but always set their eyes upon how things had improved compared with the past and how the future was bright with blessings. The hero of the novel, short story, or magazine article, confronted and overcame all barriers and was always prepared to sacrifice personal well-being, and even family and loved ones, for the sacred cause of socialist construction. The subject of representational art became the well-formed, clear-eyed and resolute son or daughter of toil, striding forward towards the sun. The images and the symbolism were all directly calculated to foster the spirit of integrated labour working together for the common good. All trades and skills, all national groups, men and women all together symbolically portrayed in endless variations the common theme of the virtue of integrated labour. The aesthetic content of this new 'socialist realism' was no more than production propaganda. It was the inspirational arm of the labour state. All those artists and writers who retained an attachment to art for art's sake, or who attempted to continue the questing and idiosyncratic inventiveness of the 1920s, were exiled from the state-directed artistic corporations. (From 1932 the Union of Soviet Writers was thoroughly dominated by the Party and it exercised a stifling monopoly over creative writing.) That they should have been denied the title 'artist' and prevented from publishing, exhibiting, or being rewarded for their work, was entirely consonant with the ethos of the organic labour state that only *socially useful work* should be published and rewarded.

It was not until Stalin's Second Revolution that the dictatorial severity anticipated in the theory of the early 1920s became a reality. It was only then that the ubiquity of the state as dictator and overseer of the mode of production was accomplished. Simultaneously, as Lenin and Trotsky had predicted, the organs of state as the theatre for what might conventionally be styled 'politics' literally ceased to function. The Supreme Soviet of the USSR met only once in the period of most drastic change from 1929 to 1935. This 'Supreme organ of state' neither discussed nor even approved the five-year plans which were to transform every aspect of Soviet social and economic life. Seventeen years elapsed between the Ninth All Union Trade Union Congress (1932) and the Tenth Congress. Nor was the Party any more vibrant in its political life. It met in Congress only three times in the decade 1929 to 1939 and by this time it had exhausted itself as an intellectual force. All its decisions were unanimously adopted, debate ceased, and its proceedings were surrounded by a mounting aura of fear which reached its peak in the crescendo of violence directed against the old guard of the Party itself between 1936 and 1938. 'According to the statement made by Khrushchev at the twentieth Party Congress, of the total of 139 members and candidates [of the Central Committee] elected at the Seventeenth Congress in 1934, 98, or 70 per cent, were thus eliminated.'[159] In such an atmosphere of purge and terror meaningful political debate was impossible, the Party itself became a cipher and power passed to the General Secretary working in conjunction with the secret police. Here indeed the state was purged of its political attributes, reduced to a monolithic uniformity and almost exclusively an instrument of coercion. The veteran leaders of the Party were annihilated in the purges and Party history was re-written to expunge their memory. The Party now became a purely executive agency of the dictatorship charged with mobilising the mass for the fulfilment of the Plan and with enforcing labour discipline. It had lost all its pretensions to be a deliberative and inspirational force and had become, as Gramsci had predicted it would in this situation, 'a police organisation and its name "political party" is pure mythological metaphor'.[160]

The revolution whose inspiration had been that of dispersing power throughout society by dismantling the hierarchical structures of domination internal to the old productive process, social structure, and governmental apparatus, had ended now in the most consummate concentration of domination, not even in the hands of a relatively predictable bureaucracy, but in the hands of one man. In torrents of sycophancy Stalin was now lauded as the only faithful comrade of Lenin, the great elaborator of Marxism–Leninism, the sole guardian of the revolutionary tradition whose thought illuminated all that was good and healthy.

It became increasingly clear, however, towards the end of Stalin's reign, that there were many features of the system that he had created that were dysfunctional to the further development of the regime's sole remaining claim to legitimacy – that it served to maximise the productive potential of society and thereby ensure the greatest material benefit to its workforce. There was, in the first place, the enormous expense of sustaining the internal policing network on the scale that it had attained. This might have been necessary in the phase of dispossessing the peasants and meeting their widespread resistance, but by the early 1950s it acted as a severe drain on the economy. There was, as important, the unsurmountable difficulty of attempting to maximise productive effiency in a climate of unpredictable arbitrariness, fear and distrust that paralysed initiative at all levels of economic and administrative life. There were, finally, widespread popular expectations that the severities, decades of civil war, internal strife, severity and world war would at last be relieved, so that the interests of the neglected consumers might be met. To some extent the regime found itself hoist on its own petard. Having insisted upon the performance-wage and having introduced carefully graduated incentive payment according to fulfilment of norms, it discovered that incentives lost all effectiveness at that point when desired consumer goods proved unobtainable. The internal logic of the organic labour state is sufficient to explain the relaxation of economic policies, the modest revival of consumer-goods industry, the restitution of the more predictable state bureaucracy and the downgrading of the secret police that Stalin's successors fairly rapidly embarked upon. What is important, however, is that these continuing changes, as we note in the Conclusion to this volume, involved no significant changes in the prevalent conception of the realm of politics, of the rights of citizens, or of the autonomy of social groups. They were, and have remained, functional adaptations of the organic labour state and not at all portents of its transformation into a 'pluralist' or 'corporatist' sociopolitical system.

NOTES

1. K. Marx and F. Engels, *Collected Works*, 50 vols (London, 1975–00) vol. 5, p. 47. Hereafter in the notes for this and subsequent chapters, *MECW*. For those of their works not yet covered by the *Collected Works*, references have, where possible, been standardised to K. Marx and F. Engels, *Selected Works*, 2 vols (Moscow, 1962) hereafter *MESW*.
2. Karl Marx, *The Civil War in France* (Peking, 1970) p. 251.
3. Ibid, p. 165.
4. Ibid, p. 166.
5. *MESW*, vol. 1, p. 520.
6. Ibid, p. 521.
7. Ibid, *loc. cit.* Compare Hoffman's analysis of the Commune as the state form of the transitional phase in the present volume, p. 132.
8. Karl Marx, *The Civil War in France*, p. 160.
9. Ibid, p. 171.
10. *MESW*, vol. 1, p. 519.
11. Ibid, p. 520.
12. Ibid, p. 522.
13. Ibid, p. 523. Marx's temporary faith in the co-operative societies to regulate national production contrasts sharply with his earlier and later disparaging remarks about the co-operative movement.
14. For a comprehensive check-list of the references to the dictatorship of the proletariat in the writings of Marx and Engels, see H. Draper, 'Marx and the Dictatorship of the Proletariat', in *Cahiers de l'Institut de Science Economique Appliquée, Serie S, Etudes de Marxologie* (Paris,

1962) no. 6, pp. 5–73. For an attempt to reconcile the Commune model with the dictatorship of the proletariat, see M. Johnstone, 'The Paris Commune and Marx's Conception of the Dictatorship of the Proletariat', *The Massachusetts Review* (Summer 1971) no. 3, pp. 447–62. For a critical examination of the problems posed by the duality in Marx's recommendations concerning the state, see N. Harding, *Lenin's Political Thought*, vol. 2 (London, 1981) ch. 5.

15. *MESW*, vol. 2, p. 24. For Lenin's extended gloss to this principle of distributive justice in the transitional period, see *The State and Revolution*, in V.I. Lenin, *Collected Works*, 45 vols (hereafter, in the notes to this and subsequent chapters, Lenin, *CW*) (Moscow, 1960–70) vol. 25, pp. 469–72.

16. K. Taylor (ed.), *Henri Saint-Simon. Selected Writings on Science, Industry and Social Organisation* (London, 1975) p. 158.

17. E. Durkheim, *Socialism* (original title *Socialism and Saint Simon*) (New York, 1962) p. 178.

18. K. Marx and F. Engels, *The German Ideology* (London, 1965) p. 48. This is, curiously, omitted from the version in *MECW*, vol. 5.

19. Taylor, *Henri Saint Simon*, pp. 166–7.

20. MECW, vol. 9, p. 212.

21. Taylor, *Henri Saint-Simon*, p. 168.

22. Ibid, p. 167.

23. Quoted in Durkheim, *Socialism*, p. 197.

24. Taylor, *Henri Saint-Simon*, p. 167.

25. A. W. Gouldner, *The Two Marxisms* (London, 1980) p. 345.

26. L. Trotsky, *Terrorism and Communism* (Ann Arbor, 1961) p. 142. We may be thankful that Trotsky in his own historical writings conspicuously departed from his own narrow maxim.

27. Taylor, *Henri Saint-Simon*, p. 165.

28. Ibid, p. 267.

29. Ibid, p. 209.

30. Ibid, p. 230; cf. the Platonic argument from techné leading to the same conclusion that politics must be made the exclusive preserve of those of appropriate aptitude and training.

31. *MECW*, vol. 6, p. 505.

32. Ibid, *loc. cit.*

33. *MESW*, vol. 1, p. 523.

34. Ibid, p. 637.

35. Ibid, *loc. cit.*

36. Ibid, *loc. cit*; and cf. Lenin, *The State and Revolution*, on the authority and subordination entailed in the complex interactions of industrial processes, Lenin, *CW*, vol. 25, p. 152.

37. Only in 1891, long after Marx's death, did Engels in his Introduction to Marx's *The Civil War in France* identify the Commune as the form of the dictatorship of the proletariat. See *MESW*, vol. 1, p. 485.

38. *MESW*, vol. 1, p. 522.

39. For a detailed account of the centrality of Lenin's analysis of international finance capitalism for his theory of revolution and his theory of the state, see Harding, *Lenin's Political Thought*, vol. 2, chs 3–6.

40. Bukharin wrote his text on imperialism in 1914, it was published in Moscow in 1917, as *Mirovoe khozyaystvo i imperializm*, and translated into English (London, n.d. [1929 or 1930]) as *Imperialism and World Economy*. On the preponderant role of the imperialist state in directing the economy, see the English edition, pp. 73–4, 108 and 179.

41. In these respects the Bolsheviks closely followed the pioneering work of Rudolf Hilferding, published in 1910 and translated into Russian in 1914 as *Finansovyi kapital*.

42. Bukharin, *Imperialism*, p. 160.

43. N. I. Bukharin, 'K teorii imperialisticheskogo gosudarstva', *Revolyutsiya prava*, sbornik 1 (Moscow, 1925) p. 21.

44. Ibid, p. 30.

45. Ibid, p. 16.

46. N. Bukharin, *Economics of the Transformation Period* (New York, 1971) p. 41.

47. The Dutch Marxist, Anton Pannekoek, had earlier arrived at very similar conclusions in his influential article, 'Mass Action and Revolution', in *Neue Zeit*, vol. xxx (1912) no. 2. See further, R. V. Daniels, 'The State and Revolution: A Case Study in the Genesis and Transformation of Communist Ideology', *American Slavonic and East European Review*, vol. 2 (1953) pp. 28–9. For Lenin's appreciation of Pannekoek's position, see *CW*, vol. 25, pp. 489–95.

48. Lenin, *CW*, vol. 24, p. 24, n.

49. Lenin, *CW*, vol. 24, p. 170.

50. Lenin, *CW*, vol. 25, p. 313.

51. Lenin, *CW*, vol. 25, p. 428.

52. Lenin, *CW*, vol. 26, p. 409.

53. Lenin, *CW*, vol. 27, p. 135.

54. Lenin, *CW*, vol. 26, p. 106.

55. Lenin, *CW*, vol. 26, p. 108.

56. Lenin, *CW*, vol. 25, p. 430.

57. Lenin, *CW*, vol. 26, p. 114.

58. Lenin, *CW*, vol. 25, p. 363.

59. Lenin, *CW*, vol. 25, p. 324.

60. Lenin, *CW*, vol. 25, p. 347.

61. Lenin, *CW*, vol. 25, p. 336.

62. Lenin, *CW*, vol. 25, p. 348.

63. M. Dewar, *Labour Policy in the USSR, 1917–28* (London and New York, 1956) p. 161.

64. Lenin, *CW*, vol. 26, p. 413.

65. An excellent recent account of just how extensive the administrative responsibilities of the Cheka were is given in George Legett's *The Cheka: Lenin's Political Police* (Oxford, 1981).

66. H. Carrère d'Encausse, *Lenin: Revolution and Power* (London and New York, 1982) p. 95.

67. For a thorough account of the atrophy of the Soviets as governmental agencies in the years immediately following the October Revolution, see O. Anweiler, *The Soviets: The Russian Workers, Peasants, and Soldiers Councils, 1905–1912.* (New York, 1974) ch. 5.

68. Lenin, *CW*, vol. 32, p. 444.

69. Lenin, *CW*, vol. 32, p. 274.
70. Lenin, *CW*, vol. 32, p. 254.
71. Lenin, *CW*, vol. 32, p. 199.
72. Lenin, *CW*, vol. 33, pp. 23–4.
73. Similar pessimistic appraisals of the degeneration of the proletariat, and similar remedies recommending greatly expanded roles for both party and state, were set out in 1920 by Trotsky in his *Terorrizm i kommunizm*, and by Bukharin in his *Ekonomiki perekhodnogo perioda*. (For details of English language publication of these works see notes 26 and 46.)
74. Lenin, *CW*, vol. 32, p. 412.
75. Lenin, *CW*, vol. 32, p. 20.
76. E. P. Preobrazhensky, *The Crisis of Soviet Industrialisation* (London, 1980) p. 26.
77. Lenin, *CW*, vol. 33, pp. 285, 290, 304.
78. Bukharin, *Economics of the Transformation Period*, p. 69.
79. Ibid, p. 75.
80. Ibid, p. 79.
81. Ibid, p. 117.
82. Ibid, p. 151.
83. Trotsky, *Terrorism and Communism*, pp. 169–70.
84. Lenin, *CW*, vol. 28, p. 241.
85. Lenin, *CW*, vol. 28, p. 235.
86. Lenin, *CW*, vol. 28, p. 238.
87. Trotsky, *Terrorism and Communism*, p. 162.
88. Ibid, p. 146.
89. L. Trotsky, *Towards Socialism or Capitalism?* (London, 1926) p. 104.
90. Lenin, *CW*, vol. 25, p. 478.
91. Lenin, *CW*, vol. 25, p. 479.
92. Trotsky, *Terrorism and Communism*, p. 135.
93. Trotsky, *Towards Socialism or Capitalism?*, p. 117.
94. Lenin, *CW*, vol. 27, p. 271.
95. Lenin, *CW*, vol. 32, p. 26.
96. Lenin, *CW*, vol. 32, p. 27.
97. The verbal savagery of Lenin's onslaught against the members of the Workers' Opposition betrayed his sensitivity to their critique and his awareness of the regime's insecurity. For the first time in his career he descended to threatening a fellow leading Communist with violence. Shlyapnikov's arguments, he asserted, would be answered with a gun. (Lenin, *CW*, vol. 34, p. 206.)
98. Trotsky, *Terrorism and Communism*, p. 108.
99. Ibid, p. 109.
100. Bukharin, *Economics of the Transformation Period*, p. 27.
101. Ibid, p. 151.
102. Trotsky, *Terrorism and Communism*, p. 146.
103. Lenin, *CW*, vol. 33, p. 189.
104. Lenin, *CW*, vol. 33, p. 191.
105. Trotsky, *Terrorism and Communism*, p. 111.
106. Lenin, *CW*, vol. 33, p. 193.

107. Lenin, *CW*, vol. 33, p. 192.
108. Trotsky, *Towards Socialism or Capitalism?*, p. 104.
109. Dewar, *Labour Policy in the USSR*, p. 179.
110. Ibid, pp. 196, 206.
111. Preobrazhensky, *Crisis of Soviet Industrialisation*, p. 22.
112. Ibid, p. 23.
113. Trotsky, *Terrorism and Communism*, p. 156.
114. Lenin, *CW*, vol. 32, pp. 448–9.
115. Dewar, *Labour Policy in the USSR*, pp. 176–7.
116. Ibid, p. 181.
117. Lenin, *CW*, vol. 31, p. 514.
118. Lenin, *CW*, vol. 32, p. 86.
119. Lenin, *CW*, vol. 32, p. 41.
120. Lenin, *CW*, vol. 32, p. 43.
121. Lenin, *CW*, vol. 32, p. 54.
122. Lenin, *CW*, vol. 32, p. 41.
123. Lenin, *CW*, vol. 32, p. 138.
124. Lenin, *CW*, vol. 33, p. 223.
125. Lenin, *CW*, vol. 32, p. 144.
126. Lenin, *CW*, vol. 32, p. 26.
127. Lenin, *CW*, vol. 32, p. 127.
128. Lenin, *CW*, vol. 32, p. 144.
129. Trotsky, *Terrorism and Communism*, p. 120.
130. Lenin, *CW*, vol. 32, p. 130.
131. Lenin, *CW*, vol. 32, p. 440.
132. Trotsky, *Towards Socialism or Capitalism?*, p. 19.
133. Ibid, p. 13.
134. Ibid, p. 14.
135. Lenin, *CW*, vol. 27, p. 349.
136. Trotsky, *Terrorism and Communism*, pp. 117–8; Bukharin, *Economics of the Transformation Period*, p. 127.
137. Bukharin, *Economics of the Transformation Period*, p. 75.
138. Ibid, p. 128.
139. Lenin, *CW*, vol. 32, pp. 244, 254; *CW*, vol. 33, p. 174.
140. Lenin, *CW*, vol. 31, p. 207.
141. Carrère d'Encausse, *Lenin*, p. 196.
142. '[By] 1927 it was apparent that the party and soviet organizations in the villages were quite powerless to assert their authority over the peasants.': Leonard Schapiro, *The Communist Party of the Soviet Union* (London, 1960) p. 383.
143. R. V. Daniels, in his 'The State and Revolution . . .', *American Slavonic and East European Review*, vol. 2 (1953) argues the case that it was Stalin who was the innovator in asserting the state's independence from economic forces. As we have seen in this chapter this proposition had long been central to the Old Bolshevik theory of the dictatorship of the proletariat.
144. Schapiro, *The Communist Party*, p. 417.
145. D. R. Hodgman, *Soviet Industrial Production 1928–31* (Cambridge, Mass., 1954) cited in Schapiro, p. 459.

146. Z. M. Chernilovky (ed.), *History of State and Law* (Moscow, 1949) p. 29.
147. T. Cliff, *State Capitalism in Russia* (London, 1974) p. 69.
148. *History of the Communist Party of the Soviet Union (Bolshevik) Short Course* (Moscow, 1938) p. 526.
149. E. A. Preobrazhensky, *Novaya ekonomika* (Moscow, 1926) vol. 1, part 1, p. 100.
150. Bukharin, in his *Economics of the Transformation Period*, had earlier observed that the enforcement of reduced sumptuary norms through state rationing had been central to accumulation under monopoly capitalism. Bukharin, *Economics*, p. 35.
151. J. Kuron and K. Modzelewski, *Open Letter to the Party*, published as *Solidarnošč: The Missing Link*? (London, 1982) p. 23.
152. E. A. Preobrazhensky, *The Crisis of Soviet Industrialisation*, p. 71.
153. Carrère d'Encausse, *Lenin*, p. 168.
154. Cliff, *State Capitalism*, p. 17.
155. E. H. Carr, *The Bolshevik Revolution 1917–23* (Harmondsworth, 1976) vol. 2, p. 226.
156. Schapiro, *The Communist Party*, p. 462.
157. Compare the critique of Kuron and Modzelewski, p. 36: 'The effective realisation of such a process of industrialisation required that all classes and social strata be deprived of the means of defining their interests and fighting for their implementation or in their own defence.'
158. *History of the CPSU (Bolsheviks) Short Course*, p. 524.
159. Schapiro, *The Communist Party*, p. 473.
160. Cited in F. Claudin, *The Communist Movement from Comintern to Cominform* (Harmondsworth, 1975) p. 103.

2 Political Power and the Soviet State: Western and Soviet Perspectives[1]

Archie Brown

It is not so very long ago that there was an almost unquestioning acceptance among Western scholars that the concept of totalitarianism provided the single key to understanding the nature of the Soviet state. That view – perhaps in a modified version, that it is the best key available – still has its defenders, but it has increasingly been challenged ever since it first came under serious attack in the 1960s. In the Soviet Union itself the same decade saw the opening shots fired in a campaign to have power relations within the Soviet and other political systems discussed more realistically and less propagandistically than hitherto in the context of the development of a discipline of political science.[2] It is only in recent years, however, that serious debate on the nature of political power and on the concepts of the state and the political system has been conducted in specialist Soviet journals and small-circulation books. One of the purposes of this chapter is to bring together such writings by Soviet scholars and the writings of Western political scientists on the nature of power relations within the Soviet system, partly on account of the intrinsic interest of both and also to see what relevance, if any, the Soviet discussions bear to Western arguments concerning the nature of the system. Some attention is paid to theoretical accounts of the relationship between state and society, a common theme in the two bodies of work.

The first of the two main sections into which the chapter is divided – they are followed by a short section of conclusions – considers briefly certain problems involved in conceptualising Soviet politics, and goes on to offer a critique of three of the major ways in which the Soviet system has been viewed by Western scholars – as totalitarian, pluralist and corporatist. The second section looks, first, at the hitherto little-known Soviet discussion of the relationship between the concepts of 'political power', 'the state' and 'the political system' and, second, at theoretical statements recently advanced by Soviet scholars on the delicate issue of state–society relations and the question of the 'relative autonomy' of the state. As part of the analysis of the different conceptualisations of the Soviet system, some recent evidence will be presented on power relations within the system and an attempt made to put these relations in a comparative perspective.

'Pluralism', which is one of the major themes of this chapter, is discussed more often by Western political scientists with an interest in the Soviet Union than by their Soviet colleagues, though Western pluralist theory (not to mention practice) attracts a fair amount of criticism in works specifically directed against 'bourgeois ideology'. In so far as Western attempts to apply the concept of pluralism to the Soviet political system are acknowledged by Soviet politicians and scholars, they tend to be given short shrift. In contrast, however, the issue of autonomy – which is of central importance in Western theories of pluralism – is well to the fore within a certain body of recent Soviet scholarship, though there is a fundamental difference in the focus of attention of Western and Soviet political scientists when they write about this. Those Western political scientists who apply the concept 'pluralism' to the Soviet polity are not generally those who pay most attention to the issue of autonomy. They emphasise, rather, the variety of influences *on* the government[3] by outside bodies, or the variety of points of view and influences *within* government of different organisations and interests. Western *theorists* of pluralism, however, tend to stress (as a central feature of pluralism) the relative autonomy of society generally, and of organisations and groups specifically, *from* control by the government. 'Autonomy from', rather than 'variety of influences on', is a major emphasis also in certain recent Soviet writing on the state – but with an important distinction from the corresponding Western work. When these particular Soviet scholars write of relative autonomy *from* control, it is the 'relative autonomy' of the state from society (not of society from the state) that they choose to stress.

In this last respect, the discussions of the Soviet scholars have more in common with those of Western Marxists (including 'critical' Marxists) than with the writings of non-Marxist political scientists. This is not surprising, for both Soviet and Western Marxists belong to an intellectual tradition in which a socioeconomic determinism has been a prominent part and in which, in the words of a Western Marxist who himself stresses the relative autonomy of the state, there remains 'an insistence on the "primacy" of the "economic base" which must not be understated'.[4] An apparent independent power on the part of the state presents, therefore, a greater intellectual challenge to Marxists than to non-Marxist political scientists, since many of the latter have long taken it for granted and have been especially conscious of the power of the state within Communist systems. The Soviet case itself has, indeed, more than any other, forced this issue on to the agenda of the serious Marxist. The stress upon the relative autonomy of 'the state' or, in other variants, of 'the political system' in some Soviet writings is frequently (though seldom overtly) part of their authors' attempts to comprehend Russian history, especially, though not exclusively, post-revolutionary history. Similarly, some at least of the emphasis among Western Marxists over the past two decades on the 'relative autonomy' or 'high degree of autonomy' of 'the state', or 'the superstructure', is a product of their attempt to come to terms with the Soviet experience.[5]

SOVIET POWER RELATIONS THROUGH WESTERN EYES

Problems of concept formation

All attempts to find one term, or one concept, that will encapsulate the essential features of power relations within the Soviet polity – or, indeed, any other – are fraught with serious difficulties. The world of real types is a more difficult one to chart than the universe of ideal types. Yet the whole thrust of the endeavour to find a model or conceptualisation that will fit the Soviet Union – in so far as such an endeavour has any point to it at all – has been to place the study of Soviet politics within a comparative perspective and to facilitate generalisations about particular types of political system, in the process clarifying what is distinctive about the Soviet system and what features it holds in common with other polities.

The major ways in which the Soviet Union has been characterised by Western political scientists – as totalitarian, as pluralist (subject to various qualifications) and as corporatist (the most recently advanced characterisation) – draw upon concepts that have been elaborated in the course of study of systems quite different from the Soviet one (as in the case of pluralism or corporatism), or which have been developed by studying the Soviet Union in association with a significantly different system (notably Nazi Germany in the case of totalitarianism). The scope of these concepts varies. Totalitarianism (in particular) and corporatism are generally regarded by those who interpret the Soviet system in either of these terms as conveying the essence of the system, as providing the best single key to an understanding of it. The variations on the pluralist theme – 'institutional pluralism', 'bureaucratic pluralism', 'centralised pluralism' and 'institutionalised pluralism' – are used by some scholars to characterise the Soviet system as a whole and by others merely to describe one important feature of Soviet life.[6]

I shall consider each of these concepts in the order in which they entered the political science literature relating to the Soviet Union (i.e. totalitarianism, pluralism, corporatism), but will pay particular attention to pluralistic and quasi-pluralistic interpretations of the Soviet political system. Such attention is justified because these interpretations have represented the most serious challenge to the understanding of the Soviet Union as totalitarian and may, perhaps, by now be regarded as the intellectually dominant type of interpretation among Western specialists. They also incorporate some important insights. Yet, at the same time, the formulation of a number of valid points in pluralist terms has tended to obfuscate important distinctions between the Soviet political system and certain Western systems, and between developments within the Soviet Union and developments in several other Communist states.

Of particular relevance to the general problem of conceptualising Communist politics is Giovanni Sartori's criticism of 'conceptual stretching'.[7] Sartori argues that when concepts that have been developed in the study of one type of political system in one part of the world are transferred to the study of another type of political system in a different part of the world, 'the gains in extensional coverage tend to be matched by losses in connotative precision'.[8] He recognises, however, that the broadening of the meaning of the concepts already to hand represents not only 'the line of least resistance' but also 'a deliberate attempt to make our conceptualisations value-free'.[9]

Indeed, the adoption of concepts and techniques of analysis from mainstream political science – a movement that seriously got underway in the 1960s – was based partly on a desire to get away from a separate vocabulary with strong pejorative connotations ('totalitarianism' being a prime example) on the part of many Sovietologists, not only because they felt that they were thereby removing a political bias which was a legacy of the 'Cold War', but also because they felt that by doing so they were making their work in some sense more 'scientific'. Many of the results of the changes that overtook Soviet studies were beneficial, but the 'conceptual stretching' involved had some serious disadvantages, for, as Sartori puts it severely, 'the lower the discriminating power of a conceptual container, the more the facts are misgathered, i.e. the greater the misinformation'.[10] One danger of conceptual stretching is that very frequently major differences between systems are played down while less important similarities are played up, with the result that the gains in universal inclusiveness are largely illusory.[11] Against these serious disadvantages, we should not, however, overlook several partly compensating benefits to be derived from scholars changing the focus of their conceptual lenses, even if the focus thereby becomes an excessively broad one. In the process of attempting to justify different ways of conceptualising and classifying the Soviet system from those prevailing hitherto, Sovietologists have come up with some new information and a number of fresh insights.

Totalitarianism

Sartori's strictures on the excessive stretching of concepts are explicitly applied to the concept of pluralism, but the disadvantages of conceptual stretching in Soviet studies are by no means confined to the use of that particular term. So far as totalitarianism is concerned, it was Alex Inkeles who pointed to one of the central dilemmas:[12] either we keep revising the 'model' in accordance with changing reality within the Soviet Union, so that the Soviet Union remains by definition 'totalitarian', or we stick with a model (or, as I would prefer to put it, an ideal type)[13] and try to ascertain how far the Soviet Union has deviated from that model (or ideal type). Though the former course can be followed and the concept refined in such a way that the Soviet Union may still not unreasonably be described as totalitarian, this procedure is, on the whole, more misleading than helpful.[14]

That is not to say that the concept of totalitarianism should be rejected as useless. In the 1960s it was sometimes discarded for the wrong reasons. Because of the part it played in anti-Commu͏ist rhetoric, it was felt by some scholars that the very concept had acquired an ineradicable bias against Communist systems which prevented its use in scholarly discussion. Yet the term, 'totalitarian', is increasingly used by Soviet and East European scholars in official publications (though not with reference to the Soviet Union and Eastern Europe). It was also used by Trotsky[15] in exile about Stalin's Russia, and it has been used to describe the contemporary Soviet Union and Eastern Europe by many formerly prominent East European Communists now in the West.[16] The concept is not, in other words, the exclusive property of any one section of the political spectrum.

The lack of agreement on a definition of totalitarianism and, indeed, the very wide variety of connotations that have been attached to it, have also been advanced as reasons for eschewing the term altogether. On that basis, such concepts as 'democracy' and 'the state' would equally be among the many that would have to be banished from scholarly discourse. (There has, indeed, been within political science over the past quarter of a century an influential school of thought that thinks that the term, 'state', serves no useful purpose and one of the arguments used against it is precisely the great variety of definitions it has attracted. David Easton, the most prominent proponent of the view that systems analysis and terminology dispense with the need for a concept of 'the state', has cited a work published in 1928 in which the author claimed to have collected one hundred and forty-five separate definitions of the state, and Easton assumes that others have been added since.)[17]

It is not, therefore, because of an alleged built-in political bias in the concept or because it has been defined in different ways that I would regard the notion of totalitarianism as a not particularly helpful way of classifying the contemporary Soviet Union or of seeking to understand it. Some of what has been written on totalitarianism is still of considerable relevance to an understanding of the Stalinist period of Soviet history. But totalitarian interpretations of the Soviet Union in the post-Stalin period in particular have tended to suffer from three major shortcomings. First, they have exaggerated the success of the official political socialisation effort *vis-à-vis* Soviet society and have implied (a) that the Communist Party is more monolithically united than in fact it is, and (b) that the party leadership controls popular beliefs and values in a way comparable to that in which it controls overt political behaviour. Second, they have paid very little attention to the policy process, suggesting, usually implicitly, that all policy emanates from the top party leadership (in saying which, I do not wish to deny that there is a heavy concentration of political power there). Third, totalitarian interpretations have contributed virtually nothing to an understanding of political change within the Soviet Union (or other Communist states), and have obscured sources of change other than change initiated by the top leader or leaders or by violent overthrow of the system.

So, though many of the works organised around the notion of totalitarianism draw attention to aspects of the Soviet system which, historically, have been extremely important and, in some measure, still are, they obfuscate as much as they reveal and are particularly unhelpful if we are interested in studying changes within the society and system. It is, nevertheless, surprising that in turning away from the concept of totalitarianism, a number of scholars (including some of the best-informed) should have seized upon its antonym, pluralism (albeit a qualified pluralism), rather than upon one of the other variants of authoritarian politics in their efforts to reconceptualise the Soviet system.[18] For while there are enough different definitions of 'totalitarianism' and 'pluralism' to choose from to make it impossible in every case to see one as the antonym of the other, the classic writings on totalitarianism emphasise total power concentrated in the hands of a single leader – or, in later modifications, in the hands of a small ruling group – whereas most definitions of pluralism have in common that they describe a system in which political power is dispersed. In this sense, totalitarianism may be regarded as an extreme sub-type of monism and pluralism as its antonym.

Pluralism

Though the concept of pluralism came later to the analysis of Communist politics than totalitarianism,[19] it has a longer intellectual history. David Nicholls, who has written a more substantial study of the pluralism of Figgis and his English contemporaries,[20] has also conveniently isolated 'three varieties of pluralism' in his short book of that title[21] – first, the theory of pluralism to be found in the writings of Figgis and Laski and others in the first two decades of this century, which he calls 'English political pluralism'; second, American political pluralism from Bentley to Dahl; and, third, the pluralism of the 'plural society', i.e. social and cultural sectionalism, or segmentalism, based upon the existence of different ethnic groups. Nicholls very usefully draws attention to the wide range of connotations that the term, 'pluralism', has carried, and for his part takes ' "pluralist state" to refer to a situation in which there are many politically significant groups with cross-cutting membership and . . . pluralism as a belief that such a state is good'.[22]

Throughout its history, pluralism has been used as both description and prescription in the context of a number of Western political systems, most frequently that of the United States. If, however, we are to consider it in its prescriptive sense, the question of whether pluralism has been accepted within the Soviet Union can be disposed of very quickly. No ruling Communist Party has accepted *unequivocally* the *principle* of political pluralism, though some of them have had to accommodate themselves to a measure of *de facto* pluralism. Individual Communist scholars within East European countries have accepted pluralism in principle[23] and various non-ruling Communist parties have pledged their support for it,[24] but not even the leadership of the Yugoslav League of Communists under Tito or his successors, the leadership of the Communist Party of Czechoslovakia under Dubček or the leadership of the Polish United Workers' Party under Kania went quite so far. Though it did not amount to an unequivocal acceptance of political pluralism – especially in the light of Tito's attitude – it is worth noting that the Yugoslavs have come closest to an official endorsement of the principle of pluralism. Edvard Kardelj, who was for long the second most authoritative spokesman of the Yugoslav League of Communists – after Tito – and the party's leading theoretician, adopted and expounded the notion of a 'democratic pluralism of self-managing interests' and took a positive view of 'pluralism' in that sense.[25]

A number of Soviet scholars have objected, *inter alia*, to the lack of specificity of 'pluralism'[26] and there is no doubt that the term is still used in very different ways by different scholars. Thus, the Polish political scientists, Jerzy J. Wiatr and Stanislaw Ehrlich, who have long accepted pluralism both normatively and as a description of political relations in Poland (and 'in other socialist countries'), define pluralism more broadly than does, say, Giovanni Sartori. Ehrlich, in an article on the relationship of Marxism and pluralism stresses that *'pluralism is not a characteristic peculiar to some concrete socio-political system or some form of state'* (Ehrlich's italics). It is the 'current' which 'opposes the uniformisation of public life not justified by need', the counterposition to 'all monolithic tendencies', to 'all attempts to monopolise social initiative'. Ehrlich concludes that while it would be 'nonsensical' to reduce Marxism to pluralism, 'negation of the pluralist character of the social and political structures of all societies (except the totalitarian) must be regarded as an extreme distortion of Marxism. Pluralism, both descriptive and normative, is inseparable from Marxism'.[27] Wiatr, in somewhat similar vein, has argued that, 'in analyzing the problems of power in the socialist society, one should direct attention to the nature of political pluralism characteristic for this system'. By political pluralism, Wiatr understands the existence in 'political life of organised forces legally expressing the interest of differentiated social groups' and holds that, thus conceived, 'political pluralism is an expression and consequence of social pluralism, socio-economic differentiation of the society'.[28]

These uses of pluralism are more precise than some of those that Sartori had in mind when he wrote: 'There is no end to pluralism, for we are never told what is non-pluralism.' They would scarcely, however, meet with his approval, for in attempting to rescue the concept from 'conceptual stretching', Sartori wishes to equate a 'truly pluralistic society' with one 'qualified by the Western use of the term', and suggests that 'a pluralistic society is a society whose structural configuration is shaped by pluralistic beliefs, namely, that all kinds of autonomous sub-units should develop at all levels, that interests are recognized in their legitimate diversity, and that dissent, not unanimity, represents the basis of civility'.[29]

If Nicholls (in his characterisation of a 'pluralist state' cited earlier), Ehrlich and Wiatr are all inclined to stretch the concept unduly by playing down or ignoring the element of *autonomy*, Sartori, by making a 'pluralistic society' one 'whose *structural configuration* is shaped by pluralistic *beliefs*' (my italics), virtually forecloses any debate on the question of whether pluralism is to be found in the Soviet Union or any other Communist state. A better starting-point is provided by Robert A. Dahl in his most recent work in which he takes the term, 'pluralism', to refer to 'organizational pluralism, that is to the existence of a plurality of relatively autonomous (independent) organizations (subsystems) within the domain of a state'.[30] The crux of the matter is *relative autonomy*, as Dahl recognises in his proposal of the following definition: 'An organization is relatively autonomous if it undertakes actions that (a) are considered harmful by another organization and that (b) no other organization, including the government of the state, can prevent, or could prevent except by incurring costs so high as to exceed the gains to the actor from doing so.'[31]

It is a weakness of 'pluralist' interpretations of Soviet politics that they have little, if anything, to say on the question of autonomy.[32]

What they tend to stress is the fact that the Soviet party and state leadership does not make up a unified elite, that it is a body in which there are numerous cleavages based, for example, upon the functional and geographical division of responsibilities among different sectors of the all-Union and republican leaderships. They can rightly point also to a body of evidence that suggests that there is substantial *diffusion of influence* within the Soviet Union.[33] However, to equate pluralism with *any* influence on a party or state leadership from outside the ranks of that leadership would mean that even the Soviet Union under Stalin was also a pluralist state – surely a *reductio ad absurdum* of such a concept of pluralism.[34] Constraints of time and knowledge and, to some degree, constraints imposed by certain social groups are present in any political system, though it seems reasonable to suppose that these constraining factors have grown in the Soviet Union during the post-Stalin years as a result of the increased specialisation of knowledge and the growth (both numerically and in the acquisition of expertise and skills) of the Soviet intelligentsia and working class.

The question, however, is not so much whether any 'elements of pluralism'[35] can ever be detected within the Soviet Union, as whether the Soviet Union should be interpreted as a 'type of pluralist system'.[36] So far as this latter and larger question is concerned, some lessons can be learned from the debate on community power and on pluralism and elites which has been waged by Western (especially American) political scientists and sociologists over many years.[37] Whatever the validity of the work of the critics of American pluralist theorists (and their writings contain many valuable insights, though evidence, too, of less-than-careful reading of some of the works they are criticising),[38] it is plain that the various criticisms of those analyses which find pluralism within the political systems of the United States or the countries of Western Europe apply *a fortiori* to pluralistic analyses of the Soviet political system. The control that Soviet leaders have over the political agenda, their control over the flow of information, their capacity to make potential issues non-issues, while not complete, are beyond the dreams even of a Richard Nixon.

Jerry Hough has been the most persuasive advocate of the view that the Soviet Union should be viewed as a type of pluralist system. He has drawn attention to what he calls 'pluralist aspects of the Soviet political system'[39] and has suggested that, 'if the Soviet and Western political systems are each visualized as types of pluralist systems, then we are led to explore the respective impact of those aspects of plural-

ism which they have in common and those on which they differ'.[40]
There are, of course, some features that the Soviet system, Western
liberal democratic systems (and, for that matter, fascist systems) have
in common. These include rivalries between branches of the
bureaucracy and varying degrees of specialist influence in the policy-
making process. The trouble with saying that it is a kind of pluralism
that they have in common is that this stretches the concept so far that
it becomes virtually meaningless, that it plays down differences that
are substantially more important than the similarities between the
Soviet system and certain Western systems and, in some ways the most
disturbing, that it lacks a comparative Communist perspective and
blurs important distinctions between different Communist states at
different times.

To illustrate this last point, Czechoslovakia in 1968 was *de facto* a
pluralistic socialist state, even if it was still a limited pluralism and not
a fully democratic socialism. Trade unions – from the Metal Workers'
Union to the Writers' Union – either changed their leaders or forced
their existing leaders to be responsive to the demands of their members. On television and radio, and in newspapers, questions were
asked and issues probed which the party leadership made clear it did
not want discussed.[41] Public-opinion polls on levels of popular trust in
individual party leaders were published in the press.[42] There was open
debate within the Communist Party itself and there were horizontal as
well as vertical links between party organisations.[43] Autonomous
political organisations, completely outside the *nomenklatura* system
of appointment or approval of office-holders,[44] emerged, prominent
among them being KAN (the Club of Committed Non-Party Members) and K231 (the organisation of former political prisoners).[45]

One of the ironies of regarding the Soviet system as being to a
significant degree pluralist is that a Soviet-led intervention by half-a-
million foreign troops took place with the express purpose of putting
an end to pluralistic socialism in Czechoslovakia, and of restoring the
'leading role' of the party as that concept was understood in the Soviet
Union. Furthermore, the subsequent political arrangements (and
those still obtaining) in Czechoslovakia did indeed become closely
based upon the Soviet model. If personal political rivalries, competition between different branches of the bureaucracy and consultation
with specialists (albeit specialists from whose ranks radical political
reformers have been purged) are to be the hallmarks of pluralism,
then contemporary Czechoslovakia could also be regarded as a
pluralist state, and the vehement attacks of their present leaders and

ideologists on the notion of pluralism might reasonably be regarded as otiose.[46]

In Poland in 1980–1, to the Catholic Church, which has long been a powerful autonomous force and alternative focus of loyalty to the party in that country, was added the independent trade-union movement, Solidarity. Between the momentous strike at the Lenin Shipyard in Gdansk in August 1980 and the military crackdown in December 1981 (and especially in the period between the fall of Edward Gierek from the party leadership in September 1980 and the ousting of his successor, Stanislaw Kania, in October 1981), Solidarity forced a whole series of concessions from party and government leaders which they were, beyond question, reluctant to make. A number of demands that were declared to be non-negotiable turned out to be negotiable, and were conceded by the Polish leadership, faced by the actual pressures of the massively supported Solidarity movement (even if some of them evidently remained firmly non-negotiable in the eyes of the Soviet leadership).[47] When this independent trade-union movement and the Church are viewed alongside the Communist Party (the official name of which, the Polish United Workers' Party, acquired an increasingly ironic ring, since the party was deeply divided and about a third of its members were at one stage members also of Solidarity),[48] it is abundantly clear that Poland in 1980–1 was, in terms even of Dahl's stringent definition, *de facto* pluralist.

It is rarely, of course, pluralism unqualified that Western scholars have claimed exists within the Soviet Union, but an 'institutional pluralism', 'bureaucratic pluralism' or, in a variant introduced by Jerry Hough, 'institutionalised pluralism'.[49] Gordon Skilling, who has taken trouble to indicate that his view that interest groups are to be found within the Soviet Union does not mean he is suggesting that 'genuine pluralism' is to be found there (or, in his opinion, in any other Communist state), nevertheless played a significant part in the introduction of the word, 'pluralism', into discussion of Soviet politics when he proposed the term, 'pluralism of elites' as one way of characterising Communist political systems.[50] It is doubtful, however, whether the term 'pluralism', even thus qualified, should be applied so comprehensively to Communist systems or applied at all to the Soviet system – not least because it blurs the distinction between, on the one hand, the main characteristics of the Soviet political system and, on the other, the clear manifestations of political pluralism that have been seen at different times in Czechoslovakia and Poland.

This is not, by any means, to reject the study of group interests and of opinion groupings (terminology that I prefer to 'interest groups' in this context) within Soviet politics, an area pioneered by Skilling,[51] and the study of institutional interests and relationships, to which Hough has made such a notable contribution.[52] If scholars are better aware than they used to be that within the Soviet Union institutional rivalries are tacitly accepted, that certain party and state institutions may have common interests which differ from those of other party and state institutions, that departmentalism and localism exist, that there is covert competition for political office on the basis of what the Czech reformists called 'cabinet politics', that federation provides an institutional base for a limited amount of ethnic diversity and promotion of 'national interests' on the part of those ethnic groups that enjoy union republican status, that there is specialist influence on policy-making, that there are opinion groupings within the party, within the intelligentsia and within the wider society, then this body of work has been of value not only for its general corrective to the totalitarian interpretation, but for the concrete details of political life it has adduced in areas that did not attract much attention from proponents of the view that the Soviet Union was totalitarian. Yet, for all that, it does not constitute pluralism.[53]

Apart from the more general objection (already outlined) to the use of 'pluralism' in the context of the Soviet political system, '*institutional* pluralism' and '*bureaucratic* pluralism'[54] suffer from severe limitations as categories of comparative analysis. First, there is the universality in advanced industrial societies of competition for scarce resources, the existence of competition in this and other respects between different branches of the executive, a rather general tendency towards the 'narrow departmentalism' so often castigated in the Soviet press. While it is useful to be aware of those features that the Soviet Union has in common with other polities, it does not take us very far. Second, not only is 'institutional pluralism' not peculiarly applicable to the Soviet system, it especially aptly characterises the government of the United States which so often (not least in Hough's work) is the implicit or explicit partner in the comparison with the USSR.

'Institutional pluralism' is not, of course, the only form of pluralism to be found in the United States. Indeed, T. H. Rigby has suggested that the limitations of 'institutional pluralism' are best appreciated if, given our acceptance that ' "bureaucratic crypto-politics" are found in the government machine of the capitalist democracies as well' as in the Soviet Union, we try to 'imagine what it would mean for "pluralism" and the structure of power generally if this were the *only* politics operating in these countries, if the whole public competitive political process were absent, and the spokesmen of all official and voluntary organisations, all communications media and all "representative bodies" presented a unanimous front of support for the current policies of the government'.[55]

The point I wish to stress here is, however, a different one. It concerns the peculiar strength of American '*institutional* pluralism', even if for the most part we disregard non-governmental institutions. Commenting on American Cabinet Secretaries' general lack of ability to manage successfully 'heterogeneous institutions with multiple and sometimes conflicting purposes' and a widespread Congressional belief that 'major bureaus should be allowed to run themselves without undue secretarial interference', Harold Seidman has remarked: 'We accept the principle of civilian control of the military profession, but not of the nonmilitary professions such as medicine, education, science and engineering.'[56] Hugh Heclo has noted that 'the administrative machinery in Washington represents a number of fragmented power centers rather than a set of subordinate units under the President',[57] and Richard Neustadt has observed that 'alone of major modern governments, the United States has had no stiffening element in its political system, no politicized army, no preponderant party, no communist cadres, no French bureaucracy'.[58] It is, we might say, the system of 'institutional pluralism' *par excellence*.

In the Soviet Union and Soviet-type systems, ministries carry out important policy and there are areas in which they play a more important part in the policy process than their counterparts in the party apparatus. The ability of the party leadership to impose their will upon the entire government network is, however, greatly enhanced by the power of their watchdogs in the Central Committee building. It could perhaps be argued, in the words of Jozef Lenárt in 1967 when he was Prime Minister of Czechoslovakia – he is now First Secretary of the party in Slovakia – that in the Central Committee building it is all talk, whereas in the ministries 'things get done'.[59] However, Zdeněk Mlynář, whose political memoirs are written from the unique vantage point of a political scientist and jurist who became a Secretary of the Central Committee of the Communist Party of Czechoslovakia and who reported these words of Lenárt's, is in no doubt of the power relationship between the Central Committee and the ministries. Writing of the Czechoslovak system pre-1968 when it was (as it is today) closely modelled on the Soviet one, he observes that it is clearly wrong to believe that 'a government minister is more important than a department head in the apparatus of the Central Committee', and warns against the 'big mistake' of judging 'political influence only, or chiefly, by formal position'. A head of department, he suggests, is in no way dependent on the minister, but the minister is in many ways dependent upon him, for the former is much closer to the real power centre, the Politburo. The Central Committee department head also has 'a decisive influence on the appointment, promotion or demotion of all the minister's subordinates, and ultimately of the minister himself'.[60]

Though the more technical ministries in the Soviet Union appear to acquire a significant degree of control within their area of functional specialisation, it can hardly be doubted that, in comparative terms, there is vastly more central direction and co-ordination within the Moscow bureaucratic establishment than in Washington. The Presidium of the Council of Ministers, the Secretariat of the Central Committee and the Politburo (for better or worse) have no functional equivalents in the United States – certainly not the Cabinet, despite the lip-service paid to it by successive Presidents upon first entering the White House, and not even the Executive Office of the Presidency.[61] One of the problems with the former is that they are, in Hugh Heclo's words, 'a government of strangers'[62] – strangers to one another and, until they enter office, often strangers to the President himself. So far as the Executive Office is concerned, 'the Watergate record', as Harold Seidman has put it, 'graphically demonstrates the consequences of allowing the presidency to speak with many voices'.[63] Richard Rose, with some justice, concluded a recent comparative study of executive power by observing: 'The fundamental fact of American government is that political power is divided among many dozens of sub-governments in Washington, whose tentacles extend throughout the federal system. The parts are greater than the whole.'[64]

Such generalisations about the United States system of government rest upon a wealth of detailed studies of institutions and policy cases, and on knowledge of the views of a great many significant participants in the policy process available to political scientists who write about Washington politics. It is important to acknowledge that we have no comparably detailed information on the relationships between institutions or on the policy process in Moscow. There is, however, more than enough evidence to enable us to conclude that the terms, 'bureaucratic pluralism' or 'institutional pluralism', fit the United States much more closely than they fit, say, the executive branches of government in Britain, France or the Federal Republic of Germany.[65] Is there less co-ordination of policy and of central direction in the Soviet system than in the West European ones? It seems unlikely. Almost everything else we know about the Soviet system, from the fact that discipline can still be imposed fairly effectively within the single party, to the impermissibility of attempts (other than under the auspices of the party leadership itself) to mobilise public opinion to support a particular department against another, suggests that the power in and around the Politburo is likely to be greater *vis-à-vis* other branches of the executive (not to speak of the legislature or judiciary where it obviously is so) than the power of the highest executive organ within Cabinet systems.

Jerry Hough has recently had second thoughts about 'institutional pluralism' but, unfortunately, it is the adjective he has proposed changing, rather than the noun. Concerned that the term, 'institutional', might imply that 'institutions are the only actors in the political process' when what he wishes to suggest is that the political process takes place within an institutional framework, that people wishing to exert influence must work through the official channels – the organisations designated for the purpose by the party and state authorities – he concludes that 'perhaps the phrase, "institutionalized pluralism" would convey the meaning better'.[66]

This, however, is less, rather than more, satisfactory and is open, in particular, to two objections. The first is that an inescapable connotation of 'institutionalised pluralism' is that of 'legitimised pluralism' and, as I indicated earlier, nothing is more certain than that pluralism has not been accepted as a legitimate concept – especially so far as attempts to relate it to the USSR are concerned – by Soviet political leaders and social theorists. The second objection is that the notion that a wide spectrum of critical views can be presented, provided that the authors of the criticisms do not bypass the official institutional channels, sounds more like corporatism than even a qualified pluralism.

Corporatism

It is worth turning to corporatism since that concept has attracted the attention of a few comparativist-minded observers of Communist politics in recent years and since there is a *prima facie* case for regarding it as just as worthy of serious attention as 'institutional pluralism'. It is precisely as a way of giving scope to particular interests to participate in the policy process without allowing competition between autonomous political groups, that corporatism assumes its potential relevance as a way of conceptualising Communist politics.

Philippe Schmitter has provided the most widely accepted contemporary definition of corporatism, which he characterises as:

> a system of interest intermediation in which the constituent units are organized into a limited number of singular, compulsory, non-competitive, hierarchically ordered, and functionally differentiated categories, recognized or licensed (if not created) by the state and granted a deliberate representational monopoly within their respective categories in exchange for observing certain controls on their selection of leaders and articulation of demands and supports.[67]

Schmitter contrasts this with pluralism, which he defines as:

> a system of interest intermediation in which the constituent units are organized into an unspecified number of multiple, voluntary, competitive, nonhierarchically ordered, and self-determined (as to type or scope of interest) categories that are not specifically licensed, recognized, subsidized, created, or otherwise controlled in leadership selection or interest articulation by the state and that do not exercise a monopoly of representational activity within their respective categories.[68]

An extensive discussion of corporatism as such would be out of place here. It may be noted in passing that there are very different types of corporatism of which the corporatism of fascist states is but one. The most common distinctions observed are those between 'liberal' and 'authoritarian' (or 'societal' and 'state') corporatism. Among those who have hinted that the corporatist model (in an 'authoritarian' or 'state' variant) may have some relevance to Yugoslavia and possibly other East European Communist states are Schmitter, [69] Juan Linz[70] and Alfred Stepan.[71]

Corporatism, however, does not fit the Soviet case particularly well, even though, in some respects, it fits a number of 'pluralist' descriptions of Soviet reality better than pluralism does. Indeed, if one were forced to choose between Schmitter's definition of corporatism and his definition of pluralism (in which his emphasis on self-determination links up with Dahl's stress on autonomy), one would have to conclude that the former corresponded more closely to the

Soviet political system than the latter. Schmitter himself, in fact, offers a definition of Leninist monism, based on the Soviet prototype, which is closer to, though not identical with, his corporatist definition, and which characterises interest intermediation in such a system as one

> in which the constituent units are organized into a fixed number of singular, ideologically selective, noncompetitive, functionally differentiated and hierarchically ordered categories, created, subsidized and licensed by a single party and granted a representation role within that party and *vis-à-vis* the state in exchange for observing certain controls on their selection of leaders, articulation of demands and mobilization of support.[72]

In the boldest and most explicit attempt thus far to see the Soviet Union as an example of a corporatist polity, Valerie Bunce and the late John Echols follow Schmitter's distinctions between pluralism and corporatism, though they ignore his own characterisation of the Soviet system as monist and his distinctions between monism and corporatism. Bunce and Echols argue that the Soviet Union may usefully be characterised as 'a mixture of corporatist types' and that 'corporatism, under the label "developed socialism", would appear to be an acceptable system with which to head into the future'.[73] They base their argument largely on the attempts at placation under Brezhnev's leadership of such powerful interests as the party apparatus, the industrial managers, the government bureaucracy, scientists and the agricultural sector, all of whom Khrushchev had succeeded in offending.[74] A leadership within an essentially monist system may, however, pursue a conciliatory policy *vis-à-vis* the most important institutional and social interests within the society without thereby introducing a systemic change in the structure of power.

A transition from a Communist Party state, organised to maintain the party's control within and *vis-à-vis* every other organisation, to a corporatist one is not, in principle, impossible, and one could argue that in Yugoslavia, and perhaps even in Hungary, we have begun to see a new type of corporatism emerging. But the evidence that this is as yet happening in the Soviet Union is extremely slender. Whether we are talking about trade unions or industrial ministries, the military or the KGB, republican party organisations or research institutes of the Academy of Sciences, it is a misleading understatement to say that the respective units of interest representation accept – as Schmitter's definition of corporatism (and, for that matter, his definition of monism) has it – 'certain controls on *their* selection of leaders' (my italics) and articulation of demands.[75] It is fundamental that in all of these organisations and associations, their head is appointed from above. The system of *nomenklatura*, according to which the filling of posts considered to be of political or economic importance requires the approval of higher authority, puts certain jobs in the *nomenklatura* of more than one body – ministries and soviets as well as party committees. But in appointments at the level of the top posts in such organisations as those mentioned above, the highest party organs have the decisive voice.[76] In no case is the leadership of the organisation or association selected or elected from below, even to the extent of choosing from a limited number of candidates, though this does not exclude some sounding of opinion from above.

Some of these posts would be filled by governmental appointment even within pluralist or liberal corporatist systems, but the trade unions may be regarded as a test case. Can one regard as even state corporatist a system in which the head of the trade unions is appointed from outside the ranks of the trade unions with the specific aim of ensuring that the trade-union movement remains a faithful executant of party policy? The case of Sándor Gáspár in Hungary, who has used his leadership of the trade unions as a support in his policy arguments with colleagues, and who has defended the interests of trade unionists and of workers as he sees them, shows, perhaps, that it is possible in principle for a Communist state to make some concessions to state corporatism. There is, however, no evidence of any recent Soviet trade-union leader playing as prominent a role as Gáspár's, circum-scribed though even that is. The chairmanship of the trade-union movement in the Soviet Union has generally been a staging-post for a prominent party official on the way up (Grishin) or way down (Shelepin). Of all heads of the Soviet trade unions since the end of the Second World War, only one (and the most recent), Stepan Shalaev, who succeeded Aleksey Shibaev in March 1982, has any substantial experience in trade-union work behind him, though for the last eighteen months before his return to the trade unions, he was a government minister.[77] It remains very doubtful whether this change at the top will make any substantial difference to the work and politic-al role of the union organisation.

It will certainly not do to infer that the trade unions are playing a role of corporatist proportions from the fact that there has been an egalitarian trend in Soviet incomes in the post-Stalin period. Roy

Medvedev has drawn attention to the fact that the call for a rapid rise in the workers' standard of living presented to the XXIV Congress of the CPSU in early 1971 showed much more concern for popular living standards than the draft prepared before December 1970. 'Undoubtedly', he notes, 'the changes were influenced by events in Poland as well as various demonstrations by workers in our country protesting against the unavailability of meat and dairy products (in Ivanovo, Sverdlovsk, Gorky and several other cities).'[78] In other words, uninstitutionalised and spontaneous protest within the Soviet Union and observation of the troubles of a neighbouring state would appear to have been the decisive influences on this occasion, rather than any influential role played by the appropriate interest representational institutions.

Poland has provided the Soviet leaders with a number of lessons on how not to proceed, and on what should be done to anticipate and prevent crises, and the most recent and most serious struggle in Poland has already led the Soviet leadership to exhort trade unionists in the USSR to be more active. In the report of the Central Committee of the CPSU to the XXVI Party Congress in February 1981 (which expressed considerable concern about developments in Poland), a far-from-complacent account of the activities of Soviet trade unions was presented. It was noted that they 'sometimes lack initiative in exercising their broad rights', and that they 'do not always act with perseverance in questions of the fulfilment of collective agreements and the rules on labour safety, and still react feebly to cases of violations of labour legislation, to bureaucratic practices, and red tape'.[79] Exhortation from above to trade unions to be more vigilant is one thing. It would, however, be quite another if the job of heading the unions were to amount to more than a differentiation of functions among the party leadership in the pursuit of their collective aims, and if trade unionists were to be allowed even a limited voice in the selection of their own leaders. There is no sign that the 1982 change in the leadership of the Soviet trade unions marks this kind of breakthrough. Until such developments have occurred, it will be premature to see the Soviet Union as an example of a corporatist state.

Totalitarianism, a qualified pluralism, and corporatism do not by any means exhaust the ways in which the Soviet political system has been conceptualised by Western political scientists in the past twenty years. Many scholars have been content to discuss and analyse aspects of the system without feeling the need to generalise about the nature of the system as a whole. Those who have felt such a need are still, however, quite a sizable group and it would be impossible to attempt a survey of their conclusions here. It is, though, worth noting that while one of the most popular ways of looking at the Soviet system is in terms of 'bureaucratic politics', those who adopt this approach are divided between writers who go out of their way to counterpose their 'bureaucratic' interpretation of Soviet politics to even a qualified pluralist characterisation,[80] and those whose study of bureaucratic politics leads them to pluralist conclusions.[81] Similarly, there are scholars who see the Soviet system as monist but not totalitarian,[82] as well as those for whom it is both monist and totalitarian.[83]

POWER RELATIONS THROUGH SOVIET EYES

Pluralism is seen by Soviet political leaders and by official party ideologists as a threat to such pillars of the system as 'the leading role of the party' and 'democratic centralism'. This became very evident in the numerous Soviet attacks on the pluralist ideas of the Czech reformers of 1968, and in 1982 pluralism was still apparently seen as a sufficiently threatening idea to attract the attention and criticism of two of the most senior members of the Politburo (though, in the case of Yuriy Andropov, in an interestingly nuanced way).[84] For these reasons, apart from any others, pluralism is not – and cannot be – explicitly commended by Soviet scholars. This does not, however, mean that the latter are confined to expressing support for a monolithic authoritarianism. I have argued that it is wrong to regard the Soviet system in political practice either as an extreme monolith or as pluralist, and such terms no more exhaust the range of conceptual alternatives than they do the scope of political reality.

In fact, since the language of democracy is sanctified in Soviet usage, many ideas are put forward and reforms proposed in the name of strengthening democracy.[85] Sceptical Western observers may be inclined to dismiss all talk from Soviet scholars about 'democratisation' as mere political rhetoric devoid of substance, but to do so would be as much of an oversimplification as to take all professions of attachment to democracy, from whatever Soviet source, at face value. Many political and social theorists in the USSR support a gradual democratisation of Soviet political life in the sense of enhancing popular influence upon political decisions (partly by providing more information to the public and also by promoting more serious and systematic investigation of public opinion,[86] and through raising the level of political participation.[87] What they do *not* advocate is *pluralism* in anything like Dahl's sense. That is to say, they have shown no inclination to promote the existence of *organisations* that can perform actions considered harmful by 'the government' (party and state leadership) and which 'the government' cannot prevent such organisations from undertaking 'except by incurring costs so high as to exceed the gains ... from doing so'.

Yu. A. Tikhomirov has written of 'the democratisation of state life' as the most important law of development of the Soviet state,[88] and Georgi Shakhnazarov has picked out 'democratisation' as the main development he expects to take place in 'socialism's political system ... in the years to come'.[89] But in distinguishing this 'from the kind of democratisation that would eventually weaken the socialist system', the same author is indicating – as he makes explicit elsewhere – that it is not *pluralist* democracy that he has in mind.[90] While various Czech, Polish, Yugoslav, Italian and Spanish (among other) Communist theorists have regarded political pluralism as perfectly compatible with a 'socialist system', Shakhnazarov has taken pains to dissociate 'the development of socialist democracy' from any link with 'political pluralism'. In an important article in the journal *Kommunist*, he wrote:

> In recent times one has met with the assertion that socialist democracy is also pluralist in nature. It seems hardly necessary to use an alien concept to characterise the features of the political system of socialism which for a long time have been quite adequately defined in Marxist–Leninist scholarship by such concepts as the needs and interests of classes and social groups, the unity and diversity of these interests, the coincidence or contradiction between them, their defence and expression, co-ordination, etc. So far as a general definition is concerned, to that vague and ambiguous term, 'pluralism', which may be interpreted in all sorts of ways, one ought to prefer the clear concept, 'sovereignty of the people' (*narodovlastie*).[91]

The political, as distinct from the literal, meaning of *narodovlastie* is, in fact, not so clear, but it is a concept that has been employed increasingly in Soviet writing on politics in recent years, though under Stalin even the very word apparently went out of use.[92] It has populist associations and, not surprisingly, is a concept to which different Soviet scholars impart different meanings. It is also one that tends to be stressed more by those who support measures of democratisation within the Soviet Union than by those who see the answer to many of the country's problems in stricter discipline and controls.

Shakhnazarov writes with some authority, for he is not only President of the Soviet Association of Political Sciences but a deputy head of the department of the Central Committee of the CPSU for relations with socialist countries. He may also be regarded as a moderate reformer within the spectrum of CPSU opinion and, along with Fyodor Burlatsky (who was first in the field),[93] he has been one of the two leading advocates in the Soviet Union of a political science that embraces not only the elaboration of political concepts and the development of Marxist political theory but also the empirical study of Soviet political life.[94]

Arguments on basic concepts

Much important discussion of concepts, including the key concept of political power,[95] has already taken place among Soviet political scientists and jurists. Indeed, the extent to which there is argument over such basic concepts as 'political power', 'the political system' and 'the state' may surprise those Western political scientists whose image of their Soviet counterparts is of an exceedingly well-drilled scholarly community. The traditional image is misleading, though not for want of attempts in the USSR to make it come true. The view that lack of agreement concerning fundamental political concepts is rather unseemly is, indeed, often expressed at conferences of Soviet scholars. Thus, at the conference held in the Institute of State and Law of the Academy of Sciences in Moscow in April 1979 to prepare Soviet scholars for the Congress of the International Political Science Association (held in Moscow in August of that year), L. A. Grigoryan 'underlined the significance of Yu. A. Tikhomirov's report for the elaboration of a united approach of Soviet scholar-jurists to the definition of the political system',[96] while V. O. Tennenbaum 'drew attention to the importance of working out a united ideological position of the Soviet delegation to the X1 World Congress of IPSA in problems of the study of political systems'.[97] (The idea that a united front in such matters is a 'good thing' dies hard, despite the fact that nothing would have impressed Western political scientists more than the public airing at the Moscow IPSA Congress of disagreements among their Soviet counterparts, even to the extent to which such debate already takes place within their specialised publications.)

The argument, however, continued. Tikhomirov's views[98] were among those criticised more recently by V. S. Shevtsov in an important book entitled *State Sovereignity*.[99] But Shevtsov's main opponent has been Fyodor Burlatsky whose record of ideological innovation includes a significant part in the conception of the 'all-people's state' in Khrushchev's time and of 'developed socialism' in the Brezhnev era.[100] Burlatsky, who – along with Tikhomirov, V. G. Kalensky[101] and others – distinguishes political power from state power,[102] defines power (*vlast'*) as follows:

> Power is the practical ability to exercise one's will in social life, foisting it upon others, if necessary; political power, as one of the most important manifestations of power, is characterised by the actual ability of a given class, group or individual to implement its will, expressed in policy and law.[103]

State power for Burlatsky is an important part of political power (though with some special attributes), but is not the whole of it:

> State power is that form of political power which has a class character, which disposes of the monopoly right to promulgate laws and other directives, obligatory for the whole population, and which leans upon a special apparatus of coercion as one of the means of securing observance of these laws and directives.[104]

In distinguishing political power conceptually from state power, Burlatsky and – in greater detail – Kalensky also distinguish between two senses of the term, 'state': a narrower one and a broader one.[105] In the first sense, the state is 'the apparatus of public power'[106] and excludes political parties; in the second sense, it is synonymous with the 'political system' and so includes, *inter alia*, parties. In the Soviet case, this means for both Burlatsky and Kalensky that the CPSU is not part of the state in the narrow sense, though it is part of the state, as these authors acknowledge, in the broad sense in which it is possible to speak of the 'Soviet state' (as of a 'socialist state' or the 'American state').[107] For both authors, and especially clearly for Kalensky, it is the second sense of the term, 'state' (which goes against the traditional, legalistic definition of the state in the Soviet Union) that is the more important one. Kalensky writes of the 'completely obvious inadequacy of the interpretation of the state as the apparatus of public power, officially consolidated in legislation, for an adequate exploration of the phenomenon of contemporary statehood'.[108] This is simply impossible, Kalensky adds, 'without an analysis of political relations, of the role of ruling parties and other politico-governmental structures, political traditions, ideology, mass consciousness, etc.'[109]

Burlatsky observes that Marx used the term, 'state', not only in the narrow sense but in the broad sense,[110], though he adds that it would be 'more precise to speak of the political system' when one wishes to convey the broader meaning.[111] Indeed, in a different work from that just quoted, Burlatsky is using 'state' in the narrow sense when, in emphasising the importance of the study of the political system, he writes: 'The traditional basic institution of the political system is the state. But the political system cannot be reduced to the state; it includes many other political institutions which exercise functions vitally necessary for its working as an independent social sub-system, above all political parties.'[112] What makes the work of these writers both significant and controversial in the Soviet context is their attempt (which, in Burlatsky's case, can be traced back at least as far as his famous 1965 *Pravda* article,[113] to put on the scholarly agenda the real political process and real political relations within the Soviet Union and elsewhere, and to break away from the legalistic approach which has been far more dominant in Soviet writing on the state and on political institutions than the so-called 'legal-institutional' approach ever was in Western political science prior to the 'behavioural revolution'. Advocating the study of the state in the broad sense, Kalensky notes in that connection that 'political parties are not simply the most important socio-political form of organisation of classes and their leaders':

> They are the principal link between society and state power, directly orientated towards participation in its implementation, towards the representation of the interests of classes and other social groups in the very activity of the state apparatus of power. They influence, by such means, the most important politico-governmental structures of the contemporary state, as the nucleus of the mechanism of political power, understood as the totality of all those diverse forms of leadership, control and influence, in which the actual role of the ruling class is given immediate embodiment in the system of political relations.[114]

V. S. Shevtsov, in contrast, had already, in 1976, attacked Tikhomirov for saying that 'social organisations may in essence appear as the direct repositories, that is the subjects, of political power'.[115] To that paraphrase of Tikhomirov's position, Shevtsov responded that 'state power, being a political power, is characterised above all by the fact that it is realised through a special apparatus, leaning on special means and measures of coercion'[116] and, further, that 'political power as such is state power and no other'.[117]

In his major work, *State Sovereignty*, Shevtsov criticises a number of Soviet scholars[118] for their 'mistaken positions' on political power and the state, and quotes approvingly[119] V. M. Terletsky's view that 'the relations of the party with society do not have a power character *(vlastnego kharaktera)*' and that 'the party leads society, relying on its moral–political authority *(avtoritet)*'.[120] Shevtsov, however, reserves his most damning criticism for Burlatsky. He cites not only Brezhnev against him but Lenin, and not just any work of Lenin's but his 'Once Again on the Trade Unions', devoted, as Shevtsov puts it, 'to a critique of the mistaken views of L. Trotsky and N. Bukharin'.[121] Shevtsov quotes Burlatsky's statement that 'the political system implements the supreme power in society',[122] gives his own précis of Article 6 of the 1977 Soviet Constitution to the effect that 'the party is the nucleus of the political system of Soviet society',[123] and concludes: 'The CPSU appears on this [i.e. Burlatsky's] interpretation as a state-power social organism.'[124] He is able to posit against the interpretation he attributes to Burlatsky, Brezhnev's position that the party's guiding role in society is 'not by virtue of power, but thanks to its high political authority and ideational influence on the masses'.[125]

If, Shevtsov suggests, political power and state power are not one and the same thing, then

> either in society there exist two political powers (the subject of one of which is the political system of the society as a whole, the subject of the other the state), or the political system must be regarded as the state organisation, with the party, the mass social organisations and the work collectives as components of the state.[126]

Burlatsky is, to a limited degree, open to this criticism by virtue of the fact that he uses the term, 'state', in different senses at different times, but the spectre that Shevtsov raises on the basis of the interpretation he places on the first of the two alternative meanings does not seem called for on the basis of Burlatsky's writings. The name of the spectre is 'political pluralism' and, writes Shevtsov, 'the very essence of the theory of "political pluralism" and "political participation", to be found at the centre of attention of bourgeois political science', consists of the fact that 'different political groups and parties, among them even oppositional *(protivoborstvuyushchie)* ones, together implement political power by their joint efforts, and in the process of mutual struggle assist the perfecting and democratisation of the existing structure of political authority *(politicheskogo up-ravleniya)'*.[127]

Shevtsov continues to pursue this argument in a lengthy article published in 1980, in which he provides the same quotations from Lenin and Brezhnev and again criticises Burlatsky. He associates the distinction between 'political power' and 'state power', including interpretations in which the former is merely a broader concept which subsumes the latter, with the idea of two powers within a state, which, in turn, he sees as tantamount to an admission of pluralism, and which cannot be a lasting basis for the structure of power within a society. He notes Lenin's characterisation of 'dual power' in the Russia of 1917 as a necessarily 'temporary and transient phenomenon'.[128]

That a determination to uphold ideological orthodoxy is consistent with reaching quite opposite conclusions from those of Shevtsov was, however, illustrated by M. Kh. Farukshin in a book published in 1980 which bore the subtitle, 'Towards a Critique of Bourgeois Sovietology'.[129] Since, for Farukshin, it is abundantly evident that among the functions of the Communist Party are some involving the use of political power, it becomes all the more important to distinguish between political and state power. He writes:

In connection with the question of the relationship between party leadership and the functions of state, economic and other organisations, great significance attaches to the resolution in theory of the problem of the reciprocal links of political and state power and of the concepts 'political power' and 'state power'. Anyone who is acquainted with the real dynamics and functioning of the political system of socialist society will hardly deny that the Communist Party carries out power functions. This results from its role of guiding and ruling party. It is enough in that connection to point to the function of selection and placement of cadres of government organs. Therefore, it seems, the identification of political power with state power, the refusal to differentiate them objectively, leads to the necessity of recognising that the party carries out state functions and, consequently, acts as a substitute for some or other state organs, which looks like ... the favourite allegation of anti-communist ideologists and propagandists.[130]

Though Shevtsov's position has many supporters, including a number of senior jurists, a majority of Soviet scholars who have explicitly addressed themselves to the relationship between the concepts of political power and state power in recent years appear to have reached conclusions different from those of Shevtsov. Yet in attacking his standpoint, they were, in a sense, attacking the 'establishment' position, for Shevtsov's views could be regarded as rather closely in line with traditional orthodoxy, and they were believed by some Soviet scholars to be also 'the view of the Central Committee'. Weight was lent to that last supposition by the fact that Shevtsov was writing from within the Central Committee apparatus – he was until 1982 a consultant in the Science and Education Department of the Central Committee – as well as by the fact that it is easier to find statements from top party leaders to the effect that the party possesses only authority and influence, than admissions that it also wields political power.

Yet the Central Committee's view is by no means so clear-cut and there are a number of signs that Shevtsov's concept of state power has not been accorded definitive and exclusive official approval. The first indicator of that is the fact that the controversy that began in the 1970s is still continuing in the early 1980s. Second, the *'diskussionnyy'* (or debatable) character of much of the writing on state power, political power and the political system is reflected in the small print runs of most of the books concerned, including Shevtsov's *State Sovereignty*.[131] Sometimes attention is quite explicitly drawn to the 'debatable character' of some of the judgements in books on these themes, and an association made between this and the low print run.[132] Third, Shevtsov's views have been implicitly criticised by Shakhnazarov (see below), who, as a deputy head of the Central Committee Department of Relations with Communist and Workers' Parties of Socialist Countries, outranked Shevtsov within the Central Committee apparatus, even though in Shakhnazarov's case (as distinct from Shevtsov's) this did not confer upon him party responsibilities in relation to academic life. (Against that, Shakhnazarov holds two academic offices, as President of the Soviet Association of Political Sciences and as head of the fairly recently established Department of Theory of Political Systems and of Political Relations at the Institute of State and Law of the Academy of Sciences in Moscow, which add further institutional weight to his opinions.) Fourth, notwithstanding Shevtsov's attachment at the time to the department of the Central Committee which oversees the Institute of State and Law, and his membership of the editorial board of the institute's journal, that same journal, *Sovetskoe gosudarstvo i pravo*, published a review of his *State Sovereignty* in the summer of 1981 which explicitly took issue with the author's narrow definition of state power. The reviewer, F. M. Rudinsky, observes that 'although the CPSU is not the repository of state *functions*, party organisations, acting within the framework of the Soviet Constitution, emerge in some cases as the *subjects* of *state-legal relations*' (italics mine).[133] As an example Rudinsky cites the part played by party organisations in the nomination of deputies in elections to soviets.[134] Fifth, after this chapter was written, and the previous four points made, Shevtsov lost his political and academic positions. From the summer of 1982 he was no longer an official within the Central Committee apparatus and between the September 1982 issue of *Sovetskoe gosudarstvo i pravo* (sent to the printer on 28 June) and the October issue (sent for printing on 28 July) he ceased to be a member of the Editorial Board of that important journal. Though the reasons for this do not appear to be connected with his theoretical views, the fact that Shevtsov has fallen from grace (and, more precisely, from positions of institutional weight) does nothing to strengthen advocates of the conservative standpoint on the socialist state. The nature of 'the state' and the problem of the party's place within or (according to the definition of the state adopted) *vis-à-vis* it, together with the meaning of 'political power', have become, and remain, legitimate topics of discussion among Soviet scholars, provided that certain conventions are observed.[135]

In a noteworthy article (alluded to in the previous paragraph) on the development of political science in the USSR,[136] written jointly by Shakhnazarov and Burlatsky, there is – though not the primary concern of the piece – an implicit reply to Shevtsov's *State Sovereignty*. In view of his considerable party standing, it is of some significance that Shakhnazarov should have established an identity of view with Burlatsky on a number of important points. Though his previously published views corresponded more closely to those of Burlatsky than to those of Shevtsov, he had not been directly involved in the debate with Shevtsov and like-minded jurists. But Shakhnazarov and Burlatsky, in their article written in 1980 and published at the end of that year, clearly resist the idea that political power is state power and nothing but state power. Thus, for instance, they write: 'The 1977 Constitution of the USSR contains a precise characterisation of the political system as embodying the power of the Soviet people. Its basic institutions are the all-people's socialist state, the CPSU, the mass social organisations, and the work collectives.'[137]

Though Shakhnazarov and Burlatsky refer once to the state 'in the broad sense'[138] (see below), they prefer to rest their case concerning the nature of political power on a broad definition of 'political system'. Having noted that 'in a certain sense of the term, the political system includes the entire sum total of strictly political relations',[139] they advance a conception of political power which is 'a logical consequence of the complex approach to problems of power and government which has been developed in legal science and the theory of scientific communism'. This 'complex approach' facilitates the overcoming of 'a certain simplification' whereby 'the entire sphere of politics was identified with the state, and the latter not infrequently reduced to the governmental apparatus'.[140] Implicitly, they would appear to be accepting that they are not going to persuade Shevtsov and jurists who share his views to accept the 'broad definition' of the state, and so they simply move the argument on. The political institutions and political relations, the entire sphere of politics with which they are concerned, have, they suggest, been given different names at different times. What was 'finally' called the 'political system' was first expressed in the concept of 'the state in the broad sense of the word' and after that in the elaboration of the concept of 'political organisation'.[141]

Shakhnazarov, like Burlatsky, has long recognised as a legal fiction the idea that all decisions of a political-power character are taken by the state in the narrow sense of the term. In his important book, *Socialist Democracy*, he notes that certain areas of policy-making involve direct party decisions, notably foreign policy and especially international crises.[142] This, and the more general picture of political power offered by 'politologically-minded' Soviet scholars clearly comes much closer to encapsulating political realities than the legalistic version of Shevtsov, Terletsky and other jurists. A Western specialist on Soviet foreign policy has noted that the Politburo 'met during summit meetings [of the 1970s] to consider specific proposals advanced by the United States delegation'.[143] Leonid Brezhnev's fairly detailed summary of the activities of the Politburo over the previous five years at the XXVI Congress of the CPSU in 1981 probably left few of his listeners thinking that the institution which he described as 'indeed the battle headquarters of our multi-million party' gave no more than influential advice to state institutions.[144]

Within a system of the Soviet type, as within Cabinet systems, there is, in fact, a strong tendency to push matters upwards for decision, a practice that produces so much documentation, presented to Politburo members a day or two before their meetings, that the documents prepared by the working groups have to be summarised for the members by their aides.[145] It is precisely because an authoritative decision by the Politburo can put an end to countless hours of argument between departments or ministries, that ministers are often anxious to take matters that are not settled to their satisfaction by Gosplan or by the Presidium of the Council of Ministers to this highest political organ.[146] Yet a minister cannot put an item on the Politburo agenda unless (as, for example, in the case of Gromyko and Ustinov in the present Soviet Politburo) he is himself a Politburo member. The great majority of ministers who are not in that position can get an item on the agenda only by approaching the Secretariat of the Central Committee and relying on their goodwill and co-operation.[147] This relationship would certainly seem to reflect the political power of the Politburo (and the Secretariat) and to indicate something a good deal more than the high inspirational value of the Politburo's deliberations.

The relative autonomy of the state

Finally, it is worth noting that one other aspect of power within political systems generally (and the Soviet system by inference) has been raised recently by Soviet theorists. That is the important and sensitive question of the degree of autonomy (from society and the 'ruling class') possessed by the political leadership and/or state bureaucrats. One of the problems for the Soviet theorist is that if he accepts that the highest party institutions stand at the apex of the power stucture within the Soviet political system, he should, logically, include these same party institutions within the political 'superstructure'. This, however, would lead to considerable tension, to put it mildly, between the notion of the party's 'leading role' and the idea that the economic base 'in the last analysis' determines the superstructure. The problem lies with the time-worn architectural metaphor of base and superstructure, which many Soviet theorists still feel compelled to use, though the reification of a figure of speech into two concrete entities (whose relationship and relative autonomies can then be discussed) is more of a hindrance than a help in political analysis.

Shevtsov circumvents the problem in much the same way as the traditional Leninist theory of the 'dictatorship of the proletariat' tends to bypass this central issue. He observes that *'the political organisation in society* possesses a relative autonomy and has the possibility actively to exert influence on the whole structure of production and ideological relations' (my italics).[148] He makes it clear that by 'political organisation' he means 'the organisation of the ruling class, of its political domination' which, in the Soviet case, stands, above all, for the CPSU. By speaking of the *influence*, rather than the *power* of 'the political organisation in society' (which he distinguishes from the state), he remains true to his emphasis on state power and upon the supremacy *(verkhovenstvo)* of the state.[149]

A rather different emphasis found in some recent Soviet writings concerns the 'enormous influence' of *state bureaucrats* on society and on *their* 'relative autonomy' from society; it is especially noteworthy that scholars who have written in this vein are among those who have pointed to the weakness of interpretations of 'the state' that exclude an analysis of 'the role of ruling parties'. Thus, by implication, the relative autonomy would include that of party officials, a point, indeed, which Shevtsov also comes close to endorsing when he writes of the 'relative autonomy' of the 'political organisation in society' (see above), though he is referring to the organisation as a whole rather than to the bureaucracy as such. Burlatsky, though his emphasis is different from Shevtsov's, is less innovative in this respect than Kalensky. In the book that he co-edited with V. E. Chirkin, *Contemporary Political Systems*, Burlatsky, after duly noting Marx's demonstration 'that material production is the base which defines the character and forms of state life', goes on to cite Engels on the influence 'of state power on economic development'. Persisting with the terminology, 'base' and 'superstructure', Burlatsky emphasises the fact that this interrelationship does not have 'a one-sided character'. The 'political superstructure' exerts in its turn 'an enormous influence *(ogromnoe vozdeystvie)* on the whole of social life'.[150] The context in which these words are written is that of a general discussion of 'the socio-economic environment and the political system'[151] and it must be assumed that they are intended to be applicable to the Soviet case, though this is not explicitly stated.

Kalensky has gone significantly further in his discussions of the relative autonomy of the *state vis-à-vis society* and its *'ruling class'*. Again, it should be noted, the author is writing about the state in general, rather than about the Soviet state specifically, but he does not appear in principle to exclude the Soviet Union from these particular generalisations. In his notably scholarly and significant book, *The State as an Object of Sociological Analysis*, he writes of 'the state bureaucracy' as being 'not simply a special exclusive social stratum and caste', but as one that 'serves as the material embodiment of state power itself' and of 'this very stratum as that which directly operates the state mechanism and implements public power'.[152] Kalensky, after drawing upon the authority of Marx, Engels and Lenin for such an analysis, goes on to observe:

> The concentration of enormous power in the hands of bureaucrats *(chinovniki)* has most serious political consequences, and leads namely to the acquisition by that special social stratum of a relative autonomy in relation to the ruling class as a whole, and to its being in certain circumstances even in conflict with it, thrusting upon it selfish interests of its own.[153]

In a more recent publication Kalensky develops that point, and also suggests that Marxist–Leninist teaching concerning the state ('notable for its genuine scientific objectivity and historical method') 'orientates the researcher to the study of political reality in all its dialectical complexity and contradictions'. This draws attention to the possibility of a situation arising when 'the public power, even though operating in the interests of the economically dominant class, possesses, however, in relation to that class a great autonomy'.[154] Kalensky also writes of public power being at times 'implemented by representatives of other classes' (other, that is, than the 'ruling class'), and here, as in his reference to the 'great autonomy', rather than 'relative autonomy', of those who implement public power, he moves beyond the position he reached in his 1977 book.[155]

Thus, in principle, if one were to apply this general formulation about the great autonomy of those who wield public power to the Soviet case, public power could be exercised by representatives of a class or social stratum other than the working class, and such a stratum could possess a great autonomy *vis-à-vis* Soviet society as a whole and the working class in particular. It must be stressed that Kalensky himself draws no such conclusion, but is putting forward a general proposition in the context of developing Marxist theory of the state. It is open to Kalensky's readers to draw their own conclusions, and his work (for he is simultaneously an outstanding Soviet authority on American political science[156] and prominent historian of political thought)[157] testifies to the liveliness and interest of a significant portion of officially published Soviet writing in recent years.

CONCLUSIONS

The Soviet literature discussed in the foregoing pages is of considerable consequence in itself, quite apart from any bearing it may have on the writings of Western political scientists discussed in the first half of this chapter. Though an excessive concern with defining terms is ultimately self-defeating, the attempts of some Soviet scholars to specify more precisely what they mean by 'the state' and 'the political system' contrasts favourably with the relatively casual way in which a good many Western political scientists decide to use one term rather than the other.[158] A more interesting contrast, however, is between the emphasis of some of the more innovative Soviet scholars on the relative autonomy of the state and the stress of Western pluralist theorists on the relative autonomy of society. They have in common the terminology, 'relative autonomy', but they are pointing in different directions. To the extent that society is autonomous from the state, pluralism is indicated; to the extent that emphasis is placed upon the autonomy of the state (with its 'special apparatus of coercion as one of the means of securing observance of [its] laws and directives')[159] from society, pluralism, it is being suggested, is curtailed or absent.[160]

A further inference that may be drawn from recent Soviet writing on political power and the state is that the suggestion sometimes made, that criticism from 'within the ideology' is no longer possible within Soviet-type systems,[161] oversimplifies considerably the position in the Soviet Union itself. Many different value preferences may be detected among Soviet writers on politics, and those who wish to see a greater emphasis upon democracy and liberty and those who take a highly restrictive view of both each draw upon the works of Marx and Lenin in support of their views. Since the positive evaluations of democracy and liberty by Marx and Lenin are numerous, and since the terminology, 'political pluralism', is not to be found in either of these classic sources, it is, in fact, a more straightforward matter for Soviet theorists to justify an emphasis on the importance of, and desirability of extending, democracy and liberty than to betray concern with the existence or absence of pluralism. Unlike, then, their counterparts among social scientists in some of the other Communist states, Soviet scholars do not make an explicit attempt to justify political pluralism in a normative sense. So far as democracy and liberty are concerned, it is worth noting Kalensky's view that, in 'the comparison of political regimes in socialist countries', special significance should be attached to information pertaining to 'the correlation between the degree of democratism and centralism in the political leadership, the ratio of persuasion to coercion in the methods of implementation of political power, and also [to] the level of legality and of guarantees of the basic constitutional rights and liberties of citizens'.[162]

The somewhat esoteric debate among Soviet political scientists and jurists concerns not only the meaning of words and is not only about approaches to the study of politics. Behind these disagreements lie, in many cases, also significant political differences. As a generalisation, it would be fair to say that those participants in the discussion who lay most emphasis on state power and state sovereignty are more conservative Communists than those who emphasise *narodovlastie* or sovereignty of the people, even though it could be argued (and is argued by those who belong to the former grouping) that there is no contradiction between the two concepts. Similarly, those scholars who call for the empirical study of political relations in their concrete reality tend to be of a much more reformist disposition than the scholars who have remained content with formalistic and legalistic accounts of Soviet political life.

It may seem strange to categorise as conservative the view that the party can but *influence* the state and that party institutions do not wield *power* over state institutions. The evolution towards such a view in Yugoslav theory (and the trend towards some limitation of the party's functions in Yugoslav practice) has, after all, been a central feature of the Yugoslav reformist 'model'.[163] Similarly, an emphasis on the party's authority, and constant need to win authority, rather than upon party power, and the enforcement of its power, is to be found in the section on 'the leading role of the Party' in the 1968 Action Programme of the Communist Party of Czechoslovakia.[164] What, then, is the distinction between, on the one hand, the standpoint of Soviet theoreticians who deny that the Communist Party of the Soviet Union exercises political power, and, on the other, 'reformist' conceptions of the role of the party held by Yugoslav and 'Prague Spring' theorists? Basically, the difference is that the

Yugoslavs and the Czechs faced up to the political reality that an enormous (and, in their view, excessive) power had, in fact, been concentrated in the hands of party organs. That is not at all the same thing as turning a blind eye to the exercise of power by party institutions and asserting that the party exercises its leading role in society *solely* by virtue of its great influence and authority.

The analysis of the argument among Soviet scholars on such matters is complicated by the fact that sometimes these academics write 'descriptively' when they would wish to write prescriptively and use an 'is' when they mean an 'ought'. Thus, in certain contexts, Soviet scholars may indeed be actually advocating a curtailment of party power when they choose to emphasise that the party cannot give orders to (for instance) soviets. It would not appear, however, in the case of the state- or party-power debate between Shevtsov and Burlatsky and others that Shevtsov wishes to see the Politburo, Secretariat and departments of the Central Committee divest themselves of all power. If that is no part of his intention, neither, it should be added, is it the wish of Burlatsky and like-minded scholars to remove political power from party organs. What makes their standpoint inimical to the conservative position is their desire to develop analysis of the Soviet political system as it is, rather than as legal textbooks on state and law have hitherto portrayed it. In essence, writers such as Burlatsky, Shakhnazarov and Kalensky recognise that in the exercise of its leading role, the party makes use of influence, authority *and* power. While they are not suggesting for a moment that the party's relationship with other institutions is *always* a power relationship rather than one of influence and authority, it is, in their view, at least as fanciful to claim that higher party organs never wield political power.

The Soviet scholars engaged in the discussions noted above are party members and they cite not only Marx and Lenin but recent party and state documents in support of their views. But, as is well known and as is further illustrated by these very discussions, the works of Marx and Lenin can be used to justify a wide range of positions and, so far as the party or constitutional documents are concerned, in a number of cases these scholars (some of whom are very prominent party intellectuals) are building upon, and extrapolating from, formulations which they themselves have helped to legitimise by inserting in the documents. The Soviet discussion of the state and its relative autonomy and of the political system and political power is, then, important not only for its intrinsic contribution to the task of conceptualising Soviet politics. It also amounts to one more piece of evidence (from a sensitive ideological area) of the diversity of view to be found within the CPSU and within various party and state institutions on matters of some consequence.

Yet, if we reject the picture of the monolithic unity of the CPSU and of the Soviet state (in the broad sense) as a great oversimplification (though one which is found equally attractive by the most conservative Communists within the Soviet Union and by their most conservative opponents abroad), there is no need to conclude as an alternative that the Soviet Union has become yet another variant of a pluralist state. While social and political forces within the broader society, and opinion groupings within the party and within various other institutions, do have an impact on public policy, the relative autonomy of institutions other than the highest party organs is (by comparative standards) fairly small, and the relative autonomy of the supreme holders of political power at the apex of the party hierarchy is (again in comparative perspective) very great.

Having rejected totalitarian, pluralist and corporatist conceptualisations of the Soviet system, I have no intention at this stage of the argument of producing a grand new conceptualisation. A large part of the problem is that Soviet reality is too complex, multifaceted and downright contradictory to be encapsulated in a word or a phrase. For those who still demand a phrase, ones that are probably less misleading, so far as the contemporary Soviet Union is concerned, than the three conceptualisations discussed in the first part of this chapter are the notion of 'diversity within monism' (Shakhnazarov's view of the system,[165] or the expression that Gordon Skilling once used, and perhaps prematurely discarded – 'imperfect monism'.[166]

Though these phrases do not take us very far, under such headings we can at least keep in mind the 'bureaucratic politics' aspect of the system, while noting, too, the limits that are imposed on it by the existence of a 'super-bureau' in the shape of the Politburo. Furthermore, the institutional rivalries and conflicts which do exist are by no means the sum total of Soviet political life. There is also an esoteric politics which includes an element of guarded debate in areas deemed by the party leadership to be of great sensitivity. This holds true, in some measure, of the debate on the state and the political system considered above. Discussion in print of Soviet foreign policy, it may be added, is of an even more esoteric nature, with differences of view expressed in somewhat veiled terms and policy changes shrouded in a mantle of continuity.[167]

In other areas of policy, where the party leadership either has an interest in a relatively free debate taking place or is not itself particularly preoccupied with the issue, there is much more open political argument, some of which is ultimately reflected in policy decisions or legislation.[168] But however vigorous the debate, the power structure remains intact. Though it would, no doubt, be wrong to exclude as future possibilities the emergence of corporatism or even a form of pluralism as the main defining characteristics of political relationships within the Soviet Union, it seems clear that to define the contemporary Soviet system in either of these terms is no less misleading than to regard it as totalitarian.

NOTES

1. This is a considerably expanded and revised version of a chapter that will appear in Susan Gross Solomon (ed.), *Pluralism in the Soviet Union* (London, 1983). It has been read in one or other of its two previous drafts by Robert A. Dahl, Neil Harding, Michael Lessnoff, Steven Lukes, Mary McAuley, David Nicholls, T. H. Rigby, Susan Solomon and Gordon Wightman. I am most grateful to them for their helpful comments.

2. See F. Burlatsky, 'Politika i nauka', *Pravda*, 10 January 1965, p. 4. For discussion of this article and some of the subsequent developments along the road to a Soviet political science, see D.E. Powell and P. Shoup, 'The Emergence of Political Science in Communist Countries', *American Political Science Review*, vol. LXIV no. 2 (June 1970) pp. 572–88; R.H.W. Theen, 'Political Science in the USSR: "To Be or Not to Be"', *World Politics*, vol. XXIII, no. 4 (July 1971) pp. 684–703; R.H.W. Theen, 'Political Science in the Soviet Union', *Problems of Communism*, vol. XXI, no. 3 (1972) pp. 64–70; and R.J. Hill, *Soviet Politics, Political Science and Reform* (Oxford, 1980).

3. I am using 'government' generically to stand in this instance for the party and state leadership.

4. R. Miliband, *Marxism and Politics* (Oxford, 1977) p. 8.

5. Illustrations from the Soviet discussion will be given in the second half of this chapter. Western Marxist statements along these lines are exceedingly numerous. See, for instance, L. Althusser, *For Marx* (Harmondsworth, 1969) p. 240; and Miliband, *Marxism and Politics*, pp. 114–16. Althusser, objecting to the concept of the 'cult of personality', places Stalinism firmly in the context of the 'relative autonomy' of the 'superstructure'. Miliband, while paying attention to the 'extreme example' of Stalin (p. 115), goes further than Althusser and writes of *'the state'* in Communist systems generally as having 'a very high degree of autonomy from *society*' (p. 116, Miliband's italics).

6. The most prominent advocate of an 'institutional pluralist' interpretation of Soviet politics (though he has also adopted the

terminology, 'institutionalised pluralism') has been J. F. Hough. See especially his *The Soviet Union and Social Science Theory* (Cambridge, Mass., 1977); and also J. F. Hough and M. Fainsod, *How the Soviet Union is Governed*, (Cambridge, Mass., 1979). Interesting 'bureaucratic pluralist' interpretations of Soviet politics include those of D. P. Hammer, *USSR: The Politics of Oligarchy* (Hinsdale, Ill., 1974); and W. Taubman, *Governing Soviet Cities: Bureaucratic Politics and Urban Development in the USSR* (New York, 1973). An example of an author who uses 'pluralist' terminology to describe institutional conflicts and rivalries within the Soviet Union, but is less inclined to make this the main defining characteristic of Soviet politics, is A. Nove: cf. his chapter, ' "Centralised Pluralism": Ministries and Regional Planning', in Nove, *The Soviet Economic System* (London, 1977) pp. 60–84, and his article, 'History, Hierarchy and Nationalities: Some Observations on the Soviet Social Structure', *Soviet Studies*, vol. XXI, no. 1 (1969).

7. G. Sartori, 'Concept Misformation in Comparative Politics', *American Political Science Review*, vol. LXIV, no. 4 (December 1970) p. 1034.
8. Ibid, p. 1035.
9. Ibid, p. 1034.
10. Ibid, p. 1039.
11. Ibid, p. 1052.
12. A. Inkeles, 'Models and Issues in the Analysis of Soviet Society', *Survey*, no.60 (July 1966) (pp. 3–17), p. 3.
13. I have elaborated on this point in my *Soviet Politics and Political Science* (London, 1974) pp. 30–41.
14. The literature on totalitarianism is very extensive. The most influential early works were H. Arendt, *The Origins of Totalitarianism* (London, 1967) (first published 1951); C. J. Friedrich (ed.), *Totalitarianism* (Cambridge, Mass., 1954); and C. J. Friedrich and Z. K. Brzezinski, *Totalitarian Dictatorship and Autocracy* (Cambridge, Mass., 1956) (2nd ed, revised by Friedrich, 1965). Among the most significant of more recent discussions are C. J. Friedrich, M. Curtis and B. R. Barber, *Totalitarianism in Perspective: Three Views* (London, 1969); L. Schapiro, *Totalitarianism* (London, 1972); and J. L. Linz, 'Totalitarian and Authoritarian Regimes', in F. I. Greenstein and N. W. Polsby (eds), *Handbook of Political Science, Volume 3: Macropolitical Theory* (Reading, Mass., 1975) pp. 175–411.
15. See, for instance, his *The Revolution Betrayed: What is the Soviet Union and Where is it Going?* (London, 1937).
16. See, for example, W. Brus, *Socialist Ownership and Political Systems* (London, 1975) esp. pp. 140–2 and 213; and Z. Mlynář, 'The Rules of the Game: The Soviet Bloc Today', *The Political Quarterly*, vol. 50, no. 4 (October–December 1979) pp. 403–19.
17. See D. Easton, *The Political System: An Enquiry into the State of Political Science* (New York, 1953) esp. pp. 106–7 and 142; and D. Easton, 'The Political System Besieged by the State', *Political Theory*, vol. 9, no. 3 (August 1981) pp. 303–25. The reference to the collector of the 145 definitions of the state (*The Political System*, p. 107) is to J. W. Garner, *Political Science and Government* (New York, 1928) p. 9.

18. For criticism along these lines, see, for example, A. C. Janos, 'Group Politics in Communist Society: A Second Look at the Pluralist Model', in S. P. Huntington and C. H. Moore (eds), *Authoritarian Politics in Modern Society* (New York, 1970) pp. 437–50; J. J. Linz, 'Totalitarian and Authoritarian Regimes', in Greenstein and Polsby, *Handbook of Political Science*, pp. 175–411; J. LaPalombara, 'Monoliths or Plural Systems: Through Conceptual Lenses Darkly', *Studies in Comparative Communism*, vol. VIII, no. 3 (Autumn 1975) pp. 304–32; and A. Stepan, *The State and Society: Peru in Comparative Perspective* (Princeton, 1978) (Part One, 'The Role of the State: Concepts and Comparisons'). See also A. C. Janos (ed.), *Authoritarian Politics in Communist Europe: Uniformity and Diversity in One-Party States* (Berkeley, Calif., 1976). For an early, perceptive and open-minded consideration of the problem, see B. Harasymiw, 'Application of the Concept of Pluralism to the Soviet Political System', *Newsletter on Comparative Studies of Communism*, vol. V, no. 1 (November 1971) pp. 40–54.

19. Its use is traced back to the 1920s by Schapiro in his *Totalitarianism*, pp. 13–14.

20. D. Nicholls, *The Pluralist State* (London, 1975).

21. D. Nicholls, *Three Varieties of Pluralism* (London, 1974).

22. Ibid, p. 56.

23. See, for example, J. J. Wiatr, 'Elements of Pluralism in the Polish Political System', *The Polish Sociological Bulletin*, no. 1 (1966); J. J. Wiatr and A. Przeworski, 'Control without Opposition', *Government and Opposition*, vol. 1, no. 2 (January 1966) pp. 227–39; J. J. Wiatr, *Essays in Political Sociology* (Warsaw, 1978); S. Ehrlich, 'Le Problème du Pluralisme', *L'Homme et la Societé*, no. V (Juillet–September, 1967) pp. 113–18; S. Ehrlich, 'Pluralism and Marxism', in S. Ehrlich and G. Wootton (eds), *Three Faces of Pluralism: Political, Ethnic and Religious* (Farnborough, 1980) pp. 34–45; and V. Klokočka, *Volby v pluralitních democraciích* (Prague, 1968). For discussion of the ideas of the advocates of pluralism within the Communist Party of Czechoslovakia, see H. G. Skilling, *Czechoslovakia's Interrupted Revolution* (Princeton, 1976) esp. pp. 333–72; F. M. Barnard and R. A. Vernon, 'Socialist Pluralism and Pluralist Socialism', *Political Studies*, vol. XXV, no. 4 (December 1977) pp. 474–90; and Z. Mlynář, 'Notions of Political Pluralism in the Policy of the Communist Party of Czechoslovakia in 1968', a product of a research project under Mlynář's direction, 'Experiences of the Prague Spring 1968', Working Paper No. 3.

24. For two East European critiques of Communists' advocacy of pluralism – the first a measured and thoughtful analysis by a Hungarian scholar and the second a much more polemical, though also interesting, attack by a Bulgarian philosopher – see P. Hardi, 'Why do Communist Parties Advocate Pluralism?', *World Politics*, vol. XXXII, no. 4 (July 1980) pp. 531–52; and A. Kozharov, *Monizm i plyuralizm v ideologii i politike* (Moscow, 1976).

25. E. Kardelj, *Democracy and Socialism* (London, 1978) esp. pp. 115–40.

26. See, for example, G. Shakhnazarov, 'O demokraticheskom tsentralizme i politicheskom plyuralizme', *Kommunist*, no. 10 (July 1979) p. 107.
27. S. Erlich, 'Pluralism and Marxism', in Ehrlich and Wootton, *Three Faces of Pluralism*, pp. 43–4.
28. J. J. Wiatr, 'The Hegemonic Party System in Poland', in Wiatr, *Essays in Political Sociology*, p. 188.
29. Sartori, 'Concept Misformation in Comparative Politics', pp. 1050–51.
30. R. A. Dahl, *Dilemmas of Pluralist Democracy: Autonomy vs Control*, (New Haven, 1982) p. 5. See also R. A. Dahl, 'Pluralism Revisited', *Comparative Politics*, vol. 10, no. 2 (January 1978) pp. 191–203 (reprinted in Ehrlich and Wootton, *Three Faces of Pluralism*, pp. 20–33).
31. Dahl, *Dilemmas of Pluralist Democracy*, p. 26.
32. Partly as a consequence, this applies also to some criticisms of 'pluralist' interpretations of Soviet politics, among them S. White's 'Communist Systems and the "Iron Law of Pluralism"', *British Journal of Political Science*, vol. VIII, no. 1 (January 1978) pp. 101–17. White provides interesting information on the number of sessions, speeches per session, etc. in the Supreme Soviet of the USSR and the Central Committee of the CPSU for the years 1954–75, but as tests of the 'iron law of pluralism' they are of but marginal relevance. The suggestion that 'an increased degree of interest articulation and aggregation within the Central Committee of the CPSU' would signify pluralism is especially dubious. Even a shift in the balance of power between leading party organs – with, say, more interest mediation taking place in the Central Committee and less in the Politburo and Secretariat – would not of itself constitute pluralism. In so far as the bare statistics of meetings tend to disconfirm anything, they might be regarded as undermining either a 'corporatist' or an 'inner-party democratisation' interpretation of developments within the Soviet Union. That they do not take us very far is, however, suggested by the extent to which formal and informal access to information (Central Committee members receive minutes, though possibly abbreviated ones, of Politburo meetings) and access to key people within the Central Committee building, whether by personal visit or by telephone, may be more important than most plenary sessions of the Committee.

A trenchant attack on the idea that the Soviet Union is 'pluralist' (except in such a broad sense of the term that Hitler's Germany and Stalin's Russia would also rank as pluralist) is contained in a more recent article in the same journal: A. J. Groth, 'USSR: Pluralist Monolith?', *British Journal of Political Science*, vol. 9, part 4 (October 1979) pp. 445–64. Groth, however, is less than fair to his principal antagonist, J. Hough, when he complains that 'Hough's discussion of the Soviet political system ... is almost wholly devoid of institutional considerations' (p. 447).
33. For a summary and analysis of the evidence available up to the early 1970s, see my *Soviet Politics and Political Science* (London, 1974) ch. 3, 'Groups, Interests and the Policy Process', pp. 71–88. Much information, relevant to this theme, is to be found in H. G. Skilling and

F. Griffiths (eds), *Interest Groups in Soviet Politics* (Princeton, 1971). For more recent contributions, see R. B. Remneck (ed.), *Social Scientists and Policy-Making in the USSR* (New York, 1977); P. H. Solomon, Jr, *Soviet Criminologists and Criminal Policy: Specialists in Policy-Making* (London, 1978); J. Löwenhardt, *Decision Making in Soviet Politics* (London, 1981); T. Gustafson, *Reform in Soviet Politics: Lessons of Recent Policies on Land and Water* (Cambridge, 1981); and L. Holmes, *The Policy Process in Communist States: Politics and Industrial Administration* (London, 1981).

34. For examples of diffusion of influence under Stalin, see T. Dunmore, *The Stalinist Command Economy: The Soviet State Apparatus and Economic Policy 1945–53* (London, 1981); A. Kemp-Welch, 'Stalinism and Intellectual Order', in T. H. Rigby, A. Brown and P. Reddaway (eds), *Authority, Power and Policy in the USSR* (London, 1980) pp. 118–34; P. H. Solomon, Jr, 'Specialists in Soviet Policy Making: Criminal Policy, 1938–70', in Remneck (ed.), *Social Scientists and Policy Making in the USSR* pp. 1–33, esp. 4–6; Solomon, Jr, *Soviet Criminologists and Criminal Policy*, esp. pp. 32–4 and 146–7; and W. O. McCagg, Jr, *Stalin Embattled, 1943–1948* (Detroit, 1978).

35. Though Gordon Skilling has been opposed to the description of the Soviet Union as a type of pluralist system, ten years ago he wrote: 'the system is operating differently than it did under Stalin, in part as a result of increased activity by political groups which have attained a certain degree of autonomy of action. In that sense Soviet society has shown signs of at least an incipient pluralism' (in Skilling and Griffiths, *Interest Groups in Soviet Politics*, p. 44). Even Schapiro, who has shown no sympathy for interpretations that make pluralism a key feature of the Soviet political system, has written of totalitarianism co-existing 'with dissent, incipient pressure groups and *some pluralism of institutions* in the Soviet Union' (my italics) in his *Totalitarianism*, p. 124. Perhaps misleadingly, in terms of Dahl's definition, which I now accept as the best way of making pluralism a somewhat more rigorous and useful concept, I have myself written of 'elements of pluralism' within the Soviet system, in *Soviet Politics and Political Science*, p. 74, and of 'a limited institutional or bureaucratic pluralism – in some areas of policy very limited indeed' – in A. Brown and M. Kaser (eds), *The Soviet Union since the Fall of Khrushchev*, 2nd edn (London, 1978) p.245. Like Skilling and Schapiro, however, I have never found it particularly useful to regard the Soviet Union as a 'type of pluralist system', even though I would interpret the concept of totalitarianism differently from Schapiro and do not find its application to the contemporary Soviet Union very useful.

36. See Hough, *The Soviet Union and Social Science Theory*, pp. 14–15.

37. Notable contributions of an empirical or theoretical nature to the debate on elites and pluralism and community power within the United States include the following: P. Bachrach, *The Theory of Democratic Elitism: A Critique* (Boston, 1967); R. A. Dahl, *Who Governs? Democracy and Power in an American City* (New Haven, 1961); G. W. Domhoff, *Who Really Rules? New Haven and Community Power Reexamined* (Santa

Monica, 1978); R. A. Dahl, 'Who *Really* Rules', *Social Science Quarterly*, vol. 60, no. 1 (June 1979) pp. 144–51; F. Hunter, *Community Power Structure* (Chapel Hill, 1953); R. S. Lynd and H. M. Lynd, *Middletown* (New York, 1929); R. S. Lynd and H. M. Lynd, *Middletown in Transition* (New York, 1937); J. J. Mansbridge, *Beyond Adversary Democracy* (New York 1980); C. Wright Mills, *The Power Elite* (New York, 1956); N. W. Polsby, *Community Power and Political Theory: A Further Look at Problems of Evidence and Inference*, 2nd, enlarged edn (New Haven, 1980); W. L. Warner *et al.*, *Democracy in Jonesville* (New York, 1949); and R. E. Wolfinger, *The Politics of Progress* (Englewood Cliffs, N.J., 1974). Four British contributions to the debate (of which only Newton's has a case-study base) worthy of note are: S. Lukes, *Power: A Radical View* (London, 1974); Nicholls, *Three Varieties of Pluralism*; K. Newton, *Second City Politics: Democratic Processes and Decision-Making in Birmingham* (Oxford, 1976); and G. Parry, *Political Elites* (London, 1969).

38. See, for instance, the exchange between N. W. Polsby and K. Newton, *Political Studies*, vol. XXVII, no. 4 (December 1979) esp. pp. 530–1 and 543; also Dahl, *Dilemmas of Pluralist Democracy*, Appendix A, pp. 207–9.

39. Hough, *The Soviet Union and Social Science Theory*, p. 5.

40. Ibid, pp. 14–15.

41. Even the party daily newspaper, *Rudé právo*, was not under the full control of the party leadership, nor, indeed, that of its editor, Oldřich Švestka. One article which was an embarrassment to the Czechoslovak party leadership, in view of Soviet sensitivities, was, for example, that on the front page of *Rudé právo*, 16 April 1968, which discussed the pros and cons of whether Jan Masaryk's death in 1948 was by suicide or murder, and held that the possibility of Soviet involvement was worth further investigation. See H. G. Skilling, *Czechoslovakia's Interrupted Revolution* (Princeton, 1976) p. 381.

42. For a graph showing the pattern of popular trust in Czechoslovak politicians, 1968–9, and discussion of it, see A. Brown and G. Wightman, 'Czechoslovakia: Revival and Retreat', in A. Brown and J. Gray (eds), *Political Culture and Political Change in Communist States* (London, 1977) (2nd edn, 1979) esp. pp. 174–6. For more extensive coverage of opinion-polling in Czechoslovakia in that period, see J. A. Piekalkiewicz, *Public Opinion Polling in Czechoslovakia, 1968–69: Results and Analysis of Surveys Conducted During the Dubček Era* (New York, 1972).

43. Thus, for example, links were established between the district committees of Prague 1 (an intelligentsia-dominated party organisation in the district in which the university and a number of research institutes were located) and Prague 9 (a predominantly working-class district).

44. Even with regard to appointments which it supposedly covered, the *nomenklatura* became a dead letter for much of 1968. It was not formally abolished, but was generally ignored.

45. See, for example, on these two organisations, Skilling, *Czechoslovakia's Interrupted Revolution*, esp. pp. 546–8; V. V. Kusin, *Political Grouping*

in the Czechoslovak Reform Movement (London, 1972) pp. 176–91; and G. Golan, *Reform Rule in Czechoslovakia: The Dubček Era 1968–1969* (Cambridge, 1973) pp. 80–82.

46. For a good general account of developments within Czechoslovakia during the 1970s, see V. V. Kusin, *From Dubček to Charter 77: Czechoslovakia 1968–78* (Edinburgh, 1978).

47. Note, in particular, the letter of the Central Committee of the CPSU to the Central Committee of the Polish United Workers' Party, *Pravda*, 12 June 1981, p. 2, and subsequent Soviet support for the martial-law regime. For four useful accounts of events in Poland in 1980–1 (the first and last of which also provide some of the essential historical context), see N. Ascherson, *The Polish August: The Self-Limiting Revolution* (Harmondsworth, 1981); D. McShane, *Solidarity: Poland's Independent Trade Union* (Nottingham, 1981); K. Ruane, *The Polish Challenge* (London, 1982); and J. Woodall (ed.), *Policy and Politics in Contemporary Poland: Reform, Failure and Crisis* (London, 1982).

48. On the overlap between PUWP and Solidarity membership, see Ascherson, *The Polish August*, p. 201.

49. See Hough and Fainsod, *How the Soviet Union is Governed*, p. 547.

50. H. G. Skilling, 'Interest Groups and Communist Politics', *World Politics*, vol. XVIII, no. 3 (April 1966) p. 449. In an article published in the same month I used the term, 'pluralistic trends', with reference specifically to Czechoslovakia in the mid-1960s. See A. H. Brown, 'Pluralistic Trends in Czechoslovakia', *Soviet Studies*, vol. XVII, no. 4 (April 1966) pp.453–72. As early as 1953, it should be noted, Karl Deutsch had raised the theoretical possibility of an 'automatic drift toward pluralization and disintegration' of 'totalitarian regimes' which, in the Soviet case, he believed could be staved off 'for a considerable time'. See K. W. Deutsch, 'Cracks in the Monolith: Possibilities and Patterns of Disintegration in Totalitarian Systems', in Friedrich (ed.), *Totalitarianism*, p. 311.

51. While recognising *Interest Groups in Soviet Politics* as a landmark in the study of the Soviet political system, I have expressed some reservations – about, for instance, the 'conceptual stretching' involved – in my 'Problems of Interest Articulation and Group Influence in the Soviet Union', *Government and Opposition*, vol. 7, no. 2 (Spring 1972) pp. 229–43, and in *Soviet Politics and Political Science*, pp. 71–4.

52. Not least in his first book, *The Soviet Prefects: The Local Party Organs in Industrial Decision-Making* (Cambridge, Mass., 1969).

53. It follows from my argument thus far that I cannot agree with Susan Solomon when she writes (in the Introduction to *Pluralism in the Soviet Union*, London, 1983, forthcoming) that because the concept of pluralism *is* being used in a variety of different senses and being applied to the Soviet Union, 'it therefore makes no sense to argue over whether the introduction of "pluralism" into Soviet studies has stretched the concept beyond its breaking point'. The Soviet Union has, after all, been called a great many things, including 'democratic', 'totalitarian' and 'fascist'. If concepts are to retain discriminating power and to be of value in comparative analysis, it *does* make sense to use them in such a way

that basic political distinctions are not needlessly blurred.
54. 'Institutional pluralism' and 'bureaucratic pluralism' are generally used interchangeably in the literature, though the latter term may focus attention more exclusively on the major party and state bureaucratic structures, whereas 'institutional pluralism' may call to mind not only ministries, departments of the Central Committee of the Party, the military, the KGB, etc., but also such institutions as research institutes of the Academy of Sciences.
55. T. H. Rigby, 'A Conceptual Approach to Authority, Power and Policy in the Soviet Union', in Rigby, Brown and Reddaway (eds), *Authority, Power and Policy in the USSR*, p. 25.
56. H. Seidman, *Politics, Position and Power: The Dynamics of Federal Organization* (Oxford and New York (3rd ed.), 1980) p. 322.
57. H. Heclo, *A Government of Strangers: Executive Politics in Washington* (Washington, DC, 1977) p. 12. See also Heclo on 'issue networks' (a concept which might well have some application in the Soviet context) in A. King (ed.), *The New American Political System* (Washington, DC, 1978) pp. 87–124.
58. R. Neustadt, *Presidential Power: The Politics of Leadership From FDR to Carter* (New York, 1980 edn) p. 242.
59. Z. Mlynář, *Night Frost in Prague: The End of Humane Socialism* (London, 1980) p. 111.
60. Ibid, p. 53; and the slightly fuller version in Z. Mlynář, *Mráz přichází z Kremlu* (Cologne, 1978) p. 69.
61. See Seidman, 'Coordination: The Search for the Philosopher's Stone', in *Politics, Position and Power*, pp. 200–17.
62. Heclo, *A Government of Strangers*. See also Heclo in King (ed.), *The New American Political System*, esp. p. 122.
63. Seidman, *Politics, Position and Power*, p. 94.
64. R. Rose, 'Government against Sub-governments: A European Perspective on Washington', in R. Rose and E. N. Suleiman (eds), *Presidents and Prime Ministers* (Washington, DC, 1980) p. 294.
65. See Rose and Suleiman (eds), *Presidents and Prime Ministers*, ibid.
66. Hough and Fainsod, *How the Soviet Union is Governed*, p. 547. See also pp. 543–55.
67. See P. C. Schmitter, 'Still the Century of Corporatism?', *The Review of Politics*, vol. 36 (January 1974) pp. 85–139, esp. pp. 93–4, and 'Models of Interest Intermediation and Models of Societal Change in Western Europe', *Comparative Political Studies*, vol. 10, no. 1 (April 1977) pp. 7–38, esp. p. 9. Among those who have used Schmitter's definition (though several of them also express certain reservations) are Linz, 'Totalitarian and Authoritarian Regimes', p. 307; Stepan, *The State and Society*, p. 66; L. Panitch, 'The Development of Corporatism in Liberal Democracies', *Comparative Political Studies*, vol. 10, no. 1 (April 1977) p. 64; and L. A. Mammergren, 'Corporatism in Latin American Politics: A Re-examination of the "Unique" Tradition', *Comparative Politics*, vol. 9, no. 4 (July 1977) p. 466.
68. Schmitter, 'Still the Century', p. 96; 'Models of Interest Intermediation', p. 9.

69. Schmitter, 'Still the Century', pp. 99–100.
70. Linz, 'Totalitarian and Authoritarian Regimes', p. 312 (though see also p. 346 where he writes of Yugoslavia as an 'authoritarian regime' in which 'the different degree of autonomy granted to different groups fits well with our notion of limited pluralism'). The distinction between corporatism (especially 'societal corporatism') and 'limited pluralism' is, of course, a far from clear-cut one.
71. Stepan, *The State and Society*, p. 15.
72. Schmitter, 'Still the Century', p. 97; 'Models of Interest Intermediation', p. 30.
73. V. Bunce and J. M. Echols III, 'Soviet Politics in the Brezhnev Era: "Pluralism" or "Corporatism"?', in D. R. Kelley (ed.), *Soviet Politics in the Brezhnev Era* (New York, 1980) pp. 1–26, esp. pp. 19–20. For a brief discussion of what he calls the 'corporate perspective' on Soviet politics, see also G. Breslauer, 'Reformism, Conservatism, and Leadership Authority at the 26th Party Congress', in S. Bialer and T. Gustafson (eds), *Russia at the Crossroads: The 26th Congress of the CPSU* (London, 1982) pp. 65–86, esp. 80–85.
74. Bunce and Echols, 'Soviet Politics', p. 14.
75. Schmitter, 'Still the Century', p. 94; 'Models of Interest Intermediation', p. 9.
76. On the *nomenklatura*, see B. Harasymiw, '*Nomenklatura*: The Soviet Communist Party's Leadership Recruitment System', *Canadian Journal of Political Science*, vol. II, no. 4 (December 1969) pp. 493–512; B. Harasymiw, *Political Elite Recruitment in the USSR* (London, 1983) (forthcoming); J. H. Miller, 'The Communist Party: Trends and Problems', in A. Brown and M. Kaser (eds), *Soviet Policy for the 1980s* (London, 1982) pp. 1–34, esp. 20–23; R.H.W. Theen, 'Party and Bureaucracy', in G. B. Smith (ed.), *Public Policy and Administration in the Soviet Union* (New York, 1980) pp.18–52, esp. 38–44; and M. Voslensky, *La Nomenklatura* (Paris, 1980).
77. *Ezhegodnik bol'shoy sovetskoy entsiklopedii 1981* (Moscow, 1981) pp. 609–10.
78. R. A. Medvedev, *On Socialist Democracy* (London, 1975) p. 404.
79. L. I. Brezhnev, 'Otchet tsentral'novo Komiteta' (report of the Central Committee of the CPSU to the XXVI Congress), *Pravda*, 24 February 1981, p. 8.
80. D. Tarschys exemplifies such an approach. See his *The Soviet Political Agenda: Problems and Priorities 1950–1970* (London, 1979) esp. ch. 2, 'The Soviet Political System: Three Models', pp. 10–39, in which he compares and contrasts totalitarian, pluralist and bureaucratic models.
81. W. Taubman is a prominent representative of this tendency. See his *Governing Soviet Cities*; and his 'The Change to Change in Communist Systems', in H. W. Morton and R. L. Tökés (eds), *Soviet Politics and Society in the 1970's* (New York, 1974) pp. 369–94. G. B. Smith's 'Bureaucratic Politics and Public Policy in the Soviet Union', in Smith (ed.), *Public Policy and Administration in the Soviet Union*, adopts a similar position.
82. This is a position that emerges clearly in, for example, the numerous

articles of T. H. Rigby over the past two decades. See, in particular, his 'Politics in the Mono-Organizational Society', in Janos (ed.), *Authoritarian Politics in Communist Europe: Uniformity and Diversity in One-Party States*, pp. 31–80; and 'The Legacy of Revolution: Models of the Soviet Socio-Political Order', *Teaching History* (Sydney), vol. 15, part 4 (January 1982) pp. 4–11.

83. Leonard Schapiro is the most prominent among the scholars who adhere to this position. See especially his 'Reflections on the Changing Role of the Party in the Totalitarian Polity', in his *The Communist Party of the Soviet Union*, 2nd edn (London, 1970) pp. 619–29.

84. See Yu. V. Andropov, 'Leninizm – neischerpaemyy istochnik revolyut-sionnoy energii i tvorchestva mass', *Pravda*, 23 April 1982, pp. 1–2 (at p. 2); and K. U. Chernenko, 'Avangardnaya rol' partii Kommun-istov. Vazhnoe uslovie ee vozrastaniya', *Kommunist*, no. 6 (April 1982) pp. 25–43 (at p. 27). In rejecting Western notions of pluralism and, in particular, any idea of 'organised opposition to socialism' being permitted 'in the Soviet Union and other socialist countries', Andropov, however, implicitly noted that the term, 'pluralism', had been used in different ways, and also went out of his way to legitimise 'within system' expression of diverse views when he observed that if by 'pluralism' all that is meant is 'the presence in society of different, divergent views and interests, then there is no society without such phenomena. That applies both to capitalism and socialism.'

85. For some examples, see Hill, *Soviet Politics, Political Science and Reform*.

86. See, for example, F. M. Burlatsky, *Lenin, Gosurdarstvo, Politika* (Moscow, 1970); G. Shaknazarov, *Sotsialistischeskaya demokratiya: nekotorye voprosy teorii* (Moscow, 1972); and R. A. Safarov, *Obschestvennoe mnenie i gosudarstvennoe upravlenie* (Moscow, 1975).

87. For examples, see Hill, *Soviet Politics, Political Science and Reform*.

88. Yu. A. Tikhomirov, 'Razvitie nauchnykh znaniy o sotsialisticheskom gosudarstve', in D. A. Kerimov, V. E. Chirkin and G. Kh. Shakhnazarov (eds), *Politika mira i razvitie politicheskikh sistem* (Moscow, 1979) p. 37.

89. G. Shakhnazarov, *The Destiny of the World: The Socialist Shape of Things to Come* (Moscow, 1978) p. 153.

90. Ibid.

91. G. Shakhnazarov, 'O demokraticheskom tsentralizme i politicheskom plyuralizme', *Kommunist*, no. 10 (July 1979) p. 107. This passage appears also in Shakhnazarov's book, *Fiasko futurologii (Kriticheskiy ocherk nemarksistskikh teoriy obshchestvennogo razvitiya)* (Moscow, 1979) p. 279.

92. The word appeared as 'obsolete' in the major Soviet dictionary produced in the 1930s, *Tolkovyy slovar' russkogo yazyka*, ed. D. N. Ushakov (Moscow, 1935). More surprisingly (and perhaps more questionably) it was classified as 'obsolete' as recently as the early 1970s in the *Oxford Russian–English Dictionary*, ed. M. Wheeler (Oxford 1972).

93. See note 2.

94. Burlatsky and Shakhnazarov have long been advocates of the social

sciences generally in the Soviet Union. See their co-authored article 'Obschestvennye nauki i zhizn'', *Literaturnaya gazeta* (24 March 1956) pp. 3–4. After writing separately over many years, they joined forces again to write an article in which they call, *inter alia*, for the establishment of a separate institution for the study of political science in the Soviet Union. See G. Kh. Shakhnazarov and F. M. Burlatsky, 'O razvitii Marksistsko–Leninskoy politicheskoy nauki', *Voprosy filosofii*, no. 12 (December 1980) pp. 10–23, esp. p. 23.

95. Cf. ibid., p. 17, where Shakhnazarov and Burlatsky write of 'political power' as 'the key indicator' in political science.

96. See N. B. Pakholenko and N. N. Efremova, 'Nauchnoe soveshchanie sovetskoy assotsiatsii politicheskikh nauk, "razvitie politicheskikh sistem v sovremennom mire" ', in Kerimov, Chirkin and Shakhnazarov (eds), *Politika mira i razvitie politicheskikh sistem*, p. 266.

97. Ibid.

98. As expressed in Yu A. Tikhomirov, *Mekhanizm upravleniya v razvitom sotsialisticheskom obshchestve* (Moscow, 1978); and in 'Sotsializm i politicheskaya vlast'', *Sovektskoe gosudarstvo i pravo*, no. 5 (1974) pp. 11–19.

99. V. S. Shevtsov, *Gosudarstvennyy suverenitet (Voprosy teorii)* (Moscow, 1979). The *tirazh* of Shevtsov's book is by Soviet standards fairly small: 2,400. The criticism of Tikhomirov's views occurs on pages 16 and 157. Shevtsov, a prominent jurist and party ideologist, was until recently an official within the Department of Science and Education of the Central Committee of the CPSU and a member of the executive committee of the Soviet Association of Political Sciences. Apart from *Gosudarstvennyy suverenitet*, his books include *Natsional'nyy suyerenitet (problemy teorii i metodologii)* (Moscow 1979); *Citizenship of the USSR (A Legal Study)* (Moscow 1979); *Obshchestvenno-politicheskoe ustroystvo SSSR* (Moscow, 1978); and *Sotsial'no-politicheskie osnovy edinstva sovetskogo naroda* (Moscow, 1975).

100. Burlatsky is the head of the Department of Philosophy at the Institute of Social Sciences which comes under the jurisdiction of the International Department of the Central Committee of the Party. Since 1982 he has held in addition an appointment at the USA and Canada Institute of the Academy of Sciences and he is a Vice-President of the Soviet Association of Political Sciences. As a young member of the party apparatus and as one of the authors of the book *Fundamentals of Marxism-Leninism* and of the 1961 Party Programme he was remarkably influential in the late Khrushchev years. When Otto Kuusinen and Burlatsky, together with other members of a group under Kuusinen's direction, first put forward the idea of the 'all-people's state' the high-level party reaction was one of shock, and the proposal was condemned as revisionist by some of the more conservative members of the leadership. The concept was, however, endorsed by Khrushchev and given the status of official doctrine in the 1961 Party Programme, though it was to suffer a partial and temporary eclipse in the early Brezhnev years. See F. M. Burlatsky, 'O.V. Kuusinen – Marksistsko-Leninskoy issledovatel' i teoretik', *Rabochiy klass i sovremenniy mir*, no. 6 (1979) pp. 99–104;

and R. E. Kanet, 'The Rise and Fall of the "All-People's State": Recent Changes in the Soviet Theory of the State', *Soviet Studies*, vol. XX, no. 1, (July 1968) pp. 81–93. The idea has been fully rehabilitated only since the appearance of the 1977 Constitution, though even then with an emphasis on the relative continuity between the 'all-people's state' and the stage of the 'dictatorship of the proletariat' which was absent in Khrushchev's time. On Burlatsky and his contributions to the formulation of the concepts of the 'all-people's state' under Khrushchev and of 'developed socialism' under Brezhnev, see also Hough, *The Soviet Union and Social Science Theory*, pp. 112 and 256; and Hough and Fainsod, *How the Soviet Union is Governed*, p. 255.

101. See especially V. G. Kalensky, *Gosudarstvo kak ob'ekt sotsiologicheskogo analiza (ocherki istorii i metodologii issledovaniya)* (Moscow, 1977), and 'Problemy sotsiologii gosudarstva v istorii politiko-pravovoy mysli', *Sovetskoe gosudarstvo i pravo*, no. 5 (1979) pp. 117–22.

102. See, for example, F. M. Burlatsky, 'Politicheskaya sistema razvitogo sotsializma', *Voprosy filosofii*, no. 8 (1977) p. 18; Burlatsky, *The Modern State and Politics*, pp. 47–51; and Burlatsky and Chirkin (eds), *Politicheskie sistemy sovremennosti*, pp. 26–7.

103. Burlatsky and Chirkin (eds), *Politicheskie sistemy sovremennosti*, p. 26.

104. Ibid, p. 27.

105. See, for example, Burlatsky, *The Modern State and Politics*, p. 50; Kalensky, *Gosudarstvo kak ob'ekt sotsiologicheskogo analiza*, p. 179; and Kalensky, in Burlatsky and Chirkin (eds), *Politicheskie sistemy sovremennosti*, pp. 34–5.

106. Kalensky, in Burlatsky and Chirkin (eds), *Politicheskie sistemy sovremennosti*, p. 34.

107. Burlatsky, *The Modern State and Politics*, p. 50; Kalensky, *Gosudarstvo kak ob'ekt sotsiologicheskogo analiza*, p. 179.

108. Kalensky, ibid.

109. Ibid.

110. Burlatsky, *The Modern State and Politics*, p. 50.

111. Ibid, pp. 50–1. L. S. Mamut, in his *Karl Marks kak teoretik gosudarstva* (Moscow, 1979) notes (p. 166) that Marx used the concept of public power in a variety of different senses. Referring (p. 178) to G. N. Manov, *Gosudarstvo i politicheskaya organizatsiya obshchestva* (Moscow, 1974) and to Burlatsky's 'Politicheskaya sistema razvitogo sotsializma', *Voprosy filosofii*, no. 8 (1977), Mamut notes that 'the state' is regarded by these authors 'as one of the institutions of the political organisation, of the political system', and for 'such a formulation of the problem', he adds, there are 'now weighty reasons'. 'However,' he goes on, 'the problem of distinguishing the state and the political organisation of society, the state and the political system, the problem of their links and relations, so controversial today, had hardly been raised so sharply in Marx's time. Therefore, he did not specially single it out and analyse it.'

112. Burlatsky, 'Politicheskaya sistema razvitogo sotsializma', p. 23. Indeed, as long ago as his *Pravda* article on 'Politika i nauka' (10 January 1965), Burlatsky made, *inter alia*, essentially this point.

113. Burlatsky, 'Politika i nauka'.
114. Kalensky, *Gosudarstvo kak ob'ekt sotsiologicheskogo analiza*, p. 180.
115. V. S. Shevtsov, 'Politicheskaya vlast' v sisteme politicheskoy organizatsii sovetskogo obshchestva', in D. A. Kerimov (ed.), *Mezhdunarodnye otnosheniya, politika i lichnost'* (Moscow, 1976) pp. 35–44, esp. p. 40.
116. Ibid.
117. Ibid, p. 41.
118. Among them, Tikhomirov (on pp. 16 and 157), L. S. Mamut (on p. 23) and A. K. Belykh (on p. 158).
119. Shevtsov, *Gosudarstvennyy suverenitet*, p. 158.
120. V. M. Terletsky, *Leninskoe ideynoe nasledie i problemy sovetskogo stroitel'stva* (Kiev, 1974) pp. 214–15.
121. Shevtsov, *Gosudarstvennyy suverenitet*, p. 160.
122. Burlatsky, in Burlatsky and Chirkin (eds), *Politicheskie sistemy sovremennosti*, p. 9.
123. The full article (which some might think implies the exercise of political power on the part of the Communist Party) reads: 'The leading and guiding force of Soviet society and the nucleus of its political system, of all state organisations and public organisations is the Communist Party of the Soviet Union. The CPSU exists for the people and serves the people. The Communist Party, armed with Marxism–Leninism, determines the general perspectives of the development of society and the course of the home and foreign policy of the USSR, directs the constructive work of the Soviet people, and imparts a planned, systematic and theoretically substantiated character to their struggle for the victory of communism. All party organisations shall function within the framework of the Constitution of the USSR' (*Constitution of the USSR*, Moscow, 1977, p. 21).
124. Shevtsov, *Gosudarstvennyy suverenitet*, p. 159.
125. Ibid.
126. Ibid, p. 158.
127. Ibid, p. 160. Shevtsov also calls upon the Bulgarian scholar, Asen Kozharov, as a witness against pluralism, referring, in particular, to Kozharov's article, 'O kontseptsii ideyno-politicheskogo plyuralizma', *Problema mira i sotsializma*, no. 1 (1977) (but see also Kozharov's *Monizm i plyuralizm v ideologii i politika*). However, since neither Burlatsky's use at times of the broader definition of the state, nor his subsuming at other times of the state, in its narrower sense, within the political system, logically entails pluralism either as a description of, or as prescription for, Soviet political life, it is not clear what purpose Shevtsov's digression on pluralism serves, unless he believes that any weakening of his central contention would be the thin end of the wedge so far as the acceptance of elements of pluralist theory is concerned, or, alternatively, is concerned merely to impute guilt by association.
128. V. S. Shevtsov, 'Sushchnost' i osnovnye napravleniya razvitiya politicheskoy sistemy sovetskogo obshchestva', in N. N. Razumovich (ed.), *Politicheskaya sistema sovetskogo obshchestva* (Moscow, 1980) vol. 1, pp. 7–64, esp. pp. 17, 19 (where Shevtsov briefly crosses swords with 'the English bourgeois sociologist, R. Miliband'), 22 and 34–6.

129. M. Kh. Farukshin, *Politicheskaya sistema razvitogo sotsializma i sovremennyy antikommunizm (k kritike burzhuaznoy sovetologii)* (Kazan', 1980). I am grateful to Ronald Hill for bringing this book to my attention.
130. Farukshin, ibid, p. 139.
131. See note 99.
132. See, for example, V. E. Chirkin (ed.), *Razvitie politicheskikh sistem v sovremennom mire* (Moscow, 1981), which has a *tirazh* of only 750 and where this point is made in a prefatory note from the editorial board.
133. *Sovetskoe gosudarstvo i pravo*, no. 7 (July 1981) pp. 142–4, esp. p. 143.
134. Ibid.
135. The Soviet literature on 'political power in Soviet society' was reviewed in a 1977 Moscow dissertation, in which the author placed Soviet scholars in three different groups in terms of their use of the concept of power 'as a general sociological category'. In this particular classification, the distinctions are between (1) those who see power as the leadership, direction and co-ordination of people's actions; (2) those (whom the author sees as composing the largest group and in which he includes Burlatsky) who define power as the 'right and possibility' or 'ability' to subordinate the wills of individuals to the predominant wishes in a given association; and (3) those who identify power directly with coercion or subordination. See V. L. Usachev, *Politicheskaya vlast' v Sovetskom obshchestve (avtoreferat dissertatsii na soiskanie uchenoy stepeni kandidata yuridicheskikh nauk)* (Moscow, 1977) esp. p. 4.
136. Shakhnazarov and Burlatsky, 'O razvitii Marksistko–Leninskoy politicheskoy nauki'. I discuss this and other recent developments in Soviet political science in a forthcoming article, 'Political Science in the Soviet Union: A New Stage of Development?'.
137. Shaknazarov and Burlatsky, 'O razvitii Marksistsko–Leninskoy politicheskoy nauki', p. 17.
138. Ibid.
139. Ibid.
140. Ibid.
141. Ibid. For an example of a book that takes a similar view of power within the political system, while using the terminology, 'Political organisation of Soviet society' for what should now, in Shakhnazarov's and Burlatsky's terms, be 'the Soviet political system', see M. N. Marchenko, *Politicheskaya organizatsiya sovetskogo obshchestva i ee burzhuaznye fal'sifikatory* (Moscow, 1973) esp. p. 40 and pp. 69–70.
142. Shakhnazarov, *Sotsialisticheskaya demokratiya: nekotorye voprosy teorii*, pp. 86–7. This distinction by Shakhnazarov of the party's role according to area of policy is also noted by R. J. Hill, *Soviet Politics, Political Science and Reform*, p. 124.
143. D. Holloway, 'Foreign and Defence Policy' (pp. 49–76) in Brown and Kaser (eds), *The Soviet Union since the Fall of Khrushchev*, p. 73.
144. *Pravda*, 24 February 1981, p. 8.
145. Mlynář, *Nightfrost in Prague*, p. 136. Mlynář is writing about the Presidium of the Central Committee of the Communist Party of Czechoslovakia, the meetings of which he attended in 1968 as a Secretary

of the Central Committee and later as a full Presidium member. He notes that 'the decision-making process was essentially the same under Dubček as it had been under Novotný' so far as this highest party organ was concerned. In an interview with the present author in Oxford on 2 June 1979, Mlynář expressed the opinion that the same practices and procedures were followed in the Soviet Union.

146. My source for this statement is a senior Gosplan official.
147. Mlynář interview.
148. V. S. Shevtsov, 'Politicheskaya vlast' v sisteme politicheskoy organizatsii sovetskogo obshchestva', in Kerimov (ed.), *Mezhdunarodnye otnosheniya, politika i lichnost'*, pp. 35–6.
149. Ibid, p. 39.
150. Burlatsky, in Burlatsky and Chirkin (eds), *Politicheskie sistemy sovremennosti*, p. 18.
151. Ibid, pp. 17–23.
152. Kalensky, *Gosudarstvo kak ob'ekt sotsiologicheskogo analiza*, p. 122.
153. Ibid, p. 123.
154. Kalensky, 'Problemy sotsiologii gosudarstva v istorii politiko-pravovoy mysli', p. 122.
155. For a discussion of the exceptions admitted by Marx to his 'general description of the state as an instrument of class domination', see also D. McLellan, 'Marx, Engels and Lenin on Party and State', in L. Holmes (ed.), *The Withering Away of the State? Party and State under Communism* (London, 1981) pp. 7–31, esp. 20–2; and for an analysis of the position not only of Marx but also of contemporary Western Marxists on 'the state as a political force', see F. Parkin, *Marxism and Class Theory: A Bourgeois Critique* (London, 1979) esp. his chapter, 'Social Cleavages and the Forms of State', pp. 119–42.
156. Apart from numerous articles, he published a well-informed book on American political science which R.H.W. Theen took as his major point of reference for an entire article on Soviet political science. See V. G. Kalensky, *Politicheskaya nauka v SShA: kritika burzhuaznykh kontseptsiy vlasti* (Moscow, 1969); and R.H.W. Theen, 'Political Science in the USSR: "To Be or Not to Be"' (see note 2).
157. His latest book is devoted to the political thought of James Madison. See V. G. Kalensky, *Madison* (Moscow, 1981).
158. Jack Hayward has suggested that both the terms, 'state' and 'society', have 'a misleadingly monolithic ring about them', that this is especially true of the former, and that this is 'one reason why many political scientists eschew the term "state" and prefer "political system"'. See J. Hayward and R. N. Berki (eds), *State and Society in Contemporary Europe* (Oxford, 1979) p. 23.
159. F. M. Burlatsky, in Burlatsky and Chirkin (eds), *Politicheskie sistemy sovremennosti*, p. 27.
160. 'Institutional pluralism', in so far as it may exist, is, of course, a special case of 'stretching' of the concept of pluralism. In Dahl's definition of the relative autonomy of organisations, the 'government of the state' is implicitly treated as *one* organisation. Institutional groupings and conflicts *within* government would not, in his terms (or indeed, in those

of most other pluralist theorists) count as pluralism at all.

161. A view expressed, for example, by Z. Mlynář, 'The Rules of the Game: The Soviet Bloc Today', *The Political Quarterly*, vol. 50, no. 4 (October–December 1979) p. 407.

162. Kalensky, *Gosudarstvo kak ob'ekt sotsiologicheskogo analiza*, p. 171.

163. For valuable accounts of this evolution, see D. Rusinow, *The Yugoslav Experiment 1948–1974*, (London, for the Royal Institute of International Affairs, 1977); and A. Carter, *Democratic Reform in Yugoslavia: The Changing Role of the Party* (London, 1982).

164. See *Akční program Komunistické strany Československa* (Prague, 1968) pp. 15–18, esp. 15–16.

165. See, for example, Shakhnazarov, 'O demokraticheskom tsentralizme i politicheskom plyuralizme', p. 108.

166. See H. G. Skilling, 'Interest Groups and Communist Politics', *World Politics*, vol. XVIII, no. 3 (April 1966) p. 449. Cf. H. G. Skilling, 'Pluralism in Communist Societies: Straw Men and Red Herrings', *Studies in Comparative Communism*, vol. XIII, no. 1 (Spring 1980) p. 84.

167. See, for example, J. F. Hough, 'The Evolution of the Soviet World View', *World Politics*, vol. XXXII, no. 4 (July 1980) pp. 509–30; M. Schwartz, *Soviet Perceptions of the United States* (Berkeley and London, 1978); and S. Bialer (ed.), *The Domestic Context of Soviet Foreign Policy* (Boulder, Colorado, 1981) esp. the chapter by A. Dallin, 'The Domestic Sources of Soviet Foreign Policy', pp. 335–408. Other writers continue to see only the undifferentiated view of 'Moscow's spokesmen'. See, for instance, S. P. Gibert, *Soviet Images of America* (London, 1977).

168. This holds true for many areas of social policy, from reform of family law to the problem of explaining and combating crime and to protection of the environment. For useful accounts of debates in these areas of policy, see P. H. Juviler and H. W. Morton, *Soviet Policy-Making: Studies of Communism in Transition* (London, 1967); P. H. Juviler, 'Whom the State has Joined: Conjugal Ties in Soviet Law', in D. D. Barry, G. Ginsburgs and P. B. Maggs (eds), *Soviet Law after Stalin*, part I (Leyden, 1977); P. H. Juviler, 'Crime and Its Study', in Morton and Tökés (eds), *Soviet Politics and Society in the 1970s*; P. H. Solomon, Jr, *Soviet Criminologists and Criminal Policy*; D. R. Kelley, 'Environmental Policy-Making in the USSR: The Role of Industrial and Environmental Interest Groups', *Soviet Studies*, vol. XXVIII, no. 4 (October 1976) pp. 570–89; and Gustafson, *Reform in Soviet Politics: Lessons of Recent Policies on Land and Water*.

3 The 'All–People's State' and 'Developed Socialism'

Ronald J. Hill

At a time when the concept of the state appears to be undergoing a reassessment among Western democratic and Marxist theorists alike,[1] political philosophers in the Soviet Union, too, are attempting to define a new theory of the state in that society. In so doing, they are presented with special problems stemming from certain contradictions and ambiguities in their ideological heritage, coupled with the persistent influence of past interpretations and practice, compounded by the political needs of the present and, perhaps, the future. Not surprisingly, in the light of these competing influences, there has been hesitancy and ambivalence in the development of Soviet theoretical pronouncements. I shall argue in this chapter that the promulgation of the concept of the state in developed socialist society reflects these various factors in Soviet political life. However, it also reflects a conviction on the part of the authorities and their ideologists that a further 'development' of Soviet society requires the existence of certain types of authoritative institutions, staffed by officials with appropriate skills and capacities, and supported by a population likewise imbued with the appropriate culture and values.

THE IDEOLOGICAL HERITAGE

The view of the state adopted by Marx and Engels is so well known as to require no extensive elaboration here. Simply expressed, throughout history the state was 'essentially a machine for keeping down the oppressed, exploited class',[2] a harmful entity, 'separated from the real interests of individual and community'.[3] This negative, class-based

evaluation of the state became a central element in the Marxist philosophy, and it followed that when classes were abolished under communism, the state too would be abolished. Political power was seen as
'merely the organised power of one class for oppressing another',[4]
therefore logically 'when class rule has disappeared there will no
longer be any state in the present political sense of the word'[5] since it
would be superfluous. Hence, in Engels's classic phrase, under communism the state would 'wither away'.

Before that happened, however, the proletariat would make use of
some form of 'state', to exercise its 'revolutionary dictatorship'
during the transition from capitalism to communism.[6] This post-
revolutionary state would exercise a monopoly of credit, through a
national bank; it would nationalise the means of communication and
transport; and it would take over factories and means of production.[7]

Lenin adopted the broad analysis provided by Marx and Engels,
which he explored in his unfinished work on the topic, *The State and
Revolution*, where he stressed the 'gradual and spontaneous nature' of
the withering away of the state.[8] He proclaimed the need for a state
during the immediate post-revolutionary period, 'a transitional state
. . . no longer a state in the proper sense of the word'.[9] But Marx and
Engels had been vague and unclear about the form that such a transitional state would take. Into the theoretical gap Lenin fitted the
Soviets of Workers' and Soldiers' Deputies, about which he wrote in
very positive terms in his 'April Theses' of 1917. The point about these
bodies, which sprang up originally as strike committees to co-ordinate
the revolutionary activity of the working class during the revolutions
of 1905 and 1917, was that they were the spontaneous creations of the
working class itself. They were therefore revolutionary and progressive bodies *par excellence*. Lenin endorsed these, and upon his return
to Russia in the spring of 1917 persuaded the Bolshevik party to press
for the revolution under the slogan, 'All power to the soviets'. The
soviets, according to Lenin, were 'the *only possible* form of
revolutionary government', and a reversion to a parliamentary republic from a soviet government would be a step backwards.[10] In the
course of the revolutionary year of 1917, the Petrograd Soviet
exercised genuine political power in competition with the Provisional
Government; the impending Second All-Russian Congress of Soviets,
fixed for 25 October, determined the timing of the Bolsheviks' seizure
of power; and the soviets were made the basis of the new regime, to
which they gave their name, as the organisational form of the
dictatorship of the proletariat.[11]

These impeccably sound revolutionary origins make the soviets –

despite radical changes in their nature since they became identified as the basis of the state – a highly evocative symbol that could not easily be dispensed with. A leader who wished to dispose of the soviets might be open to charges from political rivals that he was acting in an un-Leninist manner.

There is a further area of ambiguity in the ideological heritage, relating to the definition of what constitutes 'the state'. Marx and Engels, and subsequently Lenin, were particularly concerned about the state's centralised and bureaucratic character. Marx saw bureaucracy as the central element in the modern state apparatus;[12] Lenin too was concerned with smashing the old *bureaucratic machine* and replacing it with a new one 'that will permit [us] to abolish gradually all bureaucracy'.[13] During the transition to communism the economy would be administered 'on the lines of the postal service', i.e., in a substantially simplified form, so that any literate person could perform the tasks involved. This would lead to the abolition of the professional administrative bureaucracy, its functions being taken over by the citizens themselves, and the coercive back-up to the administrative side of the state could likewise be dispensed with. Again to quote the classic phrase, 'the government of people would be replaced by the administration of things': administration would become a matter for the society directly, and not something carried out by a state machine. There would similarly be no further need for professional parliamentarians, although direct representative institutions could be preserved.[14] Moreover, Lenin's own writings on the early Soviet state developed from seeing it as a 'Commune-type' state to being the form of the 'dictatorship of the proletariat'.[15]

This brief summary of the ideological inheritance presents certain difficulties to the politicians of today, faced with devising a policy towards the state institutions which they have inherited. There is a wide measure of uncertainty and scope for interpretation, particularly over the length of time the post-revolutionary state will exist, as developments in the society need to be assessed for their significance. Today's leaders are also influenced by the interpretations of the ideology on this and other points made by their predecessors, since continuity and loyalty within the tradition are claimed. In addition, the present generation of leaders is constrained by the practices that have become entrenched over half a century or more of Soviet statehood – plus, of course, the pressures of running a society in the present.

Since Lenin's day – and, arguably, since Marx's – it has been accepted that society will develop towards communism in certain more or less distinct phases, possibly subdivided into stages. However, the precise characteristics of the various periods and transition stages have not been determined in advance, and this opens up the possibility of intense argument among the adherents of Marxism, as well as jibes from its critics. The result of this uncertainty is inevitably that the stages of development are named and given theoretical elaboration only as they arise and are recognised; and that recognition depends as much on the political needs of the day as it does on the perspicacity of the ideologists.

PAST INTERPRETATIONS OF THE IDEOLOGY

Under Lenin, as we have noticed, the Soviet state came to be seen as representing the dictatorship of the proletariat. It was, in other words, quite openly seen as an instrument of class rule, an apparatus used by the victorious working class (led by its vanguard, the Bolshevik party) to expropriate the former exploiting classes and establish a socialist, or at least state-owned, economy. This state also served to defend the gains of the revolution from outside attack and from internal subversion and counter-revolution, in a world and a society that were largely inimical to the goals of the new regime.

In the late 1920s, following the decision to build socialism in one country, as a first stage towards building a communist society, the state of the dictatorship of the proletariat turned to the development of an industrial economy as its overriding task. By the mid-1930s, with Stalin firmly entrenched and about to launch the round-up of his last rivals for power, a further principle came into play: the 'built-in compulsion shared by all Soviet leaders to demonstrate continuous progress towards the goal of communism'.[16] This compulsion cannot be ascribed solely to the vanity of politicians (although that doubtless plays an important part): after all, building communism was the justification for the whole enterprise, so failure to advance in the appropriate direction would represent a broader failure than that of the dominant leader alone. It follows, too, that *whatever* takes place has to be justified in precisely those terms.[17] Stalin also needed to consolidate his personal authority in ideological terms, against the attacks of Trotsky and others. For such a variety of reasons, therefore, Stalin had to demonstrate that some kind of milestone had been reached. In order to do that, he declared that the dictatorship of the proletariat, introduced by Lenin, had been surpassed. The ownership of the means of production had been removed from the former exploiting classes, which, as a consequence, had ceased to exist. Using the organising capacity of the state, the new, expanded proletariat had built up an industrial base for the economy; agriculture had been collectivised and the peasantry had provided recruits for the proletariat. A new intelligentsia, likewise drawn from the peasantry and the working class, had been trained, and now placed its expertise at the disposal of the working class. There was class collaboration, rather than class antagonism, and the need for the dictatorship of the proletariat had disappeared. As two recent writers expressed it, demonstrating the continued acceptance of the Stalin (and Khrushchev) interpretation of history:

> The state of the dictatorship of the proletariat is the main weapon in building socialism. But with the construction of the basis of socialism and the disappearance of the exploiting classes, the dictatorship of the working class, having accomplished its historic task, gradually ceases to be necessary. There takes place the transformation of the state of the dictatorship of the proletariat into the state of the whole Soviet people.[18]

In other words, a new phase, or stage, had been entered with the building of the basis of socialism, and a new Constitution to reflect these realities in a modified state mechanism was introduced, on 5 December 1936, to the strains of Beethoven's Choral Symphony – the setting of Schiller's *Ode to Joy*. This Constitution introduced equal, universal, secret and direct suffrage, replaced the Congress of Soviets by the Supreme Soviet, made other institutional changes, and declared (Article 1) that 'The Union of Soviet Socialist Republics is a socialist state of workers and peasants'; it also proclaimed the principle of socialism: 'From each according to his ability, to each according to his work' (Article 12).[19]

While it may be disputed whether this stage already constituted a 'higher' stage of the dictatorship of the proletariat or a distinctly different form,[20] Stalin appears to have established certain precedents for his successors to follow. He dropped reference to Lenin's interpretation of the Soviet state as a Commune-type state, and established the notion that Lenin's formulation on the state of the dictatorship of the proletariat might be overtaken; he used the constitution as a symbolic means of indicating that one stage had been surpassed and replaced by another; he affirmed a theoretical distinction between the soviets (organs of state power) and the organs of state administration (the ministries and the local executive committees' departments); and he indicated that certain specific changes had taken place in relations between classes in Soviet society, which his successors could not deny without implying either the ideological fallibility of the party and Stalin in the 1930s, or their own failure to continue the advance towards communism.

Stalin also did something else: he added a further defining characteristic of the 'Soviet state', which was now designated 'socialist', in keeping with the stage of development that Soviet society had supposedly reached. It was no longer simply, or even primarily, an instrument of class rule, but a type of welfare state that cared for the needs of citizens on the basis of public ownership and planning of industrial production. Such a designation also served to distinguish the Soviet state from the state in other countries, at a time when the new Constitution seemed to be introducing more or less 'conventional state machinery'.[21] Whatever the reason for this further identification of the Soviet state, it is something that his successors have felt obliged to follow.

This imperative of ambition has prompted both Khrushchev and Brezhnev to emulate Stalin in the ideological field. In 1961, with the publication of the new Party Programme, Khrushchev introduced a concept that had first been used in a 1959 textbook on ideology.[22] That concept was the 'state of the whole people' or 'all-people's state', which corresponded to the new phase or stage on the road towards communism, cumbersomely named 'the unfolding building of communism'. It was Khrushchev's contribution to Marxist–Leninist theory of the state to argue that 'the state . . . has in the new, present stage become a state of the whole people, an organ expressing the interests and will of the people as a whole'.[23]

The theoretical underpinning of this pair of new concepts was as follows: since the building of socialism, further transformations had taken place in the economic base, and the full-scale building of the material basis of communism was under way; this required reflection in the theory surrounding the superstructure, including the political system. The state, it was argued, was now of a different type, one belonging to the whole people and used by them for organising their common constructive endeavour in building communism. As Churchward noted, the modified theory was expressed 'within the general framework of Stalinist formulae'.[24] Moreover, in a further emulation of Stalin, the new concept was to be enshrined in a new constitution, and a constitutional commission was set up in April 1962, with Khrushchev its chairman.[25]

Following Khrushchev's political demise in October 1964, it became politically inexpedient to retain the symbols of his period of rule. The phrase 'the unfolding building of communism' (*razvernutoe stroitel'stvo kommunizma*) was swiftly banished from the political rhetoric; the 1961 Party Programme in which it was elaborated was quietly ignored (including, notably, its concluding promise: 'The present generation will live under communism'); and the accompanying references to the 'all-people's state' became fewer and rarer. Brezhnev failed to mention it at the Twenty-Third Party Congress (1966), and although it made a brief prominent appearance at the time of the fiftieth anniversary of the revolution,[26] thereafter the phrase virtually disappeared from the language of Soviet politicians.[27] The constitutional commission, with Brezhnev now formally in the chair, likewise went into suspension.[28]

Yet Brezhnev, too, needed to demonstrate progress, while continuing to denigrate the achievements of his predecessor. From the late 1960s, the inelegant 'unfolding building of communism' was replaced by the much more euphonious, positive-sounding 'developed socialism' or 'mature socialism'. Since the phrase was first used in print, by Fedor Burlatsky, in 1966, it became the 'catch phrase' of the Brezhnev era,[29] and the concept of developed socialism has given rise to intense activity on the part of Soviet scholars. They have used it, with the encouragement of the political leadership, to explore virtually every aspect of Soviet society in the 1970s – economic, ideological, sociological, political, cultural – and the ramifications have been and are being assessed and elaborated. Moreover, in 1972 Brezhnev again revived the question of a new constitution, which was eventually promulgated in 1977 as 'the constitution of developed socialist society', introduced by Brezhnev as General Secretary of the CPSU and signed by him as chairman of the Supreme Soviet Presidium.[30]

The Constitution's prologue explains that developed socialism is 'a society in which powerful productive forces and progressive science and culture have been created ... a society of mature socialist social relations ... a natural, logical stage on the road to communism'. Commentators indicate that this stage had been reached by the 1950s,[31] although it is not explained why this was not recognised until the late 1960s, nor why the Party Programme's phrase about the 'unfolding building of communism' – a stage that *was* identified at that time, and is in fact referred to by these two writers[32] – was dropped in favour of Brezhnev's slogan. More interesting, and perhaps surprising, the new Constitution restored to the political vocabulary reference to the 'all-people's state': Article 1 states that 'The Union of Soviet Socialist Republics is a socialist state of the whole people, expressing the will and interests of the workers, peasants and intelligentsia, the working people of all the nations and nationalities of the country.'

Although it may have been politically distasteful to revert to a formulation that had been so closely associated with the disgraced Khrushchev,[33] there may have been no real alternative. Since it had been declared as long ago as 1936 that classes in Soviet society were no longer antagonistic; since the still-valid Party Programme in 1961 had referred to the 'all-people's state' as 'the organ for expressing the interests and will of the whole people' (and also the CPSU as the party of the whole people); and since Brezhnev himself had asserted in 1972 (on the fiftieth anniversary of the formation of the USSR) that 'a new historic community of people had been formed, the Soviet people', Brezhnev was trapped by the ideological pronouncements of his predecessors and by his own rhetoric.[34] The only possible alternative would have been to reassert the dominance of a particular class – presumably the proletariat – but that could scarcely have been presented as progress towards communism, under which society will be characterised by 'social uniformity' (*sotsial'naya odnorodnost'*).[35] Hence there exists the Soviet all-people's state, which is 'the first political organisation in history to direct a developed socialist society, where no social stratum is removed from power or is suppressed by the state, and where the whole people is building communism'.[36] And this is presented – as it has to be – as part of a natural, logical development, 'the direct successor to the state of the dictatorship of the proletariat', but also 'a new stage in the development of the Soviet socialist state'.[37]

In assessing the significance of this development, two things need to be borne in mind. The first is that a distinctive characteristic of the Brezhnev era has been to emphasise the 'leading role' of the working class[38] – possibly a pro forma recognition of the regime's ideological underpinnings. The second and perhaps more significant point relates to the multi-national composition of Soviet society. As has been seen, reference is made to the creation of 'the Soviet people'. Since Lenin's day a federal structure in the state has existed in order to give some symbolic (and to a certain extent tangible) recognition to national and cultural distinctions. The 1977 Constitution (as was mentioned above) explicitly refers to the nationalities as groups whose will and interests are expressed by the Soviet state. More recently, the problem of protecting nationality rights in the face of high migration levels from one part of the country to another has been recognised. Migrants, it is argued, possess the right to 'the requisite representation in party and state organs, and also the correct understanding and satisfaction of their specific needs in the field of language, culture and everyday life'. 'After all', writes the author, 'the national government represents not only the basic nationality which gave its name to the given [Soviet] republic, but in equal measure also represents the interests of people of other nationalities living within it.'[39] It may well be that the concept of the 'all-people's state' is growing to be more significant in relation to the ethnic composition of Soviet society than to its class make-up: the concept is aimed at reassuring the minor nationalities that this is their country; but it is also being seen as demanding certain concrete forms for expressing that assertion.

A further use for the concept in the Brezhnev era is to reassert the Soviet Union's leading position in the world communist movement, at a time when other socialist countries appeared to be catching up.[40] 'Developed socialism' and the 'all-people's state' can thus be seen, in part, as slogans designed to impress the outside world with the progress attained by the USSR in advancing towards the goal of communism.

This new form of socialist state is therefore presented as the product of the past, the outcome of several decades of creative collaboration by the entire Soviet people. It also has a definite future-orientated purpose: to continue the advance towards communism. However, if it is to achieve that, a number of changes have to take place in the political practices of the state, and in the qualities of the people who are involved in the running of its institutions. The degree of consistency evident in the theoretical accounts is, however, less apparent in political practice, for it is easier to think up new labels, capable of serving symbolic political ends, than to alter the behaviour of a society.

DEVELOPING PRACTICE

The state of the dictatorship of the proletariat was inaugurated in a poor, uneducated country, largely populated by peasants, who down the centuries had been all but totally excluded from participation in organised political life, except at the level of their village community. They were, as far as the national political system was concerned, essentially the *subjects*, with the attitudes and expectations (in short, the political culture) associated with that role.[41] This complicated the task of creating a participatory democracy, even given the best will in the world on the part of the leadership. This is not to deny, of course, the periodic politicisation of the Russian peasantry in revolutionary circumstances in the past; the point is, however, that a population deprived of the appropriate experience – that of functioning within the framework of representative institutions as part of its regular political life – will almost certainly not be capable of using such institutions to the best effect (at least not until the general level of this experience in the society has risen).[42] In the event, steps to encourage the development of a participant society were given a low priority, subordinated under Stalin to the drive for rapid economic and industrial development.

In place of extending the soviets as organs through which the people might rule their own affairs, the 'dictatorship of the proletariat' found its expression in the expansion of the administrative and coercive elements of the state, notably the planning authorities, the industrial ministerial empires, and the secret police. The soviets, supposedly representative institutions, remained merely symbolic bodies, elected on a restricted franchise that favoured the workers and totally excluded certain other groups, and on an indirect basis; the deputies selected by the party (rather than by the electorate) were chosen for their loyalty and hard work in building up the economy, rather than for any political flair or even interest. The introduction of the 1936 Constitution made cosmetic changes to the franchise, but had no impact on the functioning of the state institutions, and the coming of the Second World War simply confirmed the authoritarian basis of the Stalin state. By the time of Stalin's death, the soviets had shown virtually no development over their position thirty-five years earlier,[43] while the adminsitrative organs – the ministries – and the repressive agencies – the MVD/MGB/KGB – burgeoned and functioned virtually independently.

Khrushchev's populist reaction (as interpreted by Breslauer)[44] had two main goals as far as the state was concerned. First, in order to demonstrate the advance towards communism under his personal tutelage, the state must begin to 'wither away'; but the 'withering-away' state must be replaced by 'public self-administration'. In order to achieve the first of these two goals, Khrushchev swiftly downgraded the security agencies (and the post-Stalin leadership had, of course, other reasons for taking such a step), and in 1957 abolished most of the central ministries, replacing them with regional economic councils, thereby undermining at a stroke the excessive power of the economic empires of the state apparatus.[45] In addition, certain welfare and other functions were transferred from state agencies to so-called public organisations, notably the trade unions. And in order to prepare for 'public self-administration', Khrushchev took the apparently para-doxical step of introducing measures to *strengthen* the state representative institutions, the Soviets of Toilers' Deputies, essentially as a counterweight to the administrative bodies. The paradox is re-solved when it is recalled that the soviets were seen as participatory and control agencies as well as an element in the state structure.[46] Khrushchev, as part of his general appeal to 'Leninist' norms, was emphasising Lenin's dislike of bureaucracy – or at least 'bureaucratism' – which had to be brought under some form of popular control. Hence, the Twentieth Party Congress (1956), in addition to initiating the de-Stalinisation campaign, also referred to the need to 'reanimate the soviets . . . in order to raise decisively their role in economic and cultural development, in satisfying the everyday needs and requirements of the population, and in the cause of the communist training of the toilers'.[47] The last phrase was significant, and indicates how Khrushchev viewed his policy of developing the soviets: they would eventually cease to be organs of *state* power and would instead become agencies through which the population, trained in the skills required for operating them effectively, would engage in communist self-administration.

Under Khrushchev's long-term vision, therefore, 'The state "withers away" by transferring its functions to the soviets; mass par-ticipation is a goal no longer viewed chiefly in terms of activity outside the state apparatus but within it.'[48]

The 1961 Party Programme continued the trend: it called for greater care in the selection of deputies for the soviets, fixed a minimum turnover at elections, and urged the development of the 'de-mocratic' elements in the soviets. The administration, it declared, should be made far more accountable to the public representatives; it should be staffed by officials possessing integrity; and the principle of electivity (a Leninist notion) should be steadily extended until it covered 'all leading officials' in government organs.[49]

The impact of these policies was severely mitigated in practice, however, by Khrushchev's constant switches of emphasis and down-right contradictory measures, which had the effect of creating a good deal of confusion in the mind of public and officials alike, and helped to bring Khrushchev and his policies into disrepute. The ideas put forward in the scholarly literature in the early 1960s show a remarkable variety that reflects uncertainty and even confusion, rather than serious debate about the most appropriate practical application of the ideology at the given stage of development. The idea of completely abolishing village soviets was discussed, as was the notion of abolishing local soviets' administrative departments. Meanwhile, repeated administrative reorganisations, while doing little to tackle the long-standing practices in regard to the selection of deputies and providing them with the means of performing an adequate representative role, ensured that the reality did not match the rhetoric.

The more recent scholarly theorists of developed socialism, as one would expect, have given Brezhnev the credit for taking measures that would set the soviets on the road of genuine development, citing the Twenty-Third Party Congress (1966 – the first after Khrushchev was removed from power) as marking a distinct turning-point in this respect, 'towards improving the activity of the soviets and increasing their authority'.[50] Subsequent party congresses have reported general improvements in the work of the state representative institutions, and specific measures have been introduced, aimed at strengthening their material and financial base, extending their co-ordinating powers in the economic and other enterprises located on their territory, enhancing the status of the deputies and raising the level of competence of these public representatives.[51] All this can be read as implying a rejection of the claims of previous periods concerning the effectiveness and democracy of the state institutions.

Before these developments could take place, there had to be a significant change of emphasis. In particular, the haste with which Khrushchev attempted to force the pace of communist construction had to be abandoned. Soviet scholars now regularly warn against any attempts to force the pace artificially, and stress the long-term nature of the endeavour. Khrushchev's twenty-year programme has been replaced in Soviet thinking by an extended period of 'developed socialism', the name of which relieves the pressure implied in any phrase that includes the word 'communism' – as in 'the unfolding building of communism'. The transition to communism will be a gradual and relatively long process, during which the material and technical base of communism will have to be built up; socialist social relations will have to be transformed into communist ones; class boundaries will be wiped out; and the all-round-developed man will be formed.[52] It follows therefore that the 'all-people's state' will likewise remain in existence for an extended period. Indeed, it has been argued that it can finally 'wither away' only when two conditions are met: the building of a *developed communist* society, and the victory and consolidation of socialism in the international arena.[53] This, indeed, is a notion that goes back to Marx,[54] and its implication for the Soviet Union is that the 'all-people's state' is here indefinitely.

PRESENT VIEWS OF THE STATE

Such a semi-permanent view of the state under developed socialism clearly removes some of the ambiguity and ambivalence from official attitudes, and it becomes easier to argue for improvements in the functioning of the state: Khrushchev's calls to improve the work of the soviets must have carried little conviction. The state is now called upon to *develop*, as part of a broad process of development of the total *political system* – itself a concept that has only recently been accepted in the Soviet Union, in place of the static legal-institutional descriptions prevalent hitherto. Following on from this, it has been asserted that the recognition that the Soviet state requires 'the utmost strengthening' is 'another major contribution to the Marxist-Leninist theory of socialist statehood'.[55] Be that as it may, this development implies changes throughout Soviet society, as developed socialism matures still further.

In essence, Brezhnev continued Khrushchev's policy of revitalising the soviets, but in a more rational and consistent fashion, in conformity with his general approach to government. However, it is no longer argued that this presages their imminent transformation into organs of communist self-administration. As Breslauer notes, 'the emphasis is on the *political* organisation of society, achieved through the *strengthening* of the state'.[56] The state is seen as 'a powerful force without which it is impossible to build the new society and to reach its highest phase'.[57] It still incorporates both representative bodies and administrative organs, and is presented as one of the three institutional pillars of the Soviet political system, alongside the party on the one hand, and the mass public organisations on the other. Each has its specific functions, and one of the supposed key features of the developed socialist society – not well observed in practice – is the sharp delineation of fields of competence among them.[58]

Soviet writers identify a range of functions that are supposedly characteristic of the Soviet state at this time. The precise list varies from one author to another, but the following are typical: the rational management of the economy, in order to create the material basis for communism and to satisfy the material needs of the population, ensuring the application of the socialist principles of labour and consumption (work is a duty and a right, rewards are commensurate with work done), training the population in communist ideals, providing certain welfare services, maintaining socialist law and order, protecting property, and defending the rights and freedoms of citizens. Externally, the functions include defence and the provision of security, strengthening the unity and solidarity of the socialist camp, forging links with ex-colonial developing countries, and struggling for peace and peaceful co-existence. Some add the protection of the environment and the rational use of resources, and in general some of the above functions may be subdivided.[59] What is clear, however, is that all authors see a broad range of functions for the state in a sophisticated society. As D. A. Kerimov expresses it:

> In present-day conditions political, economic, social and spiritual processes are accelerating, the circle of persons drawn into this historical act is widening significantly, and the revolutionary transformational energy of the popular masses is increasing. Social progress is bringing before the socialist state ever new and more complex tasks whose resolution presupposes an all-round and profound scientific analysis of social phenomena and processes, trends and prospects for their development. All of this in turn facilitates the strengthening of the Soviet state, significantly widens, deepens and complicates its functions.[60]

In the eyes of Soviet theorists, therefore, the Soviet Union now possesses a complex society and economy whose smooth running requires the presence of a developed administrative apparatus. Moreover, since 'communist morality' has not yet been instilled into the whole population, that apparatus still needs the power of coercion:[61] it remains, in other words, a state, even though it now acts in the interests of the whole people.

It is also recognised, however, that in the face of the greater and more sophisticated demands being made upon this state administration, changes in its mode of operation have to be introduced.[62]

Relations between organs of state and the citizens are said to be based not on the old, exploitive principles of authority and subordination, but on collaboration and persuasion.[63] But since this remains still largely an *aspiration*, there is a constant need to improve the quality of personnel who staff the apparatus. This is a theme on which Brezhnev repeatedly spoke,[64] and Soviet scholars have echoed him: 'State servants', according to one authoritative book on administration, 'must in their relations with citizens be attentive, courteous and sympathetic, and display an individual approach in conformity with the culture, education and psychological peculiarities both of individuals and of various social groups ... It is particularly important that [state] servants should be disinterested, strictly maintaining the equality of citizens before the law and the state organs.'[65]

There is emerging a more competent corps of professional administrators and the role of specialist advisers is also expanding.[66] This raises the spectre of an alliance between highly trained administrators and intellectual advisers running the state as a technocratic elite. This is potentially a serious problem, in the Soviet Union no less than in the Western world, and it has been given considerable attention in Soviet writings, with phrases such as 'dictatorship of specialists', 'regime of technocracy', and even a new coining, 'acadocracy' or 'scholocracy' (*uchenokratiya*), appearing in the literature.[67] The purpose of raising this issue is ostensibly to deny its validity, on the grounds, for example, that 'government in this society loses its function of giving orders and is exercised under general control'.[68] Nevertheless, with the increasing sophistication of decision-making techniques, the information explosion, the advent of data banks and other devices under the control of administrators, it requires great ingenuity to prevent the development that is feared. 'How can all this', asked V. M. Chkhikvadze, 'be combined with the necessity of further developing democracy, with widening the participation of the masses in government ... when many questions of government are practically within the power only of specialists?'[69]

A number of proposals have been put forward to help keep the state administrators in their proper place. Special training schools have been proposed for administrative staff, who would be selected by aptitude tests, administered by personnel officers with their own special qualifications.[70] Some have called for the development of a new 'administrative culture' or 'state service ethic';[71] others for a statute to regulate the conduct of cadres;[72] and even for such appointments to be filled through public competition,[73] a practice that has apparently been introduced.[74] The study of the psychology of public servants has also been suggested,[75] and under Brezhnev as under Khrushchev, Lenin's notion of election to such posts was again broached.[76]

There can, of course, be no guarantee whatever that a better-educated, professionally more competent administrative service would be any more sensitive to the articulated needs of the public than administrators in the past have been. Indeed, the opposite might result, in an era in which society, economy and government are undergoing the 'scientific and technological revolution'. A new generation of state servants, under the pressures of running the country and its increasingly complex and large-scale economy according to the criteria of 'scientific management' as they perceive them, may find they have little time or patience to deal with the seemingly irrational and unpredictable demands of a heterogeneous public. Already there are signs that Soviet administrative theorists accept many of the values of American theorists of managerial bureaucracy.[77]

At the very least, these measures to professionalise the state service would need to be coupled with active steps to promote respect for the law, in a society where 'infringements of socialist legality' practically form part of the political culture. The causes of lawlessness in Soviet society in the past are varied. They include gaps and contradictions in legislation, ignorance of the law on the part of officials, flagrant disregard for its provisions when the meeting of production targets was more important, and the inability or unwillingness of the political authorities to enforce their regulations.[78]

Stress on the rule of law, or on law and order (*pravoporyadok*), was a significant feature of the Brezhnev period, and the immense task of codifying and updating the body of legislation was embarked upon in the 1960s. Commentators in the West tend to stress the repressive and restrictive nature of much Soviet legislation, and to see 'law and order' and 'discipline' as measures applied to restrain citizens.[79] However, much of the emphasis in Soviet discussion is on discipline and respect for the law and order on the part of state officials, and on educating citizens in their legal rights, as well as obligations. The point has been made that legality requires a well-formulated body of legislation,[80] and it is surely not coincidental that one of the amendments to the draft of the 1977 Constitution was the addition to Article 6 of the phrase, 'All party organisations shall function within the framework of the Constitution of the USSR.' Soviet legislation may be carefully drafted so as to give a good deal of latitude to the administration, and

it is certainly designed so as not to upset the present power arrangements; yet it seems indisputable that an area of administration that is
bounded by rules leaves less scope for malpractice than one that is not
– as has too often been the case in the past.

The law is only one means of restraining the administration.
Shifting the centre of gravity of government from the administration
to the public is another.[81] This can be done in two ways: strengthening
the representative institutions, and raising the public's own capacity
for involvement.

Brezhnev continued Khrushchev's policy of revitalising the soviets,
not as institutions that will shortly cease to bear state functions, nor,
indeed, as organs of genuine governmental authority, but as bodies
that can effectively check the functioning of the administration. A
spate of legislation has been introduced since the late 1960s, to
strengthen the hand of these bodies; the standing commissions have
been expanded and energised; and the literature has stressed the need
for fresh criteria to be applied to the selection of representatives – not
that the public should be given a choice over who should represent
them, but at least that individuals should be selected for their
erudition, experience of life and competence as representatives of their
constituents' interests. On top of that, in order to boost the deputies'
confidence and competence, training in legal and constitutional
matters has been or is being introduced, to supplement the various
provisions of the Statute on Deputies' Status (1972), itself regarded as
a major provision to enhance the position of the representative in
dealings with the administration.[82]

These measures to 'professionalise' the role of the representative,
and thereby provide a more effective curb on the administration, if
they were conscientiously applied, might lead to some kind of institutional 'balance'. Policy-making would remain the prerogative of the
party bodies, and that policy would be given legal force by a strengthened Supreme Soviet, which would, together with its equivalent
institutions at lower levels, supervise the correct and sensitive
application of policy by the administration (the ministries, state
committees and local departments). And by drawing in wide sections
of the population to serve as deputies or as activists working alongside
them, the level of civic awareness and responsibility – the level of
political cultural development – would be raised to a level where,
perhaps, the public might indeed be able to take over some of the
present functions of the state. That, at any rate, remains the long-term
aspiration, without the haste that was characteristic of policy twenty

years ago. It is now fashionable to quote Lenin's warnings:

> We are not utopians. We know that an unskilled labourer or a cook cannot immediately get on with the job of state administration... Politics is a science and an art that does not fall from the skies or come gratis... A vast amount of educational, organisational and cultural work is required; this cannot be done rapidly by legislation but demands a vast amount of work over a long period.[83]

Meanwhile, the gradual *democratisation* of the political system is equated with wider participation in the affairs of state,[84] and once again Lenin is cited in support: 'Politics is participation in *state* affairs, directing the state, and determination of the forms, tasks and content of state activity.'[85]

However, the prescriptions of the professional Soviet scholars – accompanied, as often as not, by a considerable measure of wishful thinking on their part – should not be read as being necessarily indicative of present policy. Although we have seen areas where the ideas of scholars have been reflected in the utterances of Brezhnev and other politicians, there is no indication of any intention on their part to effect far-reaching changes in the short or medium term that would bring about fundamental realignments of political forces within the system.[86] On the contrary: certain continuities are also emphasised, which appear to stand in the way of implementing some of the desired changes.

The first of these is the unifying principle of *democratic centralism*, which ensures that power is retained ultimately in the hands of the central authorities. Moreover, this is probably necessary so long as the present form of economic planning is retained, and certainly that particular element in Soviet socialism is always stressed. The feared alternative to planned development is spontaneity that might lead from the path of socialism, hence local initiative must be restricted.[87] Nevertheless, there appears to be some recognition that excessively burdening the central authorities with minute decisions is counterproductive, and that a significant degree of decentralisation could usefully take place. Kerimov writes of 'centralisation of leadership in major questions, with decentralisation of operative functions',[88] and the concept of 'competence' to act has been introduced into Soviet analyses of this question.[89]

And yet decentralisation of decision-making and administrative authority within the state apparatus, coupled with greater opportunities for popular input into the process of government, can have only limited impact on the way the system as a whole functions, so long as the Communist Party retains its effective dominance. There is no sign whatever that this privileged position is to be interfered with: indeed, it is asserted that as the general level of state and political activity rises, so the need for the party's influence grows.[90] The limits on the optimistic course of development outlined above, involving a possible 'balance' between the roles of different institutions, are clearly seen when it is recalled that the notion of a formal 'division of powers' is contemptuously rejected by Soviet commentators.[91] The whole process of governing would still be closely monitored and controlled by the party, acting partly as the 'nucleus' of the political system in its own right, and partly through its own members strategically placed within various state institutions. Moreover, none of the state bodies – representative or administrative – would be able to *challenge* the party's policies. From the party's viewpoint, of course, this is quite correct: since it possesses the wisdom required to lead and guide society towards communism, it has a right and a duty to exercise that wisdom; and as society's political life becomes more active under developed socialism, the opportunities for things to go 'wrong' increase accordingly. Since most officials in the state apparatus are party members, the party is in principle in a position to influence them in the performance of their duties – and that ought to be in the direction of greater competence and responsiveness, as noted above. Even when such officials are appointed by competition, as Shakhnazarov observes, the party still has the decisive influence over their selection.[92] The Twenty-Fourth Party Congress (1971) extended the rights of local party organs to examine the work of local state offices, so there is now still further scope for the party to bring a positive influence to bear over the way the country is administered.

In practice, however, the party has shown itself prone to making use of its powers to usurp the role of the state, with the inevitable result that the state officials and institutions are reluctant to act without clearance from the party and, in a vicious circle, the party willy-nilly becomes directly involved in administration. *Podmena* (substitution), petty tutelage and parallelism have thus become ingrained in Soviet political practice, and calls in the scholarly literature and the party press to respect a clear delineation of functions between party and state have had at best a modest impact.[93]

So long as the party as an institution continues to proclaim its ideologically inspired infallibility in knowing what the fundamental interests of the Soviet people are, it cannot allow the state to develop to its full potential. It may perform necessary administrative functions, it may engage in the valuable function of socialisation, it may even serve to relay to the policy-makers some of the 'secondary' demands of the population. But as I have argued elsewhere, unless the party shows that it can trust non-party bodies (including those of the state), which are led in the main by its own members, and has confidence that they can be relied on not to engage in actions that run contrary to the spirit of socialism, the state will remain in a politically subordinate position. Officials in both party and state will continue to function as though the state were subordinated to the party, and the effect is as though that were legally the case.[94]

Ultimately, therefore, despite the clear assertion that the state must be further developed, the conclusion has to be drawn that the Soviet state remains in an ambiguous position. It is surrounded by a political rhetoric that seems to acknowledge the need for such a set of institutions, both for effectively organising society and also for purposes of giving legitimacy to the regime as a whole; but it is also directed by a powerful institution – the Communist Party – that is reluctant to permit the state organs to develop the capacity to take independent decisions in response to the perceived needs of the Soviet public. The 'all-people's state' still seems to represent the worst of all worlds. It is neither a full-blown state in which the people whose name it bears could have confidence and respect, nor is it a set of institutions in the process of 'withering away' and giving way to less formal mechanisms of social regulation. Its growing professionalism tends to make it akin to the modern bourgeois state, yet it is given none of the powers of that state to run the affairs of society without guiding instructions from a quite distinct body. Those within the state structure and outside it who wish to see its development into a politically significant organ of popular power are clearly going to be fighting an uphill struggle for a long time to come.

Perhaps the most that can be hoped for in the immediate future is that the party, as a policy-making institution, will make more effective use of the new professional expertise in the various state institutions, which it has itself been promoting over the best part of thirty years. Even that modest objective would represent a significant advance on the earlier position.

NOTES

1. See C. B. Macpherson, 'Do We Need a Theory of the State?', *Archives Européennes de Sociologie*, vol. xviii (1977) pp. 223–44. I am grateful to Rick Matthews for drawing my attention to this stimulating article and for his comments on the present paper. I also wish to express my gratitude to Alex Pravda for his challenging discussion of the paper in its original form, and to others whose contributions to the debate helped my understanding of the issues raised.

2. F. Engels, *Der Ursprung der Familie, des Privateigentums und des Staats* (*The Origin of the Family, Private Property and the State*), in K. Marx and F. Engels, *Werke* (*MEW*) (Berlin, 1969–71), vol. 21, p. 167.

3. K. Marx and F. Engels, *Die deutsche Ideologie* (*The German Ideology*) *MEW*, vol. 3, p. 33.

4. K. Marx and F. Engels, *Manifest der kommunistischen Partei* (*The Manifesto of the Communist Party*) *MEW*, vol. 4, p. 482.

5. Marx, 'Konspekt zu Bakunins *Staatlichkeit und Anarchie*' (Conspectus on Bakunin's *Statism and Anarchy*) *MEW*, vol. 18, p. 634.

6. Marx, 'Kritik des Gothaer Programs' ('Critique of the Gotha Programme') *MEW*, vol. 19, p. 28.

7. Marx and Engels, *The Manifesto of the Communist Party*, *MEW*, vol. 4, p. 481.

8. V. I. Lenin, *The State and Revolution*, in V. I. Lenin, *Collected Works*, in 45 vols, (*CW*) (Moscow, 1960–70) vol. 25, p. 462.

9. Ibid, p. 463.

10. Lenin, 'The Tasks of the Proletariat in the Present Revolution' (April Theses) *CW*, vol. 24, pp. 22–3 (Theses 4 and 5; Lenin's emphasis).

11. Lenin, *The Proletarian Revolution and the Renegade Kautsky*, *CW*, vol. 28, pp. 105–13.

12. D. McLellan, 'Marx, Engels and Lenin on Party and State', in L. Holmes (ed.), *The Withering Away of the State? Party and State under Communism* (London, 1981) p. 21. McLellan refers to Marx's *Critique of Hegel's Philosophy of the State* (1843) and *The Eighteenth Brumaire of Louis Bonaparte* (1851).

13. Lenin, *The State and Revolution*, *CW*, vol. 25, p. 425; see also McLellan, 'Marx, Engels and Lenin', pp. 27–8.

14. Lenin, 'The State and Revolution', *CW*, vol. 25, pp. 426–7 and *passim*.

15. I am grateful to Neil Harding for reminding me of this point. Cf. Lenin, *The State and Revolution*, *CW*, vol. 25, pp. 42–30 and *passim*.

16. G. A. Brinkley, 'Khrushchev Remembered: on the Theory of Soviet Statehood', *Soviet Studies*, vol. xxiv, no. 3 (1973), p. 387.

17. See F. G. Casals (pseud.), *The Syncretic Society* (New York, 1980), pp. 15–20.

18. G. V. Barabashev and O. E. Kutafin, *Osnovy znaniy o Sovetskom gosudarstve i prave* (Moscow, 1977) p. 18. Cf. the 1961 Party Programme, in *KPSS v rezolyutsiyakh i resheniyakh s"ezdov, konferentsiy i plenumov TsK* (*KPSS v rez.*) vol. 8 (Moscow, 1972) p. 273.

19. English text in D. Lane, *Politics and Society in the USSR*, 2nd edn (Oxford, 1978) pp. 532–52; a text of the 1977 Constitution appears in ibid, pp. 553–84.

20. R. E. Kanet sees continuity in the dictatorship of the proletariat into the 1960s: see his article, 'The Rise and Fall of the "All-People's State"', *Soviet Studies*, vol. xx, no. 1 (1969) p. 81.

21. This is the term used by D. J. R. Scott, in his *Russian Political Institutions*, 4th edn (London, 1969) ch. 3. The similarity was further underlined in 1946 by the re-naming of the distinctively Soviet 'People's Commissars' and 'Commissariats' as Ministers and Ministries: on the origins of the revolutionary terms, see L. Trotsky, *My Life* (New York, 1960) pp. 337–8. References to the Supreme Soviet as 'the Soviet Parliament' further enhance this image of conventionality: see M. Saifulin (ed.), *The Soviet Parliament* (Moscow, 1967); at least one Soviet scholar has suggested that this is confusing: see Yu. V. Shabanov, *Problemy Sovetskoy sotsialisticheskoy demokratii v period stroitel'stva kommunizma* (Minsk, 1969) p. 92.

22. A. B. Evans, Jr, 'Developed Socialism in Soviet Ideology', *Soviet Studies*, vol. xxix, no. 3 (1977) p. 421.

23. *KPSS v rez.*, vol. 8, p. 273.

24. L. G. Churchward, 'Contemporary Soviet Theory of the Soviet State', *Soviet Studies*, vol. xii, no. 4 (1961) p. 415.

25. See J. M. Gilison, 'Khrushchev, Brezhnev, and Constitutional Reform', *Problems of Communism*, vol. xxi, no. 5 (1972) p. 73.

26. Brinkley, 'Khrushchev Remembered', p. 398, n. 2.

27. Ibid; see also Kanet, 'The Rise and Fall', p. 83; Evans, 'Developed Socialism', p. 422; J. F. Hough and M. Fainsod, *How the Soviet Union is Governed* (Cambridge, Mass., 1979) p. 255.

28. Gilison, 'Khrushchev, Brezhnev', p. 77.

29. J. F. Hough, *The Soviet Union and Social Science Theory* (Cambridge, Mass., 1977) p. 112.

30. See Brezhnev's reports: 'O pyatidesyatiletii Soyuza Sovetskikh Sotsialisticheskikh Respublik', *Kommunist*, no. 18 (1972) pp. 39–40; and 'O proekte Konstitutsii Soyuza Sovetskikh Sotsialisticheskikh Respublik', *Kommunist*, no. 8 (1977) pp. 34–44.

31. Barabashev and Kutafin, *Osnovy znaniy*, p. 18.

32. Ibid, p. 19.

33. G. W. Breslauer sees it as 'noteworthy' that the post-Khrushchev leadership continued to refer to the party and state 'of all the people', rather than reverting to Stalinist formulations; this bears witness, in his view, to the success of Khrushchev in expanding the boundaries of the political community and recognising the needs of 'all the people': see his article, 'Khrushchev Reconsidered', *Problems of Communism*, vol. xx, no. 5 (1976) p. 32.

34. On the All-People's State in the Party Programme, see *KPSS v rez.*, vol. 8, pp. 272–4; on the party as one of the whole people, see ibid, p. 301; on Brezhnev's reference to the 'new historic community of people', see 'O pyatidesyatiletii', p. 14.

35. D. A. Kerimov, *Demokratiya razvitogo sotsializma* (Moscow, 1980) pp. 53–4.

36. Barabashev and Kutafin, *Osnovy znaniy*, p. 19.

37. Ibid, pp. 19–20.

38. Ibid, p. 5; see also Kerimov, *Demokratiya*, p. 51.

39. S. Kaltakhchyan, 'Internatsional'noe edinstvo Sovetskogo naroda', *Pravda*, 2 October 1981.
40. R. J. Hill, *Soviet Politics, Political Science and Reform* (Oxford, 1980) p. 180.
41. See S. White, *Political Culture and Soviet Politics* (London, 1979) chs 2 and 3.
42. I am aware that this may be regarded as a contentious point. On the one hand, it might be interpreted as making a value-laden judgement about the desirability of functioning through parliamentary-style institutions, rather than employing other forms of political action; on the other hand, it may be used – as it essentially has been in the USSR – to justify rule by an elite of those who do possess knowledge of what needs to be done: on this point, see below. My pragmatic view holds that, given the existence of such institutions, it is desirable that they should be used as effectively as possible by the population in pursuing their legitimate interests.
43. T. H. Friedgut, 'Citizens and Soviets: can Ivan Ivanovich fight City Hall?', *Comparative Politics*, vol. x (1978) p. 464.
44. See Breslauer, 'Khrushchev Reconsidered'.
45. See D. T. Cattell, 'Local Government and the Sovnarkhoz in the USSR, 1957–1962', *Soviet Studies*, vol. xv, no. 4 (1964) pp. 430–42.
46. Churchward, 'Contemporary Soviet Theory', p. 413.
47. *KPSS v rez.*, vol. 7 (Moscow, 1971) p. 113.
48. Brinkley, 'Khrushchev Remembered', p. 396.
49. *KPSS v rez.*, vol. 8, pp. 274–6.
50. P. P. Ukrainets, *Partiynoe rukovodstvo i gosudarstvennoe upravlenie* (Minsk, 1976) p. 56.
51. See R. J. Hill, 'Recent Developments in Soviet Local Government', *Community Development Journal*, vol. 7 (1972) pp. 169–75; R. J. Hill, 'The Development of Soviet Local Government since Stalin's Death', in E. M. Jacobs (ed.), *Soviet Local Politics and Government* (London, 1983).
52. Yu. E. Volkov *et al.* (eds), *Razvitoy sotsializm* (Moscow, 1978) p. 16.
53. Kerimov, *Demokratiya*, p. 72; this is a direct quotation from the Party Programme: see *KPSS v rez.*, vol. 8, p. 280.
54. In *The German Ideology*, Marx argued that 'communism is possible only as the act of the dominant peoples "all at once" and simultaneously', and 'the proletariat can ... exist only world-historically, just as communism, its activity, can have only a "world-historical" existence': see *MEW*, vol. 3, p. 36.
55. A. Lashin, *Socialism and the State* (Moscow, 1977) p. 195.
56. Breslauer, 'Khrushchev Reconsidered', pp. 31–2.
57. N. N. Vinogradov, *Partiynoe rukovodstvo Sovetami v usloviyakh razvitogo sotsializma* (Moscow, 1980) p. 231.
58. Barabashev and Kutafin, *Osnovy znaniy*, p. 10.
59. Ibid, pp. 21–3; Kerimov, *Demokratiya*, p. 55; Ts. A. Stepanyan and A. S. Frish (eds), *Razvitoy sotsializm i aktual'nye problemy nauchnogo kommunizma* (Moscow, 1979) pp. 166–7.
60. Kerimov, *Demokratiya*, pp. 54–5.
61. Volkov *et al.*, *Razvitoy sotsializm*, p. 292.

62. Stepanyan and Frish, *Razvitoy sotsializm*, p. 169.
63. *Apparat upravleniya sotsialisticheskogo gosudarstva, chast' 2* (Moscow, 1977) p. 238.
64. See, for example, *XXV sezd Kommunisticheskoy partii Sovetskogo Soyuza: Stenograficheskiy otchet* (Moscow, 1976) vol. 1, pp. 95–6; *Pravda*, 24 February 1981, p. 6 (speech at Twenty-Sixth CPSU Congress).
65. *Apparat upravleniya*, pp. 236–7.
66. Ibid, pp. 236–7; see also Hill, *Soviet Politics, Political Science and Reform*, ch. 8; E. P. Hoffmann, 'Changing Soviet Perspectives on Leadership and Administration', in S. F. Cohen, A. Rabinowitch and R. Sharlet (eds), *The Soviet Union Since Stalin* (London, 1980) pp. 76–7.
67. For example, Yu. A. Tikhomirov (ed.), *Demokratiya razvitogo sotsialisticheskogo obshchestva* (Moscow, 1975) p. 122; the new coining is by Georgiy Shakhnazarov, in D. A. Kerimov (ed.), *Sovetskaya demokratiya v period razvitogo sotsializma*, 2nd edn (Moscow, 1979) p. 171.
68. Kerimov, *Sovetskaya demokratiya*, p. 171.
69. V. M. Chkhikvadze, 'Pravovaya nauka sotsializma', *Pravda*, 10 January 1968.
70. Kerimov, *Sovetskaya demokratiya*, p. 184.
71. A. E. Lunev *et al.* (eds), *Nauchnye osnovy gosudarstvennogo upravleniya v SSSR* (Moscow, 1968) ch. 10; Yu. M. Kozlov, *Kul'tura upravleniya i pravo* (Moscow, 1978); *Apparat upravleniya*, pp. 235–8.
72. Tikhomirov, *Demokratiya razvitogo*, p. 217.
73. Ibid, pp. 131, 218.
74. Kerimov, *Sovetskaya demokratiya*, p. 185.
75. A. Obolonsky, 'The Public Employee as an Object of Socio-Psychological Analysis', in V. Semyonov *et al.* (eds), *Political Theory and Political Practice* (Moscow, 1979) pp. 207–14.
76. Tikhomirov, *Demokratiya razvitogo*, p. 131.
77. See M. E. Urban, 'Bureaucracy, Contradiction, and Ideology in Two Societies', *Administration and Society*, vol. 10, no. 1 (May 1978) pp. 49–85.
78. See, for example, V. I. Vasil'ev *et al.* (eds), *Voprosy raboty Sovetov deputatov trudyashchikhsya* (Moscow, 1968) p. 191; *Apparat upravleniya*, p. 236; Yu. A. Tikhomirov *et al.*, *Konstitutsiya SSSR i dal'neyshee razvitie gosudarstvovedeniya i teorii prava* (Moscow, 1979) pp. 197–202.
79. For example, Breslauer, 'Khrushchev Reconsidered', pp. 31–2.
80. V. I. Remnev, summing up the opinions of a number of writers on the theme, in D. A. Gaidukov *et al.* (eds), *Aktual'nye problemy gosudarstvovedeniya* (Moscow, 1979) p. 100.
81. Kerimov, *Demokratiya razvitogo sotsializma*, p. 59.
82. A. I. Luk'yanov, *Razvitie zakonodatel'stva o Sovetskikh predstavitel'nykh organakh vlasti* (Moscow, 1978) pp. 171–2.
83. A composite quotation from Kerimov, *Sovetskaya demokratiya*, pp. 138, 140, 142; cf. Stepanyan and Frish, *Razvitoy sotsializm*, p. 174: 'Lenin more than once warned that this process must not be forced.'
84. B. Babiy and V. Zabigailo, 'Popular Participation in Government as a Criterion of Democracy', in V. Chirkin *et al.* (eds), *Political Systems: Development Trends* (Moscow, 1979) pp. 31–40.

85. Quoted in Kerimov, *Sovetskaya demokratiya*, p. 135.
86. For a fuller treatment of these points, see Hill, *Soviet Politics, Political Science and Reform*, esp. chs 8 and 9.
87. Kerimov, *Demokratiya razvitogo sotsializma*, pp. 57–8.
88. Ibid, p. 80.
89. See Hill, 'The Development of Soviet Local Government', p. 27.
90. See, for example, Volkov *et al.*, *Razvitoy sotsialism*, pp. 99–105; Stepanyan and Frish, *Razvitoy sotsializm*, pp. 38–54. This view was clearly expressed in the 1961 Party Programme: see *KPSS v rez.*, vol. 8, p. 301.
91. See, for example, Shabanov, *Problemy Sovetskoy*, pp. 109–10.
92. In Kerimov, *Sovetskaya demokratiya*, p. 185.
93. See R. J. Hill and P. Frank, *The Soviet Communist Party* (London, 1981) pp. 118–21.
94. Ibid, p. 121; see also R. J. Hill, T. Dunmore and K. Dawisha, 'The USSR: The Revolution Reversed?', in Holmes, *The Withering Away of the State?*, pp. 197–222.

4 The Coercion/Consent Analysis of the State under Socialism

John Hoffman

A NEW MODEL FOR MARXIST POLITICS?

The 1970s saw a great preoccupation among Marxists and commentators on Marxism with the question of the state, politics and power.[1]
Some have spoken of a veritable 'crisis of Marxism' and have ascribed
this crisis to the failure to develop an adequate and comprehensive
theory of the state.[2] The argument has been advanced that classical
Marxism focused too narrowly upon the state as the *coercive* instrument of the ruling class and failed therefore to analyse the ideological
and cultural aspects of political power.[3] This is why much attention
has been paid recently to the writing of the Italian Marxist, Antonio
Gramsci, for Gramsci, it is argued, inaugurated a new chapter in
Marxist political theory by developing an expanded view of the state
based upon an analysis of politics as coercion *and* consent.[4]

The idea that politics and the state can be understood in terms of a
duality between coercion and consent is a very old one, and Pateman
has argued that the conceptual contrast is rooted in the classical liberal
notion of society as a voluntary scheme whose autonomous members
acknowledge only those obligations that are self-imposed.[5] Gramsci
himself traces this dual perspective back to Machiavelli's Centaur,
half animal and half human, by quoting Machiavelli to the effect that
'there are two ways of fighting: by law or by force ... as the first way
often proves inadequate one must needs have recourse to the second'.[6]
The two sides to the state must be ever borne in mind: in Gramsci's
now celebrated formulation – 'The State is the entire complex of
practical and theoretical activities with which the ruling class not only

justifies and maintains its dominance, but manages to win the active consent of those over whom it rules.'[7] Central here, of course, is the concept of *hegemony* which Gramsci describes as intellectual and moral leadership as opposed to dictatorship or domination, and this duality expresses itself in Gramsci's two major superstructural levels as civil and political society. Gramsci regarded these concepts as relevant to both the bourgeois state and the state under socialism,[8] and those who have recently rediscovered the coercion/consent analysis follow Gramsci on this as well. In a work intended to elaborate in detail supporting arguments for the French Communist Party's new stance on the dictatorship of the proletariat, Gramsci's conception of hegemony and coercion is hailed as an idea 'as important for the conception of socialist power as it is for revolutionary struggle'.[9] Structured around the distinction between coercion and consent – what Louis Althusser has called the Repressive and Ideological State Apparatuses[10] – a series of new and challenging antitheses emerge. As formulated in Santiago Carrillo's *Eurocommunism and the State* (1977), a peaceful 'democratic' road to socialism based on electoral politics stands opposed to a revolutionary dictatorial path leading to the insurrection of a minority. The popular forces must lead rather than dominate; the old bourgeois state needs to be democratically transformed rather than smashed and rebuilt from scratch,[11] while the new state will stand as the hegemony of the working people and not, as the Marxist classics supposed, the dictatorship of the proletariat.[12] What is proposed here is a model of *democratic* socialism as opposed to political systems like the present Soviet-type ones which, ruled by a bureaucratic stratum with almost uncontrolled political power, have yet to become genuine Socialist states. These latter are indeed held to constitute a brake on the development of real workers' democracy.[13] In short, the new politics must be rooted in consent, not coercion; hegemony rather than dictatorship; democracy as opposed to a form of totalitarianism.[14]

These positions find a sympathetic echo among other Eurocommunist thinkers and parties. Lombardo Radice of the Italian Communist Party contrasts a pluralist, free, democratic type of socialism with a dictatorship of the proletariat which would suppress freedom, and urges self-management and participation in place of state socialism.[15] Etienne Balibar, a critic of the new line, has pointed to the series of contrasts and systematically opposed models central to the case for dropping the concept of the dictatorship of the proletariat from the PCF's programme in 1976: the contrast between peaceful and violent political means, between legality and illegality, the majority and the minority; 'A simple choice between two historical roads for the transition to socialism, a choice between two conceptions of socialism',[16] that is, the dictatorial and the democratic. As Lucien Sève comments elsewhere: in place of the superseded and narrow concept of proletarian dictatorship there appears the prospect of 'making socialism the conscious aim of the majority of the people'; a socialism in which, in the words of the report of the Twenty-Second Congress of the PCF, 'the state, democratic in structure and operation, will no longer be an instrument of oppression, alien and out of reach to simple people'.[17]

POLITICS AND THE STATE IN THE MARXIST CLASSICS

The reference above to a state no longer the instrument of oppression serves to spotlight the difference between classical Marxist conceptions of politics and these recent developments. Engels, for example, opposed all reference to a 'free state' on the grounds that under socialism the state is 'only a transitional institution' necessary 'to hold down one's adversaries by force': 'so long as the proletariat still *uses* the state, it does not use it in the interests of freedom . . . as soon as it becomes possible to speak of freedom the state as such ceases to exist.'[18] 'When class rule has disappeared', Marx tells Bakunin, 'there will no longer be any state in the present political sense of the word'[19] for politics is the struggle to acquire and maintain class power: power in the hands of a separate class of people who stand 'apart' from society, separated from it. In a letter to Friedrich Bolte in 1871, Marx defines a *political* movement as 'a *class* movement' with the object of enforcing its interests in a general form, in a form possessing general, *socially coercive* force.[20] The question of coercion as the product of class antagonism is more than just 'one factor' in politics, since 'political power, properly so called, is merely the organised power of one class for oppressing another'.[21] Ralph Miliband is correct when he argues that, for Marx and Engels, the state was 'above all, the coercive instrument of a ruling class'.[22] What differentiates the state from other institutions is its possession of the means of organised coercion.[23]

It is worth emphasising that this view of the state and politics as class coercion was presented in analytical or conceptual terms: as an expression, in other words, of what Marx and Engels believed constituted the essential characteristic of the state *qua* state. Hence not all the activities that a particular state undertakes are necessarily political in the strict sense in which the term is defined above. In volume III of *Capital* Marx develops the argument that under capitalism, 'just as in the despotic states',

> supervision and all-round interference by the government involves both the performance of common activities arising from the nature of all communities, and the specific functions arising from the antithesis between the government and the mass of the people.[24]

The performance of these common activities 'arising from the nature of all communities' – transport and communications, for example – does not therefore involve politics 'properly so called' except in so far as an antithesis between government and the mass of the people is also expressed. What we have, presumably, are the legitimate functions of 'the old governmental power' (as Marx refers to them in *The Civil War in France*), which, under the Paris Commune, were to be restored to 'the responsible agents of society'.[25]

GRAMSCI, THE CLASSICS AND THE 'ETHICAL STATE'

Where then do Gramsci's concepts stand in relationship to the classical Marxist view of politics as class coercion? It is revealing that in his *Prison Notebooks* Gramsci reserves the term *political* society for the coercive activities of the state, and on occasion speaks of political society as 'the State'.[26] This narrow definition accords with the classical Marxist usage, as does Gramsci's comment in 1919 that the state as the 'principle of political power will wither away all the more rapidly' under socialism, as workers become 'more united and disciplined in the context of production'.[27] While it is true that Gramsci was to incorporate civil society – 'the ensemble of organisms commonly called "private"'[28] – into his concept of the integral state, coercion still has an important role to play in Gramsci's view of politics. As Anderson has stressed, Gramsci took the Marxism of the Comintern with 'its emphasis on the historical necessity of violence in the destruction and construction of States' wholly for granted[29] and was concerned to supplement rather than supplant classical definitions. It is perhaps for this reason that Gramsci insists that the distinction between civil and political society is 'merely methodo-

logical': to treat the civil society/political society distinction as though
it were 'organic' (i.e. empirically identifiable) would lead, Gramsci
feared, to a liberal conception of hegemony as a purely autonomous
political sphere having no relationship to class interests.[30] Just as Marx
was intensely sceptical about liberal concepts of freedom and equality
since they draw an ideological veil over the inequality of class power,
so Gramsci argued that while 'hegemony is ethical-political, it must
also be economic, must necessarily be based on the decisive function
exercised by the leading group in the decisive nucleus of economic
activity'.[31] The struggle for hegemony involves a struggle for *power*:
while they may be methodologically distinguishable, 'in actual reality
civil society and State are one and the same'.[32] No organic distinction
can be drawn.

All this would seem to make it unlikely that one can derive from
Gramsci divergent political strategies and divergent models of socialism and the socialist state based simply upon a choice between force
and persuasion.

Gramsci does, for example, emphasise the importance of the
dictatorship of the proletariat under socialism, for, given the fact that
'the proletariat is little trained in the art of governing and leading', it
needs to be both dominant and to provide leadership – exercise
dictatorship as well as organise consent.[33] Yet while it must be said
that Gramsci's ideas on politics are *closer* to those of the classics than
some of his commentators would allow, there still remains his view of
the state as involving *both* coercion *and* consent. How does this dual
perspective stand in relationship to classical conceptions?

Burlatsky has commented that Marx and Engels sometimes speak of
the state in the broader sense of a political system, an organised unity,
'the official expression of civil society',[34] and this would seem to point
to the importance of factors other than coercion being involved in the
political process. Perfectly true: for Marx and Engels, the repressive
aspect of the state cannot and does not function on its own. Yet if it is
not the *only* aspect to political power, it does have analytical priority
as the core.[35] Gramsci, on the other hand, refers to a 'balance'[36]
between force and consent, and in some of his formulations it appears
that it is in *consent* rather than coercion that the root of power lies.
The state is 'hegemony protected by the armour of coercion'.[37]
Moreover, the distinction which Gramsci says should be methodological becomes more operationally practical as applied, for instance,
to the celebrated contrast between East and West where, in the case of
the West, the state is depicted as an 'outer ditch' to the 'sturdy

structure of civil society'.[38] This analogy suggests a more tangible separation between civil and political society, as does the equally famous comment that a social group must become hegemonic *before* winning governmental power.[39] It also implies that priority rests with consent and that hegemony rather than coercion is the heart of the political process.

In the *Prison Notebooks* Gramsci argues that it was Lenin who developed the doctrine of hegemony as 'a complement to the theory of the State-as-force'.[40] Yet while it is true that Lenin was concerned with the question of proletarian hegemony in the struggle for democracy and socialism, Gramsci's striking innovation was to conceptualise intellectual and moral leadership as an essential attribute of political power – a conceptual part, if not the conceptual core, of the state itself. Marx, on the other hand, speaks of power rather than will as the basis of right,[41] and this would seem to imply that consent cannot be conceived of as an independent factor which balances coercion but surfaces politically as an expression of class power. Hence freedom and consent remain highly problematic as long as the state and class divisions exist. While the mobilisation of mass support is necessary for social change, this process only really involves consent in the sense of self-determination and self-government in so far as it begins to transcend, absorb and abolish the world of politics altogether. Thus universal suffrage is transformed from 'a means of deception' into 'an instrument of emancipation' only when it offers the workers 'certainty of victory',[42] and voting is adapted to its 'real purposes' only when (as in the Paris Commune) it makes possible the replacement of the haughty masters of the people by their 'always removable servants' – that is, when it initiates the process of dissolving 'the modern State power'.[43] What therefore makes a movement political in the strict sense of the term – what makes a state a state – is not the existence of popular support or moral leadership, even though these factors will also be involved, but organised class *coercion*, the exercise of a socially coercive force in the class struggle. For this reason it would seem that the concept of civil society as an ethical state which Gramsci drew from Croce, has no counterpart in Marx's writings.[44]

It must be concluded then that Gramsci *did* introduce a new dimension into Marxist theories of politics, even though his arguments have to be oversimplified and taken out of their historical context before they can serve as the basis of 'systematically opposed models' of the state under socialism. Yet however partial or complete we judge Gramsci's responsibility for the new approach, the question still remains: how successful is the coercion/consent analysis of the state under socialism? What light does it throw on the historical development of socialist states? What insight does it offer into the way in which these states actually function?

The rest of this chapter attempts to tackle these questions in the light of some of the literature on the political history and development of the USSR.

SOVIET CIVIL SOCIETY AND 'THE BROAD, PEACEFUL VALLEYS OF CIVILISATION'

One of the most explicit attempts to employ the coercion/consent analysis to the evolution of the Soviet state appears in Harrison's 'Centenary View' of Stalin – a sustained and ingenious attempt to conceptualise some of the major landmarks of Soviet history in neo-Gramscian terms.

The argument is as follows: Lenin left the Soviet system 'a heritage containing several contradictory, alternative futures', stressing in 1922 the need to transform 'the bureaucratic traditions of the Russian people through a voluntary, co-operative road to socialism'.[45] Within the New Economic Policy and the positions taken by Bukharin, a project emerges for 'building a Soviet "civil society"' (a society based on consent), and a fierce struggle ensues in the party, between the strategy of developing rural civil society and popular democratic control from below, on the one hand, and the strategy of forced industrialisation organised from above, on the other. With the defeat of the left opposition, however, Bukharin and his supporters are compelled by Stalin to surrender to the same coercive, industrialising programme that the defeated left had developed. A model of socialism based on force is the victor, and the 'broad, peaceful valleys of community and civilisation' are submerged by the experience of 'coercive struggles and military disciplines'; two opposing roads, one based primarily upon coercion, the other upon consent, offering the historical actors of the day a political choice.[46]

How valid is this kind of analysis? Take the characterisation of Lenin's policy in 1921–2 as 'a voluntary, cooperative road to socialism'. Lenin certainly argues vigorously during this period for the New Economic Policy, for the adoption of a reformist type of method which would allow trade and capitalism to revive, but is it correct to speak here, as Tucker does for example, of a 'voluntary' Leninism in contrast to the 'coercive' Leninism of the earlier War Communism period?[47] It has to be remembered that Lenin's emphasis on raising cultural levels, developing co-operatives, and offering incentives to the peasantry arises within an essentially *political* context where the question is, as Lenin poses it in October 1921, 'Who will win, the capitalist or Soviet power?' The voluntary, co-operative road involves a stern struggle against sentiment – 'whoever now departs from order and discipline is permitting the enemy to penetrate our midst'[48] – harsh methods of education and the use of proletarian state power to keep 'a proper rein on those gentlemen, the capitalists, so as to direct capitalism along state channels and to create a capitalism that will be subordinate to the state and serve the state'.[49] Harrison himself notes that the voluntary road was accompanied by the integration of the party's Central Control Commission and Workers and Peasants Inspection into the machinery of the state,[50] while Tucker has to concede that the break with War Communism was conceived by Lenin in *military* terms, as a necessary retreat to be followed as quickly as possible by 'our subsequent victorious advance'.[51] What all this suggests, therefore, is the adoption of changing tactics for changing circumstances rather than an abstract choice between conflicting models. Lenin had spoken of the dictatorship of the proletariat in the spring of 1920 (in an argument directed against the doctrinaire conceptions of the left communists) as 'a persistent struggle – bloody and bloodless, violent and peaceful, military and economic, educational and administrative – against the forces and traditions of the old society',[52] and this implies not a choice between force and persuasion, coercion and consent, but their fluid *interpenetration*, set in the context of proletarian state power.

A similar kind of problem arises with Harrison's contrast between the NEP's strategy of developing popular control from below, and the left's strategy in the 1920s of forced industrialisation organised from above. It is true that Trotsky spoke of the need for 'a dictatorship of industry',[53] but the left opposition certainly believed that its policies of industrialisation and collectivisation could be carried out in what Isaac Deutscher calls 'the broad daylight of proletarian democracy, with the consent of the masses and "free initiative" from below'.[54] The debate between Bukharin and the left, though polarised by flights of rhetoric, turned on questions of emphasis and priorities and there was much taken for granted: as Harrison himself notes, the dictatorship of the proletariat, the one-party state and the control over the economy's commanding heights.[55] Indeed, it is for this reason that

Cohen insists (in a curiously anachronistic comment) that Bukharin's ideas cannot be deemed relevant to the ideals of Euro-communism since Bukharin was not a democrat and 'never challenged the principle of one-party dictatorship'![56] The historical record simply resists organic contrasts between coercion and consent in the assessment of Bolshevik policy, and Cohen's own reference to the 'bifurcation of Bolshevism' after 1921 into two conflicting ideological and emotional traditions, the evolutionary-reformist and the revolutionary-heroic,[57] fails to square with his actual analysis of the period. Not only does he make the point himself that the left was not anti-NEP, but he paints a fascinating portrait of the way in which Bukharin was prepared to modify and reconsider earlier positions. The snail's-pace utterance gives way to the assertion that we are 'proceeding far too slowly',[58] to be followed in 1927 with the declaration that it is now time to begin 'a forced offensive against the kulak'![59] The revolutionary-heroic tradition seem difficult to extricate from the evolutionary-reformist in the policies of a Bolshevik who, as Cohen says, while 'prepared to move in new directions', 'rejected either–or solutions' and preferred to 'walk on as many legs as possible'.[60] All this is surely most inconvenient for an analysis in terms of 'bifurcated' strategies and sharply opposed political models. Once again it is the circumstances in which the choices are made that need attention.

But what of Harrison's characterisation of Stalinism from 1929 onwards as a model of socialism primarily based on force – a model that blocked off the road to a new civil society, submerging consent and community in 'coercive struggles and military discipline'?[61] It is undeniable that the political coercion of the Stalin period was massive, macabre, and at times almost self-destructive, but does the concept of a socialism based on coercion *rather than* consent really assist in tackling the complexities of the time? If Stalinism is a model based primarily on force, how do we explain the popular enthusiasm and support so crucial for the implementation of Stalinist policies from above? Cohen speaks of there being 'substantial support for Stalinism, inside and outside officialdom, from the very beginning and through the very worst', and warns that this is a problem 'largely ignored and inconsistent with the imagery of a "totalitarian" regime dominating a hapless, "atomised" population through power techniques alone'.[62] Tucker also speaks of the importance of support 'from below', at least from among the *aktiv*, 'those who participated in the collectivisation and industrialisation drives ...enthusiastically and self-sacrificingly'. Whether support for Stalin's policies extended *beyond* this is a question that needs more research.[63] Harrison himself comments that Stalinism depended upon 'important elements of mass consent and mass participation from its birth',[64] but if coercion and consent are conceived of as conflicting polar opposites – where the presence of the one tends to exclude the other – how is their curious co-existence to be explained? Harrison can only offer an explanation that recalls Rousseau's famous paradox of men being forced to be free, for he argues that the working class 'consented to the sub-ordination of Soviet society to productive goals' and 'subjected themselves to new coercive disciplines'. Personal leaders, he adds, 'made the spread of a coercive, bureaucratic system acceptable to the working class' by, it seems, 'appealing to its anti-bureaucratic impulses and winning its participation'![65] This appears to imply that somehow or other, the workers consented to their own coercion, but if popular support for coercive policies takes place on a substantial scale, then surely an analysis of politics that 'models' one of these elements in opposition to the other is in difficulty. After all, was it not the element of coercion in Stalinist policy, projected as a necessary response to external crisis and domestic emergency, that helped to make Stalinism popular? Can it be denied that Stalin's paternalist image of steely *force* struck a strong consensual chord at the time? Bukharin's characterisation of Stalin as 'something like the symbol of the party, the rank and file workers, the people believe him'[66] epitomises the problem: would there have been more popular consent had there been less state coercion during this period? Would civil society have blossomed if political society had receded? Medvedev remarks bitterly that the 'longer this tyrant ruled the USSR, cold-bloodedly destroying millions of people, the greater seems to have been the dedication to him, even the love, of the majority of the people'.[67] Clearly, the question of political traditions, cultural levels, historical circumstances and economic necessities is critical: can these aspects be properly weighed in the balance in terms of a conflict of abstract models, each resting upon a 'political choice'?

REANALYSING THE PROBLEM: HINTS OF A 'MORE SOPHISTICATED SPECTRUM'

Commenting on the 25 000 industrial workers who were enrolled by the party to go into the villages as collectivisers during the 1930s, Tucker argues that 'at least some portion joined the movement under pressure of dire family need combined with material incentives to assist in the collectivising'.[68] This surely is the point. Whatever pure voluntarists might suppose, people do not consent to state-policies in a power vacuum: innumerable pressures, social, economic, psychological, political and cultural, influence their decisions and shape their will,[69] and in societies where economic constraint is significant and political pressures pervasive, coercion and consent are unlikely to fall neatly into opposing camps. Classically defined, the state is an institution which possesses a monopoly of legitimate violence, and it is this monopoly that, in Anderson's view, constitutes a 'silent, absent force' underpinning social relations as a whole. Deprived of this *force*, the system of cultural control expressed in terms of popular consent would be 'instantly fragile'.[70] This is why, to reiterate an earlier point, Marx and Engels appear to have resisted any analysis of politics that injects consent as a conceptual parallel to coercion, for as long as the state is historically necessary, no one is yet fully free.[71] The all-pervasive presence of the state makes for a range of pressures and constraints which cannot be classified as either coercion or consent. What of the problem of corruption and fraud, issues which, Anderson complains, Gramsci alluded to but never integrated into the mainstream of his analysis 'to form a more sophisticated spectrum of concepts'?[72] What of the fear of unemployment, pressure from the mass media, public opinion, social institutions in general?

Göran Therborn has contended that the coercion/consent conceptualisation has figured 'disastrously' in contemporary political theory. Its roots lie in the 'normative problems of the bourgeois revolution' – a revolution that presented the freedom of the individual from external authority in terms of a belief in 'consciousness as the bearer of a new social order'.[73] Individual consent is abstracted from concrete social reality. This is what consigns the coercion/consent analysis to the world of what Therborn calls normative political philosophy and renders it so imperfect as a tool of empirical political analysis. While it is certainly true that all empirical analysis has inherently normative implications,[74] the problem with the coercion/consent analysis is that it is *abstractly* normative: that is, its plea for individual freedom hinders rather than helps with an understanding of the concrete complexities of political life. Models of the state based on consent or coercion, dictatorship or democracy, totalitarianism or pluralism, bureaucracy or participation, distract attention from the question of precisely how the state under socialism (or indeed under capitalism for that matter) really does function. How much popular participation is involved in making and implementing policies? What is its quality and scope? What are the social pressures, economic constraints and political directives that provide the overall framework for popular activity and consent?

In place of what he calls the 'constrictive dichotomy of force and consent', Therborn suggests a much more differentiated spectrum for assessing citizen–state relations: accomodation to the powers that be; a sense of inevitability; a sense of being represented ('where rulers are obeyed because they are seen as ruling on behalf of the ruled');[75] deference; fear and resignation. Whereas from a normative point of view (conceived in an abstract way) there is a clear, all-important divide between force and consent, in practice, Therborn argues, the two are interrelated in a complex manner:

> the course of action to which one consents is always dependent on the situation, on what is perceived as existing and possible – in other words, on a constellation of forces. Any regime can produce its own social consent by presenting all outright opposition with impossible odds.[76]

Popular consent may not necessarily involve a sense of representation: at the same time, it need not be the product of fear. Resignation, deference, accommodation, a sense of inevitability, suggest a range of responses far more nuanced and complex than the simple political choice between coercion or consent. The line between these polar opposites is 'intrinsically blurred'.[77] Therborn develops his analysis mainly in the context of an assessment of ideology and power in bourgeois-democratic states: how useful is his critique of the coercion/consent conceptualisation in relation to the political processes of the socialist world?

THE SOVIET STATE: 'ELEMENTS OF DEMOCRACY'?

It is a curious fact that while the dichotomised models of the socialist state based on coercion and consent have been brought into prominence recently through neo-Gramscian trends in Marxist theory, academic political scientists have, since the mid-1950s, begun to move away from them. Hough commented in 1972 on a group of scholars who were unwilling to characterise the Soviet system as either a dictatorship or a democracy but who were gravitating instead towards a model of 'institutional pluralism' – a model that acknowledged a flow of ideas and power *up* the administrative hierarchy as well as down.[78] While these empirical studies have normative implications of their own (in terms for example, of a 'relaxed' attitude towards the USSR), they break significantly and fruitfully, in my view, from the *abstract* normative models inherited from the classical liberal tradition.

Here I wish to deal briefly with the question of popular participation and dissent in Communist Party states and the USSR in particular. Hough, for example, characterises the Brezhnev era as one in which citizen participation *increased* and in which public debate was fuller and more wide ranging than prior to 1964.[79] This approach at least has the merit of focusing upon real trends in a comparative way and seeks to avoid what Hough calls elsewhere 'good–evil' dichotomies.[80] Medvedev, on the other hand, despite the wealth of insights in his work, focuses less upon real development than upon the departure from abstract ideals. Marx and Engels, he argues, saw society under socialism as ordered in such a way that the free development of each serves the free development of all. 'We are still far from this ideal', he complains: 'real guarantees for the free development of each individual do not exist'; 'basic democratic rights and freedoms are absent', while the 'overwhelming majority of the working people do not participate as they should in the political life of our country'.[81] 'Real democracy' and a 'true socialist society' have yet to appear.

Given the political traditions, level of economic development and historical experience of the Soviet Union, the question has to be posed: how relevant is it to apply, as the norm of judgement, Marx's ideal of stateless communism in which 'the direct, material production process is stripped of the form of penury and antithesis', thus giving way to the 'free development of individualities'?[82] Might it not be more realistic to ask how people *should* participate in the light of how they *do* participate? Medvedev's ideal implies a state of freedom in which public power has lost its political character and class divisions have withered away. Does it not make more sense to look at the rights Soviet citizens *should* enjoy in terms of what is actually available?; to offer normative judgements in the light of concrete realities. When we do, the abstract dichotomies of coercion and consent, dictatorship versus democracy, begin to blur. If the coercion/consent analysis oversimplifies the political process under capitalism, there is reason to believe that it is even more misleading for an understanding of the politics of socialist states.

In Therborn's view, the coercion/consent analysis originates as an idealised portrait of the liberal state in a capitalist market society. It presupposes a relationship between politics and economics quite unlike that which prevails in existing socialist systems. In the socialist state, *political* leaders are charged with the responsibility for many of the functions which would be carried out by the spontaneous decision-making of the private economic sector under capitalism. This is why Therborn emphasises in an earlier work that 'existing socialist states exhibit a relationship between state personnel and citizens which is radically different from that of bourgeois states',[83] and he notes, in particular, the centrality of the cadre role – the conscious exercise of political leadership in the party, state, economy, mass organisations, scientific and cultural institutions, etc. This makes it especially inappropriate therefore to examine questions of consent and participation in terms of the spontaneous and undirected activity of private individuals, because here the very mechanisms for producing and reproducing society's goods and services are explicitly political in character. Production takes place in terms of the *plan*. This not only influences the character of participation; it also affects the question of dissent. Istvan Meszaros has noted that whereas the liberal state (in normal times) has little to worry about in the manifestation of political dissent 'so long as the impersonal mechanisms of commodity production carry on their function undisturbed',[84] the situation in the post-revolutionary states, as he calls them, is more complex. Dissent and disagreement may have a much more *direct* impact upon the economic process, since it is in the political arena that the key economic decisions are made. Developments towards accepting more dissent and organised opposition can only strengthen the planning process if, as Meszaros puts it, these trends involve an 'institutionally underpinned distribution of political power' that does not endanger 'the prevailing mode of extracting surplus labour as such'.[85] There are no invisible hands, self-regulatory mechanisms, which would allow dissenters to say what they please 'without changing anything at all'.

What this means, therefore, is that questions of participation and consent in the socialist state need to be analysed in the context of a *planned* society without the regulatory mechanism of the impersonal market. To insist that political participation can only take place if it is 'truly voluntary'[86] is highly problematical, because in these kinds of societies, activity from 'below' is always linked to conscious leadership from 'above'. This would seem to be borne out by Churchward's analysis of the Soviet system. Churchward notes growing popular involvement in Soviet politics in terms of the extension of the powers of republican and local government, the whittling-down of the police, the enlargement of citizens' rights, the attempt to strengthen legal norms underpinning government, and a broadening of the process of consultation and discussion in decision-making: yet all these changes have, he argues, *also* involved both maintaining and strengthening the 'directing role of the Communist Party'[87] – a directing role that implies *both* pressure from above and greater involvement and participation from below. Friedgut speaks of a mobilised participation rather than an autonomous participation, and in assessing the significance of the elections to the local soviets, comments that 'the people will choose, but the *apparat* will act as "guiding hand" in making the choice'. 'Neither brute force nor spontaneity are permissible'.[88] The participation is both genuine as well as limited, just as in Churchward's view, the partnership between the party and working class is a real though unequal one. On the one hand, activity is 'prompted and supervised at all levels by the Communist Party'; on the other hand, the complexity, number and scope of worker organisations in the USSR produce 'more than anywhere else in Soviet society the democratic practices of free discussion, variety of opinion and individual and group initiatives'.[89]

By defining democracy in terms of the autonomous consent of private individuals, coercion/consent theorists tend, in Therborn's view, to depict political processes in terms of 'unitary conscious subjects, legitimate or illegitimate governments, consenting or dissenting peoples'.[90] Yet the point that emerges from Stephen White's work on political culture in the Soviet Union is just how uneven and heterogenous citizen involvement and popular enthusiasm is and how unrealistic it would be to assume some kind of simple, rationalistic motivation on the part of participants. On the one hand, the regime is 'a substantially legitimate one',[91] with even dissident opinion suggesting that a high proportion of people in the USSR would continue voting for the system, even given the hypothetical opportunity to do otherwise.[92] On the other hand, elements of dissonance between the political culture and the political system still remain, in terms of the survival of religion, the strength of nationalist sub-cultures and a dissident counter-culture.[93] Greater education and non-manual occupations are closely associated with more favourable attitudes towards socio-political activity, with the better-educated and more highly qualified being more likely to participate with disinterested motives.[94] It may well be that, overall, people do not (in Medvedev's phrase) participate as they should, that is as communist-minded citizens imbued with the ideal of the free development of each as the free development of all; but on this point White's analysis recalls Marx's comment that communist societies do not develop 'on their own foundations' but *emerge* from the past 'still stamped with the birth marks of the old society'.[95] In White's view, the popularity of the Soviet political system arises less from the regime's efforts at propagating Marxist values than from the continued influence of traditional political culture with its strong Russian nationalist component, etc. 'Soviet citizens remain overwhelmingly the product of their distinctive historical experience',[96] and the complex manner in which the old norms have been carried over and transcended cannot be grasped through a series of abstract antitheses derived from classical liberalism.

Hence, for all these reasons, we would support Churchward's argument that the old designations are unsatisfactory, and that like most political systems today the Soviet polity is a mixed one that contains elements of democracy. These elements co-exist with pronounced hierarchy, for while the formally leading agencies of party and state are becoming more important, 'key national decisions, both domestic and foreign affairs, are still taken by a small body of leaders in which one person may have decisive influence'.[97]

Viewed from the standpoint of the Marxist classics, it must be said that the Soviet state is still very much a *state*. It may be that, as part of a long-term historical process, 'our statehood', as Brezhnev put it, 'is gradually being transformed into communist social self-government',[98] but for the time being, the essentially coercive state structure remains, as a framework which is *integral* to the participation and pluralism, democracy and consent which has deepened over recent years. The armour which cannot be organically separated from the hegemony which it protects. The new model of Marxist politics, with its rediscovered antinomy between coercion and consent, has certainly helped to stimulate an enormous revival of interest in the problem of the state, power, democracy and socialism, but is this model not ultimately an 'archaism'[99] which has really failed to further advance political science? As long as individuals continue to express their consent within the framework of the state, things are much more complex than the coercion/consent analysis of politics would allow.

NOTES

1. In 1977, for example, the Italian political organisation, *Il Manifesto*, organised a conference in Venice on the subject 'Power and Opposition in Post-Revolutionary Societies'. The published papers of the Communist University of London dealt with *Class, Hegemony and Party* in 1977 and *Politics, Ideology and the State* in 1978. Echoes of the debate between Ralph Miliband and Nicos Poulantzas continue to reverberate, and more recently, a bi-annual series of articles, reviews, etc. has been published entitled *Politics and Power*.

2. See, for example, L. Althusser, 'The Crisis of Marxism' in Il Manifesto (ed.), *Power and Opposition in Post-Revolutionary Societies* (London, 1979) p. 234; E. Altvater and O. Kallscheuer, 'Socialist Politics and the "Crisis of Marxism" ', *The Socialist Register 1979* (London, 1979) p. 105.

3. R. Miliband, *The State in Capitalist Society* (London, 1973) p. 8; R. Miliband, *Marxism and Politics* (Oxford, 1977) p. 43.

4. See, for example, E. Hobsbawm, 'Gramsci and Political Theory', *Marxism Today*, vol. 21 (1977) pp. 205–13; C. Mouffe, 'Introduction: Gramsci Today', in C. Mouffe (ed.), *Gramsci and Marxist Theory* (London, 1979) pp. 1–18; C. Buci-Glucksmann, *Gramsci and the State* (London, 1980).

5. C. Pateman, *The Problem of Political Obligation* (Chicester, 1979) p. 2.

6. A. Gramsci, *Selections from the Prison Notebooks* (London, 1971) p. 170.

7. Ibid, p. 244.

8. Thus Gramsci described the liberal parliamentary regime as a system 'characterised by the combination of force and consent, which balance each other reciprocally, without force predominating excessively': ibid, p. 80n. Under socialism, Gramsci considered that it would be necessary to construct 'in the envelope of the political society, a complex and well-articulated civil society in which each individual governs himself': cited by Buci-Glucksmann, *Gramsci*, p. 263.

9. J. Fabre, F. Hincker and L. Sève, *Les Communistes et l'Etat* (Paris, 1977) p. 71.

10. L. Althusser, *Lenin and Philosophy and Other Essays* (London, 1971) p. 143.

11. S. Carrillo, *Eurocommunism and the State* (London, 1977) p. 76.

12. Ibid, p. 149.

13. Ibid, p. 164.

14. Ibid, p. 158.

15. L. Radice, 'Communism with an Italian Face', in G. Urban (ed.), *Eurocommunism* (London, 1978) pp. 43, 47.

16. E. Balibar, 'The Dictatorship of the Proletariat', *Marxism Today*, vol. 21 (1977) p. 146.

17. L. Sève, 'The Leninist Development of the Strategy of Peaceful Development', *Marxism Today*, vol. 21 (1977) p. 140.

18. K. Marx and F. Engels, *Selected Works* (London 1968) p. 339.

19. D. McLellan (ed.), *Karl Marx: Selected Writings* (Oxford, 1977) p. 563.

20. K. Marx and F. Engels, *Selected Correspondence* (Moscow, 1965) p. 255.

21. Marx and Engels, *Selected Works*, p. 53.
22. Miliband, *The State in Capitalist Society*, p. 7.
23. M. Evans, *Karl Marx* (London, 1975) p. 110. Because Marx's use of the term 'politics' is so *specific* – not only in the *Communist Manifesto* but in the 'jottings' on Bakunin where he speaks of the proletariat using 'coercive means, hence governmental means' (McLellan, *Karl Marx: Selected Writings*, p. 237) – I must express my doubts about Neil Harding's ingenious argument that, for Marx, the Paris Commune had ceased to be a state-form: N. Harding, *Lenin's Political Thought*, vol. 2 (London, 1981) pp. 89–90. For Marx describes the Commune as a 'political form', albeit 'thoroughly expansive', 'essentially a working-class government': K. Marx and F. Engels, *On the Paris Commune* (Moscow, 1971) p. 75; and in the first draft of the *Civil War in France*, there is reference to the fact that the Commune does not do away with 'the class struggles' but 'affords the rational medium in which that class struggle can run through its different phases in the most rational and humane way' (Marx and Engels, *On the Paris Commune*, p. 156).
24. K. Marx, *Capital*, vol. III (Moscow, 1966) p. 384. I am grateful to Ali Rattansi of the School of Education, University of Leicester, for his comments on the way Marx developed this argument and for his more general observations about this paper.
25. Marx and Engels, *On the Paris Commune*, p. 73. The problem of the 'common activities' of the state has featured in the controversy around Eurocommunist definitions of the state. Mandel, for example, warns against 'an equation of the *social* functions of the state which it fulfils in order to satisfy the objective needs of production and the state as an instrument of class domination. Postmen and railway workers should be seen as serving the interests of "material reproduction" rather than the reproduction of a given social structure': E. Mandel, *From Stalinism to Eurocommunism* (London, 1978) p. 154.
26. Gramsci, *Selections from Prison Notebooks*, p. 12.
27. Cited by Buci-Glucksmann, *Gramsci* p. 155.
28. Gramsci, *Selections from Prison Notebooks*, p. 12.
29. P. Anderson, 'The Antinomies of Antonio Gramsci', *New Left Review*, no. 100 (November 1976–January 1977) p. 46.
30. Mouffe, 'Introduction: Gramsci Today', p. 10.
31. Gramsci, *Selections from Prison notebooks*, p. 161.
32. Ibid, p. 160.
33. Buci-Glucksmann, *Gramsci*, pp. 154–5.
34. F. Burlatsky, *The Modern State and Politics* (Moscow, 1978) p. 51. See further, A. H. Brown's discussion of Burlatsky's view of the state in the present volume.
35. E. Balibar, *The Dictatorship of the Proletariat* (London, 1977) p. 103.
36. Gramsci, *Selections*, p. 80.
37. For further discussion on this point, see Anderson, 'Antinomies', p. 26; and Fabre, Hincker and Sève, *Les Communistes* p. 71.
38. Gramsci, *Selections*, p. 236.
39. Ibid, p. 57.
40. Ibid, p. 56n.

41. Marx and Engels, *Collected Works*, vol. 5 (London 1976) p. 329. If Marx takes the side of those who regard power rather than will as the basis of politics, Gramsci is not so sure. He seems to want a much greater place for voluntarism – see his comments: Man is 'concrete will' (*Selections*, p. 360) or 'the nature of man is spirit' (p. 355) – and I incline therefore to the view that Gramsci was to a 'certain degree a party to the absorption of Marxism within idealism which it had been his intention to oppose': S. Timpanaro, *On Materialism* (London, 1975) p. 237.
42. Marx and Engels, *Selected Works*, p. 660.
43. Marx and Engels, *On the Paris Commune*, p. 154; p. 73.
44. It is true that Marx in his *Critique of Hegel's Philosophy of Right* contrasts a 'real state', 'the state as the existence of a people as a whole', with an 'abstract', 'political state' (*Collected Works*, vol. 3, London, 1975, p. 78) but this formulation disappears from Marx's work after 1843.
45. M. Harrison, 'Stalin – A Centenary View', *Marxism Today*, vol. 23 (1979) p. 23.
46. Ibid, p. 25.
47. R. Tucker, 'Stalinism as Revolution From Above', in Tucker (ed.), *Stalinism: Essays in Historical Interpretation* (New York, 1977) p. 92.
48. V. I. Lenin, *Collected Works*, vol. 33 (Moscow, 1966) p. 71.
49. Ibid, p. 66.
50. Harrison, 'Stalin', p. 23.
51. Lenin, *Collected Works*, vol. 33, p. 116; Tucker, 'Stalinism as Revolution From Above', p. 92.
52. Lenin, *Collected Works*, vol. 31, P. 44.
53. Cited by S. Cohen, *Bukharin and the Bolshevik Revolution* (London, 1974) p. 130.
54. Cited by Tucker, 'Stalinism as Revolution From Above', p. 87.
55. Harrison, 'Stalin', p. 23.
56. S. Cohen, 'Bukharin and the Eurocommunist Idea', in V. Aspaturian and J. Valenta (eds), *Eurocommunism Between East and West* (Bloomington, Indiana, 1980) p. 68.
57. Cohen, *Bukharin and the Bolshevik Revolution*, p. 129.
58. Ibid, p. 246.
59. Ibid, p. 250.
60. Ibid, p. 252.
61. Harrison, 'Stalin', p. 25.
62. S. Cohen, 'Bolshevism and Stalinism', in Tucker (ed.), *Stalinism*, p. 27.
63. Tucker (ed.), *Stalinism*, p. 324.
64. Harrison, 'Stalin', p. 24.
65. Ibid, p. 26.
66. Cited by M. Lewin, *Political Undercurrents in Soviet Economic Debates* (London, 1975) p. 28.
67. R. Medvedev, *Let History Judge* (London, 1971) p. 362.
68. Tucker, 'Stalinism as Revolution From Above', p. 101.
69. Cohen argues that the 'bifurcation of Bolshevism' he purports to discover – into 'prudent pragmatism' and 'revolutionary heroism' – echoes 'a duality in Marxism itself where voluntarism and determinism had been subtly interwoven' (Cohen, *Bukharin and the Bolshevik Revolution*,

p. 129). Yet classical Marxism sought to transcend this duality with the argument that determinism can be *dialectically* interpreted so as to both account for *action* and lay the basis for its success. As Marx puts it in *The Holy Family*: 'if man is shaped by his surroundings, his surroundings must be made human' (*Collected Works*, vol. 4, London, 1976, p. 131). I discuss this question in some detail in my *Marxism and the Theory of Praxis* (London, 1975) ch. 7.

70. Anderson, 'Antinomies', p. 43.

71. See, for example, the comment in *The German Ideology* to the effect that as long as the state is historically necessary, the proletariat 'cannot assert themselves as individuals': *Collected Works*, vol. 5, p. 80.

72. Anderson, 'Antinomies', p. 41.

73. G. Therborn, *The Ideology of Power and the Power of Ideology* (London, 1980) p. 104. Paul Connerton argues that likewise in the case of Habermas's principle of free discussion as the basis of a critical public sphere, there is a strong echo of the bourgeois abstractions of the late eighteenth century. The appeal of these abstractions to the Frankfurt School arises, he suggests, from the insecurity and lateness of liberal humanism in German history: P. Connerton, *The Tragedy of Enlightenment* (Cambridge, 1980) pp. 107, 139. Might it not be also the case that given the 'semi-feudal residues' of the southern question in Italy, Gramsci felt the need to incorporate into Marxism, Croce's ethico-political history and his liberal concept of the ethical state? Certainly Carrillo, writing in the context of a Spain about to emerge from fascism, looks to socialism to 'recover for itself the democratic and liberal values': Carrillo, *Eurocommunism*, p. 98.

74. Here I agree with David McLellan who made this point vigorously while acting as discussant when the paper was presented to the Political Studies Association Communist Politics Group at their conference on State in Socialist Society, September 1981. Therborn, on the other hand, does seem to assume that an empirical analysis implies a non-normative view (Therborn, *Ideology of Power*, p. 105). I would like to acknowledge the value of both David McLellan's comments and the general discussion at the conference in assisting me to revise this paper for publication.

75. Therborn, *Ideology of Power*, p. 96.

76. Ibid, p. 108.

77. Ibid, p. 109.

78. J. Hough, 'The Soviet System: Petrification or Pluralism', *Problems of Communism*, vol. 21 (1972) p. 28.

79. J. Hough, 'The Brezhnev Era. The Man and his System', *Problems of Communism*, vol. 25 (1976) pp. 8–9. See also the analysis in J. Hough, 'Political Participation in the Soviet Union', *Soviet Studies*, vol. xxviii (1976) pp. 3–20.

80. Hough, 'The Soviet System: Petrification or Pluralism', p. 41.

81. R. Medvedev, *On Socialist Democracy* (London, 1975) p. xvi; p. 25.

82. Marx's comment in the *Grundrisse* (Harmondsworth, 1973) p. 706. My attention was drawn to this quotation by Istvan Meszaros, 'Political Power and Dissent in Post-Revolutionary Societies', in Il Manifesto (ed.), *Power and Opposition*, p. 111.

83. G. Therborn, *What Does the Ruling Class Do When It Rules?* (London, 1978) p. 109.
84. I. Meszaros, 'Political Power', p. 123.
85. Ibid, p. 127.
86. This appears to be the position of A. L. Unger, 'Political Participation in the USSR: YCL and CPSU', *Soviet Studies*, vol. xxxiii (1981) p. 111.
87. L. Churchward, *Contemporary Soviet Government* (London, 1975) p. 304.
88. T. H. Friedgut, *Political Participation in the USSR* (Princeton, New Jersey, 1979) p. 144.
89. Churchward, *Contemporary Soviet Government*, p. 269.
90. Therborn, *Ideology of Power*, p. 102.
91. S. White, 'The USSR: Patterns of Autocracy and Industrialism', in A. Brown and J. Gray (eds), *Political Culture and Political Change in Communist States*, 2nd edn (London, 1979) p. 44.
92. White, 'The USSR', p. 42.
93. Ibid, p. 58.
94. Ibid, p. 52.
95. Marx and Engels, *Selected Works*, p. 323.
96. White, 'The USSR', p. 48.
97. Churchward, *Contemporary Soviet Government*, p. 304.
98. L. Brezhnev, *On the Draft Constitution of the USSR and the Results of the Nationwide Discussion of the Draft* (Moscow, 1977) p. 35.
99. Therborn, *Ideology of Power*, p. 100.

5 The 'Nationality Problem' and the Soviet State[1]

Peter Rutland

Any attempt to come to grips with the nature of the Soviet state must necessarily involve some explanation of the phenomenon of national identity. As the Soviet Union enters its sixtieth year, it remains a multinational state, and one in which national beliefs are strongly held. The hopes of certain Marxists that national identity would slip from the historical agenda remain a project for the distant future, rather than a description of the present.

When one turns to contemporary literature on nationalism in the Soviet Union, one finds a single model dominating the field.[2] Specialists writing in the area do not devote much time to method-ological argument, but instead advance a commonsensical and unprob-lematic view of the meaning and significance that can be attached to national identity, national animosities and prejudices in Soviet life. This can be summed up in the view that there is a 'nationality pro-blem' confronting the Soviet leadership, in that the national loyalties of the various minority nationalities, and of the Russian majority itself, give a direction to their political activities that runs counter to that desired by the Soviet leadership. Nationalism having been estab-lished as a problem, either implicitly or explicitly, the writers then proceed to chart its various dimensions, usually with an interesting and impressive marshalling of such facts as are available concerning this sensitive and shadowy side of political life.

On one hand, the various minority nationalities and ethnic groups are held to be disenchanted with their subordinate position in the Soviet family of nations. In all spheres of life – cultural, linguistic, economic, political and religious – they are seen as struggling to pre-serve their identity and win some autonomy in the face of the tremen-dous centralising tendencies of the Soviet state (and the rival claims of their neighbouring nations). On the other hand, the Russian people are held to be able to exploit the centralised state to their own advantage, because of their numerical and historical dominance.

This commonsensical approach to Soviet nationalism has a fine pedigree, and can be said to be as old as the Soviet state itself. From the very beginning many commentators, most notably the 'Promethean' movement in Poland in the 1920s, predicted that the Bolsheviks would find it impossible to maintain control over the varied and innumerable national groups which they had inherited from their Tsarist predecessors.[3] The approach also strikes a chord with popular writers today. General Sir John Hackett's best-selling *Third World War*, for example, culminates in the break-up of the Soviet state, with Central Asia going over to China, and a Ukrainian coup in Moscow.[4]

It will be argued in this chapter that such accounts are based on a serious misunderstanding of the dynamics of ethnic identity in the USSR. While it would be foolish to deny that there is a good deal of truth in these mainstream accounts, the case will be made for a more complex treatment of nationalism in the Soviet Union, in which it is shown that, in some respects at least, national identity can be channelled in ways that are integrative and system-supporting, rather than constituting a purely negative political force.

The first part of the chapter criticises the theoretical assumptions underlying the conventional treatments of nationalism in the USSR: in the second part, a more differentiated model of nationalism is developed through an examination of current Soviet nationality theory, and a look at some sensitive aspects of their nationality policy. In the final rather more speculative section it is argued that there is a need to supplement the foregoing 'functionalist' accounts of national phenomena with some attention to nationalism as symbolic activity.

PROBLEMS OF DEFINITION AND APPROACH

It would not seem unreasonable to begin such an account with a study of what is meant by the terms 'nation' and 'nationalism'. Attempts at a comprehensive definition of nationalism are notoriously unsuccessful: nevertheless, it is worth embarking on the exercise, if only because it provides an insight into the problems to be encountered in incorporating this rather slippery concept into political science in general and Soviet studies in particular.[5]

It proves to be impossible to find generally accepted objective criteria for one's definition of a nation. Neither language, territory, religion, culture, nor a 'common history' can be consistently deployed as a test of nationhood. All such definitions run into a stream of counter-examples – nations without territory, nations speaking another's language, or many languages, and so on. One solution is to abandon the attempt altogether, and retreat into history – some nations are born and grow to full maturity, others wither away, and only when the Owl of Minerva takes to the air will we be able to tell one from the other. Others turn instead to composite definitions, the most famous of which is Stalin's: '*A nation is a historically constituted, stable community of people, formed on the basis of a common language, territory, economic life and psychological make-up, manifested in a common culture*'[6] (a definition still used by Soviet writers today).[7]

Most writers, in fact, move directly to consideration of the subjective expression of nationalist beliefs, and do not see the need for any objective criteria for the definition of the object of these sentiments. Nationalism at the most fundamental level is seen as a set of beliefs held by certain individuals about their community, what Rakowska-Harmstone terms 'a collective "We" as opposed to an alien "They"'.[8] The safest definition therefore seems to be nationalism as subjective affiliation; but having established this, it is rather difficult to know how to proceed. Political scientists are rarely in a position to establish what people believe by mounting surveys and suchlike (while historians are even less likely to be in such a position!). However, this subjective sense of belonging, or of prejudice against other peoples, *is used* as a basis for political analysis, by being taken as providing the motivation for political action, and, in a more general sense, as constituting the framework, the realm of discourse, for political activity. And upon these theoretical foundations a powerful and all-pervasive model of nationalist behaviour can be raised. It is indisputable that the national framework is an integral part of modern life: there are few people in the world today who would claim no ethnic or national loyalties. However, this commonsense fact is given normative impetus by the assumption that when people express a national identity they are also subscribing to a particular view of the world: in other words, that nationalism gives a general meaning to their political activities, and supplies them with a specific set of goals.

When this interpretation of nationalism is applied to Soviet politics, one is struck initially by the fact that these personal feelings of belonging are viewed as lying outside the sphere of the state's control, and can therefore be counterposed to officially condoned political activity. In other words, a totalitarian state is not seen as relying upon the subjective affiliations of its citizenry. The state-versus-citizen argument is reinforced by a view of Soviet Marxism as a class-based ideology to which the whole idea of nationhood is anathema (of which more below). Thus, from the outset, nationality cannot fail to be a problem for the Soviet leadership.

Writers see nationalist drives at work in virtually every sphere of political, social and economic life. One occasionally finds examples of pure, explicitly nationality-based behaviour – the struggles of the Crimean Tatars for the restoration of their home republic; the demonstrations in Tbilisi in 1978, protesting at the failure to mention Georgian as the official language in the new draft Constitution. Moving on to broader cultural activity, religious dissent in the Western Ukraine and Lithuania is, clearly, inextricably bound up with the national feelings of these peoples. But commentators range still more widely in their search for evidence of nationalist behaviour. Labour migration, theatre-visiting, struggles over the state budget, book-publishing policy, faction-fighting within the Party, regional planning: in each and every one of these areas it is assumed that political agents interact within a framework of national rivalry, and are motivated by feelings of ethnic loyalty.

Thus according to what may be termed the 'narrow functionalist' approach, nationality is seen as serving (or having the potential to serve) as an all-purpose vehicle for political activity. General criticisms of such an approach to nationalism in the USSR can be considered under five main headings.

First, the concept is stipulative rather than reportive, in that evidence is collected on the prior assumption that nationalism is a 'problem'. Analysts range far and wide in their search for such evidence, and any data series, however mundane, which can be broken down on a nationality basis is marshalled as a proxy for nationalist dissatisfaction. How much meaning can be read into the fact that such statistics vary between nationalities? Take the pressing example of the contrast between the numerically exploding Central Asian population, and the stagnant Slavs. To what extent are people aware of a 4 per cent rise in the share of the population of Moslem origin over a 20-year period[9] – let alone the question of whether this is perceived as a threat. This is a very difficult question to answer: still more so if one is speculating as to the likely political sensitivity of an estimated further rise of 8 per cent (bringing the total to 23 per cent) by the year 2 000.[10] At this point the argument frequently takes on a Catch 22 quality – the problem is both that there are too many Russians (taking the best jobs in the Central Asian towns) and that there are too few Russians (swamped by the expanding native populations). It would appear that Soviet leaders are trapped in a set of insoluable dilemmas, in that just about any policy adopted by them – education, migration, economic development – is categorised as part of the problem rather than part of the solution. This situation arises because the analysis gives priority to subjective feelings over objective circumstances – I. Dzyuba, for example, is honest enough to see the problem in these terms, and criticises Ukrainian indifference to the fate of their nation in the face of social change, seeing this indifference as a more serious problem than 'Russification'.[11]

A second weakness of the 'narrow functionalist' approach to the politics of nationalism is that it is tied to a conflict model starker than that of any Marxist. Subjective affiliation to one community necessarily involves separating that community from its neighbours: thus nationalism revolves around the setting of boundaries, either social, cultural or territorial. Such a process is not intrinsically antagonistic, since most nationalisms recognise the right of other nations beyond their borders to exist. However, given that one cannot guarantee any agreement between the groups over where their mutual boundaries should lie, conflict is, in practice, inevitable. A similar point is made by a Soviet sociologist who criticises the tendency in Western writings on ethnicity to narrow the field to problems generated in the process of 'social interactions'.[12]

Cobban summarises the conflictual nature of nationalism thus: 'The ruthless either – or of the theory of the nation state does not allow for the infinite gradations of which the theory of nationality is capable.'[13] The insistence on 'one state – one culture'[14] forces nationalist movements into a single continuum: nations are either growing *or* declining, assimilating *or* remaining differentiated. In the Soviet case this means that on the one hand are arrayed the centripetal forces of the Soviet state, tinged with Russian nationalism, and on the other hand are the centrifugal tendencies of the minorities. It is, of course, impossible to have politics without conflict, but over the years many Western writers have been worried by the tendency of nationalism, both in theory and in practice, to expand to fill all the political space available, paving the way for the evils of war and genocide.[15] An example of the relatively uncritical transference of a conflict model of nationalism to Soviet society is provided by S. White. He argues that nationalist sub-cultures 'may conflict with or altogether supersede' overall national loyalties, implicitly ruling out other possibilities, such as that they might co-exist, and even supplement each other.[16]

The fallacious basis of a conflict model of national identity is illuminated by studies in the field of child psychology. Loyalty to a community develops in children over the years 7 to 12, and there is no evidence that they develop a sense of belonging to one particular community to the detriment of their other loyalties. One Scottish study showed how children are aware of themselves as Glaswegians *and* Scots *and* British.[17] It will be argued below that a similar differentiated hierarchy of national identity is at work in the USSR today.

The third criticism that can be levelled against mainstream accounts is that they give a unity and internal cohesion to the national community which it simply does not possess. Gellner points out that only in primitive societies can one talk of culture as a quality pervading all areas of community life: as soon as the social division of labour gets under way, culture itself becomes to some extent a specialised activity, one that in the modern era has tended to be the preserve of the intelligentsia.[18] There is no justification for supposing that the various social groups all share the same relationship to the cultural sphere: the nation no longer speaks with one voice. The perception of the Ukrainian nation held by Piotr Shelest, who was dismissed from his position as head of the Ukrainian CP in 1972 for, among other faults, an incorrect approach to the nationality question, will clearly differ from that held by his fellow countryman, the dissident intellectual, Valentyn Moroz, who was preoccupied with the general issue of 'the spectre of mass culture'.[19] There is some evidence (from the voting patterns of American ethnic minorities)[20] that it is those least qualified as members of the ethnic community on cultural grounds who are most likely to act politically along ethnic lines. The only general, cross-national conclusion that it is suggested be drawn from this example is the need to stress the heterogeneity of the ethnic community.

The fourth point to be made is that there is a need for careful historical periodisation. This is not merely a call for a taxonomy of 'the nation' in its journey through history: there are no grounds for assuming that the 'sense of national belonging' is the same nation at different stages of its history, nor that it is roughly comparable for different nations in the same historical period. This is not a controversial point, since all writers on the Soviet nationality issue are driven in the course of their narrative to concede that the nature of the nationality problem has shifted markedly through time, as civil war, collectivisation, the purges, Nazi invasion and socioeconomic development have pressed on different aspects of the national heritage. Likewise, it makes no sense to talk in the same breath of national cultures that are well established and in no danger of disappearing overnight (the Balt, Transcaucasian and Ukrainian); alongside others with a more precarious historical existence (Belorussian and Moldavian); and others whose national consciousness largely arrived after Soviet power itself was established (most notably in the Central Asian republics). The position of national groups without Union-Republican status is still more complex – in size alone they vary from groups of five hundred to two million.

It is felt necessary to underline here the need for a discriminating approach, simply because the frequent and traumatic shifts in the issues over the past half century, and the tremendously variegated historical experiences of the Soviet peoples, tend to be subsumed in discussions of 'the' nationality problem in the USSR. This point is stressed by Soviet theorists, who draw heavily upon Marx's condemnation of a supra-historical approach to social issues.[21] However, this contradicts the concept of nationalism as subjective affiliation, which is inherently ahistorical; ethnic identity seems to be as old as the human community itself (older still, if we are to believe the sociobiologists).

It is when these ahistorical aspects of nationalism are transferred to accounts of the way it functions within the political process that the problems really begin. For the extent to which nationalism has served as an instrument to advance political interests, and the nature of its instrumental role, have varied considerably through history. At least four phases in the functionality of nationalism can be distinguished. (Western criticisms of these functional stages will be left aside, and attention concentrated on their applicability to Soviet conditions.)[22] Initially, the nation reinforced the process of state formation in Western Europe; and then went on to serve as a force undermining the ramshackle empires in Eastern Europe. It is at this point that nationalism acquires the reputation of being a means of democratic self-expression for the masses. This view of the nation has been widespread – from Renan's definition of the nation as a 'daily plebiscite', and John Stuart Mill's view that 'free institutions are next to impossible in a country made up of different nationalities',[23] to the appeal of 'self-determination' to politicians from Woodrow Wilson to

Lenin.[24] Even Smith, writing today, refers to the nation as 'a not un-reasonable application of Enlightenment principles to the complexities of modern politics'.[25] The nation is also seen as having social and economic functions concomitant with this important political role.[26] This favourable interpretation of the nation has been carried forward to new historical circumstances – the emergence of Third World countries from colonial bondage, and the process of 'nation-building' within them. It even lives on within the imperial nations themselves, with the re-emergence of previously dormant ethnic loyalties. These are seen as being used by disaffected citizenry in need of an organising principle with which they can try to win resources from, and prevent bureaucratic smothering by, the welfare state.[27]

Given this background, it is not surprising that commentators tend to see nationalist activity in the Soviet Union in terms of the democratic self-expression of its peoples. However, the Soviet Union simply does not fit in to any of the four broad categories of nationalism in action outlined above. Interestingly, in Smith's latest work, *The Ethnic Revival*, he does not mention the USSR at all. And even Carrère d'Encausse concedes in her conclusion that there is a fundamental difference between Eastern notions of nationalism as a set of cultural characteristics, and Western understandings of it as a means of political expression – although this does not seem to have been taken into account in her preceding analysis.[28]

The USSR cannot be compared to the old Empires of Tsarist Russia or Austria–Hungary, characterised as they were by a decrepit state machine, barely able to maintain internal order, and even less able to withstand external attack. Nor are the minority nationalities, even in Central Asia, in a position comparable to that of the new Third World states. Their modernisation has been under way for sixty years, and the most traumatic phase lies behind them. It may be thought that the widespread concern with the preservation of traditional culture, combined with struggles in the economic and political spheres over plan and budget, enable the analyst to treat the movements as comparable to the ethnic resurgence currently sweeping the established states in the West. Again, however, the analogy is a false one: the extremely centralised nature of the Soviet political process precludes the sort of competing claims on resources that one sees advanced by ethnic groups in the West, not to mention the vital role played by a competitive electoral system in their emergence.[29] (See A. H. Brown's contribution to this volume on the inapplicability of pluralist models to Soviet politics.) While one cannot but be impressed by the ease with which small separatist groups can throw modern states into confusion, their success hinges on access to an open public domain. This is precisely what is lacking in the Soviet case, so that the best that groups there can hope for is that their grievances might get an airing in the West.

The argument of this first section can be summarised as follows. While it seems reasonable to have some understanding of nationalism as subjective affiliation, in the Soviet context it is unhelpful to develop this into a narrowly functional model of nationalism, whereby it serves as a conduit for a whole range of political activity.

SOVIET NATIONALITY THEORY

In this section it is argued that, by relying fairly heavily upon the accounts Soviet writers themselves give of the regime's nationality policies, a viable model of nationalism in the USSR can be constructed. The starting-point must be the recognition of the fact that 'an ideology of cosmopolitanism and national nihilism'[30] has no place in Soviet policy: they do not intend to obliterate the various ethnic loyalties within their society. It is true that Marx and Engels envisaged a future communist society where national loyalties would have no place, and that this vision was partly resurrected by Khrushchev in the 1961 Party Programme, with its talk of the 'merging' of nations, the introduction of inter-Republican economic agencies, the weakening of national borders within the USSR, and the invocation of 'the future single worldwide communist culture'.[31]

However, the position of Marx and Engels on the nation was far from unequivocal: in their concrete analyses they were prepared to treat nationalism as part of the substance of political life; and the same *Communist Manifesto* that contained the phrase 'the working men have no country' also had the disclaimer 'The Communists are further reproached with desiring to abolish countries and nationality'.[32]

The works of Lenin and Stalin are of little help in resolving this dilemma of the realisation of the future in the present. Lenin's reduction of the national question to the issue of self-determination enabled him to link national struggles to the great Revolutionary project. His aesopian pronouncements on the issue ('recognition of the right to divorce does not preclude agitation against divorce in a particular case')[33] only make sense if one subordinates national claims to the higher interests of the Revolution. Self-determination can be encouraged solely on the understanding that if it succeeds it will not have to be carried out, since the Revolution will guarantee all national rights. At least one can rescue from all this the fact that Lenin came down firmly on the side of equality between nations, against national particularism.[34]

It is not unreasonable, however, to maintain that some parts of Soviet ideology have a degree of purchase on reality while others evidently do not, and that the debate over the nature of the future communist society belongs firmly in the latter category. Looking back at the 1961 Programme, it is difficult to understand why it was so readily interpreted as a blueprint for the transformation of national relations. Khrushchev's formulations were far from extreme – for example, he recognised that 'the effacement of national distinctions is a considerably longer process than the effacement of class distinctions'.[35] Moreover, his comments were tempered in discussion by, for example, Podgorny's condemnation of spurious compaigns against Ukrainian nationalism under the 'toady and true sadist' Kaganovich.[36] The debate over the new Constitution which sporadically occupied the years 1962 to 1977 rarely reached Khrushchevian heights. The dispute was confined to the largely theological issue of the precise nature of the USSR as a federal state – whether the right of Union Republics to secede should be maintained, whether possession of a state machine of its own is an essential part of sociality nationhood,[37] and so on. The former dispute reflects a simple reluctance to depart from any of Lenin's pronouncements, and the importance of the concept of federalism itself has been grossly exaggerated. Given that it is held to be a federalism of a new and unique type,[38] it is difficult, if not impossible, to discuss it without slipping into inapplicable Western notions of dual sovereignity and so on.

The whole issue of the 'merging' of national cultures has slipped back over the future horizon of Soviet ideologists.[39] Instead, stress is laid on the other components of Khrushchev's programme – the 'flourishing' of national consciousness and culture under socialism, leading to the 'drawing together' of nations in the direction of complete unity.[40] None of these formulations envisages the disappearance of national identities in the foreseeable future, and their use seems to be governed by a set of rules that reinforce this view. Thus the 'merging' of nations is invariably linked to their 'flourishing' (usually in the same sentence); the equality of nations is underlined; and the processes are seen as 'objective', and cannot therefore be falsely speeded up – or held back.

This cautious approach to the issue of nationality draws upon a variety of sources, chief among which is the manifest impracticality of the 'merging' hypothesis, and a disinclination to indulge in Khrushchevian speculation as to the date of the final victory of communism. Thus the current policy is simply a continuation of the underlying themes of Soviet policy from previous years. Carrère d'Encausse points out that support for such a cautious policy can be found even in the writings of Stalin, since most of the components of his definition of the nation were factors of a permanent nature.[41] Leaders since Khrushchev have been careful to spell out the limitations and problems in the sphere of nationality policy. Thus, for example, Brezhnev declared that 'Nationality relations, even in a society of mature socialism, are a reality that is constantly developing and putting forth new problems and tasks.'[42]

Support for this line has come also from the international dimension: the Soviet Union is acutely aware of the intensity of the nationality question in the rest of the world, principally through its contacts with the national liberation movements, and it cannot afford to leave it in a theoretical vacuum. In addition, during the last decade a significant contribution has been made by Soviet anthropologists, who have been laboriously cataloguing the minutiae of Soviet ethnic life for many years.[43] Leading ethnographers such as Yu. Bromlei, operating within the framework of historical materialism, advance a general theory of the nature of communal loyalty, progressing from the tribe through the ethnic group to the nation. This 'ethnosociology' has now become an acceptable aspect of the study of personality formation and the dynamics of collectives in Soviet society. An interesting example is the work of A. F. Dashdamirov, where the ethnos is located in a hierarchy of loyalties, from the family to the state, tied together by an explictly structural-functional account of Soviet society.[44]

Soviet policy in practice has consistently recognised the legitimacy of national identity within the framework of the Soviet state (which anyway will find it a cheap concession to make). There have of course been a number of notable exceptions (Crimean Tatars, Chechens, etc.),[45] and at a lower level the number of ethnic designations did drop from 178 to 109 in the period 1926–59, due to the disappearance of extremely small ethnic groups such as the exotically named Svan,

Mishan and Lazy.[46] In concrete policy terms, this means that citizens have the right to register the ethnic identity of their choice at age 16, and are free to record a different loyalty in subsequent censuses. A complex administrative structure, with 53 different national organs, has been devised to give a degree of statehood to each national group.

Moving on to the terminology of the 'flourishing' and 'drawing together' of nations, these terms are endowed with a specific meaning in Soviet eyes. First, it should be noted that within the Soviet Union there is a very concrete understanding of national culture. Rather than being merely a vague sense of belonging, it is a specific set of social characteristics, whose 'flourishing' can be quantitatively measured – numbers of libraries, theatres and palaces of culture, the output of books and films in the native language, and so on.[47] That this cultural development will result in a 'merging' of national cultures can be understood in several senses. First, it is assumed that all ethnic groups will develop a level of cultural activity commensurate with their status (that is, Union Republic, Autonomous Republic, Autonomous Region or Autonomous Area), at which point they will be interacting on an equal basis. Second, given the socioeconomic goals of the Soviet state, it is seen as desirable that all nations achieve a similar level of development, as measured in terms of education standards, degree of urbanisation, share of the working class in the total population, etc. This process cannot but affect the content of the national culture (which, it is admitted, is peculiarly tied to village life).[48] Nevertheless, Rutkevich resolutely argues that 'There is no warrant for confusing the process of the wiping out of social differences with a process of the wiping out of differences between nationalities.'[49] Critics would argue that this process of social equalisation cannot but leave us with an extremely attenuated, folkloric understanding of national culture.

'Drawing together' also involves the internationalisation of certain aspects of cultural life. At a general level this involves an unobjectionable openness to the fruits of world culture, and a willingness to accept other nationalities as equals (including those outside the USSR). More specifically, it involves the promotion of common patterns of behaviour in certain areas of life[50] – for example, the encouragement of inter-ethnic marriages; the development of a common technical vocabulary through word-borrowing; the eradication of 'unacceptable' features of national life inherited from the past, such as the Moslem bride price, or *Kalym* (Stalin gives as examples the quaint Caucasian traditions of self-flagellation and the vendetta!).[51] However, most of the elements of national life will be preserved: only in certain respects will there be borrowings from the life of other nations or the international community at large. Such a process need not change the character of the national community beyond recognition.

The term 'unity' poses fewer problems than the above formulations. It has a purely political meaning, referring to the 'brotherly alliance' of Soviet nations ensured by the work of the CPSU. It does not imply any social policies that threaten their nationhood: on the contrary, 'unity' logically entails the continued existence of nations, rather than their abolition.

Discussion of internationalisation brings us to the final plank in Soviet nationality theory – Soviet patriotism.[52] It is argued that there is a 'new historical community' bestriding the hierarchy of ethnic loyalties within Soviet society: namely, the community constructed around the Soviet state itself. The Soviet community is not seen merely as the sum of the various national communities: rather, it has specific features of its own. The 'Soviet People' seem to have come into existence in 1917, and have grown 'organically' since then, It is a 'new' community, differing from all other national groupings in that it is based on the universal historical agent, the working class: Soviet patriotism becomes indistinguishable from Soviet socialist ideology in general. In the political sphere this means entry into, or at least tacit support for, the CPSU – one almost has the impression that Soviet society will have moved over into communism when everyone has become a Party member. On the economic side, it means that the whole territory is treated as a single economic unit under the central Plan, with the result that, as one recent study pointed out, 'regional inequality in personal consumption is only about two-thirds of that found in the USA and approximately half that found in Japan or France'.[53] A NATO Colloquium attributed what differences there are between regions to objective conditions, rather than any deliberate policy of fostering regional inequality.[54] An interesting example of the limited scope for the differential treatment of the various regions is the 1981 decision to introduce increased maternity benefits. Although this is clearly designed to stem the falling birthrate in the Western regions, the only clear concession to the gross differences in rates of reproduction between the Republics is to delay the introduction of the scheme by one year for the Central Asian and Transcaucasian Republics.[55]

The military dimension is also important. Historically, this refers to the forging of loyalty to the Soviet state in the course of struggle against foreign invasion, particularly in the period 1941–5. (It would be inaccurate to dismiss the war period as characterised by rabid Russification alone: special attention was also devoted to ensuring the loyalty of the national minorities.)[56] The contemporary aspect of the armed forces as 'a living embodiment of socialist internationalism' (Brezhnev) is the conscription of all young males for two and a half years into non-ethnically segregated military units.

FUNCTIONAL DIFFERENTIATION IN PRACTICE

The point of this section is to stress that the peoples of the USSR do have some sort of awareness of themselves as citizens of the Soviet Union, a fact that is frequently overlooked in much of the Western literature on the nature of national identity in that country.[57] Moreover, as J. Azrael concedes, 'national pride and Soviet patriotism..can in fact co-exist and be mutually reinforcing'.[58] One can of course disagree with Soviet estimations of the strength of feeling in this regard, and with their attempts to make it qualitatively superior to other types of national identity – for example, by calling it 'patriotism'.[59]

Thus it is argued that Soviet policy envisages two levels of national identity in the Soviet Union – a sense of belonging to a particular national group, and a sense of belonging to the Soviet state. These two can co-exist partly because there is a functional differentiation between the two, with the various communal loyalties operating in different yet complementary spheres of social life. This corresponds roughly to what Smith describes as the 'accommodation' strategy adopted by certain nationalist movements[60] (the difference being that it follows from the argument above that it is seen as being more permanent and positive than in the Smith schema). Such a functional differentiation may lead to certain tensions in people's lives, and many writers have in fact referred to the almost schizophrenic character of parts of Soviet life. (For example, Zaslavsky on the role of official and unofficial language in the propagation of the state ideology; the characters that people Zinoviev's 'Ibansk'; Hingley on the exasperating Russian penchant for tall-story telling.)[61]

Language policy is an important and useful example of how the functional differentiation works in practice. Russian is promoted for technical use in the equivalent of the 'civic culture', while the minority languages are nurtured for daily use, to preserve the commitment and involvement of the citizenry.[62] Considerable efforts have been made over the years to develop national languages and dialects up to a full literary level, and the Constitution guarantees to the citizens 'the possibility to use their native tongue' (Article 36). In fact, 93.9 per cent of all citizens now habitually speak the language of their own nationality.[63] (In practice, the opportunities to exercise this right vary considerably: while you can do an engineering degree in Uzbek, many of the small national groups below ASSR level manage only a few years' schooling.) At the same time, Russian has been actively promoted as a *lingua franca* (occasionally with excessive zeal, as in the 1959 drive). It is a compulsory subject of study in all schools, and is the language of command in the armed forces. According to the 1979 census, 62.2 per cent of the non-Russian population claim a fluent knowledge of Russian as a second language (and a further 16.5 per cent speak Russian as their native language).[64] On the political front, it is generally taken as an integral part of Soviet internationalism (in Kalinin's words, 'The Russian language is the language of Lenin'),[65] and is a prerequisite for any cadre wishing to progress up through the ranks of the CPSU. In economic life a full mastery of one's profession is rarely possible without some ability in Russian.

These various roles of the language by no means require people to adopt Russian as their native tongue – it is quite adequate for minorities to use it as a second language. Bilingualism is now a major plank in Soviet nationality policy, and, contrary to d'Encausse's view of bilingualism as 'a temporary phase', the linguist E. G. Lewis presents a convincing model of a stable, non-contradictory pattern of bilingualism in Soviet society.[66] Some authors question the exent and depth of Russian-language learning in the USSR – for example, Azrael asserts that 'the Central Asian nationalities contain a heavy preponderance of undereducated peasants with a weak to non-existent knowledge of Russian'.[67] However, another author in his collection calculates that 39.7 per cent of rural Moslems claim Russian as a second language (not that far behind the 49.8 per cent non-Russian 'Slav' nationality villagers who claim a working knowledge of Russian). And it should be stressed that from the state's point of view, the important thing is not that they should be fluent in Russian, but that they should at the minimum claim a knowledge of it, and hopefully be able to use it in their lives when necessary. Last, it should be mentioned that Soviet policy does not envisage any withering away of the national languages, and attempts to promote their drawing closer together – for example, through word-borrowing – do not seem to be pursued with any great vigour, still less with any great success. Another factor to bear in mind is the inverse of the above case – the position of the Russian diaspora. W. Forwood pointed out that 'more Russians are learning minority languages outside the RSFSR than ten years ago'.[68] The above argument refers to the general, daily pattern of language use, and by no means rules out the possibility that, from time to time, language policy may become an issue of burning political controversy.

Moving on from the language issue to the general question of a functional separation approach to nationality, Western nationality theory would presumably challenge whether such a policy would be workable in practice. Would the minority nationalities accept their 'subordinate' position? One should not rule out such a possibility in principle, particularly in the case of the native elites, who have a fair chance of crossing the boundary into the 'civic culture' (meaning the spheres of political and economic life recognised and condoned by the State). Significantly, these are the very people who are held to be the driving force behind nationalist movements.[69] Their rising self-consciousness will tend to seek an outlet in the opportunities available to them within the existing system. Few of them are likely to be contemplating seriously a political future outside the Soviet state. (And even independence would, of course, necessitate finding some *modus vivendi* with the nearest superpower.) It is widely recognised that Tsarism itself relied heavily upon the co-option of native elites for the running of its Empire, until the latter half of the nineteenth century at least.[70] Thus the tradition of political activity for the minority nationalities has been the seeking of privileges within, rather than rights against, the state structure.

The most acute problems in operating such a policy of integration of native elites are likely to occur at the interface between the regional systems which constitute the 'home base' of the native elites, and the All-Union political and economic structure, where there can be far fewer concessions to native peculiarities. Thus, writers are correct to stress the importance of a non-discriminatory cadre policy (a point frequently made in Soviet discussion of the nationality issue).[71]

However, attention usually focuses on larger and more dramatic threats to the functional separation approach. Thus, for example, the Moslem character of Central Asia is seen as providing a crucial international, cultural and historical dimension to the aspirations of the elites in those areas, which militates against the likelihood of their accepting a constrained role within the Soviet system.[72] Unfortunately, there is little concrete evidence for this. Wheeler argues that one should not share the Soviets' own initial failure to distinguish general Islamic culture from a specifically nationalist movement.[73] Reading accounts of the region, it is difficult to determine the content of Islamic culture beyond the culinary and the sartorial.[74] Bennigsen argues that, in the 1920s, Soviet Central Asia was witness to a unique fusion of communism and nationalism under the leadership of Sultan Galiev.[75] This may well be the case, but it is more significant for its demise than for the fact that it once existed. Ironically, those residues that do remain (he mentions a lingering belief in the communist ideal, for example) seem to work in favour of the existing state structure. A Soviet state that was anxious about the loyalty of its Moslem subjects would hardly have had the confidence to launch the Afghanistan operation. Nor does the state seem desperately keen hermetically to seal the area from its Eastern traditions – consider, for instance, the decision to introduce the teaching of non-Soviet oriental languages into certain Georgian primary schools.[76]

The other main challenge to the functional separation thesis comes from above. Would the Russian people be content with the limited role of *primus inter pares*, of merely providing the *lingua franca* for a multinational state, with the concomitant deleterious effects on their own language? A negative answer to this question usually follows, relying for support upon the invocation of Russian historical traditions. The exact implications of that historical experience, however, are far from clear. Russian nationalism arrived late, in European terms, in the middle of the nineteenth century, and from the beginning was tied closely to the state.[77] Thus it was very much a 'top-down' nationalism, whose penetration of the masses was not well advanced (a point recognised even by the Slavophiles). It is argued that the Russian peasantry were not, on the whole, antagonistic to ethnic strangers (the pogroms being attributed to narrowly economic causes), and that they retained a suspicious attitude towards the state as an alien import, the concoction of German advisers or whatever.[78] One cannot speak with any certainty about popular beliefs in this period, but at least it is not clear-cut that 'traditions' come in solely on one side of the argument. It could be argued that the pattern of expansion of the Russian state set it apart from the other imperialisms (shaky military expansion over vast neighbouring territories, hence close geographical and historical links with their neighbours – even to the extent, for example, of a deep tradition of the cross-migration of peoples). Thus, to risk a generalisation, it could be seen as resembling

Americanisation (introduction, albeit forced, to a new culture) rather than being comparable to British or French imperialism (involving the imposition of, or assimilation to, an existing alien culture).

That these issues are still very much alive is convincingly argued by commentators such as Amalrik and Yanov, who point to the strength of neo-nationalist ideology in the USSR.[79] However, once again the case is weakened by the problematic relationship between the extreme Russian nationalist groups and the actual dynamics of state and society. The Russian nationalists are only tolerated within narrow limits, and their predicted capture of the state seems increasingly unlikely, with the new Andropov leadership successfully installed, and Amalrik's 1984 only just around the corner. Second, as Yanov points out, only by drawing closer to the Soviet state will they stand any chance of influencing it (a dilemma dating back to National Bolshevism in the 1920s).[80] If this is the case, one wonders precisely what would be the changes in policy if the state did lurch towards Russian nationalism – the existing leadership seem perfectly capable of engineering a massive military build-up, a confrontation with China, and so on, within the confines of the ideology currently at their disposal.

The Soviet state clearly has enormous resources at its disposal in the pursuit of this policy of recognition, functional separation and Sovietisation. In simple geographical terms, the territory of the USSR is so vast that it is capable of swallowing up whole nations, almost without trace – as the experiences of the wartime years unfortunately bear witness. There is a strange incongruity running through Western Sovietology, in that a recognition of the powerful, centralised and monolithic nature of the state machine is combined with a keeness to seek out the irrepressible spirit of nationalism. A glance at one or two areas of political life should suffice to illustrate the argument that has been implicit in this chapter so far – that Soviet politics in general and the nature of the state in particular are markedly different from those of other advanced industrial societies.

The CPSU is, of course, the key to the functioning of the state. Structured in accordance with the principle of democratic centralism, it combines the mass involvement of the leading elements of Soviet society with the strict imposition of the political priorities of the centre. In all areas of life, from the economy through to social policy, there is the same combination of mobilisation and centralisation. The clearest example of the role of the state in the nationality issue is to be found in the process of political socialisation. The links in other societies between education and national identity are well documented, and date back at least to Rousseau's advice to the Poles in this regard.[81] A consistent theme in studies in the Soviet education system is the prominent place awarded to the inculcation of 'fervent patriotism' and 'socialist internationalism'. When compared to the West, the striking feature of Soviet education is not merely that the process has so much more time and energy devoted to it, nor that it is 'formal' rather than 'informal', but that the Soviet leaders, unlike their Western counterparts, have a clear and well-defined set of goals which they intend to transmit[82] (hence the space devoted above to the exposition of Soviet nationality theory). And 'political socialisation' involves not only the schools, but a whole range of socialisation agencies – Young Pioneers, Komsomol, the Soviet Army, and the agitprop work of the CPSU.

Thus the functional separation approach leads to the conclusion that the politics of nationality in the USSR are better understood as a mechanism of social regulation than as a vehicle for self-realisation. It may be objected that this leads one into an overly mechanistic view of the Soviet political process, with the state becoming a living embodiment of successful structural-functionalism. However, it in no way follows from the above that the Soviet Union is free of crisis tendencies. Such crisis tendencies as do exist, however, are markedly different from those pertaining in the West. Just as Soviet economic problems seem to take the form of gnawing structural deficiencies, rather than a wildly fluctuating cycle, so in the normative sphere one sees the state engaged in a longstanding struggle to secure honest, committed and efficient participation, rather than a periodic dramatic collapse of the state's legitimacy. (This is presumably akin to Habermasian notions of a 'motivation crisis' in advanced capitalist society,[83] although one remains unclear as to exactly how this manifests itself.) But it should be underlined that the functional separation policy only operates at the systemic level – individuals may well find it difficult to integrate their divergent roles. Thus one may expect to continue to see manifestations of national hostility – without assuming that they are going to undermine the state.

It is also necessary to point out that for the sake of clarity of argument in the above account, barriers to the state's functional separation policy have been minimised. One can recognise that there may be problems for the state, without collapsing into the paradigm of

nationalism as self-realisation. Thus, for example, any system characterised by centralisation of power will have difficulty in ensuring the
even distribution of control on a geographical basis: hence the
periodic purging of sections of the Union Republican apparat which
have drifted out of control (Shelest, Mzhavanadze and many more),
and the constant railing against the phenomenon of 'parochialism'
(*mestnichestvo*), which Brezhnev saw as 'often closely interwoven
with nationalism'.[84] This problem, however, is best understood in the
context of the centrifugal rather than the centripetal forces at work in
society – it is a product of the policies of the centre, rather than the
initiative of the periphery, and will appear in all outlying areas
irrespective of nationality. Similarly, it is conceivable that Soviet
leaders may try to manipulate nationalism for ends other than those
outlined above, without altering the role of nationalism developed
here. The clearest example of such a transgression in recent history is
Beria's attempt to cut across the entrenched patron–client networks of
the Party by appealing to the national cadres in his bid for power in
1952–3.[85]

The point being made here is that one must resist the temptation to
subsume under the heading of 'the nationality problem' all the difficult areas of Soviet political life – problems of intra-bureaucracy
control, faction fighting, religious freedom, the rights of the individual, and so on. It is up to the nationality theorists to prove that
nationalism has the ability to embrace all these diverse political
causes. There is little empirical evidence to support such a view – for
example, the surveys of emigres conducted by Inkeles and Bauer in the
1950s found class a better predictor of political attitudes than
nationality.[86]

NATIONALISM AS SYMBOLIC ACTIVITY

By way of a methodological postscript, it is worth introducing an
important yet hitherto neglected aspect of nationality politics – the
role of political symbols. The preceding analysis has been
predominantly functionalist in spirit: initially it was argued that it is
mistaken to see the nation as the instrument of self-expression of a
popular social movement, and then the case was made that it has a
role as a complex integrative mechanism in the hands of the state. Yet
this whole analysis is built up from a cautious understanding of
nationalism as subjective affiliation. If nationalism is no more than an
elusive sense of belonging, then strictly speaking it cannot serve as a

vehicle for any political interests, it cannot be a means to an end without losing its essential character. As this is clearly inadequate, the functionalist approach needs further development.

The study of mass belief systems is a rather open-ended process: as this is an essay on nationalism and the state it would be inappropriate to stray into the realms of social psychology, but there is a fine tradition of the study of political symbolism. From the ancient art of rhetoric, through Cassirer's *The Myth of the State*, to the more recent commentaries of Murray Edelman,[87] political thinkers have recognised the subjective dimension to politics, where the expressive and evocative join the instrumental as modes of behaviour worthy of investigation.[88] Nationalism itself is inextricably linked with symbolic activity, more so perhaps than any other form of political interaction. The nation has become the symbol of the state *par excellence*. A symbolic approach supplements rather than undermines the functional account: as Gellner succinctly puts it, 'social coherence may require logical incoherence'.[89]

A study of national symbols in the USSR offers many useful insights, of which only a few can be recalled here. There are a variety of intellectual approaches to the nature of symbolic behaviour: study of the role of myth, derived from anthropology; reference to the wealth of specific symbol systems, such as religion or psycho-analysis, for illuminating analogies; or a more formal approach based on a semiological analysis of political communication.[90]

Myth in primitive society is understood to be a practice that makes bearable such 'unwelcome contradictions'[91] confronting humanity as the split between man and nature, and between life and death. It achieves this by the endless repetition, in slightly varying form, of tales which do not have to pass any truth test, do not have to be 'believed in' in the conventional sense, since they derive a direct communicative power from their stereotyped nature. One could speculate that this process is not dissimilar to the manner in which Soviet historians and ideologists use political situations, not as a source of 'objective' truth, but as case studies for the unfolding of set formulae.[92] Lévi-Strauss rooted his explanation of myth in the driving force of a set of binary opposites: likewise, in Soviet theory the Marxian dialectic is explicitly deployed (Soviet patriotism yet socialist internationalism, membership of a national group yet loyalty to the Soviet state). If such circles can be squared in primitive societies, why not also in a modern state?

There are many points of contact between religious and nationalist behaviour. The very origins of the word 'nationalism' are religious: the first meaning given by the Oxford English Dictionary is 'The doctrine that certain nations (as contrasted with individuals) are the object of divine election'. A direct link is frequently perceived between the decline of organised religion and the rise of (organised?) nationalism.[93] C. Lane has recently produced a comprehensive study of the vast array of rites and rituals in Soviet life, whose sheer frequency, and rate of increase in recent years, mean that they cannot be dismissed as a trivial charade.[94] Many of the rituals involve the propagation of national symbols, both of the Soviet and minority nations.

There are a number of frameworks available for the study of political communication. The dramaturgical analogy does not offer many insights into Soviet politics, and while cybernetic models have been used ,[95] they seem too rational and positivist for our purposes in this section. A more promising approach is that of semiology – the study of the processes in language whereby meaning is given to the world. Symbols are seen as being powerful means of expression, communication and mobilisation, while at the same time the link between a particular symbol and that which it evokes is arbitrary, and the content of that evoked is ambiguous if not contradictory. The arbitrariness of the symbol adds to its 'deep' and 'mysterious' power: it also means that although the human agent can select and marshal symbols, he cannot have a completely free hand in determining their content, nor can he conjure them out of thin air. Thus patriotism during the war was just as much the creation of the Soviet people as of Stalin himself. Stalin's own attitude to the importance of political symbolism shifted markedly over the years: in 1913 he declared with some exasperation: '"National character" in itself is something intangible... "a politician can't do anything with it".'[96] Yet by 1950 he was advancing a theoretical argument to the effect that changing the way in which we describe the world is an essential part of the process of changing the world itself.[97] He was, of course, extremely well experienced in the practical manipulation of nationalism by that time, and was on the verge of launching a major antisemitic campaign to disrupt his potential successors.

Moving on to consider the ambiguous nature of the symbol, this can be seen as arising either from the fact that the symbol means different things to its many different 'readers', or that the symbol itself is the 'condensation' of many different messages. Either way, ambiguity increases the evocative power of the symbol, which resembles poetry in being resonant with different meanings. Thus the contradictions in Soviet nationality policy mentioned above may actually serve to increase rather than diminish its force.

It should be noted that the arbitrary and ambiguous nature of the symbol differs from the flexibility found in the Marxian dialectic. The latter holds that reality itself is contradictory, but that the contradictions unfold through time, and at any one moment an unequivocal and politically significant interpretation of the process can be found. Interpreters of symbolic activity do not see the process as that straightforward, still less as capable of yielding up any clear political conclusions.

An example of the problems involved in assigning a definite social role to a symbol is the classic dispute over the Coronation of Queen Elizabeth – Shils and Young seeing it as having a positive and justificatory effect, while Birnbaum held it to be a diversionary influence.[98] Precisely the same argument has recently occurred over whether participation in Soviet elections signifies powerlessness, or involvement, for the voters.[99]

A glimpse at the system of symbols of Soviet nationalism reveals all the classic elements, as laid down by Znaniecki – the people's common history, their unique links with the land, their pantheon of national heroes, the importance of defence against foreigners.[100] (Note how these themes crop up much more frequently in Soviet politics than in the West.) There are few surprises here. More problematic is the relationship with the past – vital to the generation of the symbols just listed, yet seemingly contradicting the novelty that is supposed to be the distinguishing feature of Soviet patriotism. There is an intense debate among Soviet ideologists as to the wisdom of adapting old religious rituals, and the general dangers involved in presenting a picture of a 'single stream' of Soviet culture, flowing from the past.[101] Nevertheless, somehow the past must be brought in, and despite attempts to unearth revolutionary traditions, the étatist tradition is not overlooked – we tend to hear more of Suvorov and Kutuzov than we do of Pugachev and Stenka Razin.[102] The problem of linking specifically modern activities such as education and economic achievements with the symbolic heritage of the past can be solved quite simply by the act of juxtaposition, which can work in symbolic terms without any sense of anachronism. Thus, for example, young socialist emulators are photographed alongside the war banners in the Kremlin.[103]

In conclusion, it can be seen that a purely functional or 'rational' account of nationalism needs to be supplemented by some attention to the symbolic side of the phenomenon, to bring out its contradictions and ambiguities. But overall it has been argued somewhat polemically that conventional understandings of nationalism in the USSR fail to capture the complexities of national identity, and the subtleties of the state's nationality policy. A major factor in this weakness is a methodological flaw: the simple transposition of a concept born out of collapsing empires to a new and vigorous state apparatus. Such conceptual conservatism is understandable: be the writer on the right or the left of the political spectrum, it is far safer to draw parallels between the Soviet state and its Russian predecessors, or its Western counterparts, than to tackle afresh the question of the socialist state as a new form of social organisation.

NOTES

1. I would like to thank all those who took part in the September 1981 Conference of the Political Studies Association Communist Politics Study Group, and Dr A. Shtromas in particular, for helping me to clarify my principal line of argument, and for convincing me of the strength of nationalist feelings. Mary McAuley and Archie Brown also made some illuminating comments on the final draft.
2. The following is a sample of recent work: T. Rakowska-Harmstone, 'The Dialectics of Nationalism in the USSR', *Problems of Communism*, vol. 23 (1974) pp. 1–22; I. Kamenetsky (ed.), *Nationalism and Human Rights* (Littleton, USA, 1977); R. Szporluk, 'The Nations of the USSR in 1970', *Survey*, vol. 16 (1971) pp. 67–91, also 'Nationalities and the Russian Problem in the USSR', *Journal of International Affairs*, vol. 27 (1973) pp. 23–40; Z. Katz *et al.* (eds), *Handbook of Major Soviet Nationalities* (New York, 1975); G. W. Simmond (ed.), *Nationalism in the USSR and Eastern Europe* (Detroit, 1977).
3. See P. Brock, 'Polish Nationalism', in P. F. Sugar and J. Lederer (eds), *Nationalism in Eastern Europe* (Seattle, 1969) p. 362.
4. General Sir John Hackett *et al, The Third World War: A Future History* (London, 1978).
5. For debate of these issues see A. D. Smith, *Theories of Nationalism* (London, 1971); N. Glazer and D. P. Moynihan (eds), *Ethnicity* (Cambridge, Mass., 1975).
6. J. V. Stalin, 'Marxism and the National Question', in *Collected Works*, 13 vols (Moscow, 1952–5) vol. 2, p. 307. Emphasis in original.
7. For example, A. F. Dashdamirov, *Natsiya i lichnost'* (Baku, 1976) pp. 26–7. The Stalin definition is criticised for its use of 'national character' by A. Kosing, *Nation in Geschlichte Und Gegenwart* (Berlin, 1976): Russian translation, *Natsiya v istorii i sovremennosti* (Moscow, 1978) p. 219.

8. T. Rakowska-Harmstone, 'The Study of Ethnic Politics in the USSR', in Simmond (ed.), *Nationalism in The USSR*, p. 21.
9. S. Bruk, 'Ethnodemographical Processes in the USSR', *Social Sciences* (Journal of the USSR Academy of Sciences) (1981) pp. 111–12.
10. H. Carrère d'Encausse, *L'Empire Éclaté: La Revolte des Nations en URSS* (Paris, 1978). See p. 89 of that work for a specific prediction, confirmed by J. R. Azrael, 'Emergent Nationality Problems in the USSR', in J. R. Azrael (ed.), *Soviet Nationalities Problems and Practices* (New York, 1978) ch. 12. A. Bennigsen and S. E. Wimbush argue that it will be between 16 and 30 per cent by the year 2000 – *Muslim National Communism in the Soviet Union* (Chicago, 1979) appendix F, pp. 178–80.
11. I. Dzyuba, *Internationalisation or Russification?* (London, 1968) pp. 53–5.
12. M. N. Kulichenko (ed.), *Osnovnye napravleniya izucheniya natsional nykh otnoshenii v SSSR* (Moscow, 1979) pp. 250–1.
13. A. Cobban, *The Nation State and National Self Determination* (London, 1969) p. 125.
14. E. Gellner, *Spectacles and Predicaments* (Cambridge, 1979) p. 173.
15. For example, K. R. Minogue, *Nationalism* (London, 1967) ch. 1; E. H. Carr, *Nationalism and After* (London, 1945); J. Dunn, *Western Political Theory in the Face of the Future* (Cambridge, 1979) ch. 3.
16. S. White, *Political Culture and Soviet Politics* (London, 1979) p. 144.
17. G. Jahoda, 'The Development of Children's Ideas About Nationality', *British Journal of Educational Psychology*, vol. 33 (1963) pp. 47–60.
18. E. Gellner, 'Ethnicity and Anthropology in the Soviet Union', *European Journal of Sociology*, vol. 18 (1977) p. 215. See also A. D. Smith, *The Ethnic Revival* (Cambridge, 1981) ch. 6.
19. V. Moroz, *Report From the Beria Reserve* (Toronto, 1974) p. 80.
20. T. F. Pettigrew, 'Ethnicity in American Life', in A. Dashefsky (ed.), *Ethnic Identity in Society* (Chicago, 1976) pp. 13–23.
21. For example, P. N. Fedoseev *et al.* (eds), *Leninism and the National Question* (Moscow, 1977). (Originally published in Russian in Moscow, 1974.)
22. See, for instance, W. Connor on the lack of congruence between ethnic and state boundaries, 'Nation Building or Destroying?', *World Politics*, vol. 24 (1972) pp. 319–56.
23. Cited by J. Borys, 'The Question of Political Development', in Kamenetsky (ed.), *Nationalism*, p. 38, note 16.
24. Cobban, *The Nation State*, esp. ch. 4 on 1919.
25. Smith, *Theories of Nationalism*, p. 15.
26. On the economic side – I. Wallerstein (ed.), *World Inequality* (Montreal, 1975), esp. pp. 98–111: J. Piel, 'The Current Role of the Nation State'. The classic political text is K. W. Deutsch, *Nationalism and Social Communication* (Cambridge, Mass., 1966).
27. Glazer and Moynihan (eds), *Ethnicity*, ch. 5 by D. Bell, 'Ethnicity and Social Change', and Introduction, pp. 11 ff.
28. Carrère d'Encausse, *L'Empire Eclaté*, pp. 271–2.
29. See, for example, W. R. Beer, *The Unexpected Rebellion: Ethnic*

Activism in Contemporary France (New York, 1980) pp. 114–16.
30. Dashdamirov, *Natsiya*, p. 8.
31. C. Saikovski and L. Grulion (eds), *Current Soviet Policies Volume Four: Proceedings of the 22nd Congress of the CPSU* (New York, 1962). The fullest account of the period is to be found in G. Hodnett, 'The Debate on Soviet Federalism', *Soviet Studies*, vol. 18 (1967) pp. 458–81.
32. K. Marx and F. Engels, 'Manifesto of the Communist Party', in *Collected Works*, vol. 16 (London, 1976) p. 71.
33. V. I. Lenin, 'The Right of Nations to Self Determination', in *Collected Works*, in 45 vols (Moscow, 1960–70) vol. 16, p. 71.
34. The equality theme is noted by Carrère d'Encausse, *L'Empire Eclaté*, p. 19, and is of course stressed by the Soviets – for example, E. Shevardnadze, 'Internatsionaliskoe vospitanie mass', *Kommunist*, no. 13 (1977) pp. 35–49.
35. Saikovski and Grulion (eds), *Current Soviet Policies,* p.26.
36. Ibid, p. 121.
37. For a discussion of this issue, see Kosing, *Natsiya v istorii*, pp. 211–13.
38. M. G. Kirichenko, *Edinoe soyuznoe mnogonatsionalnoe gosudarstvo* (Moscow, 1978) p. 15.
39. Carrère d'Encausse dates the dropping of the term at 1976, in 'Party and Federation in the USSR', *Government and Opposition*, vol. 13 (1978) pp. 133–50.
40. For clear policy statements, see the keynote speeches by L. I. Brezhnev, 'On the Fiftieth Anniversary of the USSR', *Pravda*, 22 December 1972, pp. 2, 3; 'Speech on the Draft Constitution', 24 May 1977, *Kommunist* no. 8 (1977) pp. 34–44.
41. For Stalin's definition, see the present volume, p. 152.
42. Brezhnev, 'On The Fiftieth Anniversary', p. 3.
43. For general commentary, see Gellner, 'Ethnicity'; also Yu. V. Bromlei (ed.), *Sovremennye etnicheskie protsessy v SSSR* (Moscow, 1975); I. R. Grigulevich and S. Ya. Kozlov (eds), *Ethnocultural Processes and National Problems in the Modern World* (Moscow, 1981). The sociological researches are summarised in Kulichenko, *Osnovnye napravleniya*, pp. 246–77.
44. Dashdamirov, *Natsiya*, p. 34. The functional theme is echoed in many works – for example, M. Kim and V. Sherstobitov (eds), *Sovetskii narod – novaya istoricheskaya obshchnost lyudey* (Moscow, 1975) p. 408.
45. R. Conquest, *The Nation Killers* (London, 1970).
46. S. I. Bruk, 'Ethnodemographic Processes in the USSR', *Soviet Sociology*, vol. 10 (1972) p. 357. (Taken from *Sovetskaya etnografiya*, 1971, no. 4.)
47. Kim and Sherstobitov (eds), *Sovetskii narod*, part two, ch. 7.
48. Ibid, p. 311.
49. M. T. Rutkevich, 'Sblizhenie natsionalnikh respublik i natsii SSSR po klassovoi strukture', *Sotsiologicheskie issledovaniya*, no. 2, (1981) p. 24.
50. A. I. Kholmogorov, *Internatsionalnye cherty sovetskikh natsii* (Moscow, 1970). (Translated in *Soviet Sociology*, vols 11 and 12, 1972 and 1973.)
51. Stalin, *Collected Works,* vol. 2, p. 341.

52. See Kim and Sherstobitov, *Sovetskii narod*.
53. A. McAuley, *Economic Welfare in the Soviet Union* (Hemel Hempstead, 1979) pp. 114–15.
54. NATO Colloquium, *Regional Development in the USSR* (Newtownville, Mass., 1979) pp. 7 and 15.
55. *Pravda*, 6 September 1981, p. 1.
56. Kim and Sherstobitov refer to a decree of September 1942 on agitprop measures for the minority nationalities. Unfortunately, A. Werth's invaluable *Russia At War* (London, 1965) deals only with Russia itself – 'Patrie en danger', pp. 377–94.
57. For example, the comprehensive Simmond collection, *Nationalism in the USSR*, apologises for overlooking Russian nationalism (p. 7) but makes no mention at all of Soviet patriotism.
58. Azrael, *Soviet Nationalities*, p. 374.
59. The Oxford English Dictionary defines patriotism as love of one's own country, as opposed to others' love of their countries. They record more derogatory uses of the word 'patriot' than of 'nationalist'.
60. Smith, *Ethnic Revival*, p. 15.
61. V. Zaslavsky, 'Socioeconomic Inequality and Changes in Soviet Ideology', *Theory and Society*, vol. 9 (1980) p. 397; A. Zinoviev, *The Yawning Heights* (New York, 1979); R. Hingley, *The Russian Mind* (London, 1979).
62. M. N. Guboglo, 'Socioethnic Consequences of Bilingualism', *Soviet Sociology*, vol. 13 (1974) pp. 93–114; Kim and Sherstobitov, *Sovetskii narod*, part 1, ch. 7; S. I. Bruk and M. N. Guboglo, 'Bilingualism and Multilingualism', in Grigulevich and Kozlov (eds), *Ethnocultural Processes*, pp. 51–90.
63. Bruk 'Ethnodemographical Processes', p. 112.
64. Ibid, p. 112.
65. Cited in Kim and Sherstobitov, *Sovetskii narod*, p. 242. For an example of heavily politicised linguistics, see the proceedings of a Tashkent conference, in F. G. Panachin (ed.), *Russkiy yazyk – yazyk druzhby i sotrudnichestva narodov SSSR* (Moscow, 1979).
66. Carrère d'Encausse, *L'Empire*, pp. 192–3; E. G. Lewis, *Multilingualism in the Soviet Union* (The Hague, 1972).
67. Azrael, *Soviet Nationalities*, p. 367. For contradictory evidence in the same collection, see B. D. Silver, 'Language Policy and the Linguistic Russification of Soviet Nationalities', ch. 8, pp. 283–5.
68. W. Forwood, in G. Schöpflin (ed.), *Handbook on the Soviet Union and Eastern Europe* (London, 1976) p. 204.
69. Smith, *Ethnic Revival*, p. 122.
70. A. Nove, 'History, Hierarchy and Nationalities', *Soviet Studies*, vol. 26 (1969–70) pp. 83–4; and S. F. Staar, 'Tsarist Government: the Imperial Dimension', in Azrael, *Soviet Nationalities*, pp. 3–38.
71. Brezhnev, 'On the Fiftieth Anniversary', p. 3; A. F. Dashdamirov, 'Natsionalnye otnosheniya', *Pravda* (7 August 1981) p. 2.
72. Carrère d'Encausse, *L'Empire*, chs 2 and 3.
73. G. Wheeler, 'Islam and the Soviet State', in M. Hayward and W. C. Fletcher (eds), *Religion and the Soviet State* (London, 1969) p. 196.

74. M. Rywkin, 'Religion, Modern Nationalism and Political Power in Soviet Central Asia', in Kamenetsky, *Nationalism*, p. 189; confirmed by D. R. Staats, 'The Minorities of Inner Asia', *Problems of Communism*, vol. 27 (1978) p. 71.

75. Bennigsen and Wimbush, *Muslim National Communism*, p. 99.

76. *Uchitel'skaya gazeta* 30 December 1980, p. 3, cited in *Current Digest of the Soviet Press (CDSP)*, vol. 33, no. 2 (1981) p. 1.

77. N. Riasanovsky, *Nicholas I and Official Nationality in Russia* (Berkeley, 1961); H. Seton Watson, *Nations and States* (London, 1977) pp. 84, 148; S. V. Utechin, *Russian Political Thought* (London, 1964) p. 72.

78. 'Stepniak', *The Russian Peasant* (London, 1894) p. 138.

79. A. Amalrik, 'Ideologies in Soviet Society', *Survey*, vol. 22 (1976) pp. 1–12; A. Yanov, *The Russian New Right: Right Wing Ideologies in the Contemporary USSR* (Berkeley, 1978); Y. Bilinsky, 'Russian Dissenters and the Nationality Question', in Kamenetsky, *Nationalism*, pp. 78–90; D. Pospielovsky, 'The Resurgence of Russian Nationalism in Samizdat', *Survey*, vol. 19 (1973) pp. 52–70.

80. One nationalist writer expressly aware of the interdependence between Russia and the minority nations is I. Shafarevich, 'Socialism in Our Past and Our Future', in A. Solzhenitsyn (ed.), *From Under the Rubble* (London, 1975) pp. 26–67.

81. Smith, *Theories of Nationalism*, p. 48; B. C. Shafer, *Nationalism: Myth and Reality* (London, 1965) ch. 10.

82. R. Clawson, 'The Political Socialisation of Children in the USSR', *Political Science Quarterly*, vol. 88 (1973) pp. 684–712; I. Volgyes (ed.), *Political Socialisation in Eastern Europe* (New York, 1975); F. O'Dell, *Socialisation Through Children's Literature: the Soviet Example* (Cambridge, 1978); V. P. Agafonova (ed.), *Patrioticheskoe i internatsional'noe vospitanie studentov* (Moscow, 1979).

83. D. J. A. Held, *Introduction to Critical Theory* (London, 1980) pp. 285 ff. For an application to the USSR see D. Lane, 'The Soviet Industrial Worker: the Lack of a Legitimation Crisis?', in B. Denitch (ed.), *Legitimation of Regimes* (London, 1979) ch. 10.

84. Brezhnev, 'On The Fiftieth Anniversary', p. 3.

85. C. H. Fairbanks, 'National Cadres as a Force in the Soviet System', in Azrael, *Soviet Nationalities*, ch. 5.

86. Cited in White, *Political Culture*, p. 149.

87. E. Cassirer, *The Myth of the State* (New Haven, 1946); C. H. Hamburg, *Symbol and Reality* (The Hague, 1956); M. Edelman, *The Symbolic Uses of Politics* (Urbana, Illinois, 1964) and *Political Language: Words that Succeed and Policies that Fail* (New York, 1977).

88. These themes are rigorously explored in T. Parsons, *The Social System* (London, 1951).

89. E. Gellner, *Legitimation of Belief* (Cambridge, 1974) p. 26.

90. For general introductions, see E. Leach, *Lévi-Strauss* (London, 1970); R. Firth, *Symbols: Public and Private* (London, 1973); P. Guiraud, *Semiology* (London, 1975).

91. Leach, *Lévi-Strauss*, p. 71.

92. 'Soviet historians have always maintained that history is a partisan

discipline, and that its cognitive and educational potentialities are directly dependent upon what class interests it expresses.': V. Pashuto, 'History Teaching in Soviet Schools', *Social Sciences*, no. 3 (1980) p. 71.

93. For example, G. L. Moses, 'Mass Politics and the Political Liturgy of Nationalism', in E. Kamenka (ed.), *Nationalism* (London, 1976) pp. 39 ff.

94. C. Lane, *The Rites of Rulers: Ritual in Industrial Society – the Soviet Case* (Cambridge, 1981).

95. Examples of the systems approach: E. P. Hoffman, 'Role Conflict and Ambiguity in the CPSU', in R. E. Kanet (ed.), *The Behavioural Revolution and Communist Studies* (New York, 1971) ch. 9; in similar vein see J. Staniszkis, who voices exasperation with the elusiveness of political language – 'the land of the slogan is the land of the blind': p. 246 in 'Adaptational Superstructure: the Problem of Negative Self Regulation', in National Deviancy Conference, *Capitalism and the Rule of Law* (London, 1979).

96. Stalin, *Collected Works*, vol. 2, p. 318.

97. R. C. Tucker, *The Soviet Political Mind* (London, 1972) pp. 144, 162 ff on Stalin's linguistic theories.

98. For this debate, see Firth, *Symbols*, p. 89.

99. V. Zaslavsky and J. Bryn, 'The Function of Elections in the Soviet Union', *Soviet Studies*, vol. 30 (1978) pp. 363–71; A. L. Unger, 'Political Participation in the USSR: YCL and CPSU', *Soviet Studies*, vol. 33 (1981) pp. 107–24. (See also elements of the controversy in John Hoffman's chapter in the present volume.)

100. F. Znaniecki, *Modern Nationalism* (Westport, Conn., 1972) ch. 4.

101. On the former, see C. Lane, *Rites of Rulers*, p. 229. The strongest Soviet attack on the 'single-stream' approach was an article by A. Yakovlev in *Literaturnaya gazeta*, 15 November 1972 (translated in *Soviet Studies in History*, no. 12/13 (1973) pp. 3–36 – 'Against Concepts that Violate the Historical Approach'). The fate of the article and its author are discussed in Yanov, *Russian New Right*, pp. 57–60.

102. 'The martial traditions of Russia as a military power could not have been more useful to Soviet Russia.': V. Kargulov, in *Nash Sovremennik*, no. 1 (January 1981) pp. 187–91. (Translated in *CDSP*, vol. 33, no. 14, pp. 5–6.)

103. V. N. Ilinsky, *Geraldi trudovoi slavy* (Moscow, 1979) p. 147.

6 Nationalism and the Soviet Multi-ethnic State

Mary McAuley

Does the existence of national consciousness in the USSR constitute an important political phenomenon and one that will have a decisive influence on its future development? With the odd exception, Western authors have stressed the seriousness of the nationality question for the Soviet leadership or have even seen it as posing insoluble problems. Although Soviet authors, while recognising that problems exist, usually emphasise the positive aspects of relationships between the nationalities, one leading scholar has recently referred to the nationality question as 'the sorest question in the history of mankind'.[1] Yet I would claim, despite the substantial literature on 'the national question', we do not find convincing answers to the opening question – either because the wrong questions are being asked, or because the assumptions are dubious (to say the least), or because the evidence is lacking.

In this chapter I try to offer not so much an answer as an approach. Before we can answer the question 'how important, politically, is the national question in the USSR?' we have to set ourselves two tasks. First, we must state what kinds of relationships between nationalities, what kinds of 'national' phenomena would constitute political problems – and we must spell out our reasons for thinking them to be such. The fact that there are approximately one hundred different nationalities in the USSR and that there is evidence of friction between some members of some of them does not, in itself, constitute a political problem. Similarly we ought to know better than to assume that anything in particular follows from changing birth-rates: the Russians ceasing to account for a majority in the total population could have any one of a number of political consequences (or none at all), but *nothing* follows from that fact in itself.[2] Furthermore, substantial outbreaks of violence by minority groups, resentful of discrimination, do not necessarily signify danger for the political system – as we in Britain or the United States well know. There is no reason why the Soviet state cannot take urban rioting in its stride, too – and I expect it will. The modern state seems remarkably unshaken by violent outbreaks of this kind. It could be that there is something about the Soviet state that makes it less able to cope with such phenomena, but it is up to us to show why this should be so. (And indeed one can hazard a guess that, on the contrary, it can cope rather better than the liberal – democratic state by using stronger doses both of repression and of palliatives.) First, then, we must specify what would constitute political threats, dangers, serious or indeed insoluble problems for the regime. Second, we must try to establish whether nationality relationships in the Soviet Union actually take, or are likely to take, such forms.

We start by asking what would constitute a serious political problem. Given that the Soviet Union is an extraordinarily diverse multicultural society, with a huge variety of language and cultural groups, yet with an all-union government in Moscow making binding decisions for the whole, the emergence of *nationalist movements* would pose a serious threat. More than one author has drawn attention to the fact that such movements, demanding political secession, would constitute the most extreme problem – and has added that none exists at the moment.[3] But if secession is out (except in the minds of some of the Ukrainian emigrés), there may still be lesser demands for more political autonomy, a looser federation, curbs on Slav migration, use of native language, which the centre may find unacceptable. The trouble here is that we do need to specify which kinds of demands really are unacceptable, incapable of being either absorbed or ignored – and these are not at all obvious. If, for example, it were the case that the regime was committed to the merging (*sliyanie*) of the nationalities with the use of the Russian language becoming compulsory, over, let us say, the next twenty-five years – then clearly serious conflict would be on the agenda. But *sliyanie* has been relegated to the far, far distant future, while the centre muddles on with its policy of pushing Russian but backing down when it touches too sensitive a nerve – as in Georgia. Yes, given the birth-rates, labour resources are in the wrong places – and there seems no real possibility of shifting them in the foreseeable future; yes, the Central Asian authorities want more investment funds and the centre is going to have to divert more funds of all kinds to Central Asia if it wishes to maintain living standards there; yes, the ethnic composition of the army is going to change, unless different recruitment policies are adopted.[4] It is also true that there is strong anti-Russian feeling in Georgia, and in some other parts of the USSR (and animosity between some smaller nationalities); it is undoubtedly the case that some groups within the Russian intelligentsia and political elite have expressed Russian nationalist sentiments. But the question is whether these very different aspects of 'the nationality question' do present the system with an impossible or even a potentially disturbing future. There seems no prima-facie case for suggesting that they do. Simply to claim that they do is not enough – whether the claim is made by a Western or Soviet author. Some multi-ethnic states manage to survive without problems of this kind producing a crisis or radical change. They may produce plenty of unpleasantness and misery for sections of the community – as US experience shows – but that is something different. Other multi-ethnic states, however, do undergo severe strain or indeed collapse. The question then becomes: when is it that relationships between different nationalities within a community become so exacerbated that they lead to political action that has far-reaching consequences? And we must then ask whether such a situation exists or is likely to come aboutwithin the USSR.

If someone can convincingly show why the changing birth-rates, a revival of Islam, outbursts of anti-Russian feeling in Georgia are necessarily or even likely to produce such a situation, then let him or her do so.[5] But in the absence of such evidence, we must turn back to surer ground. Ethnic animosity, regional bickering over resources, discrimination against minorities and urban rioting by such minorities – all seem well within the state's ability to contain. (And let us not forget the usefulness, too, of some of these to the state as a distraction for sections of the population who might otherwise identify other factors as responsible for social ills.) A nationalist movement is of a quite different order. This, I would suggest, is the only feature of the nationality question in the Soviet Union that must *necessarily* pose the regime a direct threat. What we then need to ask is: are existing relationships in the Soviet Union such that they are likely to develop in that direction? And to answer this we must set the question within a wider framework that asks: what are the causes and what maintains the existence of nationalism in the modern world? And are such factors present in the USSR? If certain combinations of factors, certain environments are conducive to nationalism – or perhaps even necessary for nationalism to rear its head – and if others seem to work against it, we have something we can start with. In order to predict whether ethnic rivalries and cultural animosities are likely to turn into nationalist demands, we must turn for guidance to other multi-ethnic states – and to analyses of nationalism based upon them.

But before proceeding any further, let me define 'nationalist demands'. A fairly standard definition would be: political demands based on the belief that it is possible to identify a long-standing cultural community and that the natural basis and guarantor of such a community is the nation state. (There is evidence of such beliefs in some of the Ukrainian *samizdat* writing, in the Baltic republics, perhaps in Georgia, and in both published and unpublished Russian writings.)[6] Notice that this is far more than a simple claim that at a particular point in time an individual is a member of a specific language group or cultural community (equivalent to the claim that he or she is a member of a religious community or social class). Notice too that this is not the same concept of a 'nation' as that which contains no reference to a cultural or ethnic community. 'The British nation', 'the American nation', or the notion of the French nation as comprising all those who owed allegiance to the King of France – in all of these membership of the state defines the nation. In talking of *nationalist* beliefs, then, we are referring to that irrational set of beliefs that acquired currency in Europe in the nineteenth century and has persisted into the twentieth century, exerting a powerful influence in many different parts of the world. As others have pointed out, one cannot define groups in terms of their special culture or members' attributes and trace these back to an ancient past — the culture changes, and hence, by its own criterion, the group disappears. Or, to make a different point, 'for most of recorded history men have been organized into castes, estates, villages, manors, tribes, cities, guilds, priesthoods, aristocracies, bureaucratic orders and the like and political units have been formed from such components with little regard for common language or ethnic identity'.[7] Finally, there is no 'natural' reason why people of the same culture or language should want to form a political state – nor any evidence that such political arrangements produce 'better', 'more just' government. But the fact that the beliefs are false is, of course, neither here nor there as far as their existence is concerned. We still have to ask which features of the modern world are responsible for creating and maintaining such beliefs.

Perhaps it is unnecessary to state this, but among those who write on the national question in the USSR there are many who seem to accept the nationalist assumption that it is somehow natural for people who share the same culture to want to build the state on that basis.[8] In part, this stems from their failure to take account of comparative research; this in its turn accounts for the unsatisfactory nature of most Western analysis of the national question in the Soviet Union. In the opening chapter of *Soviet Nationality Problems*, published ten years ago, Allworth traced the history of Western scholarship on the different Soviet nationalities.[9] Although the multi-disciplinary efforts he urged are still regrettably rare, we have seen a surge of books and articles on the nationalities. They have tended to be case studies of individual republics or language communities (and here the nationalist orientation of the writer, often himself from that community, comes out most strongly), or overall accounts which describe many of the features of the Soviet nationality scene but lack a framework of analysis. The much publicised *Decline of an Empire* by H. Carrère d'Encausse is an example of the latter.[10] It is as though someone were to write a nice description of the different aspects of the British economy, but failed to set the account within a framework that allowed the reader to predict whether the economy was about to collapse, decline, plod on or revive. But perhaps that book signals the end of an era of Western writing on Soviet nationalities – one in which most specialists ignored the findings of comparative research, failed to question their assumptions, and offered us description in place of analysis. If this seems a harsh indictment of the Sovietologists, their colleagues who study nationalism more generally hardly deserve a gentler treatment. It is still possible for Antony Smith to write a book on *Nationalism in the Twentieth Century* in which the experience of the Soviet Union since 1917 is never discussed.[11] It is rare to find a Western scholar, with an interest in nationalism, focus attention on the Soviet Union, despite the fact that one-ninth of the world's nationality groups are clustered there. Two exceptions are Kohn and Wallerstein who do place the USSR in a world context and, in consequence, produce refreshingly different perspectives.[12] It is still possible for Western Marxists to develop theories or analyses of centre–periphery nationalism, based on the existence of capitalist relationships, without asking themselves whether Soviet experience confirms or throws doubt on such theories.[13] It is, though, only recently that Marxists have again turned their attention to nationalism. Hobsbawm's comment that, 'Marxism has suffered, because, while recognizing nationalism as a phenomenon arising in the "bourgeois epoch" it has largely, because of a deep-seated lack of sympathy with it, underestimated its importance and persistence'[14] applies equally to

Marxists in the West and in the Soviet Union. Western Marxists either assumed that as a socialist society the Soviet Union had solved the national problem or, if they were Marxists critical of the Soviet Union, simply assumed that just as nationalist phenomena were a feature of the bourgeois state, so, in the USSR, nationalist activities were evidence of the new bourgeois or class character of the Soviet state. The Chinese still adopt this orthodox position: nationalism requires no additional analysis. But now that Marxists in the West have started to look again at nationalism, it is discouraging – to say the least – to find them ignoring the Soviet Union. A theory that attempts to account for the emergence and persistence of nationalism by the presence of capitalist relations, but neglects the experience of the Soviet Union, China, Yugoslavia, etc., is necessarily inadequate. If the Soviet Union is *not* capitalist, yet the same phenomena are observable, capitalism cannot be responsible. If nationalism is absent from the Soviet Union then the theoretical case *may* be strengthened. But until these questions are asked, and answered, we are not much wiser. Such strictures apply equally to other theories or explanations of nationalism – if the Soviet Union is left out, we cannot tell how good they are as explanations. To put it more strongly, the divorce that still exists between those who study the nationality question in the Soviet Union and those interested in nationalism in general must mean inadequate answers from both.

MERGER, ASSIMILATION, OR UNITY IN DIVERSITY?

The general question of nationality, and that of nationalism more specifically, are back on the agenda for academic study in the Soviet Union. 'Ethnicity' is 'in' in the USSR and the USA alike. The heated discussions of the Khrushchev period, in which authors openly advocated either *sliyanie* (the merging of nationalities) or *rastsvet* (the flowering of national characteristics), have been replaced by the adoption of an official compromise position but one that still allows for sharp differences of opinion. The official position can be outlined as follows. The world consists of ethnic communities, some of which develop into a nation with a national consciousness – usually this is associated with the development of capitalism and hence with class division, discrimination and oppression of minorities. However, within the Soviet Union, nations have been able to develop without these negative features – instead there has been friendship, with the

Russian people helping the other nationalities to develop. Finally, in the Soviet Union two processes are at work: the free development of nations on an equal basis, *and* the creation of a totally new entity, 'the Soviet people' (not to be confused with a 'nation'), which transcends ethnic and class differences. Both *sblizhenie* – the growing closer – and *rastsvet* are occurring. One day, nations will cease to exist, but that day is far off. It is not the case that the 'national question' has been solved in the Soviet Union but, to quote Brezhnev, 'the national question, in that form in which we inherited it from the past, has been solved';[15] national questions still remain very much on the agenda. Or, to quote Brezhnev again: 'That does not mean of course that all questions in the area of national relations have already been solved. The dynamic of development in such a large multi-national state as ours gives birth to many problems which require very sensitive attention from the party.'[16] The problems, it is argued, arise when individuals or groups fail to combine loyalty to their own national group with loyalty to the Soviet Union, and give priority to narrow sectional rather than to all-union interests should a conflict between them arise. This short-sighted preference for national interests takes the form of objections to central government policy (for example, an unwillingness to co-operate in the development of the USSR as one integrated economic unit – something that is crucial for its future) or an unwillingness to learn the Russian language which is one of the powerful integrating mechanisms. It also surfaces in discriminatory cadre policies, in the failure to observe the equal rights of different nationalities and in claims for the superiority of a particular nation. This in turn can spill over into nationalist demands and attitudes which are fanned by bourgeois propaganda.[17]

Within the bounds of this framework, very different positions are taken up. To advocate openly the merging of nations as a policy would seem to be outside the bounds of discussion (although a contributor to a recent discussion did feel it necessary to remark, 'Incidentally some authors still bring up the question of the merging of nations although not a single Central Committee document mentions it')[18] and the expression of overt Russian nationalist sentiments in the journals is frowned upon, but quite blatant claims for Russian cultural superiority were still recently being made. All the scholars agree that the learning of Russian should be encouraged, but we can discern two very different approaches behind the discussions which reveal very different concepts of a 'nation' – one of a nationalist hue, one decidedly not. The nationalist argument goes as follows: the spread of

Russian as the common language for the peoples of the Soviet Union rests upon an objective basis, in that a large proportion of the population is Russian, and together with others who speak Russian as their native tongue, makes up 60 per cent of the total population; furthermore, Ukrainians and Belorussians are Slavs and can learn Russian easily because the languages are so similar; Russians are to be found all over the Soviet Union, and both before and after the revolution have played a special role in helping the other nationalities economically and culturally, and consequently they have earned the love and respect of all. As Lenin pointed out, it is important to have the majority language as the medium of exchange, and it is particularly fortunate that this is Russian because 'the Russian language being the worthy expression of the spiritual culture of the Russian people is rightly considered one of the richest languages in the world'. Both Engels and Lenin recognised its richness. It enriches other languages and absorbs elements of them, and it has the further properties that it has few dialects and is spoken as it is written.[19] Now let us contrast this with the analysis being put forward by some of the ethnographers: since 1917 in the Soviet Union (whether in Russia proper or in Central Asia) there has been a gradual breaking-down of 'regionalism', that is the identification with one's village, locality or other small community. In Russia, regional identification, linked with dialect, customs, dress, architecture, type of subsistence and religious identification, rather than any *national* identification, were the important distinguishing characteristics of groups. Another process at work, which in some parts of the country pre-dates 'October' and is a general trend of modern society, is the assimilation of 'small' ethnic groups by their surrounding ones. A marked assimilation of minorities (for example, Jews, Armenians, Estonians) is taking place in the RSFSR, the Ukraine and the towns. Simultaneously other ethnic communities have acquired a new national identification and here the spread of Russian has been instrumental: by learning a second language, one's own is identified as different. Hence, on the one hand, we notice the spread of a common culture among urban dwellers opting for the same life-styles, subject to the same cultural influences, using Russian as the language of exchange, and, on the other, we see the strengthening, or even the creation, of national identification. Does the use of Russian as the international language endanger its existence as the language of Russian culture? No, because Russian culture and the Russian nation has always been a mixture of very different ethnic and cultural elements, and throughout its history has displayed an extraordinary capacity for this kind of absorption. Does this mean that this new 'international' culture is 'Western' (as some Chinese argue)? No, although of course it is true that some of the same factors (modern technology, labour migration, economic integration) that make such an 'international' culture possible also operate in capitalist societies, and there also break down regional distinctiveness, and ethnic life-styles.[20]

We can see that this approach calls into question the whole notion of historic 'nations', and stresses the mixed, culturally different, continually changing elements that go to make up a nation, itself a relatively recent phenomenon, at any particular point in time.[21] It is interesting to note that what the ethnographers have gained is official recognition that some forms of ethnic or national identification are here to stay for the foreseeable future (although the patterns are complex and always changing), and the right to carry out detailed research into changing life-styles and relationships between different communities.

Far less well researched are the causes of the negative phenomena of discrimination, national sectarianism or nationalist attitudes. Emigré propaganda, particularly in the Baltic republics, is considered one ingredient that fosters nationalist attitudes, but it is recognised that it will only have a destabilising effect if there are other grounds for discontent. One party specialist has argued that such grounds can be constituted, on the one hand, by inequalities in living standards and the excessive sacrificing of present to future needs and, on the other, by the non-observance of nationality policy by those responsible for executing it – the artificial accelerating or braking of integration, discriminatory cadre policies, refusal of equal treatment to all nationalities.[22] These may not seem earth-shattering suggestions but to propose that the government and its officials should take responsibility – not for eradicating nationalist attitudes but for *causing* them – is a far cry from the simple scenario of a progressive government struggling against the remnants of bourgeois nationalism. But still these suggestions do not get us very far.

THE RESONANCES OF 'NATIONALISM' AND 'ETHNICITY'

When we look for guidance to the writings of those who have studied the causes of nationalism, past and present, we find ourselves facing an odd fact. The different factors that are said to cause or perpetuate nationalism, the 'structural preconditions' of some authors or the 'triggering mechanisms' of others, are present in the Soviet Union in such strength and variety that it becomes difficult to imagine a more favourable environment: the USSR would seem to be a veritable nationalist's paradise.[23] Nationalism rampant might have been predicted. Yet, quite simply, this is not the case. A simple but unsatisfactory explanation of its absence might be the state's ability and willingness to crush any manifestations of nationalism. Now, this might explain the inability of a nationalist group to consolidate itself, it may be (and, we would argue, surely is) one factor that can help explain parts of the picture, but it cannot account for the very different manifestations of nationalist attitudes, or their absence, that we observe. It does not, for example, help us to explain why some sections of the Ukrainian or Russian intelligentsia should adopt nationalist positions – and at particular times – while their counterparts in Kirgizia, Armenia or Moldavia show no signs of doing so.[24]

Let us briefly list the factors that those trying to explain nationalism have suggested are important. First, whatever the reasons for the emergence of nationalist ideas in Europe in the nineteenth century, by the twentieth century these ideas are readily available as part of the world currency of ideas. This does not mean that they may not be discovered independently by a group, but their very existence as one of the available ideologies is, by the twentieth century, in itself a contributory factor. For simplicity's sake we can divide the reasons why people are receptive to such beliefs into, first, those stemming from political relationships and, second, those related to social and economic change. If the central authority in a multi-ethnic state rests on a territorial and cultural community that distinguishes it from the rest, or if a period of repressive rule is followed by liberalisation, or if the central power is unable to offer protective benefits to the minorities, then all these are conducive to minority nationalism. Other suggestions, prompted by recent outbursts of ethnic nationalism in Western Europe and North America, refer to a reaction against the contemporary state's failure to solve the problems of regional backwardness, or a simple revolt against the centralising tendencies of the state and the encroachment of officialdom on ever more aspects of everyday life. Perhaps the most serious attempt to offer an economic theory of nationalism has come from the uneven development school – and here attention is drawn to the nationalism of the centre as well as that of the minorities. But more generally many have suggested that to explain Third World nationalism we must set it in the context of slow-developers, whose new intelligentsia or army officers become aware of their being left behind in the race for a Western standard of living. Both in the nineteenth century and today, the intelligentsia is seen to be crucial for its part in producing and elaborating the ideas, and its relationship to the state is held to be a key determinant of the way it is likely to react. An intelligentsia in a multi-ethnic community, blocked in its desire for advancement and power; an intelligentsia tired of its society's backwardness and anxious to create a community mobilised around the state – both are common variants. But if the intelligentsia produces the ideas, it needs a constituency to appeal to, and this, it has been argued, is to be found in the new city dwellers – those uprooted from the rural community and thrown into a world without structure or coherence, a world in which they need to find a new identity. Although nationalists often argue that the peasant community embodies the nation's virtues and culture, peasant culture itself, with its local, religious preoccupations, is pre-nationalist. The peasant does not think in terms of a nation but of a village or region. Group identification entails, necessarily, identification of the 'others', and this is where existing economic and social relationships will be crucial in determining what kinds of identification are made. If, for example, a new urban proletariat is faced by a bourgeoisie of the same culture, class identification may seem more natural than where the bourgeoisie is of a different culture – in the latter case, discontent in the work situation can create an ethnic solidarity. But, to reintroduce a political factor, the types of political and social organisation that exist can in themselves help form patterns of group identification.

Now, from this brief listing, we see immediately that many of these conditions either have applied or still apply to the Soviet Union. First, we can draw attention to the way in which, since 1917, and for different reasons at different times, the Soviet state has given strong official sponsorship to the idea that the political unit should be based on cultural community. In the early years, despite the Bolsheviks' long-term aim of the withering-away of the state, the sponsorship took the form of creating federal arrangements that did (in good Versailles fashion) attempt to make political unit and language community correspond, by identifying the government of the republic, ASSR or lesser unit, with the titular nationality, and by placing 'nationals' sympathetic to Bolshevik rule in the governments of these territories, and by denouncing Great Russian chauvinism.[25] Much later the incorporation into the Soviet Union of the Baltic republics, whose previous and continued existence was based on the same principle, and the transformation of the nation states of Eastern Europe into people's democracies, gave a new emphasis to the idea that the socialist state was a nation state. What should not be forgotten is that during the inter-war period the development of the Soviet state was taking place in a world that was becoming increasingly nationalistic, and that this necessarily had certain consequences.[26] First, the Bolsheviks' attempts to create a socialist culture (given that they assumed that in a socialist community there would be a shared culture) *in one country* surrounded by hostile states produced the claim that in *Soviet* culture they had a distinctive culture, shared by members of their community. The assumption that cultural identity is the natural basis for the state (the nationalist assumption) took a new form – now political loyalty depended upon cultural conformity. This helps to explain the vicious attack on national minorities at a time of stress – during the Second World War – and the Soviet state's shift to fighting the war on the same terms as its opponents by dredging up Russian nationalist symbols. In the post-war period, too, the world outside intervened. This time it was the national-liberation movements of the Third World which the Soviet state found itself supporting as part of Soviet–American rivalry, thus stressing the virtues of national independence. Today, then, we find the Soviet state simultaneously sponsoring the ideas of national units and 'the Soviet people' – both derive from the assumption that cultural identity is the desirable basis for the state because it implies political loyalty or, at least, provides the best guarantee of it.[27]

But to turn to the other factors. Certainly the identification of the central power with Moscow and the Russians should create problems; certainly if minority nationalism is a response to the bureaucratic state we should expect to find it endemic to the USSR; certainly the state, at least of late, has shown itself unable to prevent particular regions remaining poor and backward. A period of repressive rule, too, has been followed by liberalisation. There are perhaps other factors that could counteract these. It is undoubtedly true that membership of the USSR, both in the 1920s and afterwards, offered benefits – whether strategic, material or cultural – to many of the minorities. But it is also true that the value of these varies enormously for the Armenians, the Ukrainians, Estonians, the Bashkirs and the Eskimos. This means that we have to treat the minorities separately. Their relationships to the centre have been and are different.

What of the social and economic factors? Again, theories of uneven development may surely be applicable. The rapid development of the more backward parts of the USSR may not compensate for their still being the poorer partners, producers of raw materials, with a gap in the standard of living that fails to close. The active creation of a new national intelligentsia is a striking feature of Soviet development, and one that takes place against the breakdown of old rural communities – the movement of the peasantry to the towns that gathered momentum at the end of the 1920s and never ceased. The process was not, however, a uniform one. The attempt to catch up with the West meant that in the 1930s resources went to Russia, the Ukraine and Azerbaijan; they went to the towns (which tended to be Russian and the Central Asian towns became even more Russian); the emphasis was on skill (again associated with being Russian) and on using Russian as the language of exchange. It was primarily the Russian peasants who did the moving – either within the RSFSR or as 'colonisers' to other parts of the country. (The better-off Ukrainian peasant moved much less; many other minorities not at all.)[28] As we can see, this could have the consequence of increasing the identification of the management stratum with one ethnic group – the Russian – or, if both management and workers became more heavily Russian, it could lessen ethnic awareness within the towns. The new intelligentsia, until very recently (and to some extent today) had differing characteristics in different parts of the country. In Central Asia in the 1930s and 1940s the tiny new elite was concentrated in the administration of agriculture, whereas in the Ukraine all sectors were expanding fast.[29] Finally, as far as social and political organisations are concerned, we could surmise that the *lack* of organisations with a strong group identity should have encouraged the adoption of national or ethnic criteria by default. The Communist Party of course offered an alternative identity but, since for so much of its existence it has only embraced a tiny proportion of even the town population, it can hardly have acted as a creator of group identity for the majority, who were then left with very vague reference points – workers, peasants, white-collar.

Clearly the analysis of nationalism (or the reasons for its absence) in the USSR is going to be very difficult. We have a number of maybe competing, maybe complementary theses or suggestions as to what causes nationalism – not one nice model against which we can set Soviet phenomena. The very different sets of social and economic relationships that exist within and between the different groups in the Soviet Union mean that a simple model would almost certainly be wrong.

By way of example let us explore the significance of 'national identification' in the Soviet Union. Nationality as it appears on the passport is determined by parents' nationality. In the case of mixed marriages, the child can opt as he or she wishes. As Zaslavsky points out, quoting from Soviet discussions of nationality policy, this can 'obfuscate' changing patterns of ethnic identification and assimilation – a wholly Russified Armenian family in Moscow still has to be 'Armenian'; a child of Ukrainian and Tatar parents living in a Russian community still has to opt for either Ukrainian or Tatar.[30] If we ask what nationality ascription means and what importance it has, we find that it 'means' different things to different communities and individuals. To a Ukrainian speaker, long-resident in Kiev, the entry 'Ukrainian' on a passport connotes a quite different concept of nationality from that implicit in the following response on a census form, 'By nationality we are Uzbeks but we are Arabs',[31] which in turn has nothing in common with that held by the child of Ukrainian–Tatar parents. In the first case, 'nationality' somehow corresponds to a sense of belonging to a language-cultural group, in the second it could refer to citizenship of a republic, in the third it is difficult to see that it means anything to the individual. Two different concepts of nationality come out in Sporluk's rhetorical statement:

> Belorussian national identity, based on a political-territorial identity is not weakening. Will Belorussians remain a separate nation even when they are Russian? [i.e. when no one any longer speaks Belorussian].[32]

The answer is that if it *matters* to be Belorussian – that is, associated with a particular political unit – then there will be Belorussians, and it is irrelevant whether they speak Russian, Polish or Lithuanian or even what Church they belong to, because these are characteristics of quite different group identifications (which may or may not exist), all compatible with being Belorussian in Szporluk's first sense.

But if the ascription of nationality means different things to different sections of the population, it can also change its meaning over time. Rates of intermarriage, population movement and assimilation will have their effect; as will the state's use of the category: that is, the importance that a particular entry in the passport has for affecting an individual's existence. Clearly, for the offspring of mixed marriages who become assimilated into another culture, it is an empty category – unless if affects educational or job opportunities where there are nationality quotas. Zaslavsky suggests that one of the reasons children of mixed marriages choose the nationality of the parent who holds the nationality of the republic they live in, is to obtain the privileges reserved for the titular nationality.[33] This sounds plausible but we need to know more about the quota system and how it operates before we can assess its actual or potential importance. If the quota system is crude (for example, preference for the titular nationality ensures 100 per cent Uzbek employment in certain jobs in Uzbekistan) it will have certain consequences; if it is finely tuned to accomodate minor nationalities within a republic, it will have other consequences. The *way* in which it operates will matter too: if bribery can cancel it out in one region, but not in another, for example. Does being a Tadjik in Uzbekistan have quite different consequences from being a Tadjik in Turkmenistan, or being a Jew in Leningrad from being a Jew in Kishinev? The state's use of 'nationality' to distribute benefits will clearly affect both the concept of nationality that people hold and, by linking privileges with nationality, can create socially divisive group identifications.[34] But other factors can also be relevant. As Zaslavsky rightly suggests, position in the social structure may be of great importance in determining how the individual views the question of nationality:

Unlike specialists, workers and peasants [in the non-Russian republics] do not need to use their own language or any other cultural marker in the competition for more lucrative jobs: given their low social status and the chronic shortage of labour power in the large and medium towns, the power of competition does not exist. The life chances of the ethnic workers are not at all affected by their membership in a non-Russian ethnic group.[35]

If this is so, then one could argue that nationality does not affect them, does not exist for them in any meaningful sense. It may be that nationality policy only has relevance for the educated and upwardly mobile. Without more evidence it is impossible to tell. Surveys among youth have shown a preference for giving the individual a free choice of his or her nationality at the age of 16 (as was the policy until the mid-1930s), which suggests the present system is felt to be artificial and unsatisfactory, and apparently in the pre-Constitution discussions some suggestions were made that the category 'nationality' be dropped altogether from the passport. Zaslavsky suggests that the leadership would hardly favour such proposals, because present practice both maintains 'dogmatic models of behaviour' and allows the 'multi-national ruling group ... an efficient means of control and regulation of the relations among nationalities' – it prevents ethnic self-consciousness developing naturally and falling prey to nationalism.[36] While agreeing that the imposition of one particular form of self-ascription will produce divisions into arbitrary ethnic groups, and that a quota system for jobs and education based on them is clearly socially divisive and may prevent wider and potentially more dangerous alliances based on class, occupation or religion from developing, it still remains to be shown that this actually *is* the case. We need to know how the quota system works, and whether, to return to Zaslavsky's point, nationality ascription only matters for the upwardly mobile. If it does, then it is *not* serving as an efficient means of control – except for one section of the community. I doubt that leadership is as consciously Machiavellian as this suggests. Moreover, if nationality policy has most meaning for the intelligentsia – the group within society most prone to think in national terms – the leadership is unwise to encourage, if not create, such attitudes precisely among that stratum. I must admit that I see the leadership as far less clever, far more trapped within 'dogmatic models of behaviour' whose consequences they ill understand.

But to return to our main task, how then should we proceed? We know we are dealing with a huge, culturally diverse society, with a centralised state which, in its territorial administrative arrangements and encouragement of language and minority cultures, has sponsored different types of national identification while simultaneously preaching supranationalism. Social and economic development in this society has been rapid, disruptive and uneven; new intelligentsias have been created. Encouragement and repression of national minorities has occurred. We know this. We also know that there have been outbursts of nationalist feeling and conflict between different cultural groups but that the picture is varied, spotty and contradictory – and that since the early years of its existence the centre has never had to face a serious nationalist challenge. We need a hypothesis that could explain both the variation and the relative success of the Soviet system in *not* creating nationalism. The foregoing discussion has provided some clues, notably that national identification has different connotations, and that the importance of 'nationality' varies for different strata within a population depending upon its relevance for them. This then suggests the following: Soviet experience shows that a multi-ethnic state, run on the basis of rigid definitions of nationality and territorial-language units during a period of rapid social and economic change, is unlikely to be faced with serious threats of nationalism, *because* nationalist attitudes will tend to be limited to the new intelligentsia who cannot form links with a wider community, whose different strata have interests that do not encourage a nationalist orientation. The only danger comes from a community where such links previously existed – and in this case nationalism is intensified.

We now try to demonstrate this by looking at three very different regions: Central Asia, the Ukraine, and the Baltic republics. Inevitably the treatment will be superficial; specialists on these regions will dislike the cavalier discussion and fault much of it. I am happy to stand corrected. My concern is to show how we should start analysing communities if we are to understand when and where nationalist attitudes exist. What we want is a theory of nationalism that can embrace the Soviet Union as well as other countries of the world.

FROM ETHNICITY TO NATIONALISM: PRECONDITIONS AND POSSIBILITIES

The Chinese argue that the Soviet regime exploits the Central Asian people in an imperialist fashion. Although it is true that Central Asia has seen considerable development under Soviet rule, the gap between living standards in European parts of the country and Central Asia remains considerable and shows no signs of closing; Central Asia is still a provider of raw materials for the industries of the north; it now has an indigenous intelligentsia and political elite but is closely supervised and controlled by Moscow, and forced to a humiliating recognition of the Russian big-brother role in the past and today. This sounds like a recipe for disaster, but let us look at the relationships between the different social groups.

Soviet authors, analysing the intelligentsia, distinguish between those occupying political-administrative posts, management personnel, the cultural intelligentsia, the scientific, and the mass-professions (school-teachers, doctors, etc.).[37] The distinctions are useful because the occupational interests of these groups do not necessarily provide them with a common interest. To take the political-administrative elite first: this is now drawn from the indigenous population; opportunity and upward mobility into republican elite positions are there for the local population. But, as Hodnett's work shows, for Central Asian nationals the republic is the limit – and there is very little movement between even the Central Asian republics.[38] Hence their horizon is the republic, their *own* republic. This means that their constituents are the people of that republic and this is where they must look to find a nation. But what kind of a nation could this be? Not one based on language, given the existence (in all the Central Asian republics) of a number of sizeable language communities. Muslim? But that does not distinguish the Uzbek community from the Turkmen. In other words, in terms of their political role, their administrative responsibilities, their position as an administrative elite of a region defending that region's interests against others and the centre, they require a territorial 'nation' – the citizens of Uzbekistan (be they Uzbeks, Koreans, Uigurs, Turkmen, or Arabs). In order to create a different kind of nation – one that suggested the citizens of Uzbekistan shared a unique culture and past – the services of the cultural intelligentsia would be needed. But in Central Asia the cultural intelligentsia, with, necessarily, its interests in art, literature and architecture, has other reference points – in language communities, religious communities or smaller ethnic groups whose boundaries do not coincide with present territorial–political divisions. The scientific intelligentsia is still small and the least tied to Central Asia; for a scientist, Moscow exerts a pull that does not exist for his or her compatriots. Russian is the language of science for him and his identification is with a much wider community than the local one. Management personnel in industry and agriculture have interests that coincide more closely with those of the political elite. Russian skills (or Slav skills) still dominate in what are often Russian towns but the local population (in line with a policy of affirmative action) have moved into management positions.[39] Hence one may find an Uzbek or a Tadjik manager welcoming Russian labour rather than local, because it has the skills. Himself a product of affirmative action, he may well object to it if it means less-skilled labour.

The urban industrial labour force is small, and still strongly Slav.[40] It is not concerned with the underemployment of the rural population; on the contrary, its interests lie in preserving its position against what could be a threatening invasion from the countryside. For its Slav members, there is the added problem that, even though they themselves may be long-term settlers, their children are going to find it difficult to move into intelligentsia jobs because these are now reserved for the indigenous population. They probably are the most alienated group in society. Their fellow workers who come from the surrounding countryside do find themselves in an alien Russian and urban environment but, for two reasons, are unlikely to develop a 'nationa-list' identification. First, because the town is so alien and the village still so near, the old village-muslim identification remains strong; second, in the workplace, they are working alongside Slavs under managers who are, for example, Uzbek or Tadjik. Hence for the new-comers it is difficult to identify the strangeness and unpleasantness of an industrial work environment with the presence of different 'rulers'. Work-force and management do not divide along the lines of 'foreign' management or local work-force, in the way they have done in most of the Third World. As for the rural population in Central Asia, here the identification is primarily village (or valley) and muslim. And for a muslim, the 'other' group includes (equally) Russians, Belorussians, Georgians, Armenians, Jews – anyone who is not a muslim. Hence the identification is simultaneously very parochial and very wide, both of which make a national identification hard to create.

What kinds of alignments then are possible or likely? It seems unlikely that an Islamic revival could unite the different sectors of the community. The political elites, and management, and the scientists have no desire to see a revival – any more than the Iranian elite or middle class did. It would not help them in their job of running their republics; it could be very threatening. They must be thankful they are part of the Soviet Union. The Central Asian elite and intelligentsia compares itself with its counterparts in their part of the world and, from this perspective, membership of the Soviet Union surely compares favourably with being under Western influence, protection, or actual rule. That is the alternative, not some ideal independence. (Suggestions that Central Asians look to China as a sympathetic Great Power are surely naive; Chinese nationality policy can hardly recommend itself and the Chinese are as 'alien' as the Russians.)[41]

A revival of interest in Islam within the cultural intelligentsia is not likely to be taken up by the rest of the intelligentsia; a revival in the countryside is not likely to find an echo in the towns. If there is sub-stantial movement to the towns from the country, movement north, experience of discrimination, or movement back to face limited employment opportunities and a Slav working class defending its jobs, then serious grievances will arise. But it is far from clear that they will produce a muslim or a national identification. If the search for jobs extends within Central Asia, 'muslims' from other than the home republic may well be unwelcome. A narrow language or cultural identification could become the key one, but so could a territorial one. But then those who will be seen to be responsible for the miserable state of affairs – political elite and management – are of those groups themselves. What will perhaps be crucial in such a situation is the composition of the elite itself: whether it is dominated or even exclusively made up of one language or cultural group within the republic (the titular nationality) or whether it is a multi-culture group – and the way its divisions correspond to those within other social strata in the population. Perhaps the political elites could turn urban unemployment to their advantage by casting the blame on Moscow and using anti-Moscow sentiments as a way of exerting greater pressure on the centre, but I doubt such a tactic would seem very attractive to them. It would provide a flimsy basis for an alliance and constitute a dangerous game. Surely it is better *not* to have a discontented, unemployed urban population (*and* the possibility of a serious Slav backlash in the towns when the locals riot), and to continue administering the republic as it is at present.

There are too many cross-pressures in Central Asia to produce anything approaching a united community or even an alliance between crucial sectors that could threaten present arrangements. The socio-political and cultural relationships produce a criss-cross of group or self-identifications – and where this happens the chances of nationalism dwindle. An individual may simultaneously identify himself as a Muslim, Uzbek, Korean, a communist and a factory manager – all have a meaning, none is paramount.

The Ukraine presents a different picture. Here the cultural intelligentsia is much more important and has shown evidence of nationalist sentiments of a good nineteenth-century kind. Although the existence of a vociferous and active emigré community, ever ready to fuel such sentiments, may be a contributory factor, we still have to ask why some members of the intelligentsia should be such ardent nationalists. We observe that the Ukrainian intelligentsia has come into existence in a community where a separate language base exists, yet an extremely insecure one given the existence and strength of Russian. Furthermore the very similarity of 'Russian' and 'Ukrainian' cultural patterns means that it is *essential* to preserve the language if the notion of a separate Ukrainian people is to be maintained. If the language goes, the differences between the communities dissolve.[42] Now this is the background to a situation in which (unlike Central Asia) the opportunities for the political, managerial aspirant are open right to the top – to Moscow, Vladivostok, New York – *provided* the individual takes the small step (and it is a small one) of adopting Russian as his or her main language. For the scientific intelligentsia, too, Moscow,

Leningrad and Novosibirsk exert a powerful pull, science is more important than language. The cultural intelligentsia can either follow suit or, if its members wish to maintain a separate identity (which is essential to their view of themselves), must see that the language is preserved. They cannot talk it just to themselves, they need an audience to grant them their identity. Language does not provide the peasant, worker, manager or scientist with his occupational identity but for many working in the world of culture in the twentieth century it does – and this is particularly the case in the Soviet Union where cultural policy has become so strongly identified with 'national cultures'. Hence it is not surprising to find the issues of language and education policy to be key concerns of the Ukrainian cultural intelligentsia, and that as part of this the historic nature of the Ukrainian nation is emphasised.[43]

What support is forthcoming from other sectors of the population? Despite the nationalist's view of the peasant, the latter's village and folk culture (however traditional – and that is perhaps the point) does not readily feed into nationalism. It is the towns that we need to look at. Here much will depend on where the Ukrainian peasantry move to – whether they move out of the Ukraine to, for example, Kazakhstan (as they have tended to), or to the towns of the Ukraine and, in this case, to which towns. There are the heavily Russian towns, and the more Ukrainian ones. It will depend where the job opportunities are, against whom they are competing, and whether Russian–Ukrainian divisions coincide with jobs, opportunities and benefits. They need not. Another division could be between the West Ukrainian peasantry (with its cultural values) facing what it sees as an alien and more skilled East Ukrainian community. But if the divide is Russian/ Ukrainian, and if the new 'Ukrainian' townsman finds himself at a disadvantage, then, given the presence of an articulate nationalist message, we would expect to see a response. And it is at this juncture that the ability and willingness of the state to suppress nationalist literature, control the media and harass opponents wil be important factors.

Let us finally consider the political elite. Could one argue, as some did in the case of Shelest, that sections of the elite are not immune to nationalism? While Shelest did flirt with the Kiev intelligentsia, it is difficult to know how to interpret this. Inherent in the job of First Secretary is the responsibility for and control of a territory; this is his fiefdom. The centre holds the First Secretary responsible, and hence the latter wants no rivals. But, in the case of the Ukraine, the three big party organisations, Kiev, Donetsk and Kharkov, do seem to act as rivals and to maintain their own links with Moscow.[44] This makes the task of First Secretary particularly difficult because he has simultaneously to defend his line to Moscow (against his rivals) and speak for the Ukraine as a whole in the competition for resources. He needs all the support he can get to present himself as *the* spokesman for the Ukraine, if he is being challenged from within – as Shelest was by Shcherbitsky. One can see how, in such a situation, a political leader may be receptive to a group that tells him there is a Ukrainian community, but only for as long as this is useful to him. His concerns are really rather different. (If one reads the republican press under Shelest and then under Shcherbitsky, it seems that Shcherbitsky fought as hard, if not harder, for Ukrainian economic interests.)

We have argued that the way in which social and political factors interact in Central Asia and the Ukraine differs, but that in neither case is the result likely to be a serious nationalist response, and, indeed, in Central Asia not one at all. But where the connections between cultural community and political territory have already been made, then the Soviet system must produce a nationalist response and conflict. We see this most clearly in Latvia and Estonia. They had a prior, recent existence as 'nation-states'. The points of comparison for their elites are Finland (for Estonia) and the East European countries.[45] Their position as the most economically advanced republics of the Soviet Union with the highest standard-of-living does not in itself have any consequences, but it can when combined with the influx of Russians and Ukrainians. It is not simply the cultural intelligentsia who fear a dilution of Latvian or Estonian culture and the loss of the language; neither management nor the indigenous industrial worker is likely to welcome the newcomers. From the point of view of management, the task of training and working with less-skilled labour, whose work-habits may weaken labour discipline and whose presence means that Russian has to be used as the language of instruction and industrial practice, is unattractive. Nor do they wish to compete with highly skilled technical and professional newcomers for what they traditionally see as their jobs. The local work-force, in turn, does not wish to see its jobs threatened, nor will it welcome new technical and managerial personnel who insist on speaking Russian.[46] The position of the scientific intelligentsia in the Baltic republics is different too: for the tiny Central Asian community, the move to using Russian and to Moscow is a leap into an advanced scientific world. For the Ukrainian, the shift into Russian is easy, involving little culture transfer. But the Baltic scientists would prefer to move straight to English, the international language of science, rather than having to make an unnecessary and unhelpful detour via Russian first. Hence the Baltic scientist will chafe at regulations requiring the use of Russian, and lend a sympathetic ear to colleagues in the humanities, striving to preserve the local language.

We see then how the interests of the different sectors of the intelligentsia and the urban working class provide a basis for opposition to rule by Moscow which has brought in its train an influx of Slavs. The political elite has to tread very carefully. If it was Slav too, then it would be even easier for the nationalist to argue that self-rule would solve the problems. Not surprisingly we find the claim that although the political leaders are nominally Balts, they are not *really*; they speak the language badly. They are, somehow, Russians in disguise.[47] Now of course it may be true that some of them have strong Russian links, but this, in itself, does not enable us to predict *anything* about their behaviour. To assume that it does, is to fall straight into the nationalist trap. A *real* patriot can only be someone who is *really* of his community's culture. It is interesting to see how this false assumption creeps into descriptions by Western authors of leaders of East European countries as 'Moscow communists' (that is, those who spent substantial periods of time in the USSR) when the author wishes to explain their failure to defend their country's interests, yet somehow is forgotten when the politician is someone such as Nagy who returned and then *did* defend his country's interests.[48] There is no evidence that identity of culture between leader and led produces a greater championing of the country's interests against an enemy than where they do not correspond. There is no reason to suppose that a political leadership made up of home-born Latvian-speakers would necessarily take a tougher line against Moscow than a culturally mixed one – other factors than *that* will determine their behaviour. What we can say is that the political elite in the Baltic republics is caught in a difficult situation, trying to reconcile Moscow's desire to see an integrated economy, Slav immigration both sponsored and spontaneous, and the local population's objections. It is not surprising that it is from this political elite that we see the strongest evidence of disagreement with Moscow, of insistence on the rights of minorities, criticism of insensitive cadre policy and Great Power chauvinism.[49]

A hypothesis that attempts to account for nationalism or its absence in the Soviet Union must include the Russians. Here too, we would argue, the social and political configuration is such that it fails to unite

the different sectors of the community, but this time there is a difference that makes the situation potentially more dangerous. For the
Russians (as indeed for the Ukrainians and to some extent the
Armenians and Jews), membership of the political elite means an all-
union elite, whose concerns and interests are Empire-wide. As rulers
of an isolated country in the 1920s, then defending the territory
against aggressors, the political elite identified itself increasingly with
the Soviet Union. But, until the break with China, there was another
strong identification – in the early days, with the proletariat and
oppressed of the capitalist states and the colonies; after the war, with
the rest of the new socialist world. With the Sino–Soviet split it
became increasingly difficult for the Soviet elite to see itself as
automatically representing either the world proletariat or the existing
world communist movement. The constituency shrank; but of one
thing the elite did remain certain: it was in charge of the Soviet Union
and responsible for defending its interests against the Americans and
the Chinese. Its members see themselves representing the Soviet
people: hence the importance placed on discussing and analysing this
entity and, given the assumption that a community should possess a
common culture, the consequent attempts to demonstrate the
common characteristics of this people. This defence of the Empire,
and the running of it, remains the dominant conccern of the political
elite and the armed forces.

Running an empire means moving resources around, co-ordinating
and controlling the separate parts, and for this a common language is
useful, if not essential. But Russian is not simply the political
language, it is also the language of industry, technology and science.
For specialists in these branches of the Russian intelligentsia, there is
no cultural divide between them and the politicians. A professional
divide there may be, and one that produces communities of 'scientists'
and 'managers' whose boundaries ignore origin, or nationality. It is
doubtful that dissatisfaction with the political system would turn the
scientists into Russian nationalists (that would be a curious jump),
although they might serve a nationalist state just as well as they do the
Soviet state. Managers are more likely to respond in a nationalist
fashion if their careers are threatened by new local engineers. But
what of the Russian cultural intelligentsia? In the 1930s this intelligentsia (which was Russian in language and culture but very mixed in
origin, with a heavy Jewish component) was still strongly inter-
nationalist, both in word and in practice. Even after a war
emblazoned with nationalist heroes and messages, when the political

climate, symbolised by the attack on cosmopolitanism, favoured a nationalist response from the intelligentsia, such a response was *not* forthcoming. It was only in the late 1960s that sections of the new Russian intelligentsia began turning to Slavophilism, thinking and expressing nationalist sentiments. The international outlook, the acceptance of Marxist tenets on the nature of society, the belief that a new progressive society was being created – all stock in trade of the intelligentsia until after the death of Stalin – worked against the forming of such sentiments. But as old beliefs crumbled, as the ideological terrain became more and more barren, the intelligentsia began to search elsewhere – at a time when the spectacular advances were over, when Chinese and Soviet leaderships were openly disputing old territory, when anti-Russian feelings were being expressed in some republics. For whom should they be spokesmen? Not surprisingly some picked up the message that the political elite had been working with for some time: that is, a society should be defined in terms of its own culture. Acceptance of this assumption led for some to the rediscovery of the Russian nation.[50]

To be influential they need a wider group to which they can appeal. As already mentioned, it is the Russian peasant who has done the moving over the last half century; men, women and children have broken with the traditional village and arrived in the towns in search of new skills and a new identity. For many, or for their children, opportunities were open. But what kind of new identities they forged is far from clear. Perhaps the nationalist wartime message got across to some. Of all the groups within the USSR, perhaps, the Russian urban worker – still a relative newcomer and now no longer facing the prospect of a better future – is the most open to new messages. Now, for the first time, the Russian nationalist has a constituency which might potentially listen. A crucial question then becomes, what else is on offer? The answer is, not much. The political elite is well aware that it needs new messages.[51] Not surprisingly, some elements within it are receptive to a Russian nationalist message; after all, they do take the value of a national culture, uniting a community, for granted. They fed this assumption to the intelligentsia in the first place. And it is convenient to encourage anti-Chinese feeling as a diversion from domestic ills. But there are more substantial reasons than this. When faced with obstruction and ingratitude, or evidence of serious maladministration in far-flung provinces, the politician at the centre (and it is irrelevant whether he is 'Russian', Latvian or Kazakh) faces a world peopled by tiresome provincials who know Russian badly, are corrupt and deceitful. How much easier it would be to run the Empire if everyone spoke Russian and behaved like a Russian; the problems are seen to stem from their being different. Hence the Politburo member flies into Tashkent and stresses the virtues, kindness and aid the Russian people has always shown to lesser people. But if the ardent Russian nationalist rejoices at this, the rejoicing is unfounded. Although the identification of central power with Moscow and the Russians disposes the all-union politician to such statements, his job of running an Empire makes him equally disposed to drawing back when there is trouble over language in the Caucasus. As a consequence of past policies, there are now administrative units run by their elites, there are firmly established language groups, and there are 'national' institutions of every conceivable kind (and a Third World impressed by them). To join hands with the Russian nationalists, feed a Russian nationalist message to the Russian workers where it might find a response, given the vacuum, would be disastrous.[52] Hence the political elite is not prepared to authorise such a message, tempting though it must seem at times. This must leave at least that section of the intelligentsia dissatisfied, alienated from the government and consequently even more prone to blame the political elite for refusing to safeguard Russian interests. It remains to hope that others within the intelligentsia and outside it can come up with an alternative message able to unite Soviet citizens into a different kind of alliance.

To conclude, we would argue that, in general, Western commentators have been too eager to see in Soviet multi-ethnic society a threat to the Soviet state. This is because of assumptions that ethnic identification, rivalry and nationalist attitudes somehow are either natural or must result from the centre's policies. If, however, one accepts that these assumptions are dubious and unproven – and that the wider literature on ethnic identification and the emergence of nationalism suggests these to be phenomena produced by a variety of complex social and political developments – then the relationship between national attitudes and the Soviet state begins to look rather different. We have argued that although some of the factors that have produced nationalist attitudes elsewhere in the world are present in the Soviet Union, there are features of the relationship between the Soviet State and its multi-ethnic society that militate against the emergence of such attitudes. The type of 'nationality' policy that has been pursued has resulted in very different kinds of self-identification, both within cultural communities and between them. The administrative arrangements, cadre policy and economic development have, in general, worked against the emergence of a shared national identification within an ethnic community, let alone a nationalist response from it. We need insights from what is happening in the rest of the world and detailed studies of the individual communities within the USSR if we are to predict the future of the Soviet multi-ethnic community.

NOTES

1. Yu. V. Bromlei, in the discussion on 'Stanovlenie i razvitie novoi istoricheskoi obshchnosti sovetskogo naroda' organised by *Istoriya SSSR*, no. 6 (1980) p. 23. See also E. Allworth (ed.), *Ethnic Russia in the USSR* (Oxford, 1980) p. xv, for a reference to a Soviet scholar's unofficial statement that the 'most crucial matter ... facing Soviet society' was the ethnic question. Opinions dissenting from the current 'crisis' view are expressed by: V. Zaslavsky, 'The Ethnic Question in the USSR', *Telos*, Fall 1980; R. Medvedev, *On Soviet Dissent* (London, 1980) pp. 45–50; P. Rutland, see present volume, pp. 150–78. J. Azrael, in his contribution to J. Azrael (ed.), *Soviet Nationality Policies and Pratices* (New York, 1978) states that he too dissents but in his subsequent analysis of the problems suggests that they are not amenable to solution. The literature on the national question, Western and Soviet, is so substantial that I shall not venture to start listing it; many key works, themselves containing good bibliographies, will be referred to in the course of the chapter.
2. As R. Lewis puts it, 'A more pertinent issue with regard to the dominance of the Russians is, so what if they were only a plurality and not a majority of the Soviet population? ... The Russians are and have been the dominant political group in the USSR and in the Russian Empire, despite their varying relative share of the population. Furthermore, there is no indication that their dominance has varied with their relative share of the population' — in Allworth, *Ethnic Russia*, p. 307; see also L. Labedz, in the same volume, pp. 201–2; and Zaslavsky, 'The Ethnic Question', p. 66, who reminds us of the unsatisfactory nature of an argument which 'arbitrarily' draws 'a political conclusion from a demographic premise'.
3. T. Rakowska-Harmstone, 'The Study of Ethnic Politics in the USSR', in G. Simmonds (ed.), *Nationalism in the USSR and Eastern Europe* (Detroit, 1977) p. 21; Z. Brzezinski, 'Political Implications of Soviet Nationality Problems', in E. Allworth (ed.), *Soviet Nationality Problems* (New York, 1971) pp. 77–8. In his article Brzezinski *asks* several of the relevant questions but then gives casual, throwaway answers, based on his guesses and not supported by evidence.
4. Azrael, *Soviet Nationality Policies*, provides a good account of these kinds of problems.
5. Labedz, in Allworth, *Ethnic Russia*, makes this point tellingly with reference to the discussion on Russian ethnicity. To return to one of the current favourites – birth-rates: maybe the changing proportion of Slavs and Central Asians and others in the population will promise a *more* stable and equal future for the nationalities in the USSR if it is the case (as

some have argued, for example, B. Denitch in Allworth, *Ethnic Russia*, p. 319) that harmony is easier to achieve where the partners are more equal. This is no more or less likely than the dire consequences so many *assume* must follow.

6. I. Dzyuba, *Internationalism or Russification?* (New York, 1968); M. Browne (ed.), *Ferment in the Ukraine* (London, 1971); for the Baltic republics, see T. Remeikis, 'Modern and National Identity in the Baltic republics', in I. Kamenetsky (ed.) *Nationalism and Human Rights* (Colorado, 1977); for Russian writings, see several of the contributions on this topic in Allworth, *Ethnic Russia*, and A. Yanov, *The Russian New Right* (Berkeley, 1978).

7. The quotation is from A. W. Orridge, 'Uneven Development and Nationalism: I', in *Political Studies,* XXIX (March 1981) p. 2. For good discussions of the origins of nationalism, and the nature of nationalist beliefs and their validity, see E. Kedourie, *Nationalism* (London, 1960); E. Gellner, *Thought and Change* (London, 1964) ch. 7. On the problem of defining groups in terms of their culture, see the introduction to F. Barth (ed.), *Ethnic Groups and Boundaries* (New York, 1969).

8. Or who see the development of nationalism as a natural phenomenon. Even Rakowska-Harmstone seems to share this view: 'minority nationalism does not exist in the Soviet Union except in a few isolated cases, partly, one suspects, because of political constraints imposed by the system (at least in the case of historical nations) and partly because the process of development of separate national identities on the part of some minorities has not yet reached this level' (in Simmonds, *Nationalism in the USSR*, p. 21). The very language we use shows how strongly nationalist assumptions have impregnated themselves. Take the popular phrase 'the awakening of nationalist consciousness', with its implication that something was there, lying dormant, waiting to be brought to life; or the suggestion that national consciousness can be suppressed by an alien power but never extinguished; it must spark to life again because it is somehow inborn. If all the writer means is that in the present twentieth-century world of nation-states and nationality movements, nationalism is a strong contender for forming group identity or that, given today's world, repressive rule by a group of an alien culture may well produce a nationalist reaction – there are no grounds for quarrel. Of course it may be sensible for such a persecuted group to argue that it would be better off if it was independent but that is *not* the nationalist's argument: for him or her it is self-evident.

9. Allworth, *Soviet Nationality Problems*.

10. First published as *L'Empire Eclaté* (Paris, 1978) (English-language edition, New York, 1979). An article which did put nationality problems in the Soviet Union in a new framework and prompted much of the later discussion was T. Rakowska-Harmstone's 'The Dialectics of Nationalism in the USSR', *Problems of Communism*, May–June 1974, but it was not followed by attempts to provide alternative frameworks.

11. London, 1979. Smith includes a chapter on 'Communist Nationalisms', which deals in part with the Third World, but there is no discussion at all of the USSR (as opposed to Russia pre-1917), despite a reference to the

Soviet Union having had 'to deal with troublesome nationalisms within and outside [their] domains' (p. 185).

12. H. Kohn, 'Soviet Communism and Nationalism: Three Stages of a Historical Development', in Allworth, *Soviet Nationality Problems*; I. Wallerstein, 'The Two Modes of Ethnic Consciousness: Soviet Central Asia in Transition?', in E. Allworth (ed.), *The Nationality Question in Central Asia* (New York, 1973).

13. See the discussion of such theories by Orridge, 'Uneven Development'. It is a pity because T. Nairn's *The Break-Up of Britain* (London, 1977) suggests many interesting avenues to pursue with reference to the USSR.

14. 'Some Reflections on Nationalism', in T. J. Nossiter *et al.*, *Imagination and Precision in the Social Sciences* (London, 1972) p. 386.

15. *Leninskii Kurs*, vol. 4 (Moscow, 1974) p. 50. The favourite quotation of those writing on the subject in the late 1970s. It is odd that some Western authors are *still* suggesting that Brezhnev referred to the national question as having been solved; he did not. His words were much more carefully chosen.

16. In his Congress speech, *Pravda* (24 February 1981) p. 7.

17. The different elements in the official position can be found coming up time and time again in, for example, articles by the republic first secretaries in *Kommunist* or *Voprosy filosofii*, although the emphasis may vary. Compare, for example, Rashidov's contribution in *Vop.fil.* (1978) no. 10, pp. 3–19 with the sophisticated article by Zimanas (editor of *Kommunist Litvy*) in *Vop.fil.* (1978) no. 3, pp. 20–9. M. Dzhunusov, *Dve tendentsii sotsializma v natsionalnykh otnosheniyakh* (Uzbekistan, 1975) combines a good statement of the official position with interesting data. For a recent discussion, see that in *Istoriya SSSR*, 1980, already mentioned, or the article by Rutkevich, in *Sotsiolog. issledovaniya* (1981) no. 2, pp. 14–24.

18. Zimanas, in *Istoriya SSSR*, 1980, p. 62.

19. V. P. Sherstobitov (ed.), *Sovetskiy narod – novaya istoricheskaya obshchnost' lyudey* (Moscow, 1975) p. 461. The 'nationalist' argument is to be found spelt out on pp. 460–1 of this work. Interestingly enough, within this edited volume there are marked differences of opinion among the contributors; in this it is similar to the Allworth (1980) volume which also contains contributions on quite different wavelengths.

20. On this latter point, Bromlei in the 1980 *Istoriya SSSR* discussion, p. 50, suggests that the Indian people should be considered an 'international entity', although capitalist. I have put together the general line of argument from various points made, for example, in *Sovremennye etnicheskie protsessy v SSSR* (Moscow, 1977) chs IX, XII, and conclusion. The journal *Sovetskaya etnografiya* carries a number of interesting articles on research in mixed communities that implicitly adopt this line.

21. This may be slightly too kind to some of the ethnographers who clearly do want to retain 'objective' historic entities, but many of them would agree (I think) with E. Keenan's conclusion to his nice article 'Royal Russian Behaviour, Style and Self-Image', in Allworth, *Ethnic Russia* – 'Russians do not commonly claim descent from Ivan the Terrible, but they do

readily express a great affinity for this unhappy man, in whom, as he is commonly represented, they sense familiar features of "our Soviet – pah – Russian man" ... There is something to this, perhaps. But the feeling would not be mutual. And those who search for the roots of the ethnic attitudes of Russians in the culture of the Muscovite court, which in so many ways did lay its impress upon modern political culture, are looking under the wrong stone. These are modern attitudes, whose mature development has a pre-requisite in the popular assimilation and refinement of the drawing-room notion of *narod* and whose most pernicious effects are, unfortunately, but part of the price to be paid, for popular sovereignty (*narodnaya vlast*)' (p. 15).

22. Zimanas, *Vop.fil.*, pp. 24–5, where he distinguishes between objective and subjective causes.

23. The literature is, of course, huge. The authors upon whom the following is based are Gellner, Hobsbawm, Nairn (already cited), Smith (also his edited collection *Nationalist Movements*, London, 1976); contributions to E. Kamenka (ed.), *Nationalism: the Nature and Evolution of an Idea* (London, 1976); Orridge (previously cited) and his unpublished paper 'Structural Preconditions and Triggering Factors in the Development of European Sub-state Nationalism', presented to the PSA Conference, April 1980.

24. The problem is recognised by S. Bialer: 'What I have said demonstrates clearly that the multinational character of the Soviet Union poses potentially the most serious threat to the legitimacy of the Soviet state and to the stability of the Soviet regime. The question is why this potential threat has not until now become more of a reality, why the nationality problem has not become a real nationality crisis. To be frank, we do not have a full answer to this question, and I have not found an answer to it in anything I have read on the subject written in the East or West. (Our detailed knowledge of local politics and local sentiments in the Soviet Union is severely limited.) I can only offer certain key elements of an answer that will explain in part the ability of the Soviet leadership to contain an incipient ethno-political crisis' (*Stalin's Successors*, Cambridge, 1980, p. 212). But, alas, *all* that Bialer offers us is some data on republican personnel – now this *might* be relevant, very relevant, but unless Bialer puts it in a famework of analysis we really cannot tell. It is not a question of needing more information; we must first specify why we should want particular types of information.

25. In Central Asia the new boundaries were drawn so as to nullify existing groups and the possibility of a Pan-Turkism movement threatening Bolshevik rule, but once drawn, the new language community was stressed as the key to the republic.

26. Kohn, 'Soviet Communism', makes this point.

27. It *could* be that such a view rests on sensible empirical investigation: i.e. where states do rest on such a community, they last longer, there is less unrest, the population is happier, etc. But to know this we should first have to establish what constitutes a shared culture, and second, decide how we measure stability, unrest, discontent, unhappiness, etc.: clearly not an easy task and not one that the politicians have undertaken. A

contrasting notion of what creates political loyalty can be seen in the British Empire where cultural diversity, different political and social relationships were quite acceptable because it was 'loyalty to the Queen' that magically united all.

28. *Sovremennye etnicheskie protsessy* chs V, VI; on the Ukraine, Lewis *et al.*, 'The Growth and Redistribution of the Ukrainian Population of Russia and the USSR, 1897–1970', in P. Potichnyj (ed.), *Ukraine in the Seventies* (Oakville, 1975).
29. *Sovremennye etnicheskie protsessy* ch. V.
30. Zaslavsky, 'The Ethnic Question', pp. 47–8.
31. Dzhunusov, *Dve tendentsii sotsializma*, p. 38.
32. In his interesting article 'Russians in the Ukraine and Problems of Ukrainian Identity in the USSR', in Potichnyj, *Ukraine*, p. 213.
33. Zaslavsky, 'The Ethnic Question', p. 50.
34. For an earlier different form of this, in the 1920s, children in Leningrad would boast that their father was a 'trade-union member', a high status symbol of the time, carrying very definite benefits, whereas they would hide the fact that he was a *lishenets*, which carried with it the danger of eviction, loss of job, etc. These were the groups that mattered and state policy created them; nationality – who cared or thought in such terms?
35. Zaslavsky, 'The Ethnic Question', p. 63.
36. Ibid, p. 49. For references to the surveys, see his discussion.
37. *Sovremenny etnicheskie protsessy* ch. V.
38. G. Hodnett, *Leadership in the Soviet National Republics: A Quantitative Study of Recruitment Policy* (Oakville, 1978) ch. 6.
39. *Sovremennye etnicheskie protsessy*, ch. V.
40. Ibid, p. 128, provides a table for 1959 showing quite how small. For example, only 4 per cent of the indigenous population was classified as industrial workers in Uzbekistan, Tadjikistan and Kirgizia. A distinction should probably be made between heavy industry (still more Slav) and light; this further complicates the relationships. It could provide the basis for an occupational/ethnic identity.
41. It was Shafarevich whose personal observation in *From Under the Rubble* (London, 1975) p. 88, provides the 'evidence' for this suggestion by some Western authors, but *he* goes on to suggest that even when making such a statement, Central Asians must know it makes little sense.
42. The Church in the W. Ukraine could, perhaps, provide a difference but then that would only help to distinguish west and east Ukrainian cultures, which is the last thing the Ukrainian nationalist wants to do – it might well turn out that *that* is the more significant divide than that between Russian and Ukrainian. On West/East Ukraine, see Y. Bilinsky, 'The Incorporation of West Ukraine and its Impact on Politics and Society in Soviet Ukraine', in R. Szporluk (ed.), *The Influence of Eastern Europe and the Soviet West on the USSR* (New York, 1975).
43. The fact that if the criterion of language and history was taken seriously the present Ukraine would lose major regions (see Szporluk, ibid) represents the typical dilemma for the nationalist, but, just as did the nineteenth-century European nationalists, so their Ukrainian counterparts avoid the problem by ignoring it. The existence of Russification policies in

education, crude chauvinist attitudes of Russian officials and political repression are rightly stressed by the Ukrainian dissidents (see Browne, *Ferment*); we are concerned here with the form the response takes.

44. On the Shelest affair, G. Hodnett, 'Ukrarian Politics and the Purge of Shelest', unpublished paper presented at Midwest Slavic Conference, May 1977; contributions by Y. Bilinsky and J. Pelenski to Potichnyj, *Ukraine*.

45. Lithuania is more complicated. On the one hand, given the Church and political past, Poland is the point of comparison, on the other, economically and also from past political connections, Belorussia is the reference point.

46. It would be good to have an occupational breakdown of the immigrants in order to get a better sense of which groups will feel most threatened. A. Kholmogorov, *Internatsionalnye cherty sovetskikh natsii* (Moscow, 1970) ch. I, suggests an influx of skilled workers and professional people but this could reflect the nature of his survey. Pavlovich in Allworth, *Ethnic Russia*, p. 296, suggests skilled technicians and professions but the reference he gives does not substantiate the claim. *The 17 Latvian Communist Protest Letter* (Berlin, 1972) p. 15, suggests all types are coming, as does a survey from Riga, quoted by J. Dreifelds, 'Latvian National Demands and Group Consciousness since 1959', in Simmonds, *Nationalism in the USSR*, P. 145.

47. *The 17 Latvian Communist Protest Letter*, p. 21; and for an elaboration of this theme, see Dreifelds, 'Latvian National Demands', p. 144.

48. An interesting wiggle in the argument, made so as to accommodate someone such as Stalin and yet leave the assumption untouched, is that an individual from a different culture often becomes a more rabid nationalist of his new country than do its own inhabitants, just as converted Catholics are the most rigid and intolerant members of the Church. Is it true? How often? Or is it quite false?

49. See Dreifelds, 'Latvian National Demands'; *The 17 Latvian*; and Zimans, in *Vop.fil.*

50. This draws in part from an earlier (unpublished) paper, 'The Soviet Leadership's Search for Legitimacy', presented at the PSA Conference, March 1978, which now seems to me either wrong or inadequate in its treatment of the subject.

51. The concern is well shown in the Central Committee edict, 'On the further improvement of ideological, political-educational work', of 26 April 1979, and subsequent conferences organised on this theme.

52. It has been rumoured that crude nationalist leaflets distributed in working-class districts in Moscow in the late 1970s were the work of political officials.

7 Institutionalisation and Political Change in Poland

Paul G. Lewis

INSTITUTIONALISATION IN COMMUNIST SYSTEMS

State power, its accumulation and exercise, has long been seen as one of the strengths of the communist political system. When Western political scientists were busily 'rediscovering politics' in the 1960s they expressed considerable respect for communist leaders and the systems they had created. It may be, wrote Paige, 'that we shall have to credit the rediscovery of politics to the totalitarians such as Lenin in Russia, Mao in China, and Kim Ilsong in North Korea'.[1] Huntington equally expressed admiration for the effectiveness of the political systems that such leaders had constructed: 'the one thing communist governments can do is govern; they do provide effective authority. Their ideology furnishes a basis of legitimacy, and their party organisation provides the institutional mechanism for mobilizing support and executing policy.'[2] It is strange that, precisely as American analysts were being impressed by communist political achievements, the durability and effectiveness of the communist machine was being sharply questioned by those engaged in running it. Indeed, with benefit of hindsight, Cocks wrote: 'The 1960s had a sobering, if not shattering effect on minds and models in Communist studies. . . Interest in social engineering and system change subsided as ruling Communist elites struggled anxiously to preserve existing structures and methods. Moreover, their ability to direct and control change either imposed from above or arising spontaneously from below declined substantially.'[3] This statement suggests that the very totalitarians (or their successors) who

211

had 'rediscovered politics' had now lost it and were desperately seeking to re-enact their former achievement.

Subsequent events suggest that they have not been wholly successful. Indeed, apart from sheer survival (itself no mean achievement), it may well be that no progress or development of their capacity to control change has occurred. We have particularly in mind the maintenance of the leading role of the Party and the evolution of new forms of leadership. With regard to the Soviet Union it was stated that, 'In many respects the task that confronts Brezhnev today resembles that which Khrushchev faced two decades ago – namely, to overcome bureaucratic inertia and ministerial resistance to program innovations, fresh approaches, and new methods in order to enahnce his own capacity (and of central authorities more generally) for executive leadership.'[4] A more recent evaluation does not give the impression that much progress has been made since then: 'As the scenario was planned, the party would put its own house in order and then rely upon its control and inspection capabilities to bring the larger and presumably even more reluctant state bureaucracy into line. The difficulty has been that the first step never has been fully taken.'[5] In Poland, leadership efforts met with even less success. A. Kraczewski of the Institute for the Study of Socialist Countries, maintained that in 1980 'the bureaucracy was brought into the greatest discredit ever in the history of our country...and that discredit applied to leading elites of interest groups forming both the economic and the political decision-making system'.[6] The Party leadership found its control over social and economic processes weakening, and appeared to be quite unable to master the central state administration, let alone improve or change its mode of operation. Thus Paweł Bożyk, the head of a group of scientific advisers summoned by the First Secretary of the Central Committee in 1977, describes how 'the government introduced an informal prohibition on the passage of information to Central Committee workers, including the group of advisers, and some members of the government used the [term] "opposition" as a kind of humorous description of them'.[7] A starker example of the failure of party leadership within communist systems would be hard to find.

But it would be unwise just for this reason to reject out of hand the approaches suggested by those proclaiming a 'rediscovery of politics', particularly in so far as that discussion concerned the central role of political institutions and the state administration. For it is precisely the inability or unwillingness of communist elites to bring about change within or between political institutions that has been responsible for many of the problems afflicting communist political systems. Moreover, these problems in many ways reflect the very success of earlier political elites in initiating and controlling certain processes of large-scale change. They are in this sense the problems of success. It was, indeed, for this reason that Huntington and Paige paid particular attention to the experience of communist states, although their primary focus was on politics in developing countries. This helps to explain why the writers quoted above seemed grossly to exaggerate the effectiveness of the communist sytsem. Nevertheless their insights may still serve to elucidate the contemporary predicament of many communist states. This is particularly the case with Huntington, whose institutionalisation thesis has already been applied to Poland by Gitelman.[8] In this discussion I propose to outline the ways in which the institutionalisation process can be seen to be applicable to communist systems, identify certain problems that arise with this application of the model, and suggest a way in which it can more usefully be applied to contemporary communist systems, taking the course of political development in Poland as an example.

Huntington's major work on this topic contains the following definition of the central process he analyses: 'Institutionalization is the process by which organisations and procedures acquire value and stability. The level of institutionalization of any political system can be defined by the adaptability, complexity, autonomy, and coherence of its organizations and procedures.'[9] On the face of it these criteria are well chosen to illuminate the issues confronting the political institutions of the communist states and to gauge the success with which their political systems are responding to pressures for change. Adaptability, for example, may be seen to refer to the ability to change from the early priorities of establishing communist control and of implementing a particular policy of heavy industrial development. Huntington also saw 'many of the communist states of Eastern Europe...grappling with the problem of adaptation to the pressures for the dispersion of power'.[10] Complexity involves the degree of organisational differentiation, both vertical and horizontal, and the capacity to involve its members in diverse ways. Here Cocks emphasised Soviet and East European regimes trying 'to integrate and manage complexity through modern organisation and technology'.[11] Autonomy is achieved by the erection of defences against the excessive influence of social forces and groups and preventing the subordination of the political organisation to their demands. The Soviet

prejudice against representative democracy and the early determination of the Soviet elite to exert their leadership role in society suggest
that autonomy is an element central to the communist model.
Coherence refers to the maintenance of sufficient unity to sustain
organisational activity and is closely related to autonomy. Taken in
conjuction the *desiderata* of coherence and autonomy would seem to
be successfully embodied in the conception and practice of democratic
centralism. As Huntington points out, 'Discipline and development go
hand in hand.'[12]

The process of institutionalisation thus seems readily applicable to
the organisations that constitute the communist political system and,
indeed, reflects a course of development that is apparently quite
advanced in the European communist countries. Coherence and
autonomy may be seen as principles that lie at the heart of
Marxist–Leninist organisations, while the requirement of complexity
would seem to be well satisified by the ramifications (indeed, excessive
bureaucratisation some might say) of the communist party organisations and their affiliated groups. The element of adaptability is also an
important aspect of political change in contemporary communist
systems, although it faces party leaderships with somewhat greater
problems. The need for adaptability, for example, can be traced to the
perceived necessity of transforming party structures and their style of
work as the initial stage of establishing communist control and constructing the basis of a modern industrial economy comes to an end.
With the abandonment of terror as a political resource and the emergence of new political and administrative tasks relating to the management of a modern economy and the government of an increasingly
urban-industrial society, new demands are made on the central political institutions of communist rule. In so far as it was the actions of the
party and its organs that played by far the major part in bringing into
being the system that generates these new demands, the effort of
adaptation, especially where it concerns the party, is correspondingly
large, and the process of change one that involves the basic nature of
the communist system. Indeed, the major upheavals in communist
systems since the death of Stalin have, in some way, been concerned
with unsuccessful or awkward attempts to adapt central political
institutions to these new demands. During the 1960s such developments included the removal of Khrushchev, which may be linked with
his attempts to reorganise the party into industrial and agricultural
sections, the better to ensure party leadership of economic development, and to other measures designed to energise party activities

which met with considerable opposition from party cadres. The upheavals of the Chinese Cultural Revolution, on the other hand, may be set within the context of a sustained onslaught on the party apparatus and its trained cadres by the leader himself, in order to counter centralism and undermine bureaucratic tendencies. In Czechoslovakia the Prague Spring can be interpreted as the belated response of the leadership to the demands of a now stagnant economy, a process in which it lost control over the changing relationship between party and society. Finally, the Polish workers' revolt of 1970 demonstrated the penalties of not confronting the need for adaptation in any way at all. Economic reform and a relaxation of the control exercised by the central party/state apparatus had been proposed several times yet never implemented, while the party's ability to control social processes had also weakened considerably. All these political developments can be seen as crises of the institutionalisation process as conceived by Huntington, in particular where it refers to the adaptation of organisations and procedures in the face of new challenges.

In his discussion of political parties Huntington seems to suggest not only that the criteria of institutionalisation can be readily applied to the communist case, but also that Communist parties are well placed to meet such challenges and thus strengthen their position as the main agents of control over a relatively developed communist society and economy. Elaborating on the topics of mobilisation and organisation, he writes, 'those twin slogans of communist action... define precisely the route to party strength. The party and the party system which combine them reconcile political modernization with political development.'[13] The relevance of the institutionalisation thesis to communist systems thus seems well established: first, because Huntington's was one of the few key works that has recently focused the attention of political analysts on institutions and organisations, obviously a fruitful line of study when the countries at issue are those that provide the most striking examples of the 'administered society'; Second, because it has directed attention to the dominant influence of political over social and economic factors, and thus represents an appropriate point of departure for the analysis of systems which have already prompted a 'rediscovery of politics' but whose current predicament has suggested a crisis in the exercise of political leadership. Nevertheless, while institutionalisation offers a potentially fruitful approach to the study of contemporary communist politics, it must be recognised that Huntington's sanguine early judgement on the effectiveness of communist political leadership and the dynamic nature of communist political systems has not been borne out by subsequent political developments. Before turning to consider institutionalisation within the Polish context it is worth noting certain problems that have been detected in applications of the thesis to other political contexts.

In an early application of Huntington's model to France, for example, it was pointed out that the implications of institutionalisation for developed societies may differ from those in systems at a lower level of political development. Thus it was suggested that the stability with which Huntington is centrally concerned is threatened in developed polities not by the underinstitutionalisation which subverts the political order of transitional societies but rather by overinstitutionalisation, whereby past successes of institutions hinder their adaptation, to new challenges.[14] This observation serves to strengthen the importance placed earlier in this discussion on adaptation as a factor helping or hindering the institutionalisation of communist organisa tions. Indeed, this is also suggested by Kesselman when he points out that 'Huntington describes how communist regimes in developing countries are adept at creating political institutions and order, but ignores the corollary: that communist regimes stifle autonomous organisations and demands long after their societies have advanced beyond the premodern condition.'[15] A second problem in applying the thesis arises from uncertainty concerning the level at which Huntington's generalisations are intended to operate. Discussion of the institutionalisation of organisations and procedures (which are the sphere within which the process is apparently conceived as operating) tends to elide with that of the polity as a whole.[16] This confusion has given thus rise to doubts concerning the feasibility of operationalising the concepts in a coherent manner and of avoiding the dangers of tautology that attend the shift from micro to macro level. A third problem centres on Huntington's dominant value orientation towards order and stability, which has been commented on from a variety of angles.[17] It is in this connection that Ben-Dor suggests that some tyranny is here being exercised by the Leninist model which leads Huntington to ingore the later problems that further development of the communist system can bring: 'The Leninist party may become dysfunctional to any sort of development other than a very narrow definition of "order", it may be overly autonomous and thus absorbed in itself, losing touch with the environment and producing corruption; it may be so complex that coordination and coherence within it may become well-nigh impossible; and it may be so "adaptable" that it will refuse to die when no longer functional.'[18] All in all, it is suggested, Huntington's thesis does little to comprehend the developmental problems inherent in the Leninist political model. The preoccupation with political order, particularly in the transitional societies of the Third World, and the evident problems – of both a theoretical and practical nature – involved in applying an American model of development to them, lead to the adoption of an idealised view of Marxist–Leninist rule as the remedy for political disorder. But in prescribing this remedy Huntington is thinking rather of Lenin's achievements and the construction of the Soviet state, which was completed under Stalin, rather than the political system administered and tinkered with by Khrushchev, Kosygin and Brezhnev. Yet it is the latter reality with which communist leaders have had to contend in Eastern Europe and the Soviet Union over the past thirty years. Let us then see how one analyst has applied Huntington's model to post-Stalinist Poland.

POLITICAL INSTITUTIONALISATION IN POLAND

Gitelman's study concerned Polish workers' councils and their successors, the Conference of Workers' Self-Management.[19] It concluded, along similar lines to Kesselman's study of France, that the network was overinstitutionalised and that for this reason it proved ineffective as a structure linking elite with masses. In the study, Huntington's view of institutionalisation as a process whereby organisations and procedures acquire value and stability is introduced and, while the *stability* of the workers' councils is documented (albeit in fossilised form since 1958 as part of the Conference of Workers' Self-Management), the rapidly declining *value* attached to them since 1956 is substantiated in summaries of various surveys and research projects: 'there were institutions not valued by the working mass, although all had manifested outward stability'.[20] Huntington's view of the process is thus challenged, as institutions are seen to persist and remain stable without value being ascribed to them. Indeed, similar connections between apparent overinstitutionalisation, stagnation of political processes and consequent outbreaks of disorder were drawn in the Polish press soon after the workers' riots of 1976. Arguing the need for 'real participation', criticism was made of

a certain lack of correspondence between well-developed institutions which are supposed to represent the population and the rather modest effects of their activity...Thus there exist silent meetings because potential contributors are overwhelmed by the authority of their governors, there are discussions which degenerate into empty chatter and there occur eruptions of demagogy which discount all reality.[21]

The account of workers' councils presented by Gitelman accords with other analyses and may be accepted as a convincing image of Polish public life.

Unfortunately, however, his conclusion is not one that can be said to rest on an analysis of *institutionalisation* – the criteria of adaptability, complexity, autonomy and coherence are not even mentioned. Indeed, it is not really this composite process that he can be said to be discussing at all. This is not very surprising. For if institutionalisation is the process whereby stability and value are acquired, this in turn implies that organisations and procedures must possess a certain degree of autonomy (as much from other political organisations as from the social forces that Huntington mentions) in order that they may operate to acquire those characteristics (or not, as the case may be). Apart from organisations already in existence or those set up under official auspices, it is difficult, under normal conditions, to identify structures whose institutionalisation may be studied within the communist system. Such constraints are, naturally, acknowledged by Gitelman, who writes that 'the councils, instead of being abolished, were coopted into the existing institutional framework...Thus, the councils had been diluted and party control, via the unions and party organisations, was assured.'[22] This incorporation was formalised in December 1958, while the first councils had been set up only in late 1956, permitting them at most 'nearly eighteen months [of existence] as relatively autonomous bodies'.[23] The point is an obvious one but it does need to be made if such an institutional study is to be carried out in the context of the communist political system – in such a bureaucratised and highly administered system there is a great difference between organisations that do wield power and fulfil some genuine function and those that exist merely as façades. There is no real point in considering the latter from the viewpoint of institutionalisation, as their fate is decided elsewhere, and they have no opportunity to acquire value by virtue of their operation.

This fact emerges clearly from the statements and actions of the Polish political authorities. Shortly before the onset of the 1980 crisis the First Secretary of a major provincial Party committee (Łódź) pointed out that when 'Party organisations and the administration fully understand and appreciate the role of the Conference of Workers' Self-Management and operate not alongside but through it, the Conference can perform a creative and positive role'.[24] Outbreaks of worker unrest serve, of course, to direct the attention of party officials to the virtues of such forms of consultation with the factory workforce with exceptional rapidity. From subsequent reports it emerged that decentralised forms of consultation were introduced in at least one Radom factory in what must have been a matter of weeks following the upsurge of discontent in 1976. According to the Secretary of the factory party committee (KZ), it was a useful innovation: 'we were convinced that people express themselves quite differently in the official forum of the Conference than on their own shopfloor. Here they are less restrained, they take up critical matters with greater boldness.'[25] Such comments support Gitelman's conclusion about the low value ascribed to the work of the Conference in general, but they also demonstrate clearly that it is party officials and those in similar posts of authority who decide whether such institutions are to be given a positive role and thus acquire a certain 'value'. The question, therefore, is less one of whether organisations operate in such a way as to acquire stability and value, than of whether party authorities choose to make use of the particular institutional means at their disposal. It is clear from his discussion of the Self-Management Conference that autonomous workers' councils were never accepted by the party authorities and that their activities were curbed at the earliest opportunity. So when Gitelman states that 'the workers were alienated from the institutions that purported to represent their interests',[26] and thereby links the councils and the Conference with the upheaval of 1970 (not to mention that of 1976), the relation can only be a tenuous one, as the capacity of the councils to represent workers' interests lasted only a few months in the fourteen-year period 1956–70.

The organisation that occupied a more central position between elite and masses and played a decisive role in mediating relations between the two groups was, of course, the Polish United Workers' Party. If, indeed, Gitelman was seeking to establish a causal link between the institutional status of the councils (or Conference) and the disorders of 1970, the pertinent question would be why, as the formal emasculation of the councils took place in 1958, the workers' revolt did not take place earlier. The important questions concerning the nature of Polish political institutions have to be directed at the party and its associated structures, for here were organisations and procedures that were encountering rather more genuine problems of institutionalisation, for, as the leadership discovered in December 1970, they had acquired neither value nor stability. Huntington's concern with political order does indeed find here some resonance in developments within the Polish political system, but in order for his thesis to be usefully applied, certain methodological distinctions need to be made. As suggested at the end of the introductory section, the first point to be borne in mind is that while insufficient institutionalisation is likely to be the major threat to political order in a developing or transitional society, in a developed society the problem is equally if not more likely to centre on overinstitutionalisation. This is particularly true of an established communist state, with a very high degree of organisational complexity and bureaucratic development. The most fruitful focus of analysis is thus less likely to be on whether young organisations are able to accommodate themselves to the diverse demands of their environment, than on whether older organisations are capable of change to a degree sufficient to enable them to process and cope with new requirements that are placed on their operation. Second, the level of analysis needs to be clearly specified. If the institutionalisation of organisations and procedures is to be seen as a factor on which political order is largely dependent, then the position of the organisation with regard to the system as a whole needs to be specified and its political significance demonstrated. If the failure of the organisation or procedure to acquire both value and stability does not undermine political order (which was the case with the Self-Management Conference) then, of course, institutionalisation will not have a direct bearing on the stability of the polity in general. More significant questions might arise, for example, in connection with the adaptation of the party to the conditions of a modern society and the management of an industrial economy. This factor, indeed, is likely to have been more influential on worker–elite relations during the Gomułka period, and manifested itself in such performance indicators as the very small rise in popular incomes during the 1960s, which was surpassed by all other Comecon countries. Pointers to the lack of adaptation can be found in such observations that specialist group representatives on the party's Central Committee in Poland, as distinct from those of other East European parties, 'during the Gomułka era (were) composed exclusively of people from universities and learning institutes'. More concerted efforts at adaptation to economic needs could perhaps be detected after 1970 with 'a significant presence of managers/technocrats on the Polish Central Committee'.[27] Third, the particularly high priority assigned by Huntington to political order and organisational persistence needs some qualification in the communist context if value *and* stability are to be regarded as more or less equal expressions of the process of institutionalisation. It is clear that communist systems greatly favour the persistence of established organisations and procedures, particularly those concerning the party, with less regard being paid (or needing to be paid) to whether they have acquired value or not. As, however, the acquisition of value is a particularly difficult process to isolate within communist societies, the dangers of tautological argument loom large. As Taubman has pointed out (though somewhat overstating his case) in connection with the related transformation-or-degeneration approach: 'it is impossible to disprove. What would constitute transformation is fairly clear, but how is one to know when degeneration has set in?'[28] But his implication that the 'day of reckoning' somehow never arrives cannot now be accepted, as recent developments in Poland have shown. It is to their institutional background that we now turn our attention.

ADAPTATION AND THE POLISH PARTY

In approaching political change in Poland within the conceptual framework of institutionalisation it is clear that the processes of change involving the organisations and procedures of the party must occupy the central place in our study. Further, it is clear both from the above brief consideration of institutionalisation in Poland and from the earlier discussion of Huntington's thesis in relation to communist states, that it is the capacity of the party to adapt to the conditions of 'established communism' that is likely to be the most fruitful focus for the analysis of change in the Polish political system. In using the term 'established communism' I am intending to emphasise the position of a party faced with a specific set of tasks peculiar to a new phase of communist state development, when (in Lowenthal's words) 'the characteristic problems of forced modernization as a revolutionary process...have come to be replaced by the new problems of a post-revolutionary, "established" single-party regime in a more or less mature industrial society'. In this context all communist parties are faced with the necessity 'sooner or later...to adapt to a new post-revolutionary role'. It should be noted that the concept of 'established communism' has certain similarities with the contemporary Soviet self-definition 'developed socialism', particularly in the importance for the latter concept of the 'economy's entirely new magnitude'. A major difference, however, is that 'established communism' envisages change occurring in the position and character of the party in the face of new demands; 'developed socialism', on the other hand, stresses more the unchanging nature of the communist party and 'the increasing identification of the ideal with the main features of actual society. As institutions become ends, goals are redefined gradually to resemble the characteristics of established structures.'[29]

As suggested earlier, the most significant political changes within communist states over the past two decades can be closely linked with different attempts to stimulate the adaptation of party organisation and procedures, in order that they might more successfully facilitate the performance of its leading role and that the party might express and satisfy the needs and aspirations of an increasingly developed communist society. In several of these cases, however, the attempt to promote the adaptation of the party came into conflict with two other factors forming part of the institutionalisation process: first, the maintenance or enhancement of autonomy and, second, of coherence. Initial attempts to redefine the role of the Soviet party following the death of Stalin, for example, unleashed forces that sought to unseat Khrushchev and led to the installation of Brezhnev and Kosygin, who disavowed Khrushchev's mishandling of the party and proclaimed their 'trust in cadres'. In the course of the Czechoslovak reform movement the party lost its autonomy from social forces and became a popular movement for change, party autonomy only being restored from without with the imposition of 'normality' under the banner of the Brezhnev doctrine. Although a rather different case and one that hardly fits the category of established communism, Chinese experiences during the Cultural Revolution illustrate the loss of coherence within the mechanisms of political guidance and control and the virtual destruction of the party as an institution. Each of these attempts thus failed to adapt party organisation and procedures to the perceived needs of the situation whilst satisfying other conditions of institutional development or survival. It should be noted that this notion of adaptation, centring on changes in organisation and procedures, differs somewhat from the later usage of Huntington, who also subsequently stressed the importance of party adaptation in the institutional establishment of revolutionary one-party regimes. In this the term was reserved for the process in which 'the party deals with legal–rational challenges to its authority', which largely involved the evolution of means to facilitate the participation of technocrats, general interest groups, intelligentsia and the masses in the sphere of party authority.[30]

But despite these experiences the need for party adaptation remained strong and was well recognised by communist leaders. Subsequent approaches to political change, however, have involved more conservative strategies of reform. In the early 1970s the keynote was set by Brezhnev who pointed to the opportunities of improved processes of direction, control and management offered by the 'scientific and technical revolution'. At the Twenty-Fourth Party Congress, Brezhnev thus stressed the importance of fusing 'the achievements of the scientific and technical revolution with the advantages of the socialist economic system'.[31] The importance of similar partial reforms and the desirability of controlled change were also expressed in Eastern Europe. This included several measures of institutional change concerning the unification of party and state hierarchies to enhance party leadership, and the simplification of party and state structures to facilitate the implementation of central decisions and top-level policy.[32] The institutional changes that were made in the 1970s were therefore of a relatively conservative nature and their consequences generally limited in their effects. As earlier statements have suggested, improvements in Soviet party procedures and controls appear also to have been minimal over this period, while Brezhnev's failure to refer to the scientific and technical revolution at the Twenty-Sixth Party Congress also probably reflected disillusion with its potentialities for enhancing party authority. But despite the limited achievements of this approach to political change, East European leaderships have mostly preserved their position in the past decade, whilst the status of the party in the communist political system has also been maintained. This, however, cannot be said of Polish developments.

The reforms made in Poland were introduced over several years, from 1972 to 1975, and were largely prompted by the awareness of the new Gierek leadership that new systems of administration and control were needed to regulate and sustain the ambitious programme of economic renovation and expansion that was envisaged for the 1970s. It is ironical in this connection to recall now that it was the years preceding and accompanying the introduction of the reforms that saw rapid economic growth, sharply rising industrial production levels and considerable improvements in popular consumption, while the situation changed with the enactment of reforms to one of economic stagnation, disequilibrium and growing popular dissatisfaction. Nevertheless, it was the firmly expressed belief of the new leadership that economic development was being held back by the existing system of administration and control. A higher degree of planning and co-ordination at *województwo* (province) level was singled out as a priority at an early stage, while excessive regional disparities were felt to call for more balance in the development of the different regions.[33] It was a major objective, stated Gierek, to create new territorial units which would 'accord with existing macroregions and take account of the developmental perspectives of industry and agriculture'.[34] Prime Minister Jaroszewicz stressed the fact that the development of political structures had not kept pace with economic development and that party policy was thus not being adequately implemented:

> Insofar as the system of state activity is delayed in its evolution in relation to the socialist development of the country, so conditions are created for the development of factors which put obstacles in the way of the realisation of the monolithic policy of the Party, weaken the services performed for society by the organs of authority, and give rise to bureaucratism and the excessive expenditure of time, effort and resources on the performance of social and economic tasks which it would be possible to carry out better, faster and more cheaply.[35]

But reform was prompted also by more explicitly political factors. As well as creating economic and developmental disproportions between regions, outdated and incoherent administrative procedures threatened harmful consequences, warping social attitudes and breeding 'particularism'.[36] The level of socio-political development of Polish society was seen to call for a new mode of political leadership. In an interesting use of military terminology the change was likened to the replacement of 'battle order' by 'scattered advance': 'socialism has now become a national programme – the system whereby the centre directs through a general transmitting mechanism is not now necessary'.[37] Gierek further emphasised the particular interest that the party had in improving the quality of administration: 'good administration strengthens state authority, that which is incompetent weakens it'.[38] As economic problems persisted, and the crisis worsened during the latter half of the 1970s with the outbreak of workers' demonstrations in 1976 and the adoption of the ill-fated economic manoeuvre (intended to restore economic stability), Gierek again indicated the importance of political factors in the resolution of economic problems:

> The decisive condition for the successful realisation of socio-economic tasks...is a good political climate which favours the participation and initiative of work-people. Efforts to strengthen our economy thus require at the same time strenuous activity in all spheres of political, state and social work.[39]

Political and economic objectives were thus interwoven in the reform measures taken in Poland during the 1970s.

The reforms may be summarised under the following headings.[40] Most important, though chronologically the last of the changes to be completed in 1975, was the abolition of the three-tier structure of administration and party control and the establishment of a two-tier one. The territorial division of the country formerly comprised 17 *województwa* (provinces), some 300 *powiaty* (districts) and several thousand rural and urban communes. The new structure comprised 49 *województwa*, generally considerably smaller than their predecessors, and (the *powiat* having been abolished altogether) more than two thousand enlarged rural communes (the *gmina*), which included around twenty villages and was intended to be autonomous in its routine administrative operation (in marked contrast to its predecessor). A second major change was the removal of all executive responsibilities from the People's Councils, which had previously been the backbone of the unified state structure, combining, in theory at least, executive with legislative functions. One-man executive management was established throughout the state structure and state executive authority thus concentrated in a single office in each unit of administration. Third, the local Party Secretary was now appointed to chair People's Councils at all levels, supposedly to enhance party leadership of society and to further self-government. By these means it was hoped to simplify the state structure and to clarify party/state relations, where the degree of overlap entailed unnecessary duplication of activity and made it difficult to assign responsibility for specific tasks.

The relevance of the reforms to the process of party adaptation, on the other hand, may be described in the following way. The establishment of the new network of rural communes was intended both to establish a strong state executive in the countryside at a level more

distant from the centre than the *powiat*, thus representing a decentralisation of state power, and also to strengthen the party network in
the rural environment. Following the abortive collectivisation
campaign that accompanied the Six-Year Plan (1950–55), well over
80 per cent of farm-land remained in the hands of private farmers.
Throughout the Gomułka period no coherent party network existed
below the level of the *powiat*, while the status of the former *gromada*
(or small commune) party committees – they were established only in
1959 – was particularly tenuous. Thus the move to establish a firmer
party base in the countryside, as well as establishing a strong state
executive, may be seen as a major step in the process of adapting to
the conditions placed on party rule by the dominance in the Polish
countryside of over three million peasant farms, and as a measure
enhancing the complexity of party organisation. As might have been
predicted, however, the role of the party secretary was not restricted
to formal PUWP activities and even less to leading the peasants' 'self-
government'. While in many cases the secretary came to play a part in
the machinery of party/state rule in collaboration with the local
executive, in others he took on directly administrative duties due to
the inadequacy of those specifically appointed to carry them out.[41]
Despite the attempt to make the most economic use of a limited pool
of qualified administrators, the supply of executives was invariably
less satisfactory than of those available for equivalent posts in the
rural (*gmina*) party organisation.

Despite the lack of power vested in the People's Councils, the
formal hegemony now exercised by the party over them should not be
viewed as significant in symbolic terms alone. The identification of
administrative responsibility with the person of the individual
executive at the various levels of the state structure, was designed both
to eliminate the ambiguities and confusion that had entered into the
diverse functions of the People's Council and its Presidium, and to
provide a complement within the state structure to the local party
chief, the pair thus personifying Gierek's otherwise simplistic slogan,
'the Party leads and the government governs'.[42] The identification of
one-man executive responsibility, and the commitment of party
authority to the organ of social control, cleared the way for more
effective supervision of the implementation of government decisions,
and for the development of a more effective state administration with
greater capacity to direct an advanced economy and social system.
The replacement of the three-tier state structure by a two-tier one may
be seen as a more direct adaptation of party structure and procedures

to the consolidation of the communist system within Poland. The bases of socialist society had now been established, the economic foundations laid and a generation raised within the institutions of the socialist system. Even if many arduous tasks lay ahead, the heavy ground-work was felt to have been completed and more sophisticated structures of leadership and administration to be appropriate. A further aspect of the change was summed up in another leadership slogan, 'the authorities closer to the people'. This rather ambiguous phrase carried a number of implications, among them that of greater effectiveness and the promise of greater social control over the administrative bureaucracy. But it also offered the hope of more direct party control over society. Babiuch, at the time party secretary responsible for cadres, was pleased to point out in 1977 that 'now, after the reform of the territorial structure of the country, over 64 per cent of Party apparat workers operate at the lower levels, having direct contact with the basic Party organisations'.[43] In a country with an overwhelming preponderance of Catholics, with a countryside dominated by private farmers and with a history of periodic worker unrest, this change represented a rather different form of adaptation. Polish institutional changes in the early 1970s thus reflected the need of the party to adapt not only to what was seen as a rapidly growing and modernising economy, but also to a society that continued to pose complex problems to mechanisms of central political control.

PARTY AUTONOMY AND THE REFORMS

Institutionalisation within the Polish context involved not only measures to facilitate the adaptation of party organisations and procedures to the demands of an essentially post-revolutionary phase of development, but also the improvement of methods of party leadership and the maintenance of its 'autonomy'. This, indeed, was the main point of Gierek's phrase, 'the Party leads and the government governs'. By unravelling the legislative and executive functions of the People's Councils and re-identifying them solely as agencies of 'social self-government' and social control (reinforced in their 'social leadership' role by the direct leadership of the Party Secretary of the appropriate organ), executive responsibilities and activities pertaining to the administration of the state became the concern of the newly appointed executives (called '*wojewód*' at province level, '*prezydent*' in most major towns, and '*naczelnik*' in the countryside). A further aspect of this clarification of responsibility was a stronger emphasis on the overall leading role of the party, and its avoidance of the temptation to substitute for administrators and managers and to become enmeshed in the over-detailed supervision of the state bureaucracy. In more concrete terms the measures enacted in Poland over 1973–5 were designed to strengthen party leadership, first by specifying more closely the persons and offices with responsibility for executing the tasks of state administration and, second, by reducing the size of each province (quite considerably in most cases) and raising their number from 17 to 49 so that more effective co-ordination of social and economic development could be achieved at local level.

Although improvement in local co-ordination and planning procedures had been one of the major objectives of the reform, it became evident at an early stage that the new provincial (*województwo*) authorities were not well equipped to perform this task. Only two years after the territorial redivision of the country, which had taken effect in June 1975, strong criticism was made by one provincial executive (*wojewód*) at a Central Committee plenum. It was, he said, impossible to co-ordinate economic activities when, as was often the case, local plants were under the control of departments lying outside the province, and local production plans were frequently being altered by the directors of production associations (*zjednoczenia*) without reference to the provincial authorities. Particular problems were experienced in the control of investment and this was because 'we have not yet worked out a well organised system of Party control'.[44] Complaints about the capacity of the provincial authorities in this respect persisted, and as the problems of Polish industry intensified in the late 1970s the local executive found himself quite unable to exert any influence over the course of economic activity.[45] His powers of control over local industry were further diminished, particularly in the early years, by the fact that plant directors had considerable influence on the levels and direction of investment, not just in the sphere of industrial production but also in the general social infrastructure and the provision of community services (roads, housing, shops, etc.). In view of the low standards of such services in Poland and their capacity to provoke disquieting levels of popular dissatisfaction, the co-operation of local plant directors in helping with their provision was not a factor that provincial executives could ignore, and this made them further susceptible to the influence of the economic agencies. Five years after the territorial restructuring the judgement passed on its consequences was a severe one: 'the transformation of Poland from one based on the *powiat* to that based on the *województwo* and *gmina* wrecked the local authorities'.[46]

The inability of *województwo* officials to co-ordinate local activities and exercise their supposed powers of control over the processes of social and economic development, affected also the local party committee and its first secretary, who was of course intended to embody the leading role of the party on the local plane. To a great extent the reforms reflected sharply contradictory intentions on the part of the central leadership in this respect. Undoubtedly the Gierek leadership was eager to enhance the role of the party in the co-ordination of economic activities and its control over processes of social development. At the same time, from the point of view of the Politburo and the incumbent First Secretary, the power of first secretaries of the 17 former *województwo* party committees (22 if those of the major towns are included) had been excessive, and their replacement by 49 secretaries having a considerably diminished power base was an undoubted political advantage. Gierek had himself used his leadership of Katowice province to great advantage under Gomułka in this respect, and he was undoubtedly keen to ensure that none should use similar political tactics against him. (It is notable in this connection that his connections with the Katowice party organisation continued to serve him well during his tenure as national leader. Katowice was by far the largest of the smaller, more numerous *województwa* – a factor partly explicable by its concentrated large-scale economic base – and its first secretary was the only one to be elected full Politburo member at the Seventh Party Congress in December 1975.) But the indications are that Gierek's desire to curb the powers of the local party secretaries took precedence over the need for them to retain sufficient capacity and authority to perform their leading role on the local plane. Certain individual cases indicate the apparent inability of local party organs to control plant and production association directors, even when their behaviour involved corruption and spilled over into illegality.[47] The reduction in size and status of the provincial party organisation, far from bringing effective political leadership closer to the local community, simply reduced the party's capacity to supervise and control economic activity at local level, and necessitated cumbersome approaches being made through the central party and government apparatus. Certainly in this respect the change in party structure did not facilitate the adaptation of party organisation to the requirements of supervising a modern and increasingly concentrated industrial sector.

But neither did the reforms serve to enhance the autonomy of the party organisation, that is, enable it to exercise its leadership more effectively by making clearer the distinction between party leadership and state executive responsibility for administrative and managerial tasks. A particular obstacle to improving the performance by the party of its leading role concerned the close relationship between key figures in the state hierarchy, particularly those engaged in management of production, and leading party figures. Just as the party and its officials at each level had important formal responsibilities for the development of industry and the supervision of economic activity, so managers and plant directors also generally played a part in the activities of the party organisation. While practically anyone who held a post of any significance in the economic hierarchy would be a party member, 60 per cent of all plant directors were also elected members of a party committee.[48] The organisational loyalties of management, however, did not lie primarily with the party, and particularly not with its local organs, and their participation in its activities frequently served to dilute party functions and vitiate its formal leading role. A local party secretary in the Warsaw Automobile Factory state boldly: 'We are afraid to put in question the authority of the director, foreman or brigade leader'. Yet it was precisely such people who warranted party criticism: the director or manager frequently presented his excuses for not attending party meetings or performing party duties, while more humble members were subject to more stringent discipline.[49] In such ways local party organs could be seen to reflect managerial interests, and the rights and duties of party membership were not distributed equally among all those who belonged to it. This tendency could be seen to run counter to the needs of institutional development: 'Political institutionalization, in the sense of autonomy, means the development of political organizations and procedures that are not simply expressions of the interests of particular social groups.'[50]

The attempt made in the reforms to enhance the leading role of the party by distinguishing different spheres of responsibility did not succeed in industry. The diminished authority of provincial party committees was merely reflected in the more independent action of management and economic administrators *vis-à-vis* local party organs. The influence of such figures in party activities emerged in a decidedly negative fashion: problem commissions set up by local party committees to supervise specific spheres of activity in the community were found to differ markedly in their effectiveness according to their composition; a distinction could be drawn between commissions led by party committee secretaries, who lent the groups' activity 'creative weight', and those

> headed by directors, often of large industrial enterprises or economic organisations. These people generally have little spare time and the honour bestowed on them of chairing a commission in practice brings about the end of its activity, with of course great harm being done to social affairs and to the effectiveness of Party activity.[51]

Further, it was elsewhere suggested that such faulty party supervision was directly responsible for poor economic results.[52] Activists were concerned primarily with what their superiors thought of them and paid little attention to the opinions of their fellow workers and party members. The doubling of offices in the party and economic structures thus continued to undermine the leading role of the party and to sap its autonomy as an institution, consequences that, it was claimed by critics, had serious deleterious effects on the economy. Certainly the symbiosis of party with management served to maintain the position of those spanning the two structures and to stifle criticism of their activities when it arose from lower party organs. Those critical of plant directors could in this way be restrained (and sometimes fired) because the object of criticism sat on the party *województwo* committee and prevented the mobilisation of the party organ against him.[53] There were occasions when the State Control Commission (NIK) uncovered criminal abuses of their posts by plant directors without any criticism, let alone sanction, being forthcoming from the plant's party organisation.[54] As Huntington reflected: 'Political organisations and procedures which lack autonomy are, in common parlance, said to be corrupt.'[55] With the greater availability of investment funds in the 1970s, the unwillingness of the central leadership to rock the political boat and the declining authority of *województwo* leaders in the weak of the reforms, such corruption spread relatively unhindered and the institutionalisation of the party was correspondingly restricted.

Other aspects of the reforms did little to mitigate the lack of effectiveness of party leadership and the low level of party autonomy in this respect. The assumption by party secretaries of the chair of the People's Councils in no way compensated for this, as the Councils were quite peripheral institutions and the secretary had, it was acknowledged, no way of working through them as initially envisaged.[56] In fact, as First Secretary Kania later admitted, 'The rights of People's Councils were reduced...as an accompaniment to the ill-thought-out reorganisation of certain areas of the economy and administration. The style of government was characterised by arrogance, an aggressive attitude to criticism and contempt for opinions and conceptions arising outside the centres of leadership'. Nowhere was this truer than in the countryside where, it was stated, 'The administration took on practically absolute power and became wholly independent of the rural community'. It was indicative in this respect that in a survey conducted in November and December 1980, 41 per cent of peasants answered 'don't know' to the question 'is self-government operative in your *gmina*?'[57] The excessive powers of plant directors, the dominance of economic specialism over local party organisations and procedures, and the total formalism of local self-government were by no means all unique to Poland, nor were they characteristic only of the Gierek period. In Yugoslavia, for example, the imbalance in local power relations occasioned by the operation of a large enterprise has also been pointed out and described as a major obstacle to the development of local democracy.[58] Continuing problems in combining party leadership with economic expertise are evident in the Soviet Union: at the Twenty-Sixth CPSU Congress, Brezhnev singled out for complaint the performance of industrial specialists within the party apparatus. They lacked, he reported, 'sufficient political experience and, in some cases, bring economic management methods into Party organs'.[59] The poor performance by managerial cadres of their relatively peripheral party role is also a common occurrence in communist systems, particularly when self-supervision and self-criticism are required. The Polish reforms, however, were responsible for lowering the status of the provincial committee and reducing the authority of the equivalent state executive during a period when plant directors and managers found their autonomy enhanced by a relatively uncontrolled flow of investment funds. It is not surprising that the reduction of organisational controls over managers encouraged abuses and threw up further obstacles to the institutionalisation of the party.

ORGANISATIONAL COHERENCE AND PARTY LEADERSHIP

If the adaptative changes made by the Polish party leadership in the early 1970s had a negative effect on the institutional autonomy of the party (or, at the very least, no enhancement of autonomy was achieved by the enactment of the reforms), then neither did any improvement in the coherence of its organisation and procedures occur. In fact, the second half of the 1970s saw a marked deterioration in this respect. Indeed, the two aspects of party change are related, and 'the two are often closely linked together. Autonomy becomes a means to coherence, enabling the organisation to develop an *esprit* and style that become distinctive marks of its behavior. Autonomy also prevents the intrusion of disruptive external forces.'[60] In similar fashion to the way that overlapping party/state responsibilities and dual-office-holding perpetuated and worsened inadequate party autonomy, so the reduced authority of *województwo* committees made them more susceptible to the influence of regional economic and departmental interests, and undermined the coherence of the party as a national institution. The ground for this development in the later 1970s was prepared by Gierek's growth-oriented economic policy and the high level of investment, often subject to minimal controls, in the first half of the decade. The forces leading office-holders at intermediate levels in both party and state levels to attempt to maximise their share of such resources were, however, well established and are rooted in the general character of the communist system. A general characteristic of the system in this respect was emphasised by Kuron and Modzelewski in the middle of the Gomułka period:

> The material power of the bureaucracy, the scope of its authority over production, its international position (very important for a class organised as a group identifying itself with the state) all this depends on the size of the national capital. Consequently, the bureaucracy wants to increase capital, to enlarge the producing apparatus, to accumulate.[61]

At local level, enterprises subject to persistent pressures from organs of central planning and co-ordination, tend to overbid and conceal resources to enhance their autonomy and safeguard their position: 'to increase their security and the certainty of being able to execute the plans, enterprises, amass reserves and extend the time-scale in which investments are made. In part this enables them to neutralise the control of the central authorities over investment and to limit their freedom of manoeuvre; they are obliged to integrate these investments in future plans.'[62]

But such tendencies are by no means restricted to those employed in the economic administration. Similar pressures are exerted on secretaries in party organs at intermediate levels: 'Party secretaries in organisations based on the territorial principle are...in a very special situation; for, even if they owe their placement to central authorities and remain under constant pressure from them, they must also take account of local needs and the interests of those institutions and organisations whose cooperation is an indispensible condition of their own success.'[63] All too often these interests concern manoeuvres and special pleading to increase local investment allocations. It has been suggested that the allocation of such resources has proved an important means of loosening such local ties:

> the main weapon against localism has been socio-economic 'development'. In the omnipresent Five Year Plan, extracting these resources from well-to-do regions and redistributing these resources to underdeveloped locales through the implantation of new industry has been used as the leading edge of the PUWP's efforts to penetrate local communities and overcome horizontal ties.[64]

With this account ignores, however, is the common interest that party officials and economic administrators at local level share in maximising the resources allocated to their area and which serves to enhance the elements of 'localism' in their mutual relations. Nor is it likely that relatively high levels of social and economic development serve to restrain these ambitions – the example of Katowice suggests, rather, that high levels of development provide only better conditions for the further pursuit of such interests.

Thus there are strong pressures on local party officials to act in concert with local economic leaders and pressure groups to secure as large a share as possible of national resources, the interests of all being furthered by gaining the allocation to the region of some national priority project, particularly one in the field of heavy industry. The inflow of capital, construction of roads, housing and other elements in the social infrastructure, the greater availability of jobs (particularly in the well-paid construction and heavy-industry sectors), the better stocking of local retail outlets with food and other consumer goods – all will contribute to the status of the local party secretary, increase his standing in the eyes of his superiors and facilitate his leadership of the local political system. In career terms he will be seen as the representative of a more populous, industrialised and richer area and will be able to show more working-class members in his returns to the Central Committee.[65] The interconnection of these factors is clearly reflected in a collection of provincial Party Committee reports and in the significance accorded to them in last years of the Gomułka administration. 'In distinction to former periods', it was recorded from the 1969 conference, 'the session of the *Województwo* Committee between the XI and XII Party Conferences did not see the inauguration of any major new industrial units. This meant that the employment problem became increasingly important in the province.' Moreover, while housing construction plans were fulfilled by 96 per cent in 1968, in the following year fulfilment stood only at 87 per cent. The rise in party membership was also slower than during the previous two sessions.[66] A similarly static picture was painted in the following year's report, with the added comments that by the end of 1969 the number of those seeking work was 21.4 per cent higher than a year before and that the housing problem was assuming greater proportions.[67]

By successfully participating in the competition for national resources the party secretary therefore succeeds in reconciling the diverse pressures acting on his position:

> he must heed his superiors and show that he can think on a national scale. After all, he should not pay attention just to his own *województwo*. But at the same time he must gain the opinion of being a good manager and must show his ability to get on with those inhabiting the territory placed in his charge. How to reconcile such requirements which frequently conflict with one another? In one way: by securing credits and resources permitting the construction in the province of heavy industrial plant recognised as essential for national economic development.[68]

This conception of the basis of success in party management emerges clearly in the accounts of numerous provincial Party Committee Secretaries.[69] A report from one party organisation clearly attributed its instability of party membership to the low level of investment in the area. Better work opportunities, improved social facilities and the hope of getting a flat attracted members to more privileged areas.[70] The recognition by party secretaries of these conditions placed on the successful performance of their role, was reflected also in the quasi-instinctive response of some newly appointed provincial secretaries to buttress their position by seeking new investment funds. This was true even of secretaries of the lowest tier.[71] One of the new *naczelnicy*, for example, described his isolation on reaching his new posting, and the lack of sympathy for him until he attracted a relatively large-scale industrial undertaking which brought considerable benefits to the community, after which he was elected to the town Council by a large vote.[72] The greater availability of investment funds in the 1970s was, therefore, a source of considerable satisfaction to local party secretaries and was the basis on which relations of mutual benefit could be formed between them and local leaders.

The new factor introduced into this situation by the reform was that party officials and the organs they were responsible for had less power to prevent and control abuses by directors and administrators of their privileged access to such funds. At the same time, given their more slender power base and faced with a deepening economic and political crisis, provincial party secretaries were under stronger pressure to ally themselves with such figures in order to protect their position. This led to a decline in the coherence of the party as a national organisation, a reduction in its capacity to perform a leading role and a diminution in its powers of control over processes of social and economic development. The diminution in the powers of local party organs, however, was only one element in the general loss of control over the economy. A year before the mid-1980 crisis erupted, the chairman of the United Peasant Party indicated the structural features involved in the economic situation. The experiences of communist development had given rise to the practice 'that particular economic units expected greater investment resources year by year. These pressures, and the lack of strong mechanisms capable of counter-acting them were responsible for frequently over-ambitious and taut programmes of development...Pressure on investment resources from below and the strategy of "hiking oneself on to the plan" led to overshooting of the financial investment plan in respect to the execution of material tasks.'[73] The unofficial 'Experience and the Future' group also pointed out that:

As legal and constitutional mechanisms have ceased to operate effectively, an exceptional significance has been gained (particularly in the 1970s, although they did exist earlier) by diverse interest groups, particularly those in the structure of power. A typical example here may be groups in the nature of industrial lobbies, which have grown up as the system of economic direction collapsed ...The ruling party (PUWP), like other political parties, is not a unified interest group. Quite the opposite, in monopolising power it is all the more riven, and has been since early days, by conflicting pressure or interest groups, enjoying in their turn the support of groups outside the Party and of various lobbies.[74]

Thus the absence of coherence in party organisation was one in a number of factors that entered the economic and political order of the late 1970s. As, however, it was the party which claimed to exercise a leading role, this lack of coherence was all the more important. This became uncomfortably apparent following the introduction of the 'economic manoeuvre', a remedial programme adopted in late 1976 as a tardy response to the considerable problems that the Polish economy was encountering.

It was the intention of the manoeuvre to restrain investment expenditure and transfer resources to favour areas of strongest public demand, that is foodstuffs, housing, and consumer goods. Ten months later the failure of this attempt was obvious and it was particularly in the investment area that the manoeuvre was proving to be most weak. 'Iron discipline' was henceforth called for in implementing the investment plan.[75] Following the IX Plenum, subsequent discussion cast light on the extent of the problems faced by the leadership. Of the investment total for 1976 some 10 per cent had been unplanned, while market imbalances due to the unrestricted amendment of prices by enterprises to boost their profits were similarly beyond the control of the central authorities.[76] Individual enterprises invariably found reason to believe that the manoeuvre did not fully apply to them and found ways to avoid its prescriptions – such attitudes being found 'at various levels of the administration, whilst higher organs often justify them when they appear in plants within their sphere of jurisdiction'.[77] In the eyes of factory workers the manoeuvre was just not being implemented: 'previously I did not know what the word particularism meant. Now I do', one is reported as saying.[78] In late 1978, two years after the formal adoption of the manoeuvre, Gierek was still calling for its acceptance and recommending it as an 'objective necessity'.[79] Indeed, in 1979, investment in the socialised economy did fall (having continued to rise during the two years following the introduction of the manoeuvre), but then only to the level of 1976.[80] This, however, was also the year of the first absolute fall in national income in post-war Poland and one that also followed a decline in workers' real earnings.

The inability of the leadership to control investment thus provides a stark example of the lack of coherence in national party organisation and of the weakness of party leadership and control over the economy. The strength of particularist interests, especially those based on regional and industrial branch groups, proved too strong for central control. Yet it is also maintained that 'Both Marxism and Leninism fit poorly, or not at all, with the accretion of local power. The requirement to maintain links with the masses leaves Communist governments no room for particularistic interests, all of which should be subsumed within broader class interests.'[81] Like Huntington's view of the Marxist–Leninist model this one also takes at face value its claims to effective control and dynamic leadership. It ignores the problems it encounters at different stages of socio-economic development and in different socio-historical contexts, and the obstacles to institutionalisation encountered by the organisation that provides the centrepiece of the Marxist–Leninist model. The objectives of the economic manoeuvre adopted by the Polish party leadership ran directly counter to the processes involved in particularism. The leadership, however, was not able to overcome these processes as it did not have the organisational means to do so. Thus, in considering Gierek's Poland, one reason for 'seemingly irrational policies was the apparent inability of the party leadership to establish firm control over the middle-rank bureaucracy and the rank and file...The result of this asymmetry between the top and middle party echelons are frequent difficulties and delays in, and even sabotage of, new policies decreed by the leadership and implemented by the middle.'[82] The incoherence of party organisation and the failure of leadership were finally demonstrated in the last weeks of Gierek's rule during the political crisis of August–September 1980 when, as was subsequently admitted, the leadership lapsed into a condition of virtual paralysis. In the post-August situation the new party leadership found its position even more difficult to maintain, as its authority was now persistently challenged by that of the independent trade union, Solidarity, which grew to include 75 per cent of those employed in the socialised economy. Reluctant to advertise its weakness by bowing to the necessity of establishing a basis of genuine co-operation with Solidarity, the Polish United Workers' Party found itself persistently powerless and increasingly lacking in organisational coherence. The Extraordinary Party Congress, held in July 1981, did nothing to restore its position. With the party unable to play its leading role there was a growth in the political significance of the armed forces, whose leader General Jaruzelski had been Prime Minister since February 1981. His assumption of the party leadership in October reflected the PUWP's inability to maintain state power, a fact that became starkly evident with the declaration of the State of War in December 1981 and the assumption by a Military Council of National Salvation of all powers of government. Shortly after the takeover a spokesman for the Military Council defined its relation to the party in these terms: 'It is clear that in recent months the party lost its authority, its credibility, and that its leading role was weakened. It keeps its leading role, but at this moment it is the Military Council which is the leading organ.'[83] It was clear in retrospect that it was only Jaruzelski's assumption of the party leadership eight weeks before the military takeover that enabled the party to make any claim whatsoever to occupy a leading role.

CONCLUSION

Gierek's reform of party/state structures and procedures during the 1970s may therefore be conceived as being centrally concerned with the institutionalisation of the party within modern Polish society and, in particular, with the attempt to facilitate the adaptation of party organisation and procedures to contemporary needs. As has been the case with other attempts to hasten the adaptation of Communist Parties, however, the autonomy and coherence of party organisation were not enhanced nor even adequately maintained, and the very survival of the party was placed in jeopardy. The crisis that erupted in August 1980 was responsible for the downfall of the particular leadership that had served as the guardian of the Polish party throughout the 1970s and also posed a grave threat to the persistence of the communist regime. Indeed, in his proclamation of military rule Jaruzelski emphasised that the Polish state itself was at risk: 'The achievements of many generations, the house erected from Polish ashes, are being destroyed. The structures of state are ceasing to function.'[84] The changes in leadership and personnel made in the wake of the August events had not been sufficient to prevent the further institutional decline of the party, let alone enhance its leading role or restore its hegemony over Polish society. Indeed, in certain respects, the post-August changes in organisation and personnel may have worsened an already disastrous political situation.

The features of party weakness identified in the above discussion – the low level of party autonomy and the lack of institutional coherence – certainly persisted under Kania's leadership. Major aspects of the post-August 'renewal' of the party themselves increased organisational problems and exacerbated lack of coherence within party activities. The renewal of party cadres at *województwo* level may be taken as a key index of this. During the nine months from September 1980 to May 1981 well over half of the First Secretaries at this level (a total of twenty-eight) were changed. Over the same period a combined total of eighty-five *Województwo* Committee secretaries and chairmen of the analogous party control commission were also replaced. But on top of this shake-up in party personnel, further turnover occurred during the elections that took place in preparation for and during the *województwo* meetings of party organs that preceded the Ninth Congress in July 1981. As a result of failure to secure election to the regional meeting, or due to electoral defeat at the meeting itself, three-quarters of those holding permanent secretarial posts at *województwo* level *as of May 1981* were again replaced. Of the 292 in post in May only 73 survived the process of election and reselection. While such a massive transfusion of fresh blood into the party authorities may well ultimately have had an invigorating effect on its activities, it was also regretted that, as a result of this process:

the organism of the apparat must, if only temporarily, be weakened. Such are the regularities not just of medicine but also of social life whose fabric is held together by the Party. It is a mistake to conclude that the replacement of whole personnel sections in the KW secretariat, executives or even committees will definitively restore confidence in the Party, or bring back its authority and depleted capacity for leadership. That can only be secured by political practice and will depend not so much on 'new people' themselves as on the skills they can draw from experience, their capacity to lead and take decisions, and their ability to control the social mechanisms regulating the life of the region and the state.[85]

Such regrets are only to be expected from an embattled party staff, but it is none the less true that wholesale turnover in key party personnel in the absence of strong national leadership, or of agreed policies of party and state reform, would do little to restore the coherence of party organisation. Certainly it did not serve to halt the reduction in party membership, which fell from 3.092 million at the end of 1980 to the 2.77 million declared in December 1981. Contributing to this decline was the expulsion or removal from party lists of 380.5 thousand between July 1980 and September 1981, as well as the resignation of 288.8 thousand.[86]

Negative consequences also appeared to flow from the composition of the leading party bodies, elected at the Extraordinary Congress in July 1981 under conditions of free election unprecedented in Eastern Europe. Of the two hundred members of the new Central Committee only eighteen had sat on the former Committee, while in composition the new body was far less representative of the *apparatchiki* and of bureaucratic officialdom than is invariably the case. This, indeed, represented a major renewal. The very newness and inexperience of the Central Committee elected in July, however, has been suggested to be a major factor in the sharpening of the political atmosphere and the polarisation that occurred in the period between the Congress and the declaration of the State of War. On the face of it, a Committee elected in full process of renewal and having far more immediate links with the party rank and file than is customary might have been expected to have created better relations with Solidarity, itself eager for reform, which also represented a mass workers' movement. But:

> just because 80 per cent of it was composed of people with experience drawn from plant or commune level, whose strength lay in their link with the Party base but who were weaker in their lack of clear vision, it is possible that more than one voice in discussion represented the aims of rank-and-file Party members without necessarily representing their views on the eventual costs that might result from the adoption of strong methods.[87]

Inexperience on the part of the new Central Committee probably did play a part in the growing frustration that was apparent in the party authorities between July and December 1981, but the problems it experienced due to its inability to act as an autonomous organisation were also relevant.

The problems of lack of autonomy that arose in the 1970s due to the susceptibility of party organs to the influence of managerial and bureaucratic pressure groups have been outlined above. After August the new context in which the party attempted to operate was even less conducive to its acting as an autonomous political force. The alternative mass working-class organisation that Solidarity constituted posed a formidable challenge to the authority of the party and its capacity for political leadership. The democratic procedures that characterised the Extraordinary Congress allowed this lack of autonomy expression in the results of elections to the Central Committee and the Politburo. Thus the inclusion of Solidarity representatives (who were, of course, also party members and activists) in these bodies reflected not only a measure of political realism but also the party's lack of autonomy in the constellation of political forces in the Poland of 1981. With the worsening of political relations in the late summer and autumn of 1981, however, the experiment of overlapping membership involving the higher organs of the PUWP proved to be untenable. At the IV Plenum, held in October 1981, two weeks after the final session of the national Solidarity Congress, those Central Committee figures who represented this overlapping membership left the trade union. Zofia Grzyb, the sole Solidarity member in the Politburo, explained her action in this way:

> I thought that the 1st 'Solidarity' Congress would adopt a critical attitude to errors committed and would direct the mass organisation on to the tracks of appropriate union activity. Things turned out differently. Quite simply, after the Congress I became convinced that I belonged to an organisation of political opposition fighting the people's power...If I had stayed in the organisation I would have had to accept not only the good it did in our factory, but also everything that extremist elements in the national and regional leadership of the union were striving for.[88]

Ten other members of the Central Committee also left Solidarity with Grzyb.

In the absence of any form of institutional compromise with Solidarity, the party required some other form of support. This was provided by the military, whose chief commander, General Jaruzelski, took over the party leadership from Kania following severe criticism at the same IV Plenum. Jaruzelski had been Prime Minister (as well as Minister of Defence) since February and the growing influence of the army in the party was detectable well before the Congress. Indeed, Kania himself commented:

> Our Party has every reason to be proud of the attitudes and ideological stance of our comrades in uniform...One of the proofs of its authority is the proportion of comrades in uniform amongst the delegates elected by *województwo* Party conferences to the Congress, as this is higher than ever before.[89]

Further recognition of this authority was afforded by the election of six vice-ministers of defence as full or alternate members of the Central Committee, and by the election of the former Minister of

Internal Affairs, holding the rank of general in the security forces, as member of the Politburo (he was also appointed Secretary of the Central Committee). Subsequently, in October, another general was appointed Head of the Cadres Department of the Central Committe. Following the declaration of the State of War he was reported as saying that henceforth the work of civil servants would be subject to regular supervision.[90] Shortly after the Party Congress another general (formerly head of military intelligence) was appointed to the Ministry of Internal Affairs, and a further military man placed in charge of the Ministry of Administration. Thus Deputy Prime Minister Rakowski's claim that 'despite diverse assumptions and speculation the government of General Jaruzelski has not undergone a process of "militarisation" over the past year' is disingenuous.[91] It was, of course, only the four military members of Jaruzelski's cabinet who formed part of the Military Council which took over the government of Poland in December 1981. Certain military members of former cabinets, moreover, had left government, only (for example, in the case of Milewski) to become a member of the Politburo and Central Committee Secretary. Thus, while the government itself had not become noticeably militarised in numerical terms, the party had become subject to increasing military influence. In so far as it lacked the autonomy to act, in practice as well as in theory, as the leading force in society, and was unable to reach a compromise with Solidarity, it was only the army that was capable of holding the party in place and, indeed, of maintaining the structure of People's Poland.

But how far can the failure of the Polish party and the virtual collapse of the communist regime from within be attributed to the weakness of the institutionalisation process? Certainly it cannot provide anything like a total explanation. As suggested in the introduction to this chapter, comparable attempts have been made at party adaptation elsewhere in the Soviet bloc without threatening the collapse of the regime. A major characteristic of the Polish attempt was the hostile nature of the political environment in which it was attempted, which left virtually no room for manoeuvre, miscalculation or accident. This, in turn, may be traced to the tenuous bases of legitimacy on which the communist regime in Poland has rested, bases whose weakness was by no means restricted to the period of Gierek's tenure of the leadership.[92] Leadership awareness of their isolation within Polish society, and the extremely limited nature of their political resources, lent a certain desperation to their approach to the political and economic problems that intensified world-wide during the 1970s. Thus the lack of political alternatives led Gierek and his entourage to permit and even encourage corruption as a means of political support, while awareness of the potential for popular opposition tempted him to a high-risk economic strategy which would have been fraught with danger even in a relatively favourable international economic climate. Another factor has been the general weakness of state development in Poland, a factor not unconnected with the persistent legitimacy problem already alluded to. Thus, despite a generally high level of socio-economic development, Poland was somewhat late in broaching the possibility of identification with the 'developed socialism' already embraced by the Soviet Union. It was only at the VII PUWP Congress in 1975 that it was suggested that Poland had entered on the stage of the construction of developed socialism, the stage preceding that of developed socialism itself. The reason for the delay was ascribed to the uneven social and economic development of the country, particularly to the persistence of its private agriculture.[93] Yet political and state-related factors also entered into this. In an apparent reference to the pre-Gierek leadership, delays in progress towards developed socialism were also associated with the fact that 'newly arising social needs did not find the appropriate response in the activities of leading organs of Party and state'.[94]

As a result of the ground that had to be covered before Poland could be considered near to the stage of developed socialism (a situation from which she is now presumably further than before following the total eclipse of the leading role of the party by the military) it was officially accepted that social contradictions were still likely to arise in the Polish political system. Particular problems identified concerned the 'socio-economic effectiveness of production and the rationality of behaviour', 'the establishment of the proper relationship between the central administration and local decisions and initiatives at various levels of social organisation', and the lack of recognition accorded to the greater maturity and heightened capacity of local activists, which led to the taking of 'erroneous decisions' and became an 'inevitable source of bureaucratism'.[95] Another eminent political scientist, discussing the Polish state apparatus, also had to admit that:

Frictions have occurred and the possibility of them recurring in the future cannot be excluded...[they] have their direct source invariably in faulty, incorrect functioning of organs of the system of organization of socialist society in this country. Frictions have also occurred within the Marxist–Leninist party itself.[96]

Recognition of the likelihood of strains developing in the Polish party/state system was seen as a measure of its distance from the harmony of developed socialism and of the weakness of state development itself. Nevertheless, the process of reform and party adaptation initiated by Gierek in the early 1970s was also intended as a response to the level of social and economic development achieved in Poland since the war. The primary intention of the institutional reforms launched by the Gierek leadership was to facilitate socio-economic growth and to achieve more harmonious political development. There can be little doubt that the failure of party adaptation and the inability to enhance or maintain the autonomy and coherence of the party organisation contributed to the general crisis of the system that became apparent towards the end of the decade.

NOTES

1. G. Paige, 'The Rediscovery of Politics', in J. D. Montgomery and W. J. Siffin (eds), *Approaches to Development: Politics, Administration and Change* (New York, 1966) p. 56.
2. S. P. Huntington, *Political Order in Changing Societies* (New Haven, 1968) p. 8.
3. P. M. Cocks, 'Retooling the Directed Society', in J. F. Triska and P. M. Cocks (eds), *Political Development in Eastern Europe* (New York, 1977) p. 53.
4. P. M. Cocks, 'The Policy Process and Bureaucratic Politics', in P. M. Cocks, R. V. Daniels and N. W. Heer (eds), *The Dynamics of Soviet Politics* (Cambridge, Mass., 1976) p. 170.
5. D. R. Kelley, 'The Communist Party', in D. R. Kelley (ed.), *Soviet Politics in the Brezhnev Era* (New York, 1980) p. 34.
6. *Polityka*, 31 January 1981.
7. *Nowe Drogi*, October–November 1980, p. 294.
8. Z. Gitelman, 'Development, Institutionalization and Elite–Mass Relations in Poland', in Triska and Cocks, *Political Development*.
9. Huntington, *Political Order,* p. 12.
10. Ibid, p. 146.
11. Triska and Cocks, *Political Development*, p. 56.
12. Huntington, *Political Order*, p. 24.
13. Ibid, p. 402.
14. M. Kesselman, 'Overinstitutionalization and Political Constraint', *Comparative Politics*, vol. III (1970) p. 22.

15. Ibid, p. 26.
16. G. Ben-Dor, 'Institutionalization and Political Development', *Comparative Studies in Society and History*, vol. XVII (1975) p. 314.
17. See, for example, M. Kesselman, 'Order or Movement', *World Politics*, vol. XXVI (1973) pp. 142–4; and D. C. O'Brien, 'Modernisation, Order and the Erosion of the Democratic Ideal', *Journal of Development Studies,* vol. VIII (1972) pp. 363–4.
18. Ben-Dor, 'Institutionalization', p. 323.
19. Gitelman, in Triska and Cocks, *Political Development*.
20. Ibid, p. 135.
21. J. Maziarski, in *Polityka*, 25 September 1976.
22. Gitelman, in Triska and Cocks, *Political Development*, p. 128.
23. G. Kolankiewicz, 'The Working Class', in D. Lane and G. Kolankiewicz (eds), *Social Groups in Polish Society* (London, 1973) p. 105.
24. B. Koperski, *Nowe Drogi*, November 1979, p. 55.
25. B. L. in *Zycie Partii*, August 1978, pp. 18–19.
26. Gitelman, in Triska and Cocks, *Political Development*, p. 128.
27. J. Bielasiak, 'Lateral and Vertical Elite Differentiation in European Communist States', *Studies in Comparative Communism*, vol. XI (1978) p. 132.
28. W. Taubman, 'The Change to Change in Communist Systems', in H. W. Morton and R. L. Tökés (eds), *Soviet Politics and Society in the 1970's* (New York, 1974) p. 379.
29. Compare R. Lowenthal, 'On "Established" Communist Party Regimes', *Studies in Comparative Communism*, vol. VII (1974) pp. 335–6, with A. B. Evans, 'Developed Socialism in Soviet Ideology', *Soviet Studies*, vol. XXIX (1977) pp. 414 and 417.
30. S. P. Huntington, 'Social and Institutional Dynamics of One-Party Systems', in S. P. Huntington and C. H. Moore (eds), *Authoritarian Politics in Modern Society* (New York, 1970) p. 32.
31. J. Smith (ed.), *Voices of Tomorrow* (New York, 1971) p. 50.
32. M. E. Fischer, 'Participatory Reforms and Political Development in Romania', in Triska and Cocks, *Political Development*; and J. Służewski, *Terenowe organy administracji i rady narodowe po reformie* (Warsaw, 1977) p. 129.
33. *IX Plenum KC PZPR* (Warsaw, 1973) pp. 105 and 124.
34. *XVII Plenum KC PZPR* (Warsaw, 1975) p. 22.
35. Ibid, p. 32.
36. Ibid, p. 52.
37. 'Tyraliera', *Polityka*, 12 June 1976.
38. Quoted in S. Gebert, *Władza i administracja terenowa po reformie* (Warsaw, 1978) p. 156.
39. *IX Plenum KC PZPR* (Warsaw, 1977) p. 25.
40. The reforms are discussed in greater detail in P. G. Lewis, 'Political Consequences of the Changes in Party–State Structure under Gierek', in J. Woodall (ed.) *Policy and Politics in Contemporary Poland* (London, 1982) pp. 76–98.
41. 'Musi być taka kreska', *Polityka*, 17 December 1977.
42. See R. Taras, 'Democratic Centralism and Polish Local Government

Reforms', *Public Administration* vol. LIII (1975).
43. E. Babiuch, in *Zycie Partii*, June 1977, p. 6.
44. *IX Plenum KC PZPR* (Warsaw, 1977) p. 70.
45. See W. Madurowicz, in *Nowe Drogi*, April 1979, p. 98; A. Zarajczyk in *Nowe Drogi*, May 1979; and J. Owczarek in *Nowe Drogi*, October–November 1980, p. 210.
46. Z. Grudzień, in *Nowe Drogi*, October–November 1980, P.93.
47. J. Fastyn, in *Zycie Partii*, March 1978, p. 17.
48. Doświadczenie i Przyszłość, *Raport o stanie narodu i PRL* (Paris, 1980) p. 59.
49. B. Lesiewicz, in *Zycie Partii*, August 1977, p. 31.
50. Huntington, *Political Order* p. 20.
51. W. Wodecki, in *Zycie Partii*, September 1978, p. 4.
52. Z. Machowski, in *Zycie Partii*, May 1977, pp.12–13.
53. J. Fastyn, in *Zycie Partii*, May 1978, p. 10.
54. J. Fastyn, in *Zycie Partii*, December 1977, p. 8.
55. Huntington, *Political Order*, p. 21.
56. W. Madurowicz, in *Nowe Drogi*, April 1979.
57. See *Nowe Drogi*, October–November 1980, p. 14; *Polityka*, 28 March 1981; and *Polityka*, 7 March 1981.
58. G. Leonardson and D. Mincev, 'A Structure of Participatory Democracy in the Local Community', *Comparative Politics*, vol. XI (1979).
59. Supplement to *Soviet Weekly*, 7 March 1981.
60. Huntington, *Political Order* p. 22.
61. J. Kuron and K. Modzelewski, *An Open Letter to the Party* (London, 1968) p. 17.
62. B. Rogulska, 'Réalisation des Plans et Politique des Salaires en Pologne de 1950 à 1975', *Revue d'Etudes Comparatives Est–Ouest*, tome X (1979) p. 162.
63. M. Hirszowicz, *Komunistyczny lewiatan* (Paris 1973) pp. 34–5.
64. D. E. Nelson, 'Subnational Policy in Poland: the Dilemma of Vertical versus Horizontal Integration', in M. Simon and R. Kanet (eds), *Background to Crisis: Policy and Politics in Gierek's Poland* (Boulder, Colorado, 1981) p. 73.
65. This became something of a fetish during the Gierek period. See G. Kolankiewicz, 'Bureaucratised Political Participation and its Consequences in Poland', *Politics*, vol. I (1981).
66. I. Caban, *Zapis trzech dziesięcioleci PZPR* (Lublin, 1978) pp. 347–8.
67. Ibid, p. 354.
68. K. Pomian, 'Robotnicy i sekretarze', in *1956: w dwadzieścia lat później z myślą o przyszłości* (London, 1978) p. 85.
69. See, for example, H. Swiderski, in *Zycie Partii*, September 1979, p. 8.
70. W. Wodecki, in *Zycie Partii*, August 1979, p. 8.
71. See 'Musi być taka kreska', *Polityka*, 17 December 1977.
72. '17 kilometrów w linii prostej od hotelu Forum', *Polityka*, 3 April 1976.
73. S. Gucwa, 'Przemiany strukturalne w trzydziestopięcioleciu PRL', *Wieś Współczesna*, July 1979, p. 8.
74. Doświadczenie i Przyszłość, *Raport*, pp. 64–5.
75. *IX Plenum KC PZPR* (Warsaw, 1977) p. 46.

76. K. Bokoszewski, in *Zycie Partii*, November 1977, pp. 3–4.
77. M. Kowalewski, in *Zycie Partii*, December 1977, p. 25.
78. J. Fastyn, in *Zycie Partii*, November 1977, P. 17.
79. *XIII Plenum KC PZPR* (Warsaw, 1978) p. 16.
80. GUS [Main Statistical Office] *Mały Rocznik Statystyczny* (Warsaw, 1981) pp. xxv–xxvii.
81. D. N. Nelson, 'Vertical Integration and Political Control in Eastern Europe: the Polish and Romanian Cases', *Slavic Review*, vol. XL (1981) p. 212.
82. A. Korbonski, 'Poland', in T. Rakowska-Harmstone and A. Gyorgy (eds), *Communism in Eastern Europe* (Bloomington, Indiana, 1979) p. 53.
83. *The Observer*, 3 January 1982.
84. *Uncensored Poland News Bulletin* (Information Centre for Polish Affairs, UK) no. 20 (1981) p. 8.
85. T. Kołodziejczyk, in *Zycie Partii*, 2 September 1981.
86. *Polityka*, 12 December 1981; *Zycie Partii*, 3 March 1982.
87. A. K. Wróblewski, in *Polityka*, 12 December 1981.
88. *Nowe Drogi*, November 1981, pp. 61–2.
89. *Polityka*, 27 June 1981.
90. *Uncensored Poland News Bulletin*, no. 2 (1982).
91. *Polityka,* 20 February 1982.
92. These issues are explored in P. G. Lewis, 'Obstacles to the Establishment of Political Legitimacy in Communist Poland', *British Journal of Political Science*, vol. XII (1982).
93. See A. Dobieszewski (ed.), *Organizacja polityczna społeczeństwa socjalistycznego w Polsce* (Warsaw, 1978) p. 341.
94. S. Widerszpil, in *Nowe Drogi,* March 1977, p. 106.
95. Ibid, pp. 116–17.
96. A. Łopatka, 'The State Apparatus in the Organizational System of Society in the Polish People's Republic', in J. Łętowski (ed.), *Administration in People's Poland* (Wrocław, 1980) p. 40.

8 Yugoslavia: Development and Persistence of the State

Sharon Zukin

Any discussion of the state in Yugoslavia is forced to confront several seemingly insurmountable obstacles: the lack of a coherent general definition of the state, the contradiction in all socialist societies between a basic assumption of 'withering away' and a continuous governing apparatus, and the striking differences between Yugoslavia and other 'socialist' states. Because criteria for comparison usually derive from Soviet practice, the *sine qua non* of such a state is taken to be a centralised authority, especially in managing the economy, and a monopoly of political initiative in communist party hands. At first glance, the centrifugal nature of political relations in Yugoslavia, as well as a diffusion of effective social control, constitute a departure from this model. But in reality, the Yugoslav leaders' attempts to respond to domestic and foreign pressures merely modify the concept of a 'socialist state'. The series of strategic choices the leaders made, or were forced to make, between 1945 and 1950 negated the only models of state power that they knew – the interwar monarchy and the Soviet Union – and slowly led to a series of innovations. In particular, the leaders' decision to withdraw from direct state management of both the economy and the society created two decisive shifts. First, despite a system founded on 'social ownership', it moved the locus of administrative control to regional, especially republican, political leaderships. Second, though retaining the policy-making role of federal party bodies, it increasingly influenced these organs to incorporate republican leaders instead of dictating to them. Emerging redefinitions of party–state and centre–periphery relations reflected some ambivalence about both theory and practice. On the one hand, political leaders did not give up the idea that only a hegemonic party-state – a true *vlast* – could control social change. On the other hand, the costs of forging such hegemony – particularly after the outbreak of 'cold war' with the Cominform in 1948 and the resulting purge of pro-Soviet activists who were most committed to the traditional model – appeared too high. The organisational and ideological compromises that ensued emphasised consensus over coercion. Eventually, they also forced additional retrenchment of the federal state apparatus in favour of local, quasi-state controls.

Until Tito's death in 1980, discussion of the state in Yugoslavia was so submerged in other issues that people might have taken the leaders at their word, and concluded that although the state had not yet withered away, it had long since been dissolved in a larger framework. A new context, social self-government, emerged parallel to but slightly lagging behind self-management in the economy. By the mid-1970s, Yugoslavs officially depicted it as part of a progressive 'de-etatisation': an evolution toward direct citizens' control of their affairs which began with the People's Liberation Committees of the Second World War, stumbled briefly during the bureaucratic period of nationalisation, collectivisation, and centralisation in the late 1940s, and has continued since 1953 – most markedly in the constitutions of 1963 and 1974 – by enlarging the institutional roles of local authorities or communes, their assemblies, and specially chosen 'interest communities' that manage most social and public services on the local level. In fact, within these broad parameters, any exercise of authority set in motion a complex array of formally autonomous institutions whose memberships, none the less, overlapped.[1]

For many years, a blind spot about the state related to general factors – the official ideology and institutions and the lack of attention in marxist theory to politics, especially in post-revolutionary states. But it also related to Tito's long dominance on the political scene. By his charismatic leadership and his personal intervention, Tito in many ways *was* the Yugoslav state. However, consideration of the state was also deflected by a common preoccupation with such heroic, early, national experiences as the Partisan War and the introduction of workers' self-management with which Tito was identified. Along with worrisome questions about what would happen after the great man's death, these factors tended to limit discussion of the state to assurances about its legitimacy. In contrast to the Soviet Union, little sense was conveyed of the weight of a state apparatus, the interdependence of its integrating and coercive activities, or the social sources, despite an ideology to the contrary, of the state's persistence and apparent growth.

Yet the Yugoslavs' constant efforts to restructure state forms implied a deep-seated belief that only political institutions could hold together a society rent by social, particularly class and national, conflicts. Indeed, co-ordinating market and federal relations has proved so problematic, in view of the general commitment to both equity and efficiency, that the most dynamic area of innovation is the attempt to express a common *political* interest which will override social divisions. The problem has grown more acute as the concept of the state as a 'dictatorship of the proletariat' has receded into a simpler past. Even Tito's return to this concept in 1972, after a decade's lapse, seemed less than persuasive. Certainly Yugoslavs describe changes in 'superstructure' as a response to changing conditions, especially economic development and the growth of social consciousness, at the 'base'. But they have always shown great sensitivity to the effect that political innovations have on this base, and the distinctive forms their socialist practice takes have all been initiated and controlled 'from the top'. As Edvard Kardelj, Tito's close associate and the leader who formulated most of the guidelines for the official ideology, wrote before his death in 1979, Yugoslavia accepted the process of the withering-away of the state as a coercive structure but 'never fell into the illusion that the role of the state and of state coercion was either a subordinate or an unimportant element in the political system'.[2] Such a frank acknowledgment suggests that resolutions to empirical problems rather than theoretical propriety account for Yugoslavia's development as a 'socialist' state.

Paradoxically, despite the aim of negating pre-socialist and bureaucratic-socialist state forms, the Yugoslavs have reproduced some of their major effects. The retention of policy-making initiative in party hands, primarily, makes Yugoslavia a 'socialist' state like any other. But decentralisation modifies the classical type. The republics' power, as opposed to that of the centre, and the growth since the mid-1960s of parity in their political representation, counter expected patterns of cultural and economic domination. This has special importance for balancing the pursuit of two priorities: social welfare and economic development. In Yugoslavia, the federation assures that the process of policy formation does not disadvantage – and even favours – the underdeveloped republics. To the extent that the policy that is adopted by the leadership responds to their demands for equity, political intervention in Yugoslavia is 'socialist' without being democratic. However, this practice of federal principles introduces into political relations another element which properly vexes socialist goals. The enhancement of local leaderships makes it difficult to enforce a general or a national interest. Particularly when federal leaders attempt to rationalise economic production or to effect a fairer redistribution of economic and social goods, they find themselves in the position of, or at least dealing with, representatives of local 'capital'. Ironically, this situation recalls a basic weakness of the interwar state.

These preliminary remarks indicate three empirical areas for comparing Yugoslavia with other socialist states: (1) political intervention in the economy, (2) political monopolies on social action, and (3) political permeation of administrative personnel. The predominance of political institutions, albeit in non-traditional forms, makes it easier to understand the criticism of domination by 'the state' to which many Yugoslavs still adhere.

POLITICAL INTERVENTION IN THE ECONOMY

No one denies that the socialist state made a decisive rupture with the institutions of the old regime that it replaced in 1946. Partly from their experience in opposition and partly from their observation of the Soviet Union, the new political leaders had learned to pay serious attention to two problems that the Kingdom of Serbs, Croats and Slovenes never resolved: first, effective representation of the ethnic nationalities, several of which lived in historically based and economically distinct territories, and second, penetration of public life, which previously had been dominated by traditional groups in the national churches and by such modern institutions as political parties that were grafted on to them. The leaders' determination to settle these problems, and their inability to sustain the use of force to do so, encouraged a confidence in institutional and ideological formulas, as well as a willingness both to circumvent and to alter them. During the early years, the Yugoslavs were constrained in their choices – nationalisation, collectivisation, centralisation – by their close relation with the Soviet Union. Negating the most hated old state forms, however, laid a basis for compromise which departed from Soviet practice. Although policy and personnel decisions remained centralised in party preserves, the leadership recognised a real commitment to the federal republics. Unlike either the interwar monarchy or the Soviet Union, the Yugoslavs rejected any form of prefectoral system. Home rule was adaptable either to expansion (in a potential Balkan federation) or consolidation of the existing state. When, after 1948, the latter goal assumed crucial importance, the leaders also began to devolve state functions from the federal centre to the republics. Their search for defensible local jurisdictions dovetailed with their attempt to find replacements for Soviet forms. Between 1950 and 1953, leaders like Kardelj and Boris Kidrić rediscovered the social utility of workers' councils and the commune. This new reliance on local jurisdictions strengthened an image of the state at the bottom as an association of equals, but it placed a premium on the ability to manage agreement at the top. Significantly, however, the leaders acknowledged the priority of reorganising the state in order to make possible substantive economic reform.[3]

The leadership was especially pressed by three basic economic problems that had plagued the old regime: modernising agriculture, developing industry, and forming a national market. The old regime had been too weak either to compel or to support the modernisation of agriculture by the large landholders, and to complete a redistribution of their property into the medium-size farms that economists of the period strongly urged. Even if it had tried to carry through this reform, the interwar government was so overextended on foreign loans and reparation payments from the First World War that it could hardly afford to finance credits for agricultural improvement. Nor did it generate political mechanisms for dealing with the demands that a new class of farmers would undoubtedly make. Moreover, the old regime failed to sponsor the development of a real industrial system. During the 1930s, Yugoslav economists agreed that only industrialisation could alleviate the burden of rural overpopulation. Not only would new industrial workers move off the land, but mechanisation would raise agricultural productivity to provide a saleable surplus. Dominated by foreign capital, however, investment aimed at extracting and exporting mineral wealth rather than developing a competent industrial base. The consumers' goods that were manufactured domestically, mainly in the northern industrial centres of Slovenia and Croatia, lacked a domestic market. Dependent on low agricultural prices, the south and the highlands could not absorb them. Despite the expansion of the major cities following the First World War, continuous urban growth did not affect regional and urban–rural imbalance. Finally, the old regime never created a unified national market. Political centralisation proved grossly inadequate to this task when local capitalists in each region showed little interest in developing sources or generating orders outside their traditional markets.[4]

Decisions by the new Communist political leaders reversed these patterns of economic failure without transforming their structural causes. As in the old regime, basic problems were caused, first, by capital formation without centralised, coercive, economic power and, second, by labour mobilisation without a market system. In agriculture, the retrenchment of collectivisation that began in the early 1950s resulted in the dominance of relatively inefficient peasant smallholdings. These had also been the major result of the pre-war agrarian reform. During the 1950s, in the aftermath of decollectivisation, no political institution initiated an overall modernisation program that would link these small producers within a framework orientated towards increasing production or improving marketing. By contrast, in industry, state-financed investment dramatically increased productive capacity. Industrialisation created jobs, raised the standard of living, and inducted all segments of the society into a cash economy. To a large extent, work in industry helped individual families finance improvements on rural property. But without a system of national planning, productive investment led mainly to increased consumption, through the domestic production of consumers' goods, imports, and the purchase of foreign licences. No political inducements countered the easiest path to profitability by aligning investment with the relative need for capital and labour in different regions or by balancing the buying power of industrial and non-industrial consumers. Furthermore, regional markets duplicated capacity. Difficulties of large-scale capital formation within the country influenced each region and even each prodcution unit to relate its needs outward to foreign investors, buyers, and suppliers. In comparison with the old regime, however, the degree of economic decentralisation permitted by current leaders intensified a pressure for central political intervention noted by the economist Rudolf Bićanić fifteen years ago: enterprises or republics that sink in an enlarged market run to the centre for help, while those that swim with the tide call for looser ties.[5]

Significantly, the means that have been chosen to promote de-etatisation of the economy, particularly in investment and taxation, contradict the stated ends. Since the late 1960s, for example, investment functions have been transferred from the state to local banks, hence indirectly to the communes' control. But because there is no free capital market in which projects could compete for funds, local control creates a pressure to generate investment capital locally. Officially encouraged by decentralisation, local functionaries unofficially commit themselves to investment in their communes, and press local banks, even if they are already overcommitted, to back them up. In the absence of either municipal or commercial bankruptcy, there is little reason for this strategy to change or for any commune to act differently. The resulting 'territorialisation' politicises investment decisions. The lack of economic sanctions for making wrong decisions leaves a gap to be filled by higher-level political action. In this case, the political system affirms a role for the state on two levels. First, the investment process creates a power base for local 'capital' made up of commune officials and local banks. Second, problems of over- and under-investment necessitate the centre's intervention. The sort of local clientelism that has evolved condemns the federal leadership to an unpalatable choice: either to take repressive measures against local economies (as it did during the 1970s by forcing republics to pool their foreign-currency earnings and forcing communes to pass new taxes to cover the costs of new investment), or to bargain with local political 'machines'. The use of military troops to quell the sustained resistance in Croatia and the Albanian region of Kosovo suggests that there are limits, on the one hand, to the efficacy of economic coercion and, on the other hand, to the leaders' tolerance for bargaining. When local leaders appeal outward toward a broader public, rejecting established lines of center–periphery command and intra-party communication, their behavior is considered tantamount to rebellion. Only within the proper framework are local communities supposed to replace 'the state'.[6]

The tax system also demonstrates the difficulty of managing centre–periphery relations through quasi-state institutions. Though published data about tax rates are unclear, both corporate and individual taxpayers assert that their rates are incommensurate with the services they receive and the autonomy (or self-management) they supposedly enjoy. Furthermore, as fiscal responsibility has increasingly devolved on communes and interest communities, these local authorities have turned to raising revenue through levies that are termed, Orwellian-style, 'self- (or voluntary) contributions' (*samodoprinosi*). Although citizens decide on the imposition of such taxes in referenda, social and political pressures influence both a high turnout and a largely favourable vote. Moreover, the parallel structures of economic and social self-management amplify dissatisfaction with the fiscal system. First, Yugoslavs are taxed – indirectly, for the most part, on enterprise rather than personal income – in the work unit as well as the residential community. Second, neither the enterprise nor the locality provides the collective goods Yugoslavs need.

It is true that over the past fifteen years enterprises have suffered from chronic liquidity crises that have led them to pour most of their cash into wages and simple reproduction, leaving fringe benefits aside. At the same time, local communities' budgets have been so strained that they have cut back on vital services (for example, public transportation) and new public works (for example, plans for a subway and a train station in Belgrade). Citizens rightly ask where their tax monies go. Certainly service on the $20 billion foreign debt, import and export subsidies, and inflationary increases in fuel and labour costs for the public sector take their financial toll. But equally problematic are the costs of the state's purchases (especially for defence), its administrative costs, and its direct investments channelled through republican and federal funds specifically earmarked for the less developed regions. Political conflict arises over the latter issue, for the most part because it meshes the social with the national question. It leads to criticism of the wisdom of state-financed investments as well as the equity of their distribution. Since 1980 this criticism has been heightened by the drain of foreign currency earnings to pay for fuel and raw material imports.

Nevertheless, in Yugoslavia, no form of political intervention institutionalises the conflict between localism (of enterprise as well as territory) and national capital formation. Since the mid-1950s, for example, neither a planning ministry nor a council or congress on any level has had jurisdiction over projects and disputes. To some degree, over the past few years, *ad hoc* committees drawn from the federal legislature (the *Skupština*) and the federal administration (the Federal Executive Council, or FEC) have acted as a locus of interrepublican and federal–local negotiation. But the quality of their intervention – the sources of their recruitment and the way discussions are carried out – leaves a gap, again, for higher-level political action. Delegates to the *Skupština*'s main body, the Chamber of Republics and Provinces, come from the republican assemblies, and the interrepublican committees of the FEC are drawn from the republican administrations. According to American researcher Steven Burg, the administrators have a greater commitment to federal co-ordination. Their relative disinterest may be offset, however, by the regional advocacy of their legislative colleagues,[7] and even a suggestion of cross-cutting cleavage between functional and regional interests may assume a clearer role-division than officials themselves are likely to define. After all, their negotiations take place in secret sessions and personal communications.

As Burg suggests, it may well be that these norms assure the cohesion necessary to reach a compromise as well as to generate – without a chief like Tito – a commitment to enforce it. But despite the effort to replace individual with collective authority, such forms of negotiation, serious as they are for Yugoslavs, hardly represent an institutional advance over top-level decision-making in any other party-state. Moreover, the bargaining process in Yugoslavia imposes costs on both the party and the state. First, it lengthens the time required for reaching important policy decisions, or even preparing the guidelines for party congresses, and makes it more difficult for the party to assume its 'guiding' role.[8] Second, it necessitates a central financial mechanism to compensate the 'losers' in policy decisions. This is particularly important when the losers are republics and autonomous regions and their compensation takes the form of subsidy. As long as these federal entities are able to exact compensation, they adhere to the political rules. In that case, however, the normal policy-making process forces an expensive strategic reversal. Although in most societies economic underdevelopment legitimises the opportunity for state intervention, in Yugoslavia the opportunity to exact compensation suggests, contrary to expectation, that state intervention legitimizes underdevelopment.[9]

Under these conditions, political intervention in the economy 'from the top' continues to be necessary, costly, and cumbersome. Compromise at the centre frequently demands mobilisation at the periphery, and, as sociologist Josip Županov points out, the implementation of policy decisions creates an atmosphere of cyclical 'campaigns' that the leadership supposedly wants to avoid.[10] Successful local economies and industrial sectors seem to flourish *despite* political intervention, while political pressure on economic decisions creates permanent dependence on welfare. These relations reach acute political form when they mobilise national or ethnic fears. On the one hand, Albanians in Kosovo, a region whose budget is almost entirely subsidized by federal funds, have reacted violently against the state for 'exploiting' their dependency. On the other hand, regional leaders in Vojvodina, a region whose economic viability owes little to federally financed investment, criticise the state for 'exploiting' their success. The major justification for political intervention in a decentralised economy is to rationalise decisions on production and distribution. But the less rational the whole process seems, the more it impinges on the political system's legitimacy. Here at least, Yugoslavia's problems coincide with those of other states.

POLITICAL MONOPOLIES ON SOCIAL ACTION

Like the search for defensible local jurisdictions, the Yugoslavs' contributions to a general concept of politics arise less from theory than from pragmatic concerns. In particular, Yugoslav leaders confront a need to differentiate their political system from those of other socialist states. Normally, this requires an effort to contrast their ideas to the absence, in the Soviet Union, of a viable concept of politics. But in extraordinary times, as in the Polish events of 1979–81, the Yugoslavs also contrast their ideas to the concept of 'civil society'. Because the Yugoslav leaders have tried to institutionalise authority outside a traditional, centralised state, they regard both alternatives – the absence of a concept of politics in a centralised state and the presence of a civil society in opposition to the state – as subversive of the political order. Pressed to formulate a positive statement of their goal, they show some uncertainty. A political-science professor recently proposed, for example, in the authoritative journal *Socijalizam*, 'the political system of a post-state society'.[11] To the extent that this expression has any meaning, it refers to the framework the Yugoslavs have already established: the state's withdrawal from control over 'social capital' in favour of non-state organs made up of citizens (in localities) and workers (in production units). Adopting new terms for these participatory local authorities (the 'socio-political community' for territorial, and 'basic organisations of associated labour' for sub-enterprise units) indicates at least nominally the non-directed political system the Yugoslavs intend. The question remains, however, to what extent a political system may appear to be free of manipulation without losing its sense of social direction.

The unobtrusive directing role of political institutions was Edvard Kardelj's lifelong concern. Though he never relinquished a view of the state as a form of coercion and a source of social control, as one of the architects of a 'post-state' politics Kardelj influenced a new view of the state as a reservoir rather than the font of power. This approach conceives of state power as residual. The state may act as a 'partner', a means of 'adjustment', and the ultimate 'defender' of the social system. But it neither owns the means of production nor directs the social institutions and it does not even hold a monopoly on the political system. Indeed, politics more properly belongs to a wider realm. It is the distinctive mark of Yugoslav self-management, for instance, to suggest both the rules of 'the political system' and its equitable, desired end. Even among Yugoslavs, these distinctions cause some confusion. Theoretically, though not in the official sources, there appears to be a tripartite division. First, *sovereignty*, as the 1974 constitution states, derives from 'the working class and all working people'. Second, *authority* inheres in 'self-management', especially in three fundamental institutional zones: the economy (through the basic organisations of associated labour), the locality (through the socio-political community), and ideologically-based social action (through socio-political organisations like the party, the Socialist Alliance, labour unions, and veterans' and youth associations). Finally, these institutional zones, particularly their elected assemblies, are where the *exercise of sovereignty* takes place. But as political intervention in the economy suggests, power is really exercised through narrower and frequently informal channels.

A divergence from the formal assumptions appears in the familiar distinction between participation and power. During the 1970s, political institutions were restructured to increase the number of participants and the number of 'organs' in which they could take part. To a degree, these reforms corresponded to perceived needs: dissatisfaction with 'technocratic' control over workers' councils by directors and their staffs, disaffection from 'bureaucratic' control in Belgrade and local capitals, and the growth of blue-collar grievances, due especially to variations in real wages and a rise in taxes. In response, Kardelj and his associates developed the idea of circumventing the power bases of both bureaucratic and technocratic forces and refocusing political struggles in different forms. They particularly wanted to enlarge the competence of legislative assemblies. But these assemblies were not to be restricted to the legislative branch of government; instead, they would have jurisdiction over all areas of policy-making and their implementation. In certain ways the Yugoslavs seemed to revert to eighteenth-century political theory, by making the 'self-manager' into a modern version of the universal legislator.

For years, of course, each commune as well as the republics and the federation was governed by a *skupština*, or assembly. After the reforms of the 1970s however, the federal *skupština* in Belgrade no longer had priority over the *skupština* on any other territorial level. So now each socio-political community was sovereign in its area. Furthermore, each assembly was divided into three 'functional' chambers corresponding to the three self-management zones. The first chamber was elected by citizens in their residential locality, the second by work units, and the third by local branches of the socio-political organisations. Moreover, by 1978, almost 5000 interest communities, each with its own assembly, had been established, for the most part, in the communes. Of course, the work organisations had their own system of assemblies. Assuming state approval for each new 'community' to be formed, the possibilities of increasing the number of assemblies seemed infinite. By the beginning of the 1980s, social researcher Neca Jovanov estimated that two-and-a-half million Yugoslavs were involved in some fashion in these assemblies' work. Probably half of them participated in self-management institutions in the economy.[12]

Power, however, is not so widely dispersed. In three key areas – budget formation, policy initiation, and the exponential growth of their administrative staffs – the assemblies reproduce conditions conducive to technocratic and bureaucratic control. Neca Jovanov has been particularly critical in this regard. Their share of social resources, as he demonstrates by their budgets, makes the interest communities a considerable 'power centre' in society. Furthermore their 'administrative-managerial apparatus', as Jovanov says, 'overpowers its own assembly by its social power'.[13] To a certain extent, these charges ring true. Rather than disappear, budget and personnel lines have merely been transferred along with formal competence from the federal to the local level. Understandably, as the assemblies' functions grow and the society they regulate becomes more complex, a higher level of expertise is required to carry out their work. The official ideology decrees that ordinary people do more in running the society. But in reality, as Jovanov has consistently pointed out, the assemblies succumb to the professionalisation and the entrenchment of their administrative apparatus. Even official writings admit to some doubt as to whether the 1970s reforms instituted the Paris Commune or a New Leviathan.

Tito's concern about this problem gave rise, toward the end of his career, to the priority of 'deprofessionalising' political office. Again, empirical problems influenced reform, especially because white-collar-dominated bodies had to deal with blue-collar grievances and, even worse, members of such bodies tended to stay indefinitely in these positions. Three changes were made. First, at the end of the

1960s, constitutional amendments mandated that the majority of representatives in all elected organs be blue-collar workers. Second, pressure was put on the bureaucracy, too, to be more 'representative' by
requiring that top-level administrators – the members of the executive
councils – be elected by their respective assemblies. Third, following
the so-called 'Tito initiative', new rules activated the rotation of all
political personnel. Always sensitive to charges of bureaucratism, the
leadership had previously adopted similar rules. Now, however, the
imminence of Tito's death and the desire to avoid another 'cult of the
personality' lent fresh impetus to their enforcement. Curiously,
according to these norms, leaders who wished to cloak themselves in
Tito's mantle had to move out of their political office. More sensibly,
perhaps, leaders who felt at a relative disadvantage in political
bargaining – at either federal or republican level – may have favoured
rotation as a possible means of changing the balance of forces arrayed
against them.

On paper, at least, the increase in staff size also seemed control-
lable. Some interest communities began to share administrative
personnel. Yet bureaucratic recruitment continues to be problematic
on at least two levels. First, the scarcity of jobs, especially for lower-
secondary-school graduates, and the relative protection of jobs in the
public sector, make it hard for a socialist government to reduce the
number of clerical personnel. On another level, despite the rules, it is
still difficult to remove high office-holders from these or equivalent
positions. When people in this stratum are *not* re-elected, it's a news
story of 'Man-bites-dog' magnitude and arouses some notice in the
national press.[14]

It is harder to evaluate the content of political decisions. Jovanov
criticises the interest communities and various assemblies for
furthering bureaucratic rather than social interests and for aiding and
abetting 'the state'. 'In fact they are part and parcel of the state', he
says, 'and are objectively its political gears.'[15] Indeed, in cases where
popular opinion was known in advance to oppose a policy proposal,
such as the reform of the higher education system in 1978, the
assembly system did not prevent its enactment. Similarly, in the
current round of decisions to build nuclear power stations around the
country, local assemblies (notably in Zadar) have been able to delay
such plans, but their long-term effect is far from clear. From the
beginning, in fact, the procedure for choosing the assemblies and
making policy through them suggests that their freedom of action was
blocked.

First, all assemblies above the most 'basic' or local level are constituted by indirect elections. Officially, the Yugoslavs call this delegate system 'the most direct' form of democracy, but the election of each higher territorial assembly by delegations in a lower organ really excludes mass participation at all but the neighborhood level. Second, votes are cast by delegations rather than by individual delegates, so voting within the assemblies is done by blocs. This enables the Yugoslavs to avoid the bargaining and brokering of classical parliaments and the Burkean individualism on which such representation is based. By practically requiring prior consensus within delegations, the bloc-vote principle reduces the delegates' opportunity to represent specific interests. Such brokering as occurs, however, must take place between as well as within delegations.

Although in theory each assembly chamber has the right to veto decisions that are taken by another assembly body, in practice this veto power is never used. Like the bloc vote, a veto creates an all-or-nothing situation with which most delegations would not want to get involved. Nor is there much time for involvement. Because assembly delegations, in contrast to assembly staffs, meet only a few days each month, they can engage in only limited discussion. Observers generally note that members of the most important assemblies, that is the federal and republican *skupštine*, tend to meet more frequently and for longer sessions than in the past, and to use interviews in the press for the strategic purpose of publicising their views. However, important decisions are delegated to special negotiating committees, where the administrative staff (especially the Federal Executive Council) is known to play a key role. The FEC, in fact, together with other high-level organs, initiates most of the bills the *skupština* considers. Finally, even the most active participants in this process hold few illusions about their effect. Often they have little confidence, given the Yugoslav penchant for reform, that a law will stand for several years. If they do show such faith in legislation, they have little reason to believe that people will violate their self-interest to obey it.[16]

Ironically, Kardelj's formulation of the Yugoslav political system was founded on the acknowledgment that people act in their own self-interest, and that the major task of politics is to reconcile conflicts between them.[17] This position has always been presented as a theoretical advance over the Soviets' 'all-people's state', first for the recognition of conflictual interests under socialism it provides, and second for the opportunity it gives the political system to resolve social conflicts. But Kardelj pursued his insight so as to stifle conflict rather than express it. In this sense, the proliferation of assemblies, the indirect selection of the delegations, and the constitution of their bloc vote all suggest means of manipulation. Because Kardelj himself limited the meaning of interest to 'political interest' broadly founded on social role, he separated the concept from its traditional marxist class context.[18] By eliminating social class from 'interest', however, Kardelj could not only speak of a healthy 'pluralism of interests' in socialist society at large – regardless of the persistence of social classes – but also build upon the plurality of every citizen's roles. Democracy under these conditions, according to Kardelj, consists of multiple functional representation, or a political representation of citizens in all their social roles. By contrast, the lack of democracy consists, on the one hand, in acknowledging the sway (or the 'monopoly') of any single interest (as in both capitalism and state socialism) or, on the other hand, in denying the validity of a general social interest borne by the working class. Certainly differences of opinion and alternative proposals are expected to emerge from discussions in the assemblies and even in the executive councils. But under no circumstances are they supposed to generate an organised opposition. Kardelj expressly and permanently excluded the creation of political parties. 'Any other political system', he says, 'would really be a negation of self-management itself.'[19]

The tricameral organisation of functional representation is merely the most recent Yugoslav attempt to match self-management with control. Prior to the reforms of the 1970s the leaders had tried several different forms of representation within legislative assemblies, combining statism with syndicalism in varying degrees. During the first, 'etatist' period (1946–53), the *skupštine* were unicameral. Their action was necessarily considered as the unitary expression of the centralised party-state. The introduction of workers' self-management, in 1950, inaugurated a period of unsteady institutional innovation. Received ideas were challenged, but it was not clear by which or whose ideas they would be replaced. On one side, old communists and labour union activists probably exerted pressure by claiming either greater stringency from the party or wider latitude for 'workers' control'. In another area, Milovan Djilas in the leadership, as well as some workers and younger intellectuals, grew disillusioned with what they saw as a lack of idealism in everyday life. The leaders chose to respond by a compromise of sorts. They consolidated *workers'* representation in a system channeled by the *state*. In 1953, for example, a constitutional change made the assemblies bicameral; in addition to a chamber of locally elected representatives, a producers' chamber (*veće proiz-vodjača*) was chosen by employees at their place of work. Within a few years, however, this form of representation no longer enjoyed official approval. Several possible reasons account for its abandonment. It may have detracted from a growing emphasis on the commune or conflicted with a relaxation of hard-core Leninist ideology. (This was the period of the reorganisation of the League of Communists and the official resurgence of labour unions.) Alternatively, producers' chambers may have offered too direct and too radical a channel – in conjunction with the First Congress of Self-Managers (1957) and the first workers' strike (1958) – for the representation of working-class interests.

In any event, the 1963 constitution introduced a more differentiated functional representation, primarily by making the assemblies multicameral. Although the federal *skupština* in Belgrade had five chambers, four specialising in a particular area (economic policy, social welfare, education and culture, socio-political organisations), in practice the general assembly (the Federal Chamber) did most of the legislative work. The flourishing of 'constitutionalism', as some foreigners called it, and the seeming autonomy of the *skupštine* from party control, marked the beginning of a period often referred to as 'liberalisation'.[20] Yet in retrospect, in comparison both with the possibilities opened by the producers' chambers and with the realities of the eventual delegate system, the reorganisation of the *skupštine* in 1963 appears to have been a means of tightening control. For the first time, *skupština* members were elected indirectly, by members of lower territorial assemblies. In addition, though symbolically, the constitution removed sovereignty from the *skupstina* and placed it in the self-management 'system'. This move effectively eliminated the possibility of political representation in a broadly elected legislative system.

But even the multicameral assembly proved too hard to control. Like the old producers' chambers, the new economic chambers offered an opportunity to the enterprises – and, apparently, to the directors and managers who gained seats in the assemblies – to write their own policy.[21] By the end of the 1960s, streamlining the *skupštine* to three chambers facilitated both legislative efficiency and political control. Certainly the three chambers assure access to state power for the three basic institutional zones of social action: the economy, the locality, and ideologically based political groups. Furthermore, the assembly system links them, as the leaders say, 'horizontally' on each level and 'vertically', through their analogues up to the federation.

But contrary to first impressions, each zone is not an autonomous field. None is free from interference from the other zones, particularly from the socio-political organisations; nor is an opportunity granted for the checks and balances of liberal constitutions. Instead of replacing a traditional state with freer forms, the tripartite organisation of representation really creates three 'global states', each asserting a certain sovereignty, an internal system of representation, and an independent means of identifying the individual in relation to society. More significantly, the three institutional zones *together* define the limits of the global state. Outside these three zones, no legitimate social action is possible. In another sense, social action often requires the co-ordinated participation of all three zones.[22]

Implicitly, of course, the delegate system excludes the creation of other political zones. But in addition, two alternate means of legitimising or delegitimising social action constrain expression that might foster an attempt to create new zones. First, any entry into public life via the establishment of a journal, a radio or television broadcast or a film, or a public meeting of any committee that advocates a specific cause, must be sponsored by a legally constituted organisation in one of the three zones. Though sponsorship is important for obtaining operating funds, it is crucial for the right to operate. Possibilities for expression suffer if sponsorship is denied or withdrawn, as in the cases of the journals *Javnost* (in Belgrade) and *Argumenti* (in Rijeka), respectively, or if the sponsorship procedure is made complicated or obscure, as in the recent confusion surrounding the 'licensing' of a private citizens' committee against capital punishment (in Belgrade).[23] The second means of constraining social action outside the three zones is the state's residual right, as the defender of self-management, to exclude it. Though repression may be sporadic rather than certain, and lenient compared with the past, the possibility of arrest and prosecution reinforces self-restraint. In this sense of social control, the semi-legitimate status of strikes offers a good example. No longer repressed by imprisonment, strikes are none the less disowned by all three zones. First, the localities claim they are not relevant to 'economic' demands; second, the work communities are the entity being struck against; and third, the socio-political organisations – in this case, the labour unions – are held responsible for preventing strikes before they occur. The Yugoslavs have discovered that, in practice, strikes are impossible to avoid. But it is possible to contain them, without denying their validity, by excluding them from the three institutional zones.[24]

These ideas about the political system grew out of the leadership's early strategic choices. Diffuse delegation is a new, possibly less costly form of political mobilisation and control. By the late 1940s, when it became obvious that neither physical coercion nor moral incentives produced the desired results in productivity and social cohesion, the leaders at the time (Kardelj, Kidrić, and Djilas) began to invent alternate forms. Though they never relinquished as antipodal ideal types the 'council' of revolutionary tradition and the 'parliament' of bourgeois rule, each of these forms was too closely connected, for the Yugoslavs' purposes, with a single class interest. Each type also challenged party or single-party rule. Driven by theory and buffeted by practice, the Yugoslavs took some time to invent new forms. As late as 1970, political theorist (and later judge) Najdan Pašić tried to describe representative institutions of a new 'direct' type, consistent with a 'socialization of politics' founded on 'the decentralization and de-etatisation of social life'. Clearly, however, despite his efforts, the delegate system was still just a gleam in Kardelj's eye.[25]

POLITICAL PERMEATION OF ADMINISTRATIVE PERSONNEL

In common with leaders of other socialist states, the Yugoslavs warn against 'bureaucratic' and 'technocratic' influence on policy. More fundamental a motivation than ideological purity is a desire to block all professionalisation outside political control. Certainly the delegate system was intended as part of a programme to deprofessionalise political institutions, making them more responsive to or more reflective of manual workers' demands. But the reforms of the 1970s were also connected with a reassertion of political authority over professionals in non-political fields. This effort was directed not only toward their incorporation in political institutions but also toward eliminating the opportunity they had forged during the 1960s to express their interests in public discussion. Just as the *skupštine*'s economic chambers served as a vehicle for the interests of economic managers, so journals, public meetings, and even sessions of professional associations became forums for intellectuals of the most varied views. The two major offenders, in the party's books, were economists and sociologists, whose infiltration of public life was related to an ideologically based critique which came dangerously close to impinging on the party's role.[26] Political leaders attacked these professions on several fronts: by reorganising the representative system, by redefining the role of party members, and by reinstitutionalising control over the recruitment and circulation of political personnel.

To begin, Kardelj carefully and explicitly inserted the party into the new political system while formally underlining its absence from direct social and political control. Basic to the Kardeljian system was a regenerated communist party that bore the 'long-term, general interest' throughout all functional disputes. Kardelj also conceived of the party as a forum for discussing policy *before* it was considered by the delegations. After party bodies 'democratically' debated and decided upon their position, each party member was obligated to enter the public arena, especially by being elected as a delegate, and 'fight for' adoption of the party view. Both at the time and later, Kardelj's ideas caused some confusion. Though the party still adhered to the principle of democratic centralism, members had grown used to a degree of autonomy from centralised control. But Kardelj intended to tighten the reins. On the one hand, his reformulation bound members more stringently to party positions. On the other hand, it mobilized them as in the old days to 'fight' for the party's will. These conditions had obvious implications for party control over 'nationalist deviations'.[27]

The new political system also asserted the party's right to control political personnel. Though nominations for delegations are made at open meetings in the constituencies, lists of candidates are drawn up in advance by people from the socio-political zone. Without their imprimatur, it is practically impossible to get elected. In the economic zone, as well, nominations for directorships are cleared by local party co-ordinating commissions. Another means of control applies to the executive councils. They serve at the assemblies' pleasure. Because its members stand for election by the assembly every two to four years (depending on the particular republican or federal mandate), an executive council is considered to be held accountable, albeit indirectly, to popular control. In reality, of course, it is accountable to the people who control the assemblies. But the key point about the administration is that it is neither dependent on the (collective) presidencies that make up the executive branch, nor autonomous in the manner of a classical civil service. Indeed, the official texts depict the executive council as a technical instrument rather than a professional corps.

Prior to the 1970s, though, the administration tended to be the most professional of all the political elites.[28] Frequently, federal administrators spent their entire career in the administration. Even if they were recruited to administration from party office or another professional field, they remained in the civil service, where their experience in administration in a single area of expertise contrasted with the generalist's career more typical of party leaders. Administrators also came from higher social strata than members of the other political elite. They were better educated, and their families had white-collar rather than working-class backgrounds. Subjecting them to election and rotation like other political personnel was intended to break down the autonomy that these patterns implied. Although too little time has elapsed for a clear assessment of the reforms' results, several factors probably thwart administrative 'deprofessionalisation'.

First, it is difficult to recruit capable personnel who meet or are willing to meet politically imposed requirements. No less than in other countries, university graduates in Yugoslavia want high-status positions with job security. For the most part, highly educated Yugoslavs, especially those with technical degrees, choose to work in the economic rather than the public sector. Those who do make a career in the civil service apparently experience difficulty in recruiting similar personnel. Another problem in deprofessionalising the administration is due to the continued tendency of most high-level administrators to stay in the civil service. In part, these may be officials with special functions or areas of expertise who cannot easily be transferred; the foreign service corps, the planning experts, and the higher judiciary exemplify this type of personnel. Furthermore, in a small country like Yugoslavia, the entire pool of qualified administrators is fairly small. At any time, under such conditions, high-level personnel tend to be a self-selected group.

This is especially true of political personnel who work on the federal level. As foreign observers frequently note, members of the non-Serbian nationalities do not like to go down to Belgrade. When they must, they minimise discomfort by maintaining their residence in their home republic and spend only a few days each month on business in the capital. On another level, these cultural predilections lead to a self-recruitment of federal personnel. Although patterns of ethnic chauvinism are much less marked than in the interwar period, when Serbs monopolised almost all the ministerial posts, Serbs and Montenegrins are still the only ethnic group that readily enter the federal apparatus. Otherwise, a 'republican key' for equal representation in the highest political and administrative organs, and proportional representation in less important bodies, assures recruitment to the federal level of all national and ethnic groups. Serbs and Montenegrins are however the only groups that circulate in republican-level positions outside their home republic.[29]

Despite official norms of deprofessionalisation and de-etatisation, patterns of recruitment and interaction suggest the outlines of a Yugoslav state apparatus. First, the apparatus is firmly multinational, though geographical representation appears to be enforced rather than freely chosen. Furthermore, each sector of the state–administrative, legislative, and socio-political organisations – tends, unless checked by rotation, to perpetuate itself. Although highly-educated, higher-class Yugoslavs avoid political positions entirely, there is a stratification of the social backgrounds of political personnel. While people from white-collar families enter the administration, Yugoslavs of working-class origin choose careers in the socio-political organisations. On all levels and in all organisations, clerical staffs are drawn from a mixed white-and-blue-collar stratum. Sociometric data from the late 1960s suggest additional, political stratification. Each sector of the state apparatus tends to interact most among its own members. More than party leaders, administrators have a wide field of interlocutors, consulting across organisational lines within their field of expertise. Politicians seem to keep to themselves. This tendency is most marked among leaders in the highest positions. Exerting their influence on the other sectors they, none the less, consult only with each other. During the 1970s, there were suggestions of some widening of interaction, mainly because of interrepublican negotiations. The likelihood, however, is that these negotiations are also stratified. This would be consistent with the impression, due to the lack of career specialisation among political leaders, that in Yugoslavia power still inheres in individuals rather than in positions.[30]

Two professions that challenge incorporation into the state apparatus are the intellectuals and the military. The former group is more easily placed in the Yugoslav political system. Social councils affiliated with the interest communities recruit intellectuals in their specific areas of expertise. Through these councils, intellectuals are given a function and a chance to influence policy without formulating an autonomous expression of their own. Some intellectuals criticise this as a means of corporatism, but others find it, in certain places, a useful, non-co-optive means of integration.[31] The military presents a more difficult case for incorporation. In view of a heightened

Yugoslav perception of and response to foreign threat, the most likely approach incorporates the society into the military rather than incorporating the military into the state. Aside from the former Partisan heroes who made their careers in party or government work, there has never been marked circulation or interaction among military and political offices. There remains the exceptional gesture: the nomination, after the imposition of military rule in Poland, of a general at the head of the Serbian government. More important, however, since the late 1970s, has been an expansion of the concept of civil defence. Under this rubric, military and quasi-military functions devolve on ordinary citizens in the communes and the work organisations. For example, all local authorities and workplaces have civil defence committees, part of whose job is to control the admittance of outsiders, especially foreigners, and to report on all contacts these outsiders make. The universal obligation of an annual tour of active military duty adds not only to a pervasive sense of civil responsibility but also to a sense of militarisation in everyday life.

In contrast to civil defence, the police are not at all incorporated into the interest communities. Without an obligation of even formal accountability, the police none the less command great access to governmental resources. Despite the famous removal from public life in 1966 of former secret-police chief and political leader Aleksandar Ranković, and the subsequent decentralisation of police command, the organisation that he headed has continued to expand. The police control a modern, computerised data-retrieval system, and in the past few years they have recruited supplementary, para-military troops. (In an alleged regenesis of the lumpenproletarian role, these troops are said to be recruited from the prison population. They were used to put down the Albanian riots in Kosovo in 1981.) In addition, police powers affect private expression and freedom of movement, which are constitutional rights. Since the 1970s, for example, advocating an anti-state act even in the privacy of one's home has been considered a crime. Juridically, the point is not that a critical remark has been made (in private), but – if the remark is overheard by someone passing in the street below – that it is held to have been made *in public*. In the early 1980s the compulsory registration of residence was tightened up, so that citizens must now report to the local police station annually instead of once every five years. Yet despite these factors it does not seem possible that either a police state or martial law could be established. However, the current course suggests a continued coupling of 'self-management' and national defence both with specialised police controls and a general militarisation of society.

Neither decentralisation nor de-etatisation ensures the state's impermeability from 'political' forces. The leaders would have it understood though, given the marxist view of every state's lack of neutrality, that their state is firmly biased toward the working class. Yet the way personnel are recruited to the state or the quasi-state apparatus, and the role the League of Communists continues to play, suggest a different sort of political permeation. On the one hand, state and quasi-state administration grows in size and function. The apparent reduction in political activists at its helm is offset by the weight, the persistence, and the professionalisation of its staff. On the other hand, the state administration and the self-managing interest communities that manage local affairs are subject to party control over both policy and personnel. In contrast to some other societies, Yugoslavs tend to incorporate the society into the army rather than the army into the state. Like many states, however, the Yugoslavs also entrust extensive coercive controls to the police.

IN LIEU OF CONCLUSION: THE 'WEAK' SOCIALIST STATE

Short of asserting that they have entirely eliminated the state, Yugoslavs officially claim an evolutionary 'withering' process. De-etatisation of both economy and society, decentralisation of administrative rule-making and its implementation, and deprofessionalisation of political personnel supposedly mark the new 'post-state' political system. Nevertheless, to critics who take marxism seriously, evolution has not been so clear. Because the League of Communists continues to monopolise political power, they find the state hardening its position as the embodiment of *poredak* rather than *pokret*: the party of 'order' triumphant over 'movement'. Moreover, the socialisation of production, in their view, has not been the pathbreaking departure from bureaucratic collectivism the leaders claim. For the most part, it has merely socialised the costs of running the state instead of reducing its power. Critics find the old state apparatus living on in the assemblies, the interest communities, and the local political *aktiv* (especially the commune president and the party secretary). Its 'social power' is wielded, with no apparent opposition from the party, against the interests of the working class. Attempts to analyse the apparatus without developing a theory of the state have led critics to define it in terms of a party-based bureaucracy, a class-structured 'politocracy' and quasi-state and quasi-capitalist 'power centres'.[32] Regardless of terminology however, some distinct, self-conscious, and expanding social force – that claims to derive from working-class sovereignty – skims off the economic surplus and thrives on a fear that individualism, if left unchecked, would lead to anarchy. This practice, in contrast to Yugoslav ideology and institutions, generally evokes the image of state capitalism associated with centralised socialist states. Yet faced with their own foreign and domestic problems, Yugoslav leaders modified the Soviet state practice they had thought to inherit. Their need to establish credibility *vis-à-vis* both domestic and foreign audiences incited an early departure from established models and laid the basis for new relations in and around the state. Innovation was influenced by an inability to use traditional coercive forms. In particular, the Yugoslavs replaced centralised state controls with a looser, though complex, set of norms. Their practice was bounded, and is bounded still, by two types of integration: of centre and periphery, on the one hand, and state and party, on the other. Despite de-etatisation, their unwillingness to depoliticise society led the Yugoslav leaders to structure social action around three zones: the economy, the locality, and the socio-political organisation. In contast to official ideology, the zones that were intended to parcellise social interest assumed universalising characteristics, so that each of the three functional zones appeared as a global state. In accord with official intentions, however, these zones performed a useful function because they limited legitimate social action to those forms they monopolised, licensed, or at least did not exclude. The political system's effect on professionalisation offers a final, interesting point. Though socialist states are structured to assure political control over extra-political professional groups, Yugoslav institutions have an ambiguous effect. On the one hand, politics in Yugoslavia is directed toward incorporating professional groups; on the other hand, it leaves open some 'social space' for these groups to form and express their interests. Surely this is emblematic of Yugoslavia's development as a socialist state.

NOTES

1. For a compendium of explanations of the current political system, see J. Djordjević *et al.*, *Društveno-politički sistem SFRJ* (Belgrade, 1975). The effort to trace this system back to wartime Partisan practice is remarkable (pp. 248ff.).
2. E. Kardelj, *Pravci razvoja političkog sistema socijalističkog samoupravljanja* (Belgrade, 1978) pp. 192–3.
3. In the division of labour that they practised, Kardelj worked more on government proper while Kidrić devoted himself to the economy. On the re-organisation of the state, see B. Kidrić, 'O reorganizaciji državnog upravljanja privredom' (1950) in his selected essays *Socijalizam i ekonomija* (Zagreb, 1979) pp. 67–73.
4. The history of the interwar period is due for critical re-examination; see the historiographical essay by M. Zečević, 'A New Outlook on the Formation of the Yugoslav State in 1918', *Socialist Thought and Practice* (Belgrade) no. 4 (April 1981) pp. 45–62. On the political economy of the interwar period see J. Tomasevich, *Peasants, Politics, and Economic Change in Yugoslavia* (Stanford, 1955) esp. pp. 338–41, 369–82; and V. Dedijer, 'Putevi ujedinjavanja i borba za socijalnu revoluciju', in I. Božić *et al.*, *Istorija Jugoslavije* (Belgrade, 1973) esp. pp. 412–26.
5. R. Bićanić, *Economic Policy in Socialist Yugoslavia* (Cambridge, 1973) pp. 20–1; empirical detail in E. Comisso, *Workers' Control Under Plan and Market: Implications of Yugoslav Self-Management* (New Haven, Conn., 1979).
6. For a clearsighted analysis of the Yugoslav economy, see K. Mihailović, *Ekonomska stvarnost Jugoslavije*, 2nd edn (Belgrade, 1982) esp. pp. 125ff. On territorialisation of investment and other problems, see S. Zukin, 'Beyond Titoism', *Telos*, no. 44 (Summer 1980) pp. 5–24; see also R. Marinković, *Ko odlučuje u komuni* (Belgrade, 1971); L. D'Andrea Tyson, 'Liquidity Crises in the Yugoslav Economy: An Alternative to Bankruptcy?', *Soviet Studies*, vol. 31 (1979) pp. 3–22; and on the behaviour of regional leaderships, S. L. Burg, 'Regional Constitution-Making in Yugoslav Politics', *Publius* (forthcoming); cf. the Central Committee's report, 'Political Stabilization and Socio-Economic Development in the S.A.P. of Kosovo' (Belgrade, 1981).
7. S. L. Burg, 'Yugoslavia Without Tito: Prospects for Stability', paper presented at the annual convention of the International Studies Association, Philadelphia, March 1981, and reprinted in *South Slav Journal* (1981).
8. These difficulties are endemic in the effort to write a long-term policy to contain inflation, a medium-term economic plan (for example, the five-year 'social plan' for 1981–5) and in the short run, the draft resolutions for the XI Conference of the League of Communists (1982). Nevertheless, the 'loss' in efficiency may be compensated for by a 'gain' in consensus. As the economist Slaven Letica says about one area of policy-making, 'There is no doubt – at least from the economic point of view – that the new conception of Yugoslav [economic] union is less efficient than the earlier one. However, it has a variety of non-economic, i.e. political and

social, advantages: a guarantee of the justice and sovereignty of specific republican and regional interests, as well as the public nature and the openness of expressing these interests and making them agree.': 'Republički interesi i jugoslavenska zajednica', *Naše teme*, vol. 25 (1981) p. 1934.

9. This is an implicit criticism made by some Yugoslavs, particularly economists, and is not connected with the so-called market reforms of the 1960s. See the discussion of the political debate over 'objective' economic indicators of underdevelopment in Mihailović, *Ekonomska*, pp. 139 ff.

10. J. Županov, 'Teze o društvenoj krizi', *Revija za sociologiju*, vol. 9, no. 3– 4 (1980).

11. V. Vasović, 'Država i samoupravna socijalistička demokratija', *Socijalizam*, vol. 23, no. 7–8 (1980) p. 71.

12. N. Jovanov, 'Pledoaje za dijalog o državi u socijalizmu', in ibid, p. 100; numbers of delegates and interest communities published in *Trideset godina samoupravnog razvoja Jugoslavije 1950–1980; Statistički prikaz* (Belgrade, 1981).

13. Jovanov, 'Pledoaje za dijalog', pp. 80, 95.

14. In 1982, for example, the failure to re-elect local party officials in several small towns prior to the national party conference generated such comment.

15. Jovanov, 'Pledoaje za dijalog', pp. 93–4.

16. In autumn 1981, for example, an FEC member who was called to the *Skupština* to explain why the administration had not completed the preparation of certain legislation by the deadline the *Skupština* had set, caused a stir by saying that the law would not be acceptable because it would never work. Nevertheless, the attempt to make legislation and to hold the FEC responsible for preparing it according to the *Skupština*'s reading of the situation shows the legislators' willingness to fulfil their functions.

17. The authoritative text is Kardelj, 'Pravci razvoja'.

18. See the criticism in M. Lazić, 'Pluralizam i jedinstvo samoupravnih interesa', *Kulturni radnik*, vol. 31, no. 2 (1978).

19. Kardelj, 'Pravci razvoja', pp. 194–5. The six areas in which the 'democratic pluralism of self-managing interests' can be expressed are, according to Kardelj (p. 115), work and occupation; social policy, including health, education, and culture; the residential community; the sub-federal, territorial nationality (i.e. the republic and the region); ideology (i.e. the socio-political organisations); and the delegate system or 'the organs of state power and general social self-management'. 'Of course,' Kardelj says, 'each of these areas of self-managing interests represents a complicated democratic system *for itself*' (emphasis added).

20. The most knowledgeable presentation of the 'liberal' characterisation of this period is in D. Rusinow, *The Yugoslav Experiment 1948–1974* (Berkeley, 1977).

21. Rusinow, ibid, p. 155, reports that a party member who supported the market-oriented economic reforms of the mid-1960s told him, 'When we realized that we would never be able to count on the Party machinery, we put our boys into the assemblies.' On general doubts about the efficacy of

the multicameral assemblies expressed by Yugoslavs even before their establishment, see F. W. Hondius, *The Yugoslav Community of Nations* (Paris and The Hague, 1968) pp. 286–91.

22. For example, in cases where a work organisation experiences business difficulties or labour problems. On the former, see the case studies in N. Pašić et al. (eds), *Socijalističko samoupravljanje u Jugoslaviji* (Belgrade, 1978) esp. p. 274; on the latter, see N. Jovanov, *Radnički štrajkovi u SFRJ* (Belgrade, 1979).

23. On the journals, see S. Zukin, 'Sources of Dissent and Non-Dissent in Yugoslavia', in J. L. Curry (ed.), *Dissent in Eastern Europe* (New York, 1983).

24. See Jovanov, *Radnički štrajkovi*, and S. Zukin, 'The Representation of Working-Class Interests in Socialist Society: Yugoslav Labor Unions', *Politics and Society*, vol. 10 (1981) pp. 281–316.

25. N. Pašić, *Političko organizovanje samoupravnog društva* (Belgrade, 1971). Rusinow, *Yugoslav Experiment* (pp. 331–2) finds 'the core of the Kardeljian distinction [between the Yugoslav and other representative systems]' in two provisos: first, that the Yugoslav delegates maintain constant contact with their constituents, and second, that they must not be professional politicians.

26. From this point of view, on the problematic professionalisation of sociologists in Yugoslavia, see V. Rus, 'Jugoslovenska sociologija izmedju politizacije i socijalizacije', *Sociologija*, vol. 23, no. 3–4 (1981) pp. 215–27; on the long struggle against another professional group, see T. Oleszczuk, 'Convergence and Counteraction: Yugoslavia's "Anti-technocratic" Campaign and Electoral Results, 1957–1974', *Comparative Political Studies*, vol. 13 (1980) pp. 205–33.

27. See Kardelj, 'Pravci razvoja', p. 217. On the ambivalence this role-definition causes party members, at least in Serbia, see A. Milić et al., *Svest i angažovanost komunista* (Belgrade, 1981); for an outline of ideological statements about the party's role over time, see T. Oleszczuk, 'Group Challenges and Ideological De-radicalization in Yugoslavia', *Soviet Studies*, vol. 32 (1980) pp. 561–79.

28. Discussion of careers is based on an unpublished analysis by R. Rosen and S. Zukin of data collected in 1968 by the Research Project on Yugoslav Opinion-makers, Columbia University (New York) and Institut društvenih nauka (Belgrade).

29. Ibid; cf. Rusinow, *Yugoslav Experiment*, p. 147: 'local government tended to attract and hold a higher proportion (and federal apparatuses a correspondingly lower proportion) of ambitious and/or talented people than would have been the case in other circumstances'. On the interwar period, see L. J. Cohen, 'The Social Background and Recruitment of Yugoslav Political Elites, 1918–48', in A.H. Barton et al. (eds), *Opinion-Making Elites in Yugoslavia* (New York, 1973) pp. 25–68. The post-1970s' use of rotation may have decreased these tendencies.

30. This conclusion is reinforced by data in C. Kadushin and P. Abrams, 'Social Structure of Yugoslav Opinion-makers; Part I, Informal Leadership', in Barton et al., *Opinion-making Elites*, and is not contradicted by S. L. Burg, 'Yugoslavia Without Tito' (see note 7). A comparison of

Yugoslav and Soviet political careers suggests that Soviet personnel are more highly specialised in functional fields.

31. For example, planning councils in Slovenia (see V. Rus, 'Jugoslovenska sociologija', pp. 224–5).

32. Over the years the key terms in this critique have changed, from the 1950s analysis of 'bureaucracy' in M. Djilas's, *The New Class* (New York, 1957), to 'politocracy', in the 1960s essays of intellectuals associated with the journal *Praxis* – see, for example, N. Popov, 'Les formes et le caractère des conflits sociaux', *Praxis*, International Edn, no. 3–4 (1971) p. 367 – to the 1970s discussion of 'power centres' in the articles of N. Jovanov – see, for example, his discussion in *Marksistička misao*, no. 6 (1978). A succinct critique of the current and coming crisis is J. Županov, *Marginalije o društvenoj krizi* (Zagreb, 1983).

9 State Reforms in the People's Republic of China Since 1976: A Historical Perspective

David S. G. Goodman

Since the death of Mao Zedong in 1976, and particularly since the 1st session of the 5th National People's Congress (NPC) in early 1978, the leadership of the Chinese Communist Party (CCP) has implemented various political reforms in the People's Republic of China (PRC). The explicit context of reform has been a reaction to the political practices and policies pursued during the period of the Cultural Revolution, 1966–76. In particular, state reforms have been presented as the means to encourage a revitalised and autonomous (but by no means independent) structure of government, and a return to the political status quo of the early 1960s. Some commentators have regarded the word as the deed, arguing, moreover, that the PRC has returned to the orthodox 'Leninist–Stalinist' model it had adopted during the early 1950s, and which exists in other communist party states.[1] It is, of course, too soon to assess what the actual impact of state reforms will be, as opposed to their intention, not least since many have only just been implemented and it is reasonable to assume that more reforms are on the way. However, it is possible, by considering recent reforms not only in their immediate context but also from a wider historical perspective to assess the limits of their possible significance. Specifically, it is possible to consider further the claims that those reforms may lead to the state's relative autonomy, a return to the administrative and political framework of the early 1960s, and even a return to the 'organisational orthodoxy' of the Soviet Union and Eastern Europe.

Although the concept of 'the state' is clearly open to a variety of interpretations, Western political studies of the PRC have tended to regard the state in the very specific and limited sense of government organisation, the state *apparat*. In that definition, the terminology employed within the PRC has to a large extent been adopted. When applied to the PRC itself that terminology differentiates relatively clearly between, on the one hand, the state, and on the other, party, nation, and the more general political (or social) system.[2] In general, it is only when the PRC is considered in comparative perspective, or in description of other polities that the state is less clearly or more widely defined. The conceptualisation of the state in the PRC as government is reflected in two commonly used terms. The first and more abstract is *guojia*, usually translated as 'the state', that entails the organised strength of centralised and united political power, and stresses its coercive functions. For example, a recent political encyclopaedia provides as its examples of the state's most important institutions 'the armed forces, police, law courts, and prisons'.[3] The second is *zhengfu*, usually translated as either 'government' or 'administration', that refers to the administrative units of the state's organisation, from the central to the basic level. Somewhat paradoxically, the notion of the state *apparat* in the PRC is even narrower than it is more generally conceived, for it does not include the People's Liberation Army (PLA).[4] As Schurmann, among others, has pointed out, the CCP has viewed the PRC's political system since 1949 as comprising three major hierarchies; namely the CCP, the PLA, and the state.[5] It is the last of those three that is the focus here. First, the context and nature of state reforms will be outlined. Thereafter, the limits of their potential significance will be considered through an examination of party–state relations since 1949; a comparison of the state structure before the Cultural Revolution and since 1976; and a discussion of the peculiarities of the PRC as a communist party state.

THE CONTEXT OF REFORM

With respect to the state *apparat* recent reforms have had two stated aims. One has been the desire to promote 'socialist democracy and legality' as opposed to the 'autocracy, bureaucracy, love of privileges, the patriarchal style of work, and petty-bourgeois individualism'[6] that is now said to have existed during the period of the Cultural Revolution from 1966 to 1976. That decade is now virtually written off as a period of 'feudal fascism' for which the 'Gang of Four' are held responsible.[7] Curiously, from any Marxist perspective, that appellation is presented with little discussion of the relation between base and superstructure or the prevailing mode of production. In general, it has been described as 'feudal' because there were no laws, the rule of an emperor (in effect), no courts, arbitrary arrest and torture.

The specific criticisms of a leading party theoretician, Li Honglin, in 1979 are particularly interesting. He pointed out that the NPC had not met often enough; and that as a 'democracy' the system, far from being socialist, did not even measure up to that of capitalist democracies. Moreover, Li criticised not only the Cultural Revolution's decade as feudal, but also by implication included the years 1958–1961, thereby obliquely attacking Mao since all those years are clearly recognisable as times of his ascendancy.[8] Two years later, the CCP was more openly hostile to both Mao and the Cultural Revolution. The 'Resolution on Certain Questions in the history of our Party since the establishment of the PRC' was adopted by the 6th plenum of the 11th central committee of the CCP in June 1981.[9] It criticised Mao generally for his personal arbitrariness, held him responsible for the evolution of the Cultural Revolution, and regarded that decade as an almost unqualified disaster. Though the resolution recognised Mao's contribution to the Chinese revolution, it criticised his political activities, particularly after 1958, and drew a distinction between the ideology that bears his name (Mao Zedong Thought) and his personal activities to such an extent that it explicitly condemned Mao for having contravened Mao Zedong Thought during the Cultural Revolution.[10]

The second expressed aim of state reforms has been the need for economic revival, recognised in the campaign to achieve the 'Four Modernisations' – that is, of industry, agriculture, science and technology, and national defence. Though the slogan of the 'Four Modernisations' and its general content had first been coined in the early 1960s and even supported by Lin Biao in his foreword to Mao's 'Little Red Book', during the mid-1970s it became associated with those opposed to the economic policies of the Cultural Revolution. Although the extent of economic problems during the 1970s has only become apparent, at least partially, since 1976, by all accounts the economic situation during the Cultural Revolution was certainly not as healthy as had been claimed at that time.[11] In the summer of 1975 a series of policy documents was drafted as the first stage in a programme for economic revival and the achievement of the 'Four

Modernisations' by the end of the century. Though they fell foul of the intraleadership conflicts of 1975–6 and were removed from the political agenda along with Deng Xiaoping in April 1976, they re-emerged and were enlarged after Mao's death and the arrest of the 'Gang of Four'. In essence the economic policies of the Cultural Revolution have been criticised for 'placing politics in command' too much, not 'paying attention to economic laws', and for a lack of adequate economic planning.[12]

STATE REFORMS SINCE 1976

Diagnosis of the PRC's economic, political, and administrative problems has led to changes throughout the state *apparat*. The re-orientation of economic perspectives since 1976 has resulted in an expansion of the state's central organisational framework – that is, the ministries and commissions directly under the State Council, whose ministers are members of that body; the introduction of a new system of economic administration; and the creation of new co-ordinative planning units. In 1975–6 there had been 25 ministries, but as of 1 April 1981 there were 38. With two notable exceptions, that expansion has resulted directly from the renewed concern with administration of the economy.[13] The exceptions are the re-establishment of Ministries of Justice, and Civil Affairs, that are undoubtedly an integral part of the programme to promote 'socialist legality'. However, perhaps of greatest significance, seven new commissions (there had only been four during 1975–6) have been established for the explicit purpose of co-ordinating economic activities across ministries.[14] At the basic level, economic enterprises formerly under the close direction of local government have been encouraged to experiment with a greater degree of freedom in their management and administrative procedures. Flexibility has been the keyword in planning, purchasing, distribution and pricing policies.[15] At the regional level, the six large economic co-ordinative regions (each covering several provincial-level units) that existed in the late 1950s and early 1960s have been re-established.[16] As before, it would appear that their intended function is to attempt regional (as opposed to provincial) economic self-sufficiency, while maintaining both continued and centrally directed economic growth.[17]

From an administrative perspective the post-1976 critique of current ills and the Cultural Revolution has been directed at the overconcentration, both institutionally and associationally, of functions and powers within the politico-administrative system; and at previous policies on cadres, their appointment and terms of office. Putative reforms have included the restructuring of local (That is, non-central)[18] government, and the adoption of new policies towards cadres. A major administrative problem facing the PRC increasingly during the 1970s was the guaranteed employment and lack of compulsory retirement for cadres. The results have included not only the emergence of a significant gerontocracy and the lack of an adequately trained administrative successor generation (particularly given the relative youth of cadres on attaining power in 1949),[19] but also considerable overmanning. As one complainant described the general behaviour of cadres in a letter to the *People's Daily*: 'With tea to drink and fags to puff, The daily paper's work enough!'[20] Though noises have been made to end cadres' guaranteed employment, little has so far emerged. On the other hand, Deng Xiaoping and several other elderly vice premiers led the way and resigned their official positions in the state *apparat* at the 3rd session of the 5th NPC in 1980[21] in order to encourage other older cadres to do likewise, and the cases of those who have followed received considerable publicity.[22]

The restructuring of local government has been a necessary consequence of the rejection of the Cultural Revolution. At its very start the Cultural Revolution involved, outside the centre, the dismantling of the previous organisational frameworks of both party and state, and their replacement by what at that time was described as 'the brand new proletarian organ of power', the revolutionary committee. Though the functions of the revolutionary committees (which originally replaced every administrative unit from the basic to the provincial level) changed considerably during the 1970s, they were originally conceived as joint agencies of party and state. Despite the recreation of a party *apparat* at local levels after 1969, the lack of differentiation between party and state characterised the period of their existence. In addition, despite the revolutionary committee's claim to be 'representative' there would appear not to have been any pretence of election. Thus, for example, after 1965 and until 1977 no people's congresses were convened to elect or approve people's governments at the various levels of local government, as they had been before the Cultural Revolution. Between 1977 and 1980, the pre-Cultural Revolution structure of local government was re-established at all administrative levels. People's congresses were re-convened and have continued to hold approximately annual sessions. That has followed the practice of the 5th NPC, elected in 1978, for although a 4th NPC had been elected in 1975, it had not (unlike its pre-Cultural Revolution predecessors) held annual sessions. Local people's congresses have elected permanent standing committees (as representative bodies) and people's governments (the executive branch of the state *apparat* at each level). In line with the new principles of clearly differentiating between the roles both of institutions and of individuals, and of not over concentrating functions and powers, an attempt has been made to minimise the overlap between people's congresses and people's government. For example, at provincial level, no individual holds a leadership position on both the standing committee of the people's congress and in the people's government, and that would appear to be generally the case at lower administrative levels.[23]

The concern with promoting 'socialist democracy and legality' and the consequent state reforms have perhaps received the greatest publicity within the PRC. The legal system has been refurbished. As previously noted, ministries of justice and of civil affairs have been re-established; the law courts have been regularised, and to be a lawyer has once again become respectable.[24] Moreover, the attempt to codify and regularise the PRC's laws has been started, with several new major laws, notably the Criminal Code, Marriage Law, and Electoral Law, drafted and implemented.[25] The emphasis has been on a 'socialist rule of law' (contrasted to the tyranny of the decade of the Cultural Revolution); and on 'equality before the law', despite the apparent paradox that similar sentences were prescribed for Yao Wenyuan (one of the 'Gang of Four') and Wei Jingsheng (a leading radical dissident of Beijing's Democracy Movement during 1978–9).[26] Though the trial of the 'Gang of Four' was a clear symbol of both emphases they have also been pursued in other ways. For example, the state has prosecuted officials for corruption; and held cadres responsible for apparent mistakes, even of delegated responsibility. Thus, Wang Shouxin, manager of a county fuel company was imprisoned after having been found guilty of misappropriating approximately £160 000;[27] and Song Zhenming, Minister of the Petroleum Industry, was dismissed following the capsizing of an oil-rig in the Bohai Gulf.[28]

Regularisation, accountability and responsibility have been the keynotes of political reforms in the state *apparat*. A completely new Electoral Law has been adopted,[29] quite apart from a revised state constitution.[30] The new Electoral Law provides for competitive elections, on the grounds that competition 'would prevent officials becoming "masters of society"', a constant complaint during the late 1970s. In principle there are to be more condidates than places to be

filled in any election, and there are even regulations covering the
numbers of candidates. For direct elections the number of candidates
should be 50–100 per cent above the number of places to be filled; in
indirect elections, 20–50 per cent higher. The Electoral Law also
stresses the accountability of cadres to their electorates, and provides
for the possibility of recall meetings and elections. Finally, the new
law provides for direct elections, not only at the basic level as before,
but also (in a new departure for the PRC) in county elections. Since its
national adoption, the new law would appear to have been implemented, at least formally.[31] Moreover, considerable emphasis has been
placed on the 'democratic' implementation of not only the Electoral
Law but all the reforms in the state structure. Thus, for example, 'by-
elections' (*buquexuanju*), as had occurred during the 1950s but not
thereafter, have once again been held; and elections have been
declared null and void on the grounds that there had been undue
outside interference, notably from the CCP.[33] For similar reasons
great stress has been laid on the need for regular sessions of people's
congresses at all levels, *inter alia* to receive and approve government
work reports, plans and budgets.[34] Though that practice had generally
occurred before the Cultural Revolution, it had not thereafter until
late 1977. Since then, however, people's congresses have met on a
more regular basis and their published proceedings have included
government work reports, plans and budgets.[35] All in all, then, the
long-term aims of reforms in the state *apparat* since 1976 have been its
revitalisation: to create a separate and functioning structure of
government, capable of fulfilling the tasks allotted to it by the CCP.[36]
It is interesting that the revival of concern with the state *apparat* has
been reflected in recent attempts to establish political science as an
academic field of study in the PRC. Though other aspects of Western
political studies are, and have been for some time, studied under other
academic subject headings (for example, philosophy, political
economy and history),[37] the state has not been a focus for academic
work or political science studied more generally since 1949. However,
in May 1980, steps were taken to establish the study of political science
within institutes of higher education and research. The inaugural
meeting of the Chinese Political Science Society proclaimed (perhaps
somewhat optimistically by Western standards):

Political science is an independent basic branch of learning in the
social sciences. However, since the founding of the People's
Republic, political science has not been given the importance it

merits ... As a result, there is insufficient research on such important theories and practical questions in political science as 'the institution of the state', 'the organization of governments', 'the functions of legislative, executive and judicial organs and their mutual relations', or 'the cadre system'. The lesson is profound.[38]

PARTY AND STATE

If viewed in isolation, the potential of any government organisation, let alone the whole state *apparat*, may clearly be magnified. However, almost by definition, in a communist party state it is the state *apparat*'s relationship with the communist party that is of key significance. Ever since the establishment of the PRC, except for a brief period during 1967–8 when its position was ambiguous, the CCP has held to the theoretical position that the party makes policy but the state implements it. If nothing else, that distinction between two parallel hierarchies preserves the party's vanguard role.[39] In a speech in 1952, the veteran communist Dong Biwu emphasised that 'The CCP should issue general directives to the government administration but the party does not directly conduct the affairs of the state.'[40]

However, ever since 1949 that distinction has proved difficult and sometimes impossible to maintain in practice. Speaking in 1951, Gao Gang, the then chairman of the State Planning Commission complained bitterly that cadres were not maintaining any distinction between party and state and concluded, 'We must understand that party organs should not and cannot replace state organs.'[41] If anything, the party's tendency to subsume the state *apparat* has increased with time. For example, in 1957 the Tangqi *xian* (country) CCP committee (in Zhejiang province) stated that, 'At present the phenomenon of replacing the government with the party is tending toward becoming a tradition', and criticised the situation that had arisen when 'A meeting of *hsiang* [village] magistrates recently summoned for the purposes of discussing work on grain was monopolised by the Department of Trade and Finance of the *hsien* [County Party] committee.'[42] During the Great Leap Forward and early 1960s, as Barnett indicates, there was a recurring tendency for the CCP

to go far beyond acting as director and supervisor of other political organizations, and has constantly encroached upon government administration as such. In short, on many occasions and in many fields the party has not simply supervized the running of things but has tended to step in and run them itself.[43]

Explanations of the tendency for the CCP to subsume the state *apparat* vary from the cultural to the institutional and political. A cultural explanation is provided by Pye in his research into Chinese political culture. He has argued that in the PRC political power is not only undifferentiated and indivisible, but also that it has a tendency to drift towards its nominal location.[44] Though to a certain extent such findings would imply that within the state *apparat* political power would come to be concentrated in the hands of leading cadres, they also suggest an explanation for the party's over-dominance.

The maintenance of the distinction between party and state has not been aided by the attitude of CCP itself. Even before the Cultural Revolution, several of the CCP's practical policies created ambiguities. Though the overlap between the leadership of party and state organisations before 1966 was not as complete as it became in the following decade, none the less it was considerable. At every level of the politico-administrative system the majority of leading state cadres were also leading party cadres. It was not just that there were exceptionally few non-CCP members in leadership positions within the state *apparat*, (particularly after 1954), or that most leading state cadres were party members, but that taken as a whole there was considerable similarity between the top decision-makers in the party and state organisations at each level. Though *the* leading cadre in one *apparat* at any given level more often than not was not *the* leading cadre in another *apparat*, they were extremely likely to have been a leading cadre in the other *apparats*. Thus, for example, before 1966 it was almost a rule that a provincial governor (the leading cadre in the state *apparat*) was also the 2nd secretary of the party committee in the same province.

Though it is clearly possible for an individual to wear two or more hats, it is also reasonable to assume that when it occurs on as large a scale as in the PRC before 1966 considerable confusion ensues, at least occasionally. However, that is as nothing compared with some of the institutional reforms implemented by the CCP, in terms of blurring the distinction between party and state. Two of considerable significance were the decentralisation measures of 1957–8, and the introduction of the rural people's communes in 1958. Conceived as administrative decentralisation within the state *apparat,* the 1957–8 measures were designed to increase local flexibility and initiative. Several of the central economic ministries were closed down and their functions devolved to provincial level. However, an essential concomitant of the decentralisation of state functions was that the provincial party committees were directed to act as co-ordinating committees for all state activities within the province.[45] The contribution of the rural people's commune to blurring the distinction between party and state was even simpler. Right from its inception in 1958 the rural people's commune was conceived as the basic-level unit jointly of party and state.[46]

It would of course be easy to overestimate the extent to which the party subsumed the state before 1966. However, it would appear that outside the centre the distinction between party and state often existed more on paper than in reality. In that context the changes introduced during the Cultural Revolution, and particularly by the institution of the revolutionary committee in its early stages, can be seen more as a natural development from earlier practices than as a radical break with the past. In that context too, it would seem likely that it will take more than rhetoric to ensure that the more recent reforms of the state *apparat* result in a clear and continuing distinction being maintained between party and state. Certainly the evidence from provincial people's congresses held in early 1980 and early 1981 would seem to suggest that either in formulation or in implementation the party–state distinction remains confused in many respects.

BEFORE AND AFTER THE CULTURAL REVOLUTION

As already noted, the officially stated context of all reforms and not just those concerning the state's organisation, has been the reaction against the Cultural Revolution. To quote Hu Yaobang, when General Secretary of the CCP (Hu became Party Chairman in June 1981):

> the decade between 1966 and 1976 of the so-called great cultural revolution was a period of catastrophe. There was nothing correct nor positive about these ten years. The whole thing was negative. Tremendous damage was done to our economy, culture, education, political thinking and party organization. The only positive factor, if we may call it that, is that we have learnt some lessons from the mistakes made during this decade.[47]

The apparent implication of Hu's statement, and indeed those of other national leaders during recent years, is that reforms are intended to restore the status quo of the early 1960s, now regarded as a 'golden age' in the PRC's development. Thus in an important speech delivered in January 1980, Deng Xiaoping rejected not only any other more radical solutions to the PRC's problems but also those practices implemented during the 1950s. Instead, he emphasised the strength of the PRC during the early 1960s – 'Under the united leadership of the CCP, we quickly overcame the grave difficulties of 1959, 1960 and 1961. It is worth recalling that.'[48] Certainly, the resolution adopted at the 6th plenum of the 11th central committee of the CCP in June 1981 contained a similar judgement on the respective merits of the periods of the Cultural Revolution and the early 1960s.[49] Finally, the impression of a return to the early 1960s has been reinforced by the large-scale rehabilitation, sometimes even posthumously, of those who had been leading cadres at that time but who were attacked and removed from office during the Cultural revolution.[50]

However, even on a very superficial analysis it is clear that recent reforms in the structure and operations of the state do not obviously represent a return to the early 1960s. Though it is undoubtedly true that there are similarities between the intentions of the reforms recently adopted and the first half of the 1960s, there are also significant differences. Though there had formally been a judicial and legal system in the period immediately before 1966, it had largely been in disgrace following the 'Hundred Flowers Movement' of May 1957, and could hardly be regarded as a lively part of the state *apparat*. Similarly, though people's congresses existed between the Great Leap Forward and the Cultural Revolution, they met infrequently (often without even annual sessions) and in considerable secrecy.[51] Except for the NPC, no government work reports, budgets and plans were published, and even at national level such statements were couched in very general terms. Indeed, from 1961 to 1977 there was almost no official publication of economic statistics and similar detailed information. Certain aspects of the new Electoral Law introduced since 1978 have no precedents before 1966. For example, previously, even elections to the county people's congress had been indirect rather than direct; and though there had been no regulation concerning the number of candidates for each place to be filled, it had not been the usual practice for there to be more candidates than places. Again, though the seven so-called 'Democratic parties' (That is, those accepting the CCP's leadership after 1949, and, in the party's theory, representing 'non-antagonistic' classes other than the working class and peasantry) formally participated in the state's organisation during the early 1960s – for example, Zhou Jianren (Lu Xun's brother and a biologist of international standing) was Governor of Zhejiang province – in fact they too were criticised in the wake of the 'Hundred Flowers Movement' and their involvement decreased thereafter. However, as part of the recent reforms, not only have the 'Democratic parties' been revived as organisations, but for the first time since the early 1950s they have started to recruit new members.[52] Finally, the introduction of a certain amount of economic decentralisation to enterprise level is a completely new departure. Although that had been under discussion during the mid-1950s and provided for in the first draft of the 2nd Five Year Plan, in fact it was never implemented. In its place, as already noted, administrative decentralisation to the provincial level was introduced during 1957–8.[53]

The significance of those differences to the situation as it existed immediately before the Cultural Revolution, is that it suggests more of a return to the mid-1950s than to the first half of the 1960s. Before 1958 the state was a more functioning organisation, even given the limits imposed by the CCP's direction and involvement, than it was later to become. At all levels, people's congresses had met regularly and more openly, receiving government work reports, plans and budgets. Moreover, there had been a functioning judicial and legal system; and the 'Democratic parties' could be considered active, if restrained, political organisations. However, the real relevance of the mid-1950s to the more recent reforms is that the earlier period was one of debate and discussion. Between the 2nd session of the 1st NPC in the summer of 1955 and the 3rd plenum of the 8th central committee in the autumn of 1957, the CCP decided to abandon the soviet model of development and debated its replacement. Though that debate was primarily concerned with economic development, it necessarily entailed discussion of the state's organisation. Thus, a major topic of discussion was the extent and form of decentralisation.[54] In the wider debate, reforms were proposed and adopted, though never implemented after 1957, that in many ways are the direct ancestors of the reforms promoted since 1976. For example, Chen Yun, probably the most important architect of economic policy since 1976, first outlined his programme for economic development during 1956. Thus, one of his proposals was for decentralisation, not just administratively to provincial level, but also economically to the basic level, in both industry and agriculture.[55] It is interesting to note that though Zhao Ziyang, the current premier, has received considerable publicity for his experimental implementation of economic decentralisation to the basic level in Sichuan when he was that province's first party secretary after 1975,[56] that reform had been promoted not only by Chen Yun but also by Li Jingquan,[57] one of Zhao's predecessors in Sichuan, during 1956.

More important still are the reasons for the non-implementation after 1957 of the reforms agreed in 1956. Before 1976, it was fashionable for Western academic scholarship to argue that the severity of the economic crisis that became apparent in the second half of 1957 enabled Mao to persuade the rest of the national leadership to adopt his programme for economic development (as later enshrined in the Great Leap Forward), rather than the more gradual (and probably more realistic) Second Five Year Plan.[58] However, since 1976, with the re-evaluation of PRC history both inside and outside China, considerably greater emphasis has been placed on Mao's role in abrogating organisational and political norms. Thus, for example, Teiwes has argued that it was during 1955–7, that Mao changed the rules of politics within both the CCP and the PRC in general. In his view, the post-1976 reaction to the Cultural Revolution, and its subsequent reforms, are in fact a reaction to the process initiated by Mao during the mid-1950s.[59] It is a view shared by at least some of the current leadership of the PRC, in substance if not in rhetoric. Though it is the 'pernicious influence of Lin Biao and the Gang of Four' that is held responsible for the emergence of 'feudal fascism' in general, that phenomenon is not limited to the decade of the Cultural Revolution. As previously noted, Li Honglin has traced the origins of 'feudal fascism' back to the Great Leap Forward in 1958, and, by implication, Mao's personal intervention. Nor is he alone in appearing to take that stance against Mao's disrespect for organisational and political norms. A conference organised in early 1979 by the CCP Propaganda Department shortly after the decisive 3rd plenum of the 11th Central Committee, concluded that Mao had been guilty of 'left adventurism' after 1957. It is a conclusion that seems to have gained wide support. For example, Lu Dingyi, in an article to the memory of Zhou Enlai, criticised Mao's behaviour at the Lushan Plenum of 1959;[60] and the leading economist Xue Muqiao, in a major speech to a conference organised by the State Economic Commission, took Mao to task for insisting on the pursuit of his policies no matter what, pointing out that a 'leftist' error was not necessarily the best antidote for a 'rightist' deviation, for in the final analysis it was still an error.[61] Though there can be little doubt that Mao's post-1976 critics disagreed with the contents of his policies, they disliked his methods even more.

Two reasons may be suggested for the CCP's reluctance to 'reverse the verdict' on the whole of the period since 1957, and its apparent continued insistence on a return to the status quo of the early 1960s. The first is the question of legitimacy. Deng Xiaoping, and other national leaders, have repeatedly stressed that a 'crisis of faith' in the regime by the population has become manifest and must be resolved.[62] In a real sense Mao can be seen as both the cause of that 'crisis' (through the Cultural Revolution) and its solution (as author of the regime's ideology). Thus the resolution of the 6th plenum of the 11th central committee of the CCP, as has already been noted, deliberately created a distinction between Mao Zedong Thought and Mao's political activities. If somewhat cynically, clumsily, and in a not altogether convincing manner, that resolution does attempt to differentiate between criticism of Mao and criticism of the Cultural Revolution. However, criticism of the 1950s would necessarily challenge any basis for the newly refurbished Mao Zedong Thought. It is for that reason that the 'spirit of the 8th party congress' (of 1956) has been re-invoked and heavily publicised in the approach to the 12th national party congress. The historical irony of that situation is that whereas the CCP's new draft constitution claims 'Marxism–Leninism, Mao Zedong Thought' as its guiding ideology, that of 1956 omitted any reference to the latter.[63] The second reason, that perhaps could be related to the first, is that there may well be a divide within the national leadership. Clearly there are those, particularly among the economic planners – for example, Xue Muqiao and Sun Yefang – who regard the policies pursued from 1957 to 1977 with extreme disfavour. On the other hand, there are those, like Deng Xiaoping, who for various reasons at least publicly have a more positive attitude towards Mao and the policies of the late 1950s. In other words, it seems possible that the leadership is united only in its opposition, and not in its prognosis, and so the rhetoric of politics reflects their lowest common denominator.

THE PRC AND THE SOVIET MODEL

The argument that recent state reforms in the PRC represent a return to the 'organisational orthodoxy' of the Soviet Union and Eastern Europe seems rather unconvincing, not least because it is difficult to ascertain when, if ever, the PRC had conformed. Though the PRC adopted a Soviet model for its development during the early 1950s, it is largely a myth that it subsequently implanted the Soviet Union's organisational forms *in toto*, or that those which were adopted remained permanently. It is certainly true that during the first four years of the First Five Year Plan (1952–7) the PRC's economic administration was highly centralised and the central ministries dominant in the state *apparat*. However, an over-simplistic model of a communist party state as a centralised political system in which the party hierarchy parallels the state *apparat* has never really been an appropriate description of the PRC. As far as its state *apparat* is concerned the PRC's lack of conformity is revealed through even a brief consideration of its non-central government, and the relationships between the state and other hierarchies.

An obvious but none the less important determinant of government and politics in the PRC has been its guerilla heritage from before 1949. Both before and after the Long March (1934–6) the communist movement had established base areas not only for military purposes but also in order to create rural soviets. However, the requirements of guerilla warfare meant that the communist movement's cadres had to be soldier, administrator, political leader, as well as peasant. For long periods the CCP was in effect the Red Army (the PLA's forerunner) and vice versa.[64] The lack of differentiation between the party and administrative hierarchies in the base areas, and between cadres' roles in the CCP and local governments, undoubtedly helps to explain why the maintenance of a party–state distinction has proved so difficult since 1949. Those who came to power at all levels of the politico-administrative system in 1949 had been trained in and emerged from the guerilla tradition. In 1949 the PRC's cadres were relatively young, and to a large extent the generation that came to power then have remained in office ever since.[65] Though it might be reasonable to assume that the technicalities of state administration after 1949 would have created greater role differentiation, that was to a certain extent counter-balanced by the success of Mao's appeal to revive the guerilla heritage (the 'Yanan tradition'), an integral part of his vision for the PRC's future development from the mid-1950s on.

Moreover, just as the guerilla heritage had influenced party–state relations, so too has it affected party–state–military relations. As already noted, the PRC has described itself as comprising three major hierarchies, one of which has been the PLA. Ever since 1949, except for a brief period during 1955–7, the PLA has played an active role in civilian politics. At times, such as between 1949 and 1952[66] and during 1967–71,[67] the PLA *qua* organisation has been institutionally involved in the state's administration. Throughout, PLA cadres (that is, currently serving PLA cadres, and regardless of the not insignificant fact that most post-1949 cadres of any description had a military background) have held civilian positions in both party and state. Conversely, party and state cadres have held positions in the PLA. Thus, for example, since the mid-1950s it has been common practice for the posts of party secretaries (CCP) and political commissars (PLA) in any one province (each province is also a military district) to be held by the same individuals.[68] Although the extent of PLA involvement in civilian affairs has varied over time, largely as a result of changes in the CCP's general line, none the less it has remained considerable.[69] Even during the period since 1976, when role differentiation has been emphasised, the by now traditional relationship between military and civilian has been retained. Thus, for example, as of April 1978, 10 per cent of provincial party secretaries and almost 11 per cent of provincial leading cadres in the state *apparat* were also currently-serving PLA cadres.

A further effect of the CCP's guerilla heritage has been an appreciation of the need for considerable local flexibility in implementing policy, which to some extent has countered the over-centralisation usually associated with the 'Soviet model'. Before 1949 each communist base area operated more or less independently, and on occasion had to in order to survive. Though attempting to maintain political and ideological unity through rectification campaigns, the CCP also recognised the need for a high degree of local flexibility. In the early 1940s, the CCP adopted the administrative principle of 'Do the best according to local conditions' for the implementation of central policies and directives. Since 1949, that administrative principle has quite explicitly been retained. Generally, in any campaign, the centre lays down the broad outlines for policy implementation but leaves the concrete arrangements to the localities.[70] It is even possible for some areas either to fail or to be excused from implementating policies on the grounds that 'local conditions are not suitable at present'. Thus, for exemple, during the early 1950s when land reform was national policy, those areas inhabited by non-Chinese peoples were largely exempted from the campaign since it was claimed that other social reforms (such as the abolition of slavery) were of a higher priority.

Finally, the applicability of an over-centralised 'Soviet model' to the PRC is brought into question by the roles of the regional and provincial levels of administration since 1949. From 1949 to 1952, the PRC was administered to a large extent by the six regional military and administrative committees; whose boundaries largely resulted from the PLA's pattern of final conquest, with each region having been occupied by one of the PLA's Field Armies. Each region covered several provinces; its government involved CCP, state, and PLA cadres, as well as leading local notables sympathetic to the CCP without actually being members; and its responsibilities were wide-ranging. In 1952 a major attempt to establish central economic ministries was launched, and military involvement in regional administration decreased. None the less, until 1954 the region remained as a counter-balance to centralisation.[71] Though it is true that the state *apparat* was at its most centralised immediately after 1952 with the introduction of the administrative principle of 'vertical rule', that changed in and after 1956. Discussions at the 3rd session of the NPC in the summer, and at the 8th national CCP congress in September 1956, revealed the near-unanimous criticism that the system was too inflexible and centralised.[72] Two reforms followed. At the regional level economic co-ordinative areas were established.[73] Though little is known about their specific activities, it is certain that they existed until 1961, and probable that their functions were taken over by the regional party bureaux that operated from 1961 to the Cultural Revolution.[74] More important were the adoption of the administrative principle of 'dual rule', and of the decentralisation of the functions of many of the central economic ministries, both of which resulted in the enhanced importance of the provincial level. Whereas previously within the state *apparat* each unit at any level had been subordinated solely to the unit at the immediately superior level within the same organisation (the former had, in other words, been the branch agency of the latter), 'dual rule' additionally subordinated each unit to the party committee at the same level. Decentralisation reduced the number of central economic ministries, devolved many of their functions to the provincial level, and transformed the provincial party committee into a co-ordinating committee for state as well as party activities. Though equivalent in many ways to centralisation at the provincial level, central ministries have since had to share authority with provincial administration.[75]

FINAL OBSERVATIONS

There can be little doubt that the intention of recent state reforms in the PRC is for radical change. However, unless it is assumed that the

PRC's past experience is completely irrelevant to its future, the impact of those reforms is likely to be more limited than may at first sight seem apparent. Those reforms have officially been presented as a reaction to the Cultural Revolution. Here it has been suggested that in interpreting the possible results of those reforms it is their wider historical context that is of greater importance. Rather than concentrating on recent reforms as a reaction to the Cultural Revolution, it is perhaps more useful to see them as a reaction to Mao-dominated politics from the mid-1950s to his death. As has been noted here, and elsewhere, it is easy to overemphasise the organisational and associational changes wrought by the Cultural Revolution.[76] Without for a minute wishing to minimise the dramatic impact of some aspects of the Cultural Revolution (particularly during 1966–9), it is none the less possible to argue that the political changes it invoked were not as revolutionary as is often claimed, and were in many ways a development of practices pursued (by at least some members of the national leadership) since the mid-1950s. In that context, the apparent resurrection of the state *apparat* becomes the re-assertion of the CCP as an organisation in its own right. Mao bent and broke the rules of organisational behaviour, and after his death the CCP is attempting to regularise its own internal politics and its leadership of the state and society in general. Deng Xiaoping, in a report to the Politburo during August 1980 (that first became available outside the PRC in April 1981) concerning the reforms in party and state leadership, was relatively explicit: for example,

> From the Tsunyi Conference to the period of socialist reformation, both the Central Committee of the Party and Comrade Mao Tse-tung paid greater attention to the practice of collective leadership and democratic centralism ... It is a pity that these good traditions have not been sustained, nor were they developed into a strict and perfect system ... After ... [1958 and 1959] democratic life in the Party and the state gradually became abnormal. This gave rise to the patriarchial phenomena characterized by one man speaking for all, the deciding of important questions by an individual, the personality cult, the riding of an individual on the organization, etc. ... without thorough elimination of this patriarchal work style, there can be no intra-party democracy or socialist democracy to speak of.

Having outlined the reforms under consideration, Deng concluded:

To change the leadership system of the party and state is not aimed at weakening the party's leadership or slackening the party's discipline; on the contrary, it is for upholding and strengthening the Party's leadership as well as discipline ... The core of the four principles to which we must hold fast is the party's leadership. The problem is that the Party must be skilled in leadership.[77]

The parallel with the revival of 'party life' in the Soviet Union following Stalin's death is too obvious to avoid. Whether, despite the PRC's peculiarities as a communist party state, such parallels can be taken further is a task for the future.

NOTES

1. For example: R. L. Walker, 'PRC Under Teng: Back to Leninist Organization', *Issues and Studies*, vol. 16, no. 8 (1980) p. 12.
2. For example, see Zhou Fang, *Woguo guojia jigou* (*Our Country's State Organization*) (Beijing; 1955), the most widely known PRC source on the state. For a more recent set of comments emphasising such distinctions, see Peng Zhen, 'Explanation of the Seven Draft Laws', *Main Documents of the Second Session of the Fifth National People's Congress of the People's Republic of China* (Beijing; 1979) pp. 190–220, p. 201.
3. *Cihai: zhengzhi jingjixue (The Encyclopaedia: Political Economics)* (Shanghai, 1978) p. 60.
4. The PLA includes not only the army, but also the navy and air force, and all the armed forces.
5. H. F. Schurmann, *Ideology and Organization in Communist China*, 2nd edn (Berkeley, 1968) pp. 532 and 557 ff.
6. Peng Zhen, 'Explanation of the Seven Draft Laws', p. 190–1.
7. Chen Zihua, 'On China's Electoral Law', *Beijing Review*, 37, (1979) p. 15.
8. *Guangming ribao* (Guangming Daily) 11 March 1979, p. 3.
9. *Beijing Review*, no. 27 (1981) contains the text of the resolution.
10. D. S. G. Goodman, 'The 6th Plenum of the 11th Central Committee of the CCP: Look Back in Anger?', *The China Quarterly*, 87 (1981) p. 518.
11. For a stimulating re-assessment of the PRC's development, see N. Eberstadt, 'Has China Failed?', *New York Review of Books*, vol. 26 (1979): no. 5, p. 33; no. 6, p. 41; and no. 7, p. 39.
12. For example: Hu Qiaomu, 'Anzhao jingji guilu banshi, jiakuai shixian sige xiandaihua' ('Speedily realize the Four Modernizations, through acting according to economic laws'), *Renmin ribao (People's Daily)*, 6 October 1978; and Wei Xinghua, *Zenyang zhengque kandai geming he shengchan (How to correctly regard revolution and production)* (Beijing, 1978).
13. Three former ministries – Forestry and Agriculture, Petroleum and

Chemical Industries, Water Conservancy and Electric Power – have been subdivided into their constituent parts; and further economic ministries established, for Agricultural Machinery, Building Materials, Food, Geology, Railways, State Farms, Land Reclamation, and an 8th Ministry of Machine Building.

14. The seven are commissions for: Foreign Investment Control, Imports and Exports, Agriculture, Economics, Finance and Economics, Machine Building, and Science and Technology.

15. Much has been made of the role of Zhao Ziyang, former provincial first party secretary of Sichuan and now Premier, in promoting that experimentation. An account of Zhao's so-called 'Sichuan experiment' may be found in Zhao Ziyang, 'Principles for All-round Economic Re-adjustment', *Eastern Horizon*, vol. 19, no. 5 (1980) p. 5.

16. Yu Qiuli, 'Speed Up China's Industrial Growth, Strive to Catch Up With and Surpass Advanced World Levels', *Peking Review*, 21 (1977) p. 17.

17. D. J. Solinger, 'Some Speculations on the Return of the Regions: Parallels with the Past', *The China Quarterly* no. 75 (1978) p. 623.

18. Although the PRC constitution defines all non-central government as 'local' this is something of a misnomer, since it includes the provincial level which is more of an intermediate than a local level of government as generally understood.

19. L. Pye, 'Generational Politics in a Gerontocracy: the Chinese Succession Problem', *Current Scene*, vol. 14 no. 7 (1976).

20. Li Desheng, 'Shiyong ganbu yeyao "jieyue"' ('The use of cadres must also be "economized"'), *Renmin ribao* (*People's Daily*, 4 December 1978, p. 2.

21. *Beijing Review*, no. 37 (1980) p. 3.

22. 'The system of lifelong leadership must be abolished': *Beijing Review* no. 46 (1980) p. 20.

23. D. S. G. Goodman, 'The Provincial Revolutionary Committee in the People's Republic of China, 1967–1979: An Obituary', *The China Quarterly*, no. 85 (1981) p. 78–9.

24. See, for example, Li Yunchang, 'The Role of Chinese lawyers', *Beijing Review*, no. 46 (1980) p. 24.

25. For example: Peng Zhen, 'Explanation on the Seven Draft Laws', p. 190; and Peng Zhen, 'Report on the Work of the Standing Committee of the National People's Congress of the People's Republic of China', *Main Documents of the Third Session of the Fifth National People's Congress of the People's Republic of China* (Beijing, 1980) pp. 86 and 209.

26. Wei Jingsheng was given a 15-year gaol sentence and deprived of his political rights in October 1979; Yao Wenyuan was sentenced to 20 years' imprisonment and deprived of his political rights for five years in January 1981.

27. *Guangming ribao (Guangming Daily)*, 17 October 1979.

28. *Beijing Review*, no. 36 (1980) p. 7.

29. Chen Zihua, 'On China's Electoral Law', p. 18.

30. *Documents of the First Session of the Fifth National People's Congress of the People's Republic of China* (Beijing, 1978) p. 129–72.

31. Of particular interest is Tian Sansong, 'Election of Deputies to a County

People's Congress', *Beijing Review*, no. 8 (1980) p. 11.

32. See, for example, the report of by-elections to people's congresses within Shanghai at ward and country levels, broadcast by the municipal broadcasting service, 13 July 1980, *BBC Summary of World Broadcasts*, part III, The Far East (SWB FE 6478) 23 July 1980.

33. See, for example, the account of a county election reported in *Liaoning Daily* and broadcast on 13 November 1980 by the provincial radio service (SWB FE 6604) 18 December 1980.

34. 'China's Structure of State Power', *Beijing Review*, no. 20 (1979) p. 18.

35. At the time of writing most provincial-level units had just held, or were about to hold, the 3rd sessions of their 5th people's congresses. See, for example, the reports from Liaoning (SWB FE 6662); Hubei (SWB FE 6665); Guizhou (SWB FE 6665); Anhui (SWB FE 6670); and Guangdong (SWB FE 6677).

36. Feng Wenbin (Deputy Director of the Central Party School), 'Reforming the Political Structure', *Beijing Review*, no. 4 (1981) p. 17.

37. T. P. Bernstein, 'Political Science', in A. F. Thurston and J. H. Parker (eds), *Humanistic and Social Science Research in China* (New York, 1980) p. 130.

38. *Xinhua xinwen (New China News Agency)*, 10 May 1980, translated in SWB FE 6421.

39. For example, Schurmann, *Ideology and Organisation*, pp. 98 and 109 ff.

40. *Renmin ribao (People's Daily)*, 30 January 1952, p. 1.

41. 2 June 1951, in Xinhua yuebao (*New China Monthly*), vol. 4, no. 4, pp. 839–1.

42. *Chin-hua Ta-chung*, 11 June 1957, translated in *Joint Publications Research Services*, 664 (1958) p. 59.

43. A. D. Barnett, *Cadres, Bureaucracy and Political Power in Communist China* (New York, 1967) p. 429.

44. L. Pye, *The Dynamics of Factions and Consensus in Chinese Politics* (Santa Monica, 1980) p. 120 ff.

45. Schurmann, *Ideology and Organization*, p. 194 and 362.

46. Ibid, p. 487ff.

47. 'Bright Prospects for China's Reforms', *Beijing Review*, no. 51 (1980) p. 11.

48. SWB FE 6363, 6 March 1980.

49. Goodman, 'The 6th Plenum', pp. 518–27.

50. D. S. G. Goodman, 'Changes in Leadership Personnel after September 1976', in J. Domes (ed.), *Chinese Politics after Mao* (Cardiff, 1979) p. 64.

51. F. C. Teiwes, 'Provincial Politics in China: Themes and Variations', in J. M. H. Lindbeck (ed.), *China: Management of a Revolutionary Society* (London, 1972) p. 116.

52. See, for example, the report on activities in Jiangsu, in SWB FE 6701, 16 April 1981. Perhaps equally significant is the fact that of 624 individuals holding leadership posts in the revised state structure at provincial level, 108 are not members of the CCP.

53. Schurmann, *Ideology and Organization*, pp. 173 ff; and A. Donnithorne, *China's Economic System* (London, 1967).

54. For a detailed account of that period see R. MacFarquhar, *The Origins of*

the Cultural Revolution, Vol. 1: Contradictions Among the People, 1956–1957 (London, 1974).

55. Schurmann, *Ideology and Organization*, p. 86.
56. Tian Yun, 'More Authority for Enterprises Revives the Economy', *Beijing Review*, no. 14 (1981) p. 21.
57. Li Jingquan's speech to the 8th national congress of the CCP may be found in *Xinhua Banyuekan (New China Semi-Monthly)*, 20 (1956) p. 52.
58. MacFarquhar, *The Origins*, pp. 293 ff.
59. F. C. Teiwes, *Politics and Purges in China* (Folkestone, 1979) p. 601 ff.
60. *Renmin ribao* (People's Daily), 8 March 1979, p. 2.
61. 'Economic Work Must follow the Laws of Economic Development', *Documents in Communist Affairs, 1980* (London, 1981) pp. 146–7.
62. In his speech on 16 January 1980; SWB FE 6363, 6 March 1980.
63. *Issues and Studies*, vol. 16, no. 9 (1980) p. 85.
64. For an interesting account of that relationship see E. Snow, *Scorched Earth* (London, 1941) p. 240 and pp. 317–23.
65. D. W. Klein, 'The "Next Generation" of Chinese Communist Leaders', *The China Quarterly*, 12 (1962) p. 57.
66. D. J. Solinger, *Regional Government and Political Inegration in Southwest China, 1949–1954* (Berkeley, 1977) p. 132.
67. J. Domes, 'The Role of the Military in the Formation of Revolutionary Committees, 1967–68', *The China Quarterly*, no. 44 (1970) p. 112.
68. Goodman, 'Changes in Leadership Personnel', p. 51.
69. E. Joffe, 'The Chinese Army after the Cultural Revolution: The Effects of Intervention', *The China Quarterly*, no. 55 (1973) p. 450.
70. V. C. Falkenheim, 'Provincial Leadership in Fukien: 1949–66', in R. Scalapino (ed.), *Elites in the People's Republic of China* (London, 1972) pp. 218–22.
71. Solinger, *Regional Government and Political Integration*, p. 254.
72. MacFarquhar, *The Origins*, p. 122.
73. See the common foreword to the various regional economic geographies (one for each economic co-ordinative area) published during the late 1950s and early 1960s. For example Sun Jingzhi *et al.* (eds) *Xinandiqu jingji dili (An Economic Geography of Southwest China)* (Beijing, 1960).
74. P. Chang, 'Patterns and Processes of Policy-making in Communist China, 1955–1962: Three Case Studies' (Ph.D.: Columbia University, 1969) pp. 269–70.
75. Schurmann, *Ideology and Organization*, p. 210.
76. D. S. G. Goodman, 'The Provincial First Party Secretary in the People's Republic of China, 1949–78: A Profile', *British Journal of Political Science* no. 10 (1980) p. 72, and 'The Provincial Revolutionary Committee', pp. 50–64.
77. Deng's report of 31 August 1980 was circulated by the CCP central committee on 11 September as Central Circular No. 66 (1980): translated in *Inside China Mainland* (April 1981) pp. 6–7 and p. 11 respectively.

10 Conclusion

Neil Harding

We need not invoke either too lofty or too base a view of human nature to explain the durability and stability of the state formations of Communist regimes. We need only accept the commonplace, that in most times most men are guided by a prudent concern for their own welfare and for that of those who are close to them. It is, therefore, unremarkable that where all the prospects for advancing that welfare are in the hands of the state, and where it is clear that the condition for advancement is support for its policies, then few will rebel. These state forms have at their command a comprehensive and graduated hierarchy of benefits and sanctions the allocation of which penetrates every aspect of the educational, vocational, social and economic life of the individual and of his family. Everyone in such a society cannot but be aware of these potential benefits and sanctions, behaviour patterns are formed accordingly. What we are presented with is not merely 'an example of prudential conduct', but entire societies in which prudence (that is, avoidance of sanctions)[1] becomes a lifetime vocation. The higher one's status and reward in such a society, the more important and publicly visible one is, the greater the fear of sanctions and the more prudent one is likely to be in avoiding them. Those who have children at university have more to fear than those who have not, those with jobs in Moscow and Leningrad more than those in Uzbekistan, managers and engineers more than foremen, and foremen more than manual workers, and so on.

It is perhaps in these terms that one might wish to reconsider the 'false dichotomy' between coercion and consent that Hoffman discusses. It is not a matter of dispute that direct coercion and deprivation of liberty have (since Stalin's day at least) generally featured less and less as weapons of social and political control. Coercion had to be used wholesale to *achieve* state dominance over the whole of economic and social life, but in the proportion that that goal was

299

achieved it rendered coercion if not redundant then increasingly unnecessary and dysfunctional. Its utilisation as a last resort now became a signal of the failure of the range of moral, vocational, educational and economic sanctions in the hands of the state, and a testimony to the fact that *some* men and women are guided by motives other than the prudential.

It is fairly evident that dissident behaviour in any society meets with sanctions of some sort – be it only rebuke and popular censure – but the extensiveness of the welfare sanctions available to and utilised by Communist regimes is different both in degree and in kind from those available to any other regimes; different in kind because they are purposefully utilised by the organic labour state to induce habitual patterns of thought and behaviour supportive of the state's dominance, and therefore, by definition, constitutive of 'socialist morality'.

Much the same pattern of astute distribution of welfare incentives and sanctions that so effectively conditions the behaviour of individuals can be applied (as both McAuley and Rutland demonstrate) to minority nationalities within the state. Their integration into a single economic plan and their specialised contribution to it make the prospect of separation an ever-receding possibility. The more developed the integrated all-Union plan becomes, the less plausible the dreams of economic autarchy that nourish nationalism. Indeed, to the extent that the minority nationalities were relatively backward in economic development and have been brought up to the level of the dominant group, they feel themselves affirmed by unity. They have, for the most part, never enjoyed separate statehood and hence have no historic memory of ethnic identity being derived from it. (The experience of most of the countries of Eastern Europe and of the Baltic Republics of the Soviet Union is, on both scores, different.)

There are, as McAuley points out, powerful incentives, especially for the educated national elites, to strengthen and preserve the Union. Their dedication and endeavour in fulfilling the Plan is the condition for their mobility and preferment. But the better they fulfil the Plan the greater the social surplus in the hands of the central political bureaucracy that allocates it and, therefore, the stronger its grip on the periphery. As with the individual so with national groupings, the careful distribution of welfare incentives is the key to their conformity to the goals of the organic labour state.

It is clear that the effectiveness of what we might term 'welfare inducement' as a means of social and political control is a function of unequal distribution. A good only acts as an inducement if it is not universally available. It follows, therefore, that a condition for the stability of Communist regimes is their ability to sustain differentials between different categories of labour and a hierarchy of status within society. This accords, as we have seen in the introductory chapter, with the basic principle of distributive justice in the organic labour state that material reward, status and honour, should be distributed according to functional contribution towards the productive goals of state and society. The more industrially advanced such states become, the more complex their social division of labour, the more are economic and status differentiation encouraged by the state. The dangers of egalitarianism that Lenin and Stalin discerned as fatal hazards to the regime are still bitterly opposed.[2] Competition for the welfare inducements proferred by the state constitutes what is always referred to as 'socialist emulation', which is, especially under 'developed socialism', held to be the main motor of increased productivity.

The formal political life of state formations of this sort cannot be analysed as if it served liberal-democratic purposes, nor criticised for failing to fulfil them. It is, for instance, evident, though rather fatuous to complain, that elections in Communist regimes hardly serve the purposes of calling the government to account, canvassing alternative national strategies, or of advertising the grievances of citizens. Such strictures, though true, mistake the functions of elections in these regimes. Elections in the organic labour state serve to advertise the plans drawn up for the social system of production and to enthuse and mobilise the citizenry behind them. They are prolonged bouts of production propaganda and fanfares for plan fulfilment. As we earlier observed the very notion of who is to count as a citizen and to participate in elections is itself contingent upon the state's definition of socially useful work. Elections are opportunities for the organic unity of society to express itself and 99 per cent confirmatory votes are occasions for rejoicing that such unanimity exists. The results of elections serve, similarly, to advertise the organic unity of society so that there is invariably achieved a nicely balanced and 'representative' cross-section of peasants and workers, minority nationalities, skilled and unskilled, men and women and so on. The intentions are not to canvass and elicit differing, contending views, platforms and plans, but to symbolically confirm the importance of all functional and ethnic groups in the smooth working of the social system of production. 'The essence of Soviet democracy', Brezhnev reminded the 26th Party Congress, 'lies in concern for the common work, for the development of production.'[3]

Elected delegates are, therefore, (as Hill observes) almost never distinguished by those features that generally count as political – oratorical skill, charisma or persistence in putting a particular viewpoint. In the case of non-party deputies they are almost invariably selected as exemplary workers in their particular field. Since 'Soviet society is a society of working people' it is entirely appropriate that its representative and deliberative assemblies should be composed of those possessing an 'exemplary understanding of social duty, heroism and dedication to work'.[4] It is, however, precisely this mode of preferment that makes deputies and representatives so depressingly lack-lustre and inadequate as mass communicators. Politics as theatre, as a spectacle, being so entirely predictable and exhortatory, is debased. Communist regimes bear witness to the debilitating effects of Lenin's strictures about 'political fireworks' and against the media's fixation with personalities.[5] Politics as merely 'concentrated economics' becomes an anaemic sanitised process and the mass to whom it addresses itself (as Party leaderships constantly lament) retreat into apathy and indifference to public affairs. It results in 'a degree of privatisation exceeding by far the extent of depoliticisation of individuals in capitalist society'.[6]

The formal political structure rests, therefore, upon the use of a theory of virtual representation. That is, that in so far as all significant occupational, regional and ethnic groups are represented in the legislatures, and in so far as this 'supreme body' of state unanimously assents to the plans laid before it, then the whole citizenry thus mirrored in its representatives is deemed to have so assented. There seems to be little doubt that, as far as the majority of Soviet citizens are concerned, this structure of state and government it felt to be neither irksome nor inappropriate. Even among Soviet exiles in America and Israel there is a marked antipathy to the political dissensions and industrial confrontations typical of Western regimes.[7] Opinion surveys of emigrés all suggest that Soviet citizens accept the need for a strong stable and authoritative state which ought not merely to reflect popular inclinations but to mould and improve them. In particular they value most highly the guarantee of employment and the security that the state welfare services afford to all.[8] 'It was... the achievement of the Soviet government in these fields which respondents were most likely to credit in its favour.'[9] The conclusion is fairly clear, that so long as the state continues to furnish its citizens with job security, comprehensive social services and a tolerable standard of living then it is felt to be doing its job.

Our conclusion may be easily arrived at but the problems entailed for the state are daunting and, some maintain, increasingly unrealisable. There is, in the first place, the question of whether, with the growing complexity and sophistication of economies as vast as these, the whole business of planned direction and co-ordination from the centre is even feasible. There are empirical and theoretical grounds for believing that, beyond a certain extensiveness and complexity, centralised direction of this sort might impede rather than promote the efficiency of the economic system.

As the economy and social services grow in extensiveness it follows that so, too, do the planning, organisational, supervisory and mobilising functions both of the state and of the party. It cannot be otherwise, given the objectives of the organic labour state and the sorts of expectations it generates to legitimate its rule. The growing responsibilities and powers both of state and of party have become so clear and demonstrable in everyday life that their new roles have had to be theoretically and constitutionally confirmed. One of the casualties of this development has been the antiquarian and altogether inconsistent commitment to 'the withering-away of the state'.[10] The 1977 Constitution of the USSR allots specifically to the state the task of promoting 'the transformation of labour into the primary vital need of every Soviet person',[11] and charges it with ensuring 'the growth of labour productivity, the increase in production efficiency and work quality, and the dynamic, *planned*, and proportional development of the national economy',[12] so that 'The economy of the USSR shall constitute a single national economic complex embracing all links of social production, distribution and exchange in the territory of the country.'[13] The fiction that these tasks were increasingly to devolve upon trade-union, industrial and social bodies, has been sharply rebuffed. It is now constitutionally acknowledged that far from society supervising and progressively appropriating state functions, the state shall now supervise society – 'The state shall further the strengthening of the social homogeneity of society'.[14] Under Article 62 of the Constitution every citizen 'shall be obliged to safeguard the interests of the Soviet state and to further the strengthening of its might and authority'.[15] The growing might and authority of the state is a necessary entailment of its presumption to organise and direct the whole of economic and social life, and this was clearly presaged in the formulations of the organic labour state by Lenin, Bukharin and Trotsky in the 1920s. There were, even at that time, some commentators astute enough to recognise the inherent dangers and difficulties of a state form of this sort. As MacIver noted: 'That the state should maintain unity in difference is a hard enough task, that it should itself constitute the unity of social life is a vain ideal.'[16] The 'all-people's state' explicitly sets itself this goal and its Constitution acknowledges the *growing* 'might and authority' of the state. The potentially dangerous theoretical fiction of the dictatorship of the proletariat – that it was a temporary and transitional institution fated to wither away when the stage of developed socialism had been attained – has been the most significant casualty of recent theoretical developments. The state has now, quite unambiguously, been allotted a *permanent* role as *the* directing agency of all political, economic and social life. For the first time since the 1920s, as Brown's thorough commentary reveals, the autonomous power of the state has re-emerged as a principal issue in theoretical debates. 'When these particular Soviet scholars write of relative autonomy *from* control, it is the "relative autonomy" of the state from society (not of society from the state) which they choose to stress.'[17] They are at last acknowledging the internal logic of the organic labour state, by bringing theory into accord with practice and by jettisoning the last vestiges of the discordant Commune model so briefly espoused by Marx and Lenin.

Only the Yugoslavs recognise both in theory and, to a more limited extent, in their practice, that society does and ought to have a diversity of interests that need a degree of autonomy from state control for their proper development. Zukin's chapter makes plain that Yugoslav commitment to de-etatisation and progressive withdrawal of the state from the detailed management and control of society and of the economy, has sprung from a mixture of motives, has had a chequered historical career and is partly counterbalanced by centralising restraints, but there is no doubt that the ethos and the general tendency is different from the rest of communist regimes. The Yugoslavs alone are prepared to accept not only that a plurality of social and economic interests is a sign of health, but to pursue this to the extent of allowing dissension, particularly within provincial legislatures. The state 'neither owns the means of production nor directs the social institutions and it does not even hold a monopoly on the political system'.[18] Politics in Yugoslavia has, consequently, partially escaped from the anaemic condition to which the fiction of organic unity between state and society condemns it elsewhere. It is revitalised by a frank acceptance of a clash of interests within society which its task is to reconcile.

It is evident, given the presuppositions and objectives of the organic labour state, that the size and the powers both of the state and of the Party apparatus must grow in proportion to the development of the economy. That this should be confirmed in the latest Soviet Constitution should come as no surprise. The problem that critically arises, however, relates not so much to the physical extensiveness of the agencies of State and Party, nor to the extent of their powers, but to their functional adaptation to the changing demands of expanded social services and an ever-increasingly complex industrial base. These are, of course, very large problems for *any* system of government but are especially acute in regimes where the state is the sole organiser and controller of the means of production. It follows from the internal logic of the organic labour state that when the regime no longer has at its disposal extensive welfare inducements to dispense, it can no longer oblige its citizens. Economic obligation and political obligation being fused, they must collapse together, as they have so dramatically in Poland. In this case it was the regime's inability to devise administrative structures sufficiently stable to guarantee that minimum of predictability necessary for forward planning, yet sufficiently flexible to accommodate unforeseen local difficulties, alterations in the world market, changes in consumer demand, etc., that had so disastrous an effect. The institutions of this sort of state cannot, as Lewis demonstrates, remain static when what they are administering is constantly evolving and becoming more complex. Nor can they, as was the case with Mao's China in the Cultural Revolution (and, to a lesser extent, the Soviet Union under Khrushchev), be radically and suddenly transformed with impunity, for this too, as Goodman notes, can lead to economic and social dislocation on a massive scale. It follows, then, that the problem of institutional adaptation is raised in especially high relief in the organic labour state precisely because that which is to be administered is itself constantly changing.

Of itself, however, institutional adaptation, no matter how intelligently implemented, would be of little avail unless the right people with appropriate dispositions and qualifications were in the right place. The more complex and extensive the management, planning and control mechanisms of the state become, the more important the training and placement of its personnel. Since the principal functions of the party are to draw up the Plan and to supervise and mobilise the whole economy, it must bring to these tasks the appropriate expertise. Both party and state are engaged in a constant uphill struggle to fuse political reliability with technical and managerial expertise. The results are predictable enough. There has been a constant and irreversible escalation of qualifications for cadre entry to all levels of the party and state administrations. Hardly a Party or Soviet Congress passes without calls from the leadership to bolster the technical and managerial expertise not only of cadres but even of elected non-party deputies who now, increasingly, are required to undergo specialised training. Even elected representatives are being 'professionalised'. Such a concern for expertise and the 'cult of diplomas'[19] is natural and inevitable given the enormous managerial functions that states of this sort have taken upon themselves. It cannot be otherwise, given that their legitimacy and stability rests upon their ability efficiently to manage a centralised economy. Even where positive steps have been taken to decentralise economic decision-making, as in Yugoslavia, the same problems arise; 'as the assemblies' functions grow and the society they regulate becomes more complex, a higher level of expertise is required to carry out their work.'[20] And yet this very necessary concern for qualifications and appropriate education must progressively distance deputies and state and party cadres from the mass of ordinary people. The regimes themselves are certainly quite aware of the potentially dangerous gulf between governors and governed which a succession of socialist critics have voiced and theorised. They reject as idle demagogy the claim that there has arisen a new class of ruling bureaucrats and specialists exercising a 'dictatorship of experts' or 'scholocracy'.[21] The organic unity of interests binding workers, peasants and intelligentsia in pursuit of common productive goals which are to their mutual advantage, is indeed the axiomatic starting-point of the theory of the all-people's state. The rule of the people, (*narodovlastie*), it is asserted, is confirmed rather than impaired through its fusion with expert knowledge, and unthinkable without it. But such rejoinders have quite failed to still the voices of criticism that in one way or another reject the premises of technocratic marxism.

It was Marx's contemporary and adversary, Bakunin, who first prophesied that any government so arrogant as to pretend that it could embrace 'the infinite multiplicity and diversity of the real interests, aspirations, wishes and needs whose sum constitutes the collective will of a people', would issue in an organisation that 'will never be anything but a Procrustean bed upon which the more or less evident violence of the State will force unhappy society to lie down.[22]

Specifically, the Marxian 'dictatorship of the proletariat' was bound, in Bakunin's view, to lead to the most odious tyranny of white-coated experts.[23] His themes were taken up by the anarchist movement generally, and elaborated into a sophisticated theory of education as the new preponderant form of capital in the workers' state by Jan Waclav Machajski who predicted the exploitative tendencies of the 'intellectual worker'.[24] With increasing frequency and cogency East European marxists (or former marxists) like Djilas,[25] Konrad and Szelenyi, Kuron and Modzelewski, Vajda, and Bahro,[26] have reflected upon the common theme of the rise to unchallengeable pre-eminence of a new class of educated experts, disposing of the social surplus and manipulating the founts of patronage they command to confirm their own power. Even some Soviet theorists guardedly concede that the bureaucracy that 'serves as the material embodiment of state power itself'[27] may well develop its own particular interests and a potentially dangerous autonomy.

The general presumption of the dissident socialist critique is that if only the representative bodies of 'existing socialism' could be revivified and socialist legality enforced so as to ensure widespread popular participation 'and guarantee public control over important decisions',[28] then a genuinely socialist society could yet be realised. Much the same sort of animus informed the ill-fated Action Programme of the Czech Communist Party of 1968. Such sentiments are admirable and have cost the brave men who uttered them dearly of their liberty. But there is another honest, if thoroughly discordant, voice that better captures the intractable logic of the organic labour state. It argues that the sheer dimensions and complexities of the problems of accumulating and interpreting the manifold information required for the centralised state-planning and direction of mighty economies, have long since put them beyond the capacity of the average man to comprehend let alone resolve:

> How can all this be combined with the necessity of further developing democracy, with widening participation of the masses in government. . . when many questions of government are practically within the power only of specialists?[29]

The answer to Chkhikvadze's loaded and rhetorical question was provided by Lenin, who, in his turn, merely formulated in categorical terms the implications of the tradition of technocratic Marxism: 'Industry is indispensable, democracy is not.'[30]

I began the introductory chapter to this volume noting the dangers of brief attempts to define or characterise the nature of Soviet-type state formations. Archie Brown, in Chapter 2, disposes of the most widely discussed current models with his customary rigour. It seems almost foolhardy therefore to proffer another: yet the pedagogic and psychological need for a more adequate characterisation now becomes more pronounced. I will conclude with a concise and schematic account of the Organic Labour State:

1. The Organic Labour State exercises an exclusive monopoly over the planned development of the economy of a territorially delimited area in order to maximise the economic surplus at the disposition of the state authority.

2. Ownership and control of the principal productive forces must be in its hands, and it acknowledges that this precondition may often necessitate a period of expropriation effected through state-directed coercion. Its ideological justification is socialism defined as that system of state direction of the economy that best conduces to the maximisation of production.

3. It conflates and identifies the objectives of society and state, in that society is conceived of as an organically developing system of production relations whose planned co-ordination is made possible only through the agency of the state. Within its logic the social, productive and political spheres of life have no separable identity.

4. In order to maximise the economic surplus available to it the Organic Labour State must itself be the sole agency dictating the measure of labour and sumptuary norms of society. It cannot allow producers' or consumers' organisations to have effective sanctions over it in this regard. It cannot accommodate autonomous trade unions or tolerate the organised withdrawal of labour from the social system of production.

5. Within society and state the duration and intensity of labour is the principle of distributive justice. Economic reward, honour and status are ideally distributed according to functional contribution to the productive goals shared by society and the state. Egalitarianism is corrosive of its structure.

6. The overwhelming majority of the inhabitants of the Organic Labour State are reliant upon it for employment, promotion and pensions. The state is, effectively, the sole distributor of social welfare benefits in the realms of health, education, housing, culture and recreation. Welfare inducement and welfare sanction constitute its most potent and pervasive weapons of social and political control, and their efficient management is the principal guarantee of its stability. Resort to extensive coercion is not intrinsic to its structure but symptomatic of its adolescence (see point 2) or of the failure of the graduated hierarchy of sanctions available to its mature formation. Prudence – that is, the avoidance of sanctions – is the distinctive mark of its social and political conduct.

7. Citizenship is conditional upon socially useful work and political and social preferment based upon its exemplary fulfilment. Citizens' rights are expressly confined in their exercise to those activities that serve to strengthen the social system of production superintended by the state. They may not be exercised to challenge or limit its prerogatives nor to canvass alternative formulations of its proper objectives. Unanimity rather than dissent is characteristic of its civility and is taken to confirm the organic unity of society and state.

8. The homogeneity of social interests, in pursuit of productive goals realisable only through planned associated labour, is expressed in the single political party that is the vehicle of socialist ideas, the inspirational force of society, planner of the economy and mobiliser of the populace for the fulfilment of state directives. The functions, personnel, prerogatives and modes of social control of party and state are tightly interwoven. In particular, the party is the principal advisory agency for the allotment of welfare benefits and the application of welfare sanctions.

9. Elections within the Organic Labour State are ritualised occasions for registering the unity of society, party and state, for advertising the plans drawn up for the socialised system of production and for enthusing the populace to fulfil them. Dissidence and conflict are taken as signs of individual morbidity or social malaise, outside, rather than constitutive of, politics.

10. The growth of the socialised system of production in extensive-

ness and complexity prompts constant escalation of technical and managerial qualifications for cadre entry to all levels of the party and state apparatuses. Such experts, technicians and managers have an interest in predictable and rational decision-making (as against the arbitrary predominance of a single leader) in which their own functional contribution becomes increasingly indispensable. In any event, the functions, powers and organisational complexity of state and party constantly grow rather than diminish.

NOTES

1. R. E. Flathman, *Political Obligation* (London, 1972) p. 171.
2. See, for instance, the reports of the spring 1982 symposium on 'Economic Development and Social Progress at the Present Stage of Socialist Construction', attended by high-ranking delegates of the Comecon countries who 'noted the presence of some "egalitarian" elements and the need to overcome these', and re-affirmed the principle that 'scrupulous observance of the duty to work for the benefit of society and the right to receive remuneration according to the quantity and quality of labour (and in no other way!) continues to be one of the basic tasks of the present stage of socialist construction': *World Marxist Review*, vol. 25 (May 1982) p. 79. Brezhnev, in his Report to the 26th Party Congress, similarly complained of 'all sorts of levelling and instances of paying wages solely for appearing at work and not for its results'. Rewards, he insisted, had to be tied more firmly to the quantity and quality of work so that 'Those who want to live better should work more and better. I think this is clear to all.': *Report of the Central Committee of the CPSU to the XXVI Congress of the CPSU* (Moscow, 1981) pp. 78–9.
3. Brezhnev, *Report of the Central Committee*, p. 86.
4. Ibid, pp. 76–7.
5. Lenin, *CW*, vol. 32, p. 130.
6. M. Vajda, *The State and Socialism* (London, 1981) p. 137.
7. S. White, *Political Culture and Soviet Politics* (London, 1979) pp. 100–9. When faced with strikes and industrial conflict (as in Czechoslovakia in 1968 or in Poland from 1980) Soviet leaders consistently complain of 'anarchy'. For such a situation really is a departure from constituted government in their tradition. Amalrik recalls the forceful (perhaps typical) response of a Russian worker to the turmoil in Czechoslovakia in 1968: 'What sort of a government is it that tolerates so much disorder? Power must be such that *I* live in fear of it – not that *it* lives in fear of me!': A. Amalrik in G. R. Urban (ed.), *Eurocommunism* (London, 1978) p. 239.
8. A. Inkeles and R. A. Bauer, *The Soviet Citizen* (Cambridge, Mass. and London, 1959) pp. 236–42.
9. White, *Political Culture*, p. 100.

10. On the theoretical and historical background of this inconsistency see Chapter 1 of the present volume and the valuable collection of essays edited by L. Holmes, *The Withering Away of the State* (London, 1981).
11. A. L. Unger, *Constitutional Development in the USSR, A Guide to the Soviet Constitutions* (a useful compendium of the four Soviet constitutions) (London, 1981) p. 236.
12. Ibid, p. 237.
13. Ibid, p. 236.
14. Ibid, p. 237.
15. Ibid, p. 245.
16. R. M. MacIver, *The Modern State* (London, 1926) p. 463.
17. See the present volume, p. 52.
18. See the present volume, p. 259.
19. G. Konrad and I. Szelényi, *The Intellectuals on the Road to Class Power* (Brighton, 1979) p. 228.
20. Zukin, in the present volume, p. 260.
21. Hill, in the present volume, p. 118.
22. M. Bakounine, *Oeuvres* (Paris, 1910) tome IV, p. 260.
23. M. Bakunin, *Gosudarstvennost i anarkhiya* in *Archives Bakounine* (ed. M. Lehning) vol. III (Leiden, 1967) pp. 148–9.
24. J. W. Machajski (A. Volsky, pseud.), *Umstvenniy rabochiy*, 2 parts (Geneva, 1905).
25. M. Djilas, *The New Class* (London, 1966).
26. R. Bahro, *The Alternative in Eastern Europe* (London, 1978).
27. Quoted by Brown in the present volume, p. 83.
28. Konrad and Szelényi, *The Intellectuals*, p. 232.
29. Quoted by Hill in the present volume, p. 118.
30. Lenin, quoted in Chapter 1 of the present volume, p. 28.

Index